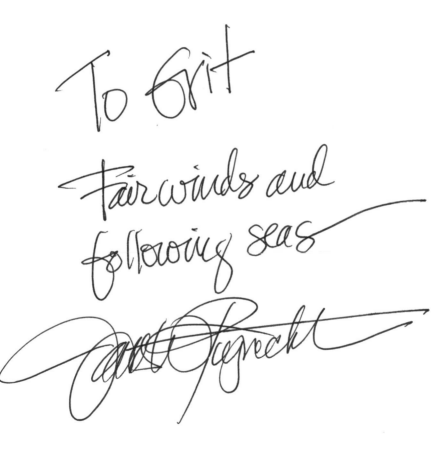

To Grit

Fair winds and
following seas

*Jim has written a crisp and entertaining book on leadership and leading organizational change. Told through the lens of Jim's own experience, the book is a collection of time tested theories and practical methods explained with terrific quotes, entertaining stories, and theoretical frameworks generated from the world's best leaders, business thinkers, and historical figures.*

**Dave Marver,**

President & Chief Executive Officer,

Cardiac Science Corporation

*Here is a leader who has been in the trenches and shares what works and what doesn't. As evidenced by his history of successful leadership roles in an impressive variety of companies, spanning the full range of economic conditions, Ruprecht's approach to getting things done is honest and straightforward. He knows that a leader is not there to replicate the status quo even when they may be the very person who gave the quo its status. Windward Leadership is food for the thoughtful leader, written with great style about making things better for the organization and all stakeholders by how one leads and serves.*

**Dr. Bowen White, M.D.**

Physician, teacher, consultant, speaker, clown, and author of *Why Normal Isn't Healthy: How to Find Heart, Meaning, Passion & Humor on the Road Most Traveled*

*What other books on leadership promise, Ruprecht actually delivers—an insightful, strategic yet pragmatic approach for changing your organization to create competitive advantage. A truly compelling read!*

**Michael A. Boylan**

Founder & Chief Executive Officer,

Accelerant International, LLC

Author of: *The Power to Get in*; *TEETH, Does Your Value Proposition Have Any*; and *Accelerants*.

*Windward Leadership is a thoughtful, pragmatic, sometimes irreverent look at what it takes to successfully lead an organization through change. Ruprecht has synthesized leading organizational theories and thinking from his experience implementing them. It's a book that provides guidance where the rubber meets the road—and is indispensable for those who are charged with implementing and leading change efforts. He demonstrates what it takes to be successful, and not from a lofty theoretical perspective, but from someone who's been there and lived it.*

**Kim Albee**

Founder and President

Genoo, LLC

*Drawn from his years of hands-on experience, Windward Leadership brings Ruprecht's pragmatic approach to leadership of business and technologies. He is experienced with a broad range of businesses from new ventures and start-ups through Fortune 100s. He is an inspiring leader, has assisted in business turn-arounds, and has successfully nurtured organizations from introverted, mediocre performers to highly energized, business engaging, consultative, service-driven contributors.*

**Rick Strahl**

VP, Business Development

Quality Systems Integrators, Inc.

# WINDWARD LEADERSHIP

*Taking Your Organization into the
Prevailing Winds and Political Seas*

# WINDWARD LEADERSHIP

*Taking Your Organization into the
Prevailing Winds and Political Seas*

## JAMES W. RUPRECHT

TWO HARBORS PRESS

MINNEAPOLIS

Two Harbors Press
212 3rd Avenue North, Suite 290
Minneapolis, MN 55401
612.455.2293
www.TwoHarborsPress.com

Windward Leadership Associates
windwardleadership.com

ISBN - 978-1-935097-65-5
ISBN - 1-935097-65-2
LCCN - 2009939944

Cover Design and typeset by Kristeen Wegner

*Printed in the United States of America*

# DEDICATION

To my folks, Bill and Jeanne Ruprecht. From them I learned to avoid the easy path of intellectual laziness, acquiescence to the unacceptable, and the importance of strength and honor, wit and play. Their fingerprints are all over this book.

To my daughters, Rebecca and Jessica. I didn't limit my experimentation with the concepts and methods described in this book to just the teams I led in the workplace. Rebe and Jess had to endure my experimentation in our home life as well, and I don't know who learned more from whom. Their fingerprints are all over this book, as well. They have had the additional burden of having to endure the ongoing embarrassment of hearing me tell stories about them as I've spoken and written about this leadership and organizational change stuff, but they have done so with grace and good humor.

To my soulmate, Dr. Annalisa Wirth. Annalisa encouraged me to take the risk and make the effort to gather all of the lessons that I had long been sharing with others and record them in as coherent and engaging a fashion as possible in the form of this book.

To my professional colleague and good friend, Scott Nintzel. Scott, too, was dogged in his persistence and encouragement to write this book.

Finally, to my kitchen cabinet, the "Bagel Shop Brain Trust"—the group of friends with whom I enjoy spirited but civil debate each morning at Bruegger's bagel shop in Woodbury, MN. They keep me honest, they keep me humble, and they keep me from falling.

# Acknowledgements

Several people were most influential in my professional development and the experiences that have culminated in this book.

First are my colleagues Pat Irestone, Jim Kubiak, and Pete Meyers. Pat was my boss at several different points in my career, and quickly became and remains my lifelong mentor and great friend. Many of my "on the job," or OJT, lessons were courtesy of Pat. Jim and Pete were my consulting partners. They taught me more than just the ins and outs of the consulting profession; they helped me to adapt to a life where, if we didn't work, we didn't eat—an experience everyone should go through because it recalibrates your perspective towards service and the customer. All three taught me the importance of putting my values on the line when working with someone found to be engaged in unethical practices—a very real test, especially during those times when you eat only when you work.

Next there are two amazing entrepreneurs in the field of executive education, Jim Ericson and Tom Miller. A major source of my leadership learning in a classroom setting came from a program that they originated in 1987; at the time it was called, "The Masters of Executive Excellence," but now it is known simply as, the "Masters Forum®." What makes the Masters Forum distinctive, what made it incredibly valuable to me, is Jim and Tom's ability to identify leading-edge thinkers well before they appear on the radar screen of the popular press.

Finally, while my work draws upon an eclectic plethora of work done by many others, there are a select few whose work I draw upon most heavily: Dr. Stephen R. Covey, Dr. Steven Kerr, Lawrence M. Miller, and Dr. Roger Rosenblatt. My learning from them and their work is shamelessly prominent in this book, and used with their permission.

# TABLE OF CONTENTS

# PART I:

# CALIBRATION

# 1

# Introduction

*Without deviation from the norm progress is not possible.*
**Frank Zappa**
American composer, electric guitarist, record producer, and film director
1940 – 1993

# A KEY MEASURE OF SAILING PERFOR-

mance is the degree by which you can go to windward. The higher performing the vessel, the crew, and the captain, the more directly they can sail into the wind. A decision to lead an organizational change is a decision to sail into the organizational wind, and a key measure of leadership performance is the degree to which one can take their organization windward.

This is a book about leadership; more specifically, it is about organizational leadership and leading cultural change. I know what you're thinking: "There are several things the world just doesn't need another of. We don't need another belly-button-bearin', or crotch-clutchin' singer. We don't need another hollerin'-head, rage-raisin', reason-reducin' talk show. We don't need yet another blade in our shaving razors. We certainly don't need another version of Microsoft Word. And, for the love of God, we don't need another book on leadership."

## WHAT MAKES THIS BOOK DIFFERENT

I realize that the subject of leadership and cultural change, particularly in the context of business organizations, has received much attention. Much research has been done; many concepts and theories have been formally postulated; many gurus complete with their own discipleships have emerged; many articles have been published in everything ranging from the Harvard Business Review to airline magazines; many books have become best sellers; many conferences and seminars have been given; and much money has been made (although I am unsure of the "money-made to good-done" ratio).

So what makes this particular book on leadership and leading cultural change different? Pragmatism.

Most of the material on leadership and organizational change that I have seen has been written by people from one of two points of view: that of an academician or consultant, or that of a CEO. It's not that the academician's, the consultant's, or the CEO's perspectives are bad; theirs are certainly instructive points of view—the ideas, theories and strategies they espouse are expert and thought-provoking. However, the academician's and the consultant's work (like that of sportscasters, reporters, and other professional spectators) is based on observing, not doing—their view is from the press box. The CEO's work (like that of a team owner) is based on their experience applying leadership concepts and theories with all of the authority and influence that comes with being the CEO (i.e., a lot)—their view is from the owner's suite.

In contrast, this book flows from the lessons I've learned throughout my thirty-plus year career "on the field." If you'll forgive my American football analogy, I have run the plays sent into me from the sidelines and I have called audibles[1] at the line. I have had plays breakdown for big losses, and I have had plays breakaway for big gains. I have been fortunate to lead organizations of varying size, of varying scope, at varying levels in the larger organizational hierarchy at various companies. While most of the positions I've held have been in technical functions like IT and engineering, most of my career has involved forming new organizations, renovating under-performing ones, and invigorating neglected ones. Much of my career has been spent sailing into the prevailing organizational winds and in waters that were not always politically safe.

I make extensive use of analogies and metaphors. However, very few of them are from business organizations; most are from sports, history, and, because it has been the dominant organization throughout history, the military. I do this in hopes that it will do for you what it does for me: learn by

---

[1] In American football, the quarterback usually runs the play that a coach on the sidelines has sent in. However, even after calling that play in the huddle, the quarterback still has the discretion to run a different play if he sees something about the other team's defense that tells him that the play they are planning to run won't work, or that a different play will work much better. Because they have already broken from their huddle, the quarterback must inform the rest of his teammates about the new play they are going to run via coded voice commands that he shouts as he takes his position behind the center. This kind of play is referred to as an audible.

getting out of your normal context—seeing things in a different light, thus thinking differently about them. Let me use an analogy to explain. Imagine you go to a Chinese village, gather the villagers together, ask them to select their ten smartest members and tell those ten folks to design the very best house they could imagine. Price is no object and material is no object—if they can conceive it, and if physics permit it, they can build it. What are the odds they'll come back with a Williamsburg Colonial? Zero—it is simply not going to happen. It may well be the very best house ever to come out of that Chinese village, but it is still going to be a Chinese-looking house. So it would also be if we asked the same of villagers in Virginia. The point is that we all live in our own "Chinese village," and I use analogies and metaphors in an effort to help you think beyond yours.

Finally, many of the existing books on leadership and organizational change talk about the need for strong board and/or executive support, diligent management, and high trust subordinates. This is another example of how this book differs from others in a pragmatic way. Frankly, if you have strong board and/or executive support, diligent management, and high-trust subordinates I don't know why you would bother reading this or any other book on the subject—everything works in that kind of environment. This book will be valuable only for those who live in a highly political, neurotic, time-starved, resource-poor organization.

## WHAT THIS BOOK IS AND WHAT IT IS NOT

I do not pretend to pose any brave new concepts in this book. You won't read any bold new theory here, so don't work hard to find any new conceptual underpinnings—I don't think they're there. The theories that you will find in this book have all been said before, and said better, by others with more impressive pedigrees than mine.

What I do intend to do is share those theories and concepts that I have found to be practical. More importantly, I will share what I have found to be important in successfully putting them into practice.

I have studied the works of most of the marquis authorities in this field, and going beyond just reading their articles and books, I've made a point of attending courses, seminars, conferences, and/or lectures that they have personally led. However, as you know, while an expert's ideas may look good on paper, that does not mean they work in practice. Using Shewhart's "Plan-Do-Check-Act," or PDCA, cycle, I have experimented with the authorities' ideas—I've even come up with a few of my own. I have taken those theories from the safe, predictable confines of the conceptual laboratory to the irregularities and ambiguities of real life.

This book is my report on my years of lab and field results. I will cite the principles, concepts, theories, strategies and other ideas that I have found to be of value, and sometimes I will cite those I have found to be empty or dysfunctional. However, I will move quickly from that philosophical context (where the rubber meets the sky) to the pragmatic issues of putting it into practice (where the rubber meets the road). So, while little new theory is presented, what is presented is original work on how these various concepts and theories can be woven together for the purposes of real-life application.

In the spirit of real-life application, I will tell you that the object of the kind of change presented in this book isn't to make people feel better—that was never the object of any of the change efforts I have led. If making people feel better is the object of your change effort, then my friendly suggestion to you is to think again. Here's my first lesson for you: "hard" always drives out "soft." The object of your change effort better be to improve the performance, the contribution, of your organization. If your people aren't becoming more productive, if the value your organization is contributing isn't increasing, then you need to fix or kill your change effort. This is about improving productivity and increasing value. So, you should hold the ideas I present up to a pretty rigorous standard. With that understood let me also tell you that with the kind of change that I share in this book you'll find that people will feel better—their morale and satisfaction will go up.

## MY PURPOSE FOR THIS BOOK

As a person who has spent most of his career sailing into the prevailing organizational winds and political seas, I wrote this book for two reasons.

First, I want to share my experience and point of view with those others who also find themselves sailing into the wind, or aspire to do so. I believe that the ideas presented here have broad applicability. While I may focus largely on business organizations, the concerns, arguments, concepts, methods and tools I present in this book apply to organizations of all kinds, of all sizes, and at levels in an organizational hierarchy: businesses, unions, political and religious organizations; public or private; profit and non-profit; government and non-government; from huge global enterprises to small single facility organizations; from entire companies to business units within a company to functions within a business unit, to departments within a function, and to teams within a department.

My other reason for writing this book is that I am concerned that organizational leadership today is on a bad course. There is an ill leadership wind prevailing in many organizations today, and practices, which I regard as sins of leadership, have become the object of admiration and handsome rewards.

For example, just as we know that large, heavy ships with tall structures cannot go well to windward, whereas smaller, lighter, lower-built ships can go more directly to windward, we also know that the same is true with organizations. Too many organizations today are too large; some are so large that our society cannot allow them to fail. Too many organizations are too tall with many unnecessary levels of management. Too many organizations are top heavy with executives who are compensated disproportionately to the workers at the bottom—their center of gravity is too high. We have leaders whose talent is limited to reducing costs versus increasing value. We have leaders who do not take a leadership share of the sacrifices that must be made during times of adversity and hardship. We have leaders who are tough on their own employees but ineffectual against the competition. We have leaders rewarded for making short-term decisions that are detrimental to the long-term vitality of the organization, and to make matters worse they are rewarded in ways that insulate them from the long-term consequences of their short-term decision-making.

This book is my modest effort to affect a course correction, and is written for those leaders whose conscience compels them to sail into that prevailing ill wind—be they senior executive, one of the distributed leaders sprinkled throughout organizations, or an up-and-coming member of the next generation of leaders. This book is a manifesto for change from wherever you are in the organization. This book is about breaking the passing of dysfunctional, intergenerational leadership tendencies from the current generation to the next. This book is about trying to make whatever little corner of the world, which you have the good fortune to lead, a better place.

## IT'S NOT THE NOTES; IT'S THE MELODY

There is an essential difference between the kind of change intended more to make a splash, and the kind of change that is intended to yield durable results. Making a splash simply requires a visibly dramatic change in some under-performing process, and many individuals have made lucrative careers out of doing just that as they flit from low-hanging fruit to low-hanging fruit. However, leading change that produces enduring results requires not only process changes, but also cultural change. There is an essential difference between what is technically possible and what is culturally doable. This book is about changing what is culturally doable.

Leading cultural change is hard to do—anyone who thinks cultural change is easy should try this experiment: tell the loved-one with whom you're sleeping that you want to switch sides of the bed.

I love baseball and I find that leading enduring organizational change is a lot like hitting a baseball. Hitting a baseball is probably the hardest thing to do in sports. On the surface it is a simple function of just two things: hand/ eye coordination, and bat speed. Unfortunately, however, there are thousands of little things that go into doing each of those two things well enough to "hit safely." The same is true about leading organizational change. On the surface it is a simple function of just two things: changing how your organization technically does its work (i.e., its processes—its technical system), and changing how your organization socially governs its conduct of that work (i.e., its culture—its social system).

Let me explain how hard it is to hit a baseball. For one thing, you're trying to hit a five-ounce sphere measuring nine inches in circumference with a cylinder no more than forty-two inches in length, averages thirty-two ounces in weight, and is only about two and one-half inches in diameter at its "sweet spot" (i.e., the place on the bat where you want to make contact with the ball). In addition, you have to hit the ball so it stays within a ninety-degree angle for it to be considered "fair," and you have to hit it in a way that avoids the play of the nine opposing players in order to "hit safely." Further, when thrown from a mound that's ten and one-half inches high and sixty and one-half feet away, and depending on the speed and the rotation the pitcher puts on the ball when thrown, the 216 stitches on the baseball give it aerodynamic properties that can cause it to curve, slide, flutter, or fall away.

Or, it can just come at you high and hard at ninety-plus miles per hour. In which case, you have about one hundred milliseconds for your eye to see the ball and send an image to your brain. Your brain has another seventy-five milliseconds to process that information and gauge the speed and location of the pitch, another twenty-five milliseconds to decide whether to swing, another twenty-five milliseconds to decide on a swing pattern, and fifteen more milliseconds to let the rest of your body know and get into the act (e.g., start your stride). Your swing itself takes 150 milliseconds.

During the first fifty milliseconds you can stop, but after one hundred milliseconds, the bat is moving too fast and your swing cannot be checked. Then, swinging your two-pound bat at eighty miles per hour, you must deliver about nine horsepower of energy within an eighth of an inch of the dead center of the ball at precisely the right millisecond. To hit a ninety-mile-per-hour pitch, the whole process will take about 400 milliseconds, but if your swing is seven milliseconds too late or too early, the batted ball will sail foul past the first or third base lines respectively (i.e., outside of that ninety-degree angle).

That's why hitting a baseball is so hard. This is why a batter who consistently hits safely only three times out of ten is considered among the best in the game. When leading organizational change, I don't think your odds are even that good.

Yogi Berra, the great catcher and later coach said, "Baseball is ninety percent mental; the other half is physical." Leading organizational change is similar: ninety percent is cultural; the other half is technical. Baseball is also the only game where the defense controls the ball. Similarly, when leading organizational change, you'll find that legacy controls the ball. Baseball is the only game where points aren't scored by an object but by people. Similarly, when leading organizational change, you'll find that success isn't a function of land, capital, technology and what's technically possible, but of people and what's culturally doable.

I said that hitting a baseball is simply a function of two things: hand/eye coordination and bat speed. However, doing this well, batting .300, requires a career spent working diligently on those thousands of things that go into doing those two things well.

I've said that leading enduring organizational change is also a simple matter of two things: changing how your organization technically does its work and how it socially governs the conduct of that work. I will spend the rest of this book sharing the thousands of things that I found go into doing those two things well. I share them with you, not as a sportscaster or team owner, but as someone who has spent his career on the field.

If you don't like baseball, here's another analogy for you. Leading enduring organizational change seems to me to be like composing and playing music. The theories are like musical notes; however the melody comes from how you blend those concepts and theories together and the methods and techniques with which the instruments are played. I certainly didn't invent any new notes, but I have experimented with composing, conducting and playing numerous and various melodies. I'll share the constructs I've used when composing, along with the methods and techniques I've used while conducting and playing. I'll also share with you those melodies that I've found harmonious and those that struck me as sour.

Leadership is not about the notes; it's about the melody.

# 2

# Biases

*What gets us into trouble is not what we don't know;*
*it's what we know for sure that just ain't so.*
**Samuel Langhorne Clemens [Mark Twain]**
American author and humorist
1825 – 1910

## LET ME WARN YOU OF TWO MAJOR

biases that liberally lace my thinking.

First, I firmly believe that businesses have a social purpose: to increase the wealth of society. Real wealth is created when new products and services are created—products and services for which people will voluntarily trade their hard-earned money. This creates new jobs and adds wealth to the aggregate of society. I also argue that there is no other single economic lever that can cure more social ills than job creation. Creating wealth is what gives businesses their license to exist. If they aren't creating wealth—if they're simply manipulating wealth—then they are goofing off, and if it were up to me they would lose their license to practice.

This concept of wealth creation doesn't apply only to companies within an economy; it also applies to organizations anywhere within a company. Internal organizations have customers, too, and they should aspire to be their customers' vendor of preference, not a vendor of force. If a business' social purpose is to create wealth, then the social purpose of those organizations within that business is to add value in ways for which their internal customers would be willing to voluntarily trade their hard-earned budgets.

Second, I firmly believe that if leaders adopt a pattern of decision-making that creates value for one stakeholder group at the expense of another, then they devalue the organization. Every organization has multiple stakeholders; some have more than others, but all have at least these five: customers, employees, owners, vendors, and the various communities to which that organization belongs. Very often the pattern is to create short-term benefit for the shareholders at the long-term expense of some other stakeholder.

I can certainly understand why a company struggling for its life would take the drastic action of conducting layoffs; and, of course, every organization needs to guard against becoming "over weight." However, I find something immoral about a firm that lays off personnel while they continue to throw a boatload of cash into the bank each quarter, or while they continue their wildly disproportionate compensation practices, so they can deliver a couple of extra pennies in shareholder dividends.

Whenever I hear a CEO proclaim, "Our number one priority is to make money for our investors," it pegs my worry meter. I worry that he or she has forgotten the natural order of things. Customers occupy the top spot on capitalism's food chain. Everything depends on the customer—if your organization produces a product or service for which customers are willing to trade their hard earned money, then you will prosper; otherwise you will and should decay. So, your first priority has to be your customers. Next comes your human resources. The production of products and the delivery of services that customers value is work that is done by people—be they labor you own (i.e., employees) or labor you lease or rent (i.e., consultants and contractors). Your second priority has to be your human resources. Then, if you take care of your people and you take care of your customers, your investors will be taken care of as a natural byproduct.

I will grant you that it is possible to so grossly mismanage, or fraudulently manage, an organization such that, even though it takes care of its customers and takes care of its people, the investors still get screwed. But the incidence of this occurrence is rare. Whereas the incidence of the opposite occurrence—where an organization is so grossly mismanaged, or fraudulently managed, that even though it takes care of the stockholders, the organization's customers and people get screwed—is not so rare.

I am much more worried about the very accepted practices of sacrificing product and service quality, sacrificing ongoing investments in research and development (R&D) and over-relying on acquisitions, capping or reducing wages and benefits, restructuring pensions, and various financial and accounting tactics to manipulate results for the sake of earnings per share (EPS).

Look at the current practice of publicly forecasting quarterly EPS—it is amazing to me that companies do it. First, it is not required. Yet many companies choose to do it, and then they spend precious cultural energy manipulating numbers at the end of the quarter to make sure they hit the forecast they weren't required to make in the first place. Second, it is unnatural. I can think of no other competitive human endeavor in which a team strives to achieve a specific score. Can you imagine a football coach telling his team that it isn't good enough to simply beat the other team, but that they must also meet or beat the bookies' point spread? It's unnatural.

What is the difference between a coach betting on his own team and then managing their performance over the course of the game to meet or beat the point spread, and a CEO with stock options managing the company's performance over the course of the quarter to meet or beat the EPS forecast? Tell me the difference between an EPS forecast and a point spread. Tell me the difference between a bookie and a stockbroker. If companies were football teams and CEOs were head coaches, those CEOs who forecast EPS would be barred from the sport for life, would have no chance of getting into the hall of fame, would probably spend some time in court and might even enjoy an extended stay in the gray-bar hotel.

Such behavior is an example of a pattern of decision-making that creates benefit for one stakeholder group at the expense of another, and in the long term, I believe it devalues the organization. And I am not a new or lone voice in this regard.

Elmer L. Anderson was CEO of H.B. Fuller, a Minnesota company, which, under his leadership, enjoyed outstanding corporate and community performance, and became a global company before it was fashionable to be one. He also went on to become governor of Minnesota. In his book, *A Man's Reach*[1], he explained his management philosophy. While there is no doubt that the management of the company was interested in producing profit for their shareholders, the company also counted other important constituents—customers, employees, and the community. In fact, Anderson listed these four main constituents in their order of importance: the customer, the employee, the shareholder, and the community. Certainly all four were important, but Anderson cited the customer and the employee as more important because it was they that produced the business and the profits that paid the investors and served the community.

Michael Treacy, a former professor at the MIT Sloan School of Management, is an internationally known expert on corporate strategy and

---

[1]   Elmer L. Anderson and Lori Sturdevant, Lori, *A Man's Reach* (Minneapolis, Minnesota: University of Minnesota Press, 2000).

11

business process transformation. He pioneered a whole new approach to customer, industry, and competitive analysis known as "value disciplines." He presents this approach in his 1997 *New York Times* bestseller, *The Discipline of Market Leaders: Choose Your Customers, Narrow Your Focus, and Dominate Your Market*. He has followed this with his latest book, *Double-Digit Growth: How Great Companies Achieve It—No Matter What*. In his 1998 Masters Forum lecture, "Value Leadership, Strategic Agility and Organizational Greatness[2]," Michael Treacy asserted that you can drive value for shareholders or you can drive value for customers. If you drive value for customers, value for shareholders will be an inevitable byproduct. The opposite is not true.

For too many companies the primary purpose of their annual planning and budgeting process is to show Wall Street that the EPS forecast they have set for themselves is at least plausible; or it is to show Wall Street that it has a plausible plan to hit the EPS target that Wall Street has set for them. A company building its annual plans around an EPS target, thus focusing on EPS rather than products, services, customers, and employees is like an athlete playing tennis by focusing on the scoreboard.

Unfortunately, the sect of those who worship at the altar of EPS is a growing one, and it will be tough to cleanse because whenever you take from Peter to give to Paul, you will always have the support of Paul. For example, most members of corporate leadership are rewarded in the form of cash bonuses, stock options, and grants. The cash bonuses reward short-term results and the stock options and grants are meant to reward long-term results, but have a decidedly tilted bias in favor of the shareholders.

Yes, it is true that companies award bonuses, stock grants and options to people at lower levels in the organization, and many also have employee stock purchase programs. This way, in hopes of aligning interests, all employees may also be stockholders. However, I believe that the disparity between the stock awards and ownership opportunities at the executive level and those at the lower levels is too great—that disparity is so great that as you go deeper in the organization the rewards alignment meter barely moves.

James B. Stewart, former Page-One editor at *The Wall Street Journal*, and 1988 Pulitzer Prize winner for his reporting on the stock market crash and insider trading, makes this point in his book, *Disney War*, which chronicles the internal politics at Disney during the rise and fall of Michael Eisner:

> *In corporate America, in 1997, it wasn't all clear that board*

---

[2]  Michael Treacy. "Value Leadership, Strategic Agility and Organizational Greatness," (Speech. The Masters Forum, Minnetonka, MN, 27 Oct. 1998).

*members at major corporations typically gave the shareholders much thought, unless the shareholders happened to be Sid Bass, or Warren Buffett, or other billionaires holding such large blocks of shares that they couldn't be ignored. The long-running bull market, interrupted only briefly by the 1991 recession, had lulled shareholders into complacency and masked a steady erosion of shareholder democracy. Entrenched executives who managed their companies for their benefit rather than for shareholders had helped bring on the takeover wave of the 1980s, when many of them were thrown out by new owners, but the lofty stock prices of the mid- and late 1990s discouraged hostile takeover bids. Corporate governance experts had urged companies to align the interests of management and shareholders by using stock options rather than cash as compensation. The theory, enthusiastically embraced by Eisner and many other CEOs, was that executives would focus their efforts on raising the stock price, which would benefit all shareholders at the same time it lifted their compensation. In practice, few recognized that the interests of someone who owns millions of shares in a company are far different from someone who owns several hundreds or thousands.*

*Nowhere was this more evident than at Disney. From the beginning, Eisner had embraced stock options as his primary means of compensation, and in some years they had made him the highest-paid executive in the country. Eisner often pointed out that he only became wealthy by making shareholders rich. By the time Ovitz was fired, stock options had made Eisner the company's second-largest individual shareholder, eclipsing even Roy and other members of the Disney family. Only the Basses held a bigger stake. At the same time that his ownership was growing, Eisner had consolidated power by isolating board members, compromising their independence and stripping them of any real oversight function. The Disney board had become a travesty of independent governance.*[3]

Eisner and the Disney board during his reign may be the exception rather than the norm—maybe not. Either way, it is not surprising that the board of directors and senior executives give the interests of the stockholders priority over the other stakeholders, for "the interests of someone who owns millions of shares in a company are far different from someone who owns several hundreds or thousands."

---

[3]  James B. Stewart. *Disney War*. (New York: Simon & Schuster, 2005.) p278-279

# 3

# ASSERTIONS

*I don't want someone shoving his views down my throat,*
*unless they're covered in a crunchy candy shell.*
**Stephen Colbert**
American comedian, satirist, actor, and writer
b. 1964

# THERE ARE THREE ASSERTIONS THAT

represent my thesis. The first is that culture is the key to competitive advantage. The second is that leadership is the key to culture. The third is that actualizing values, not implementing a program, is the key to leading cultural change.

## ASSERTION #1: CULTURE IS THE KEY TO COMPETITIVE ADVANTAGE

Paraphrasing observations made by organizational change agent, author, and consultant Lawrence M. Miller, in his 1989 Masters of Executive Excellence lecture, "Managing for Tomorrow: Visions of a New Corporate Culture,[1]" there have been several stages of competitive advantage throughout history.

## ADAM – 1850: PROPERTY

From the time of Adam to around 1850, property was the key to competitive

---

[1]  Lawrence Miller. "Managing for Tomorrow: Visions of a New Corporate Culture." (Speech. The Masters of Executive Excellence. Minnetonka, MN, 22 Aug. 1989).

advantage. We hunted on it; we fished on it; we grew crops on it; we mined it, and we built military force to conquer and defend it. Today, however, the measure of a country's or an organization's possession of property is no longer a measure of their competitive advantage. Unless they are in the mining, oil, or gas business, you won't hear an organization argue that it needs to acquire property in order to build competitive advantage. The Soviet Union had a lot of property; it didn't have any competitive advantage. Meanwhile, Japan and South Korea don't have much property, but they certainly have competitive advantage.

Global sourcing has made natural resources fluid, and once something becomes fluid it is no longer a competitive advantage because it can flow to the next guy as easily as it can flow to you.

# 1850 – 1950: CAPITAL

From 1850 to 1950, capital was the key to competitive advantage. In the industrial age capital was the deal—if you wanted to build a steel mill or if you wanted to build a railroad, you needed a lot of money. This was the true age of capitalism, and capital was concentrated in a few families like the Carnegies, Mellons, Morgans, Rockefellers, and Krupps. But, if you took a random poll today, how many people (outside those in the financial sector) do you think would even recognize names like Kohlberg Kravis or any of the other equity firms that can raise billions of dollars in a matter of days.

Capital is no longer a competitive advantage because global capital markets have made it fluid. Generally, there is money looking for a place to land. If you have an idea, you can get money; if you can't get money, it's because you don't have a good enough idea or don't know how to sell it. (Or, there is a total meltdown of the global financial markets, in which case money isn't flowing to anyone.)

# 1950 – 1980: TECHNOLOGY

From 1950 to 1980, technology was the key to competitive advantage. This was the heyday of companies like AT&T and IBM. But technology, too, has become fluid. I guarantee you that if you come up with the next big microprocessor today, the "Zip Chip 1000," someone else will come up with the "Zip Chip 2000" tomorrow. Technology has become fluid, and patent laws and copyright laws do not protect. If they did, we'd all still be using VisiCalc[2].

# 1980 – TODAY: CULTURE

From 1980 to today, culture has become the key to competitive advantage. What is not fluid, what transitions slowly, is human competence and culture. Cultivating an organization's culture requires a quantum increase in leadership capability over managing property, capital or technology. If General Motors or Ford or Chrysler could buy Honda or Toyota's culture, they would pay a dollar or two. But money is not what gets you a culture that is growing and conquering—the key to a growing and conquering culture, is leadership.

# THE ASSET CURVE AND THE CULTURE CURVE

I'll talk about this in greater detail in a later chapter, but it is pertinent here to observe that an organization's accumulation of wealth over time is a curve that lags the curve representing the health and strength of its culture over time. As illustrated in Figure 1, the asset curve depicts the civilization's/organization's accumulation of wealth. The other curve, the culture curve, depicts the civilization's/organization's power to produce wealth.

*Figure 1: The Asset and Culture Curves*

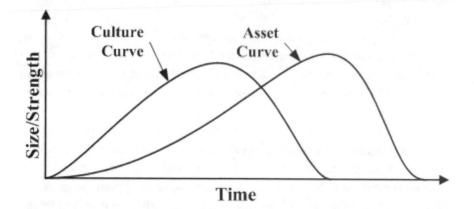

Source: Lawrence Miller. "Managing for Tomorrow: Visions of a New Corporate Culture." (Speech. The Masters of Executive Excellence. Minnetonka, MN, 22 Aug. 1989).

[2] For you younger readers, VisiCalc was the first spreadsheet software; it was dethroned by Lotus 1-2-3. Lotus fought off the challenge of Borland's Quattro, but was ultimately dethroned by Microsoft Excel.

There are a couple of things worthy to note about these curves. First, the culture curve leads and the asset curve lags. For example, Hadrian's Wall was built across the width of Great Britain's mid-section in the years 122 - 130 AD by order of the Emperor Hadrian. Yet, while Hadrian's Wall represents the outer most reach of the Roman Empire, one could easily argue that this was 300 - 400 years after the Roman culture had begun to set into a state of decline. Similarly, a meritorious argument could be made that GM, for example, began losing its creativity and became complacent thirty to forty years before it began to lose market share.

Second, these two curves bear a striking resemblance to the P/PC metaphor used by Stephen Covey to define "effectiveness" in his work, *7 Habits of Highly Effective People*, where Covey defines effectiveness as "P/PC balance," where "P" represents production (i.e., your desired results), and "PC" represents production capability (i.e., your power to produce your desired results) [3]. Covey uses Aesop's fable of the goose that lays the golden eggs as a metaphor for effectiveness, where the golden eggs represent "P," and the goose represents "PC." The asset curve above is analogous to Production, P (the assets you want—the eggs), and the culture curve is analogous to Production Capability, PC (the capability to produce the assets you want—the goose). Effectiveness, Covey says, is achieved through balanced attention to both, and he goes on to remind us of the consequences of focusing on one over the other. Certainly, when the poor farmer focused solely on the golden eggs and sacrificed the goose, the consequences were clear. Conversely, focusing on the goose without regard to realizing any golden eggs is just as fateful––no margin, no mission.

Yet, what do we watch and measure? We watch and measure the asset curve because that involves linear thinking and "objective" measures (or so we tell ourselves); whereas understanding the health of the culture requires non-linear thinking and subjective measures. It is true that some organizations will try to measure the health of their culture through instruments like employee surveys. However, my experience is that most of this is only lip service. Companies may conduct employee surveys in earnest, but it is hard to tell if these surveys ever beget any constructive and substantive action. I have seen no organization that treats issues arising out of disappointing employee survey results with the same gravity they do issues arising out of disappointing financial results.

The accumulation of wealth represents the golden eggs for a business

---

[3] Stephen R. Covey. *The 7 Habits of Highly Effective People* (New York: Simon and Schuster, 1989), p52-54.

organization; but the culture of that organization represents the goose.

Assertion #1: Culture is the key to competitive advantage.

## ASSERTION #2: LEADERSHIP IS THE KEY TO CULTURE

While an organization's culture is the key to its competitive advantage, leadership is the key to an organization's culture. Let me share a historical example that demonstrates this assertion. It is a story about Vice Admiral Horatio Lord Nelson.

Like many leaders, Nelson was not the uncomplicated person we would like our leaders to be. Nelson's personal life was visibly flawed; it included a loveless marriage, and an affair which he lived openly and which produced a daughter. But his professional life—his military career—is, I believe, a case study in leadership creating a culture of competitive advantage.

In his course, "Design for Total Quality[4]," Lawrence M. Miller, shared the following story about Lord Nelson as an example demonstrating culture as key to competitive advantage and effective leadership as a key to a high-performing leadership.

> *Throughout history there are hundreds of examples of leadership gaining advantage over superior material force. Perhaps there is no better example than the contrasting leadership of the British fleet and the combined French and Spanish fleets of Napoleon at Trafalgar in 1805—a battle that determined the dominance of the sea (i.e., competitive advantage) for the next one hundred years.*
>
> *Materially the fleets were almost equal. There were twenty-seven ships in Nelson's fleet and thirty-three in French Admiral Villeneuve's fleet. There was no advantage of technology, tools or equipment. There was, however, an advantage in method and communication. Nelson had devised a new signaling system that provided more immediate and frequent instructions.*
>
> *The difference that resulted in catastrophe for the combined French and Spanish fleet by the day's end was in people, not things. In the British fleet, 449 were killed and 1,214 wounded out of 18,000. Among the French and Spanish there was slaughter. Vil-*

---

[4]  Lawrence M. Miller. "Design For Total Quality," (Seminar. The Miller Consulting Group. Atlanta, GA, Oct. 1990).

*leneuve's lead ship alone lost 400, with 200 wounded. Another ship lost 450. The total lost is not known, but it was many thousands. The battle eliminated the threat of Napoleon launching an invasion of Britain and extending his empire beyond the continent of Europe.*

Can a leader make this difference? Villeneuve thought so.

*When he [Villeneuve] saw that it was Nelson's flag carried atop the lead ship he wrote in his diary, "The battle is lost. It is Nelson!"*

What was the contrast?

*Before the battle, Villeneuve called a war council on his ship attended by the French and Spanish captains, at which insults were exchanged and distrust expressed. On the other hand, Nelson and his captains were known as a "band of brothers" who rose through the ranks together, repeatedly fought together, knew each other and trusted each other as brothers.*

*The combined French and Spanish fleet had adhered to the standard accepted order of battle for the past one hundred years. They formed the traditional "line of battle" and expected the enemy to do the same. Nelson, to the contrary, innovated and surprised his opponents by sailing perpendicular, running straight at their line. This strategy resulted not in fleet against fleet fighting, but in the chaos of ship against ship. It required absolute trust that each captain would make his own on-the-spot decisions, would have the courage and judgment to pursue the battle, and that "every man would do his duty," as Nelson's last and most famous signal message conveyed.*

*Nelson was unquestionably one of the most successful military leaders in history. He was a "tough boss." At Trafalgar, he stood on deck with one arm shot off, the loss of one eye, and refused to leave the deck even when the enemy was firing broadside directly across the deck.*

*However, while Nelson was tough on his competition, he was not tough on his own men. There was an intimate relationship, affection and affiliation, between him and his companions. For ex-*

*ample, at Trafalgar, Nelson walked the decks of his ship, Victory, before the battle and found a common seaman sitting unhappily. When asked the reason for his despair, he said that his letter to his family had failed to make the mail ship, the last to leave before the battle. Nelson then ordered the recall flag hoisted to bring back the mail ship that was already sailing off in the distance. Stories such as this, stories of Nelson's concern for the common seaman, were what men died for.*

*The loyalty was so strong that upon Nelson's death, the seaman refused to allow his body to be taken from the ship, insisting that they who sailed with him into battle would sail his body back home.*

*Perhaps the most significant advantage at Trafalgar was the skills of the men—both officers and enlisted. The French officer corps had suffered from the excesses of the French Revolution and many lacked fighting experience. The British officers had all been at sea since they were fourteen-year-old midshipmen, experienced and well-drilled. However, more significantly, the British seamen had been so well-drilled in manning their guns that their rate of fire was twice that of the French and Spanish. Although the British were outgunned, effectively they had almost twice the firepower due to the cycle time of the crews working the guns. The effectiveness of the British broadsides at close range was totally devastating.*

*It was the effectiveness, the spirit, and the skill of people conditioned by their leaders that determined competitive advantage for the next one hundred years.*

Do you see any analogies between this brief Nelson leadership vignette and leadership in your organization? Do the leaders in your organization grow through the ranks together, have a history of fighting the competition together, know and trust each other; or has your leadership corps been decimated by the excesses of cost cutting, and do you now rely on collaboration among mercenary leaders who you have signed-on for the time being? Are your leaders tough bosses in the sense that they are tough on the competition, or are they tough bosses in the sense that they are tough on their own people? Do your leaders innovate and take risks, or is the height of their aspiration to conform to accepted best practices? Do your leaders play to win, or do they play to not lose?

In business competition, the conditions may be different, but the principles are the same. The ability of leaders to influence their people is the key. Nelson and his men were unified and trusted one another. Nelson innovated; he took risks by attempting new tactics and new methods. Nelson delegated and relied on the abilities of his fellow officers. Nelson created advantage through training, human competence, and commitment. In short, Nelson created the stronger culture.

And so it also is in today's world, culture is the key to competitive advantage, and the organization's culture flows from its leadership.

Assertion #2: The key to culture is leadership.

# ASSERTION #3: ACTUALIZING VALUES IS THE KEY TO LEADING CULTURAL CHANGE

Building a healthy and prosperous culture, building a culture that is growing and conquering, isn't about faithfully executing each step in five three-ring binders of some program of that some consultant or guru is peddling, then expecting that your organization will be magically transformed like you're some sort of David Copperfield. Building a culture of any kind is not about implementing a program—it is about actualizing values.

If you were around in the 1980s, you'll remember the Total Quality Management (TQM) movement that arose in the U.S. when Japanese companies began eating American companies' lunches. There were those who treated TQM as if it were a program to be implemented, only to watch it take its deserved place in the dustbin of their company's history as it degenerated from a serious intent into a fading fad. Plant managers quickly learned that no matter what question they were asked, the acronym "TQM" better appear somewhere in the first ten words of their response. But there were also those who realized that TQM was not a program to be implemented but was really a set of values to be actualized, and it became woven into their cultural fabric, it became second nature, organizational habit.

Then we had "Six Sigma" and "Lean" programs, even "Lean Sigma" hybrids. Plant managers quickly learned that no matter what question they were asked, the words "Six Sigma," "Lean," or "Lean Sigma" better appear somewhere in the first ten words of their response. There still are those who treat it like a program to be implemented, and those who treat it like a set of values to be actualized. In the words of Yogi Berra, "It's like déjà vu all over again!"

Assertion #3: Actualizing values is the key to leading cultural change.

# PART II:

# LEADING, FOR A CHANGE

# 4

# Abuses and Usurpations

*It is hard to get someone to understand something,*
*when their salary depends on them not understanding it.*
**Upton Sinclair**
Pulitzer Prize-winning American author
1878 - 1968

# Too many organizations are led

by the people at the top largely for the enjoyment of people at the top. This is my profound insight on the state of organizational leadership based on my decades of observational leadership. This insight is worth remembering for two reasons. First, it will help you make sense of leaders' decisions that otherwise don't make sense. Second, remember it because it is not leadership.

Here's some root cause analysis for you: organizations that are in trouble are in trouble because their problems are over-managed and their people are under-led. The disturbing leadership trend in too many organizations is one of repeated abuses and usurpations.

- There is an excess of "me first" leadership and a deficit of "we" leadership.
- There are too many leaders who lack strength of vision and strength of values—personal gain is their vision, and expediency is their guiding value.
- There are too many leaders who lack commitment to their organization's mission, and lack loyalty to their people—they work for the money. There are too many leaders who are just-passing-through

mercenaries, and they will sign on to a different ship in a different navy when offered a more lucrative contract.

- There are too many leaders who are tough on their crews, but weak on their competition. There are too many leaders who do not take a leadership share of the sacrifice required during times of adversity and they enjoy a disproportionate share of the rewards during times of plenty.

- There are too many leaders that camouflage their intellectual laziness with testosterone-fueled decision-making.

- There are too many leaders who rely more on the art of manipulation and spin and don't value the virtue of truth-telling and authentic communication.

- There are too many one-dimensional managers in leadership positions who only know about, only care about, or who don't have the leadership wherewithal to do much more than cut costs. There are not enough leaders who have the intellectual capability and the intestinal fortitude for path-finding and innovation—not innovation in cost-cutting, but innovation in value creation.

- There are too many leaders who do not understand, or don't care about, the importance of safety to risk—they play not to lose rather than playing to win.

- There are too many leaders who don't grasp, or don't care about, the concept of self-interest rightly understood.

- There are too many leaders who don't understand, or don't care, that business has a social purpose—to increase the collective wealth of society, and it does that by creating products and services and jobs of value.

- There are too many leaders who don't understand, or don't care, that when they practice a pattern of decision-making whereby they create benefit for one stakeholder at the expense of another, they are devaluing the organization.

# A BLUEPRINT FOR TROUBLE

In the mid-twentieth century, British historian, Arnold J. Toynbee, published his analysis of the rise and fall of civilizations, *A Study of History*[1]. It is a

---

[1]  Arnold J. Toynbee. *A Study of History: Abridgement of Volumes I - VI by D.C. Somervell*, and *A Study of History: Abridgement of Volumes VII - X by D.C. Somervell,* (Oxford: Oxford University Press, 1946).

synthesis of world history based on universal rhythms of rise, flowering and decline, and examines history from a global perspective. One of the conclusions Toynbee reached as a result of his research was that civilizations die by suicide, not murder.

Toynbee is not alone in this conclusion. In his address at TED2003 (the Technology, Entertainment and Design, or TED, conference in February 2003), Jared Diamond, award-winning scholar of ecology, biology, history, and best selling author of *Guns, Germs and Steel*, gave a glimpse at his research behind his subsequent book, *Collapse: How Societies Choose to Fail or Succeed*. With lessons from the Norse of Ice Age Greenland, deforested Easter Island, and present-day Montana, Diamond addressed the question, "Why do societies fail?"

> *One blueprint for trouble, making collapse likely, is a conflict of interest between the short-term interests of the decision-making elites and the long-term interests of society as a whole—especially if the elites are able to insulate themselves from the consequences of their action. That is, when what is good in the short run for the elites is bad in the long run for the society as a whole, there's a real risk of the elites making decisions that will bring the society down in the long term.*[2]

Toynbee and Diamond's work pertained to the decline, decay, and death of cultures in civilizations at a macro level. I will argue that this blueprint for trouble also pertains, on a micro level, to cultures in smaller organizations as well--to economies, governments, political parties, churches, industries, companies, unions, for-profit and non-profit organizations of all types and kinds.

Simon Johnson, a former Chief Economist for the International Monetary Fund (IMF), makes this very point in his article, "The Quiet Coup," which appeared in the May 2009 issue of *The Atlantic*. The IMF is generally the stop of last resort for countries on their last economic breath—private capital has abandoned them, regional trading-bloc partners haven't been able to throw them a strong enough lifeline, and last ditch attempts to borrow from friendly, more prosperous nations have fallen through. In his experience with the IMF he has observed, "Typically, these countries are in a desperate

---

[2] Jared Diamond, "Jared Diamond: Why Societies Collapse," TED Ideas Worth Sharing, February 2003 (posted October 2008): http://www.ted.com/index.php/talks/jared_diamond_on_why_societies_collapse.html

economic situation for one simple reason—the powerful elites within them overreached in good times and took too many risks."[3] Further, he observes, "In its depth and suddenness, the U.S. economic crisis [2008-09] is shockingly reminiscent of moments we have recently seen in emerging markets (and only in emerging markets): South Korea (1997), Malaysia (1998), Russia and Argentina (time and again)... But there's a deeper and more disturbing similarity: elite business interests—financiers, in the case of the U.S.—played a central role in creating the crisis."[4]

This blueprint for trouble also applies to the subcultures of organizations comprising larger organizations. Too many of our leaders today, at all levels, prosper by making decisions that ultimately devalue the organization they serve. They sacrifice long-term goals in favor of short-term results.

> *"Stanley O'Neal, the CEO of Merrill Lynch, pushed his firm heavily into the mortgage-backed securities market at its peak in 2005 and 2006; in October 2007 he acknowledged, "The bottom line is, we—I—got it wrong by being overexposed to subprime, and we suffered as a result of impaired liquidity in that market. No man is more disappointed than I am in that result." O'Neal took home a $14 million bonus in 2006; in 2007, he walked away from Merrill with a severance package worth $162 million, although it is presumably worth much less today.[5]*

Making matters worse, the fact that these elites are rewarded so handsomely without apparent regard to their actual short-term performance, and certainly with a blind eye toward the future, has two further detrimental effects. First, it insulates them from the long-term consequences their short-term decision-making has on the customers, employees, vendors, communities, and all of the others who have a stake in the organization's success. As we learn at an early age, focusing on the golden eggs, to the exclusion of the health of the goose that lays them, inevitably leads to the death of the goose. Second, because this pattern of decision-making is richly rewarded, it therefore becomes the object of emulation by those who aspire to leadership positions in that organization. It results in the passing of a dysfunctional intergenerational tendency from one leadership generation to the next.

---

[3]  Simon Johnson, "The Quiet Coup," *The Atlantic*, May 2009, http://www.theatlantic.com/doc/print/200905/imf-advice
[4]  Ibid.
[5]  Ibid.

*Works like Barbarians at the Gate, Wall Street, and Bonfire of the Vanities—all intended as cautionary tales—served only to increase Wall Street's mystique. Michael Lewis noted in Portfolio last year that when he wrote Liar's Poker, an insider's account of the financial industry, in 1989, he had hoped the book might provoke outrage at Wall Street's hubris and excess. Instead, he found himself "knee-deep in letters from students at Ohio State who wanted to know if I had any other secrets to share. ...They'd read my book as a how-to manual."[6]*

# DENOMINATOR MANAGEMENT VS. NUMERATOR LEADERSHIP

The standard definition of productivity is outputs divided by inputs. In business this translates to:

$$Productivity = \frac{Revenue}{Costs}$$

It is this equation that led Gary Hamel to coin the term, "denominator managers." Denominator managers are managers who, either through limitations in their vision, creativity, courage, or skill, focus on cost reduction (i.e., the denominator), and neglect value creation (i.e., the numerator). I'm sure you've seen the species.

Denominator managers worship at the altar of quarterly EPS. They know how to manipulate wealth, but are impotent when it comes to creating wealth. They know how to cut fat, but not how to build muscle. They know how to harvest, but not how to plant. They know how to gut and slaughter, but not how to track and hunt. They put conformance before creativity, productivity before quality, and administrative efficiency before customer service.

Denominator managers employ cost-cutting as a strategy, rather than the tactic of desperation that it is. If cost-cutting were a strategy, then companies would be at the height of their profitability when they padlocked the doors. Cost-cutting is nothing more than a tactic by which you retreat and regroup after being outsmarted by the competition or surprised by the market, so you can develop a new strategy to replace the one you either didn't have, or the one you did have but which didn't work.

I've adapted a story told by Minnesota businessman and author, Har-

6  Ibid.

vey McKay, which illustrates the vision impairment from which denominator managers suffer. When asked how he enjoyed the previous night's performance of Schubert's Unfinished Symphony, the denominator manager offered the following report:

1. For considerable periods, the four oboe players had nothing to do. Their number should be reduced, and their work spread over the whole orchestra.
2. Forty violins were playing identical notes. This seems unnecessary duplication, and this section should be drastically cut. If a larger volume of sound is required, this could be achieved with an electronic amplifier.
3. Much effort was expended in the playing of demi-semi-quavers. This seems an excessive refinement, and it is recommended that all notes be rounded to the nearest semi-quaver. If this were done, it should be possible to use trainees and lower-grade operators.
4. No useful purpose is served by repeating with horns the passage that has already been handled by the strings. If all such redundant passages were eliminated, the concert could be reduced to twenty minutes.
5. If Schubert had attended to these matters, he probably would have been able to finish this symphony after all.

Too many organizations are over-populated with denominator managers because the cultural ecosystem in most organizations encourages their propagation. I attribute this to several things. Chief among them is the fact that cost reduction is easy to do, easy to measure on a quarterly basis, and can be achieved by an individually motivated mercenary. This then has both a direct and a vicarious effect on others who aspire to leadership positions in that organization—they learn to emulate that behavior that they see is so richly rewarded.

Value creation, on the other hand, is incredibly hard to do and even more difficult to quantify on a quarterly basis. Value creation requires greater strength of leadership than cost reduction because value creation requires visionary teamwork and very often involves changing the competitive rules, even changing the game, in the organization's marketplace.

Numerator leaders are mindful of the denominator because they understand that without a margin there is no mission. However, they also understand that you don't sacrifice long-term goals for short-term objectives. Numerator leaders worry about cost effectiveness, not merely cost reduction.

They employ creativity to grow, and conformance to protect. They know that quality comes before productivity because if you chase quality, you can get productivity, but if you chase productivity, you won't get quality—producing crappy products faster and cheaper than you did before still leaves you with crappy products. They put customer service before administrative efficiency for the same reasons—pissing off customers more efficiently than you did before still leaves you with pissed-off customers. Numerator leaders look at an organization as a holistic ecosystem, not as a decomposition of discreet parts.

One example of where this tension between numerator leadership and denominator management has manifest is in the tension between innovation and operational efficiency. Unfortunately, too many leaders see innovation and operational effectiveness as mutually exclusive, an either/or tradeoff. For example, in his June 6, 2007, blog post, "Told You So!" Tom Peters stirred the ire of Six Sigma devotees with a comment on a quote from page 307 of his 1997 book, *The Circle of Innovation*:

> *I was riffing on the problems associated with ISO 9000 certification, and unearthed the perfect quote to match my sentiments, courtesy Richard Buetow, then director of corporate quality for business systems at Motorola:*
>
> *'With ISO 9000 you can still have terrible processes and products. You can certify a manufacturer that makes life jackets from concrete, as long as those jackets are made according to the documented procedures and the company provides next of kin with instructions on how to complain about defects. That's absurd.'*
>
> *What's particularly interesting about that, in addition to the amusing-but-deadly-serious content, is that the speaker is a Motorolan. Long before Welch at GE, Motorola was the poster child for wholesale adoption of Six Sigma quality processes. And, though the process worked wonders on quality in the short term, it apparently starved innovation, an under-tended priority for historically innovative Motorola...*[7]

Innovation and operational effectiveness are not mutually exclusive; they can peacefully co-exist. However, if you chase cost reduction you won't get innovation, but if you chase innovation you can realize cost effectiveness.

---

[7]    Tom Peters, "Told You So!" *tompeters!*, June 6, 2007: http://www.tompeters.com/entries.php?note=009788.php

Where denominator managers give their energy to cost reduction, numerator leaders give their energy to both. In fact, on the very same day as Peters' post, *Business Week* editor Bruce Nussbaum posted, "Six Sigma Fights Back In The Debate Over Efficiency vs. Creativity." In this post Nussbaum talks about "parallel pathing" and refers to the need for organizations to be ambidextrous:

> *The black belt Six Sigma folks are steaming that they were cast as "anti-innovation" and are providing lots of examples of how they can be creative. At the same time, we are getting lots of examples of how Six Sigma rooted out creativity in company after company. One letter came in from a top NBC exec describing how the network lost it when GE applied Six Sigma to programming, took out all the variation in local news, and sent ratings plummeting.*
>
> *The truth, of course, is that you can get all kinds of great incremental innovation from Six Sigma. But you're not likely to get any breakthrough, paradigm-changing innovation from a process-focused system that reduces variability and risk.*
>
> *The best way for big companies to get what they need is through parallel-pathing (I like that term). Jeneanne Rae discusses this in her essay in "Inside Innovation" on "ambidextrous" corporations. Bank of America, Starwood, and other companies do this very well. Put Six Sigma and innovation on two parallel tracks organizationally and then meld them.*
>
> *Both tracks have separate needs so keep them separate. Finance both adequately (don't stint on innovation as many companies do). Appoint an ambidextrous manager to oversee the two tracks. When the innovation track generates a scalable breakthrough concept or product, shift it to the larger process-oriented track for implementation.*
>
> *Just remember that the return on breakthrough innovation projects is far higher than the return on incremental innovation. According to the Blue Ocean folks[8], only 14% of all projects in companies can be considered "radical" innovation but they generate 38% of revenue and 64% of profits.*
>
> *Parallel-pathing is hard to do. Finding ambidextrous managers is hard to do. It's all hard to do—but the payoff is enor-*

---

[8] A reference to the 2005 book, *Blue Ocean Strategy*™, written by W. Chan Kim and Renée Mauborgne, and the accompanying body of work produced by the INSEAD Blue Ocean Strategy Institute.

*mous. Just think of what the iPhone is about to bring to Apple—
and how it is going to change the world of cell phones for Verizon,
Nokia, and other players.*[9]

Steve Jobs, Apple's CEO, is perhaps the consummate numerator
leader. For example, recall the state of the economy during the latter half of
2008: stock markets were on a wild roller-coaster ride; credit markets were
stalled; governments across the globe were taking unprecedented action to
bailout their respective financial institutions, and they were collaborating with
other governments in unprecedented ways to deal with these interdependent
market systems in as coherent a fashion as their leadership capability could
muster. In October 2008, Apple reported their fourth quarter financial results,
and held their quarterly call with financial analysts. In his October 21, 2008
*Mac Word* post, "Steve Jobs Holds Court", *Macworld* Editorial Director, Jason
Snell, offered this report of that call:

> *It's not often that Steve Jobs appears on an Apple finan-
> cial-results phone call. But there he was this past Tuesday, appear-
> ing as a surprise "special guest" as Apple unveiled its fourth-quarter
> earnings.*
>
> *And Jobs held court, making some scripted pronounce-
> ments, parrying with questioning analysts, and offering enough
> vague tidbits to whip Apple Kremlinologists into a frenzy.*
>
> *Among the biggest issues Jobs confronted was the ongo-
> ing global financial climate. Jobs opened by saying, "Some remark-
> able things are happening at Apple, but everything is set against
> this remarkable economic slowdown." Later, he said, "We are not
> economists. Your next door neighbor can likely predict what's going
> to happen as well as we can."*
>
> *But in general, Jobs was about as optimistic as he could
> be about Apple, given the global economic conditions. He said that
> Apple customers are the "smartest, most product-aware customers
> in the market." While they may postpone purchases, he said, they're
> unlikely to abandon Apple and would more likely just delay pur-
> chases rather than switch to a competitor.*
>
> *More importantly, Apple's cash reserves—Jobs said the
> company has almost $25 billion dollars in the bank, and is free of*

---

[9]  Bruce Nussbaum, "Six Sigma Fights Back In The Debate Over Efficiency vs. Creativity," *Business-
Week*, June 6, 2007: http://blogs.businessweek.com/mt/mt-tb.cgi/6714.1412814389

*debt—will help the company invest its way through the downturn and emerge with better products and a stronger position over its competitors, as it did during the last economic downturn. Apple, always conservative when it comes to estimating future financial results, was especially conservative this time out. Jobs, again, had an explanation: "There's a lot of prudence in [our forecast]," he said. "And it's also October. October has always been a foggy month for us. Sales don't often take off until November sometime.... We think we're doing the right things, and we think we know what the results may be, but there's a lot of prudence built in. We're not economists and we read the same newspapers you do."*

*One analyst suggested that Apple could use the cash to buy back its own stock, but Jobs intimated that the money would be better used for funding R&D and perhaps even acquiring other companies or talented employees. Or even better, much of it could remain as a safety cushion. "It [the cash] isn't burning a hole in our pocket," he said.*[10]

Rather than using their cash to buy back their own stock, which would have certainly helped the immediate stock price, as one analyst suggested, Jobs intimated that Apple's money would be better used for funding research and development, and perhaps even acquiring other companies or talented employees. This is how numerator leaders think.

Bill George is another numerator leader. Currently professor of management practice at Harvard Business School, he is a former chairman and CEO of Medtronic. He joined Medtronic in 1989 as president and COO, and was elected CEO in 1991, serving in that capacity through 2001. He was chairman of the board from 1996 to 2002. Under his leadership, Medtronic's market capitalization grew from $1.1 billion to $60 billion, averaging 35 percent a year. He is the author of three best-selling books: *Authentic Leadership: Rediscovering the Secrets to Creating Lasting Value*, *True North: Discover Your Authentic Leadership*, and his most recent, *Finding Your True North: A Personal Guide*. He was professor of leadership and governance at IMD International in Lausanne, Switzerland, and executive-in-residence at Yale University's School of Management.

In his March 15, 2008, *Wall Street Journal* article, "Seven Lessons for Leading in Crisis," Bill George reminds us, "[A] crisis offers the best opportu-

---

[10]   Jason Snell, "Steve Jobs Holds Court," *Mac Word*, October 21, 2008: http://www.macworld.com/article/136286/2008/10/jobs_analyst_phone.html

nity to change the game in your favor, with new products or services to gain market share. Many people look at a crisis as something to get through, until they can go back to business as usual. But 'business as usual' never returns because markets are irrevocably changed. Why not create the changes that move the market in your favor, instead of waiting and reacting to the changes as they take place?"[11] This is how numerator leaders think.

Clearly, being a numerator leader takes much greater strength of leadership than does denominator management, so effective numerator leaders are harder to find and/or develop. To make matters worse, in many companies the life span of a numerator leader at any level is often abbreviated. In too many business organizations numerator leaders are endangered and they are not on the firm's protected species list.

# "TOUGH BOSSES"

In addition to the over population of denominator managers, and the endangerment of the numerator leader, I am also concerned about the prevailing fascination with "tough bosses." It's not that being tough is bad; my concern is with how people define "tough." The trouble is, while most of these tough bosses may be tough on their employees, they are eunuchs when it comes to being tough on the competition. Denominator managers are frequently tough on their employees. Numerator leaders are tough on the competition.

A tough, denominator manager is coaching a "right-sized" worker: "Do you see the beautiful home on that idyllic hill overlooking the water? And do you see the armored vehicle delivering that truckload of money to that home? Just look at it, and just imagine… If you work a little harder—you may even have to double your efforts—but if you work hard, someday, all of that will be mine!"

In sports and in business, I happen to think that how tough a person is on the competition is far more important than how tough they may be on their fellow team members. Yet, for reasons defying any logic I can muster—other than laziness on the part of their boards—organizations hire these denominator tough guys and pay them as if they were franchise players. Worse yet, these guys seem to be awarded these obscene bonuses and incentives no matter how well their organization performs—even if their organization tanks, and even if it takes their whole industry with them, they reap quite handsome rewards.

---

[11]  Bill George, "Seven lessons for Leading in Crisis," *Wall Street Journal*, March 15, 2009. http://online.wsj.com/article/SB123551729786163925.html

# THE EXCESSES OF EXECUTIVE ARISTOCRACY

Following the infusion of $350 billion in U.S. taxpayer money into the U.S. financial industry, courtesy of financial bailout package officially known as the "Emergency Economic Stabilization Act of 2008," the excesses of executive aristocracy in the U.S. financial sector became so egregious that it even compelled comment from then newly elected U.S. President Barack Obama, "We don't begrudge anybody for achieving success. And we believe that success should be rewarded. But what gets people upset — and rightfully so — are executives being rewarded for failure. Especially when those rewards are subsidized by U.S. taxpayers."[12]

John Thain, former CEO of Merrill Lynch, has the unfortunate distinction of achieving poster boy status for the excesses of executive aristocracy. J. Robert Brown's January 26, 2009 blog post, "Executive Compensation and John Thain", on TheRacetotheBottom.org[13], provides a quick recap:

> *This [John Thain] is the same person who was listed by AP [Associated Press] as the highest paid CEO in 2007 ($83.1 million) and only a month or two ago, after a disastrous year, proposed that he receive a $10 million bonus. Now, it turns out, that in early 2008, he had his office suite (office, two conference rooms and a reception area) redecorated. According to CNBC, the redecoration cost $1.22 million, with the single biggest chunk paid to the interior decorator, Michael S. Smith Design, apparently the same firm used by Steven Spielberg, Michelle Pfeiffer, Cindy Crawford, Sir Evelyn de Rothschild, and, apparently, Michelle Obama.*
>
> *As for the materials actually used in the redecoration, the amounts included: Area Rug $87,784, Mahogany Pedestal Table $25,713, 19th Century Credenza $68,179, Pendant Light Furniture $19,751, 4 Pairs of Curtains $28,091, Pair of Guest Chairs $87,784, George IV Chair $18,468, 6 Wall Sconces $2,741, Parchment Waste Can $1,405, Roman Shade Fabric $10,967, Roman Shades $7,315, Coffee Table $5,852, and Commode on Legs $35,115.*
>
> *CNBC also noted that some who work for Thain did very well. His driver received $230,000 for one year's work, "which*

---

[12] Stephen Labaton and Vikas Bajaj, "In Curbing Pay, Obama Seeks to Alter Corporate Culture," *New York Times*, February 4, 2009, http://www.nytimes.com/2009/02/05/us/politics/05pay.html?_r=2

[13] Race to the Bottom is a collaboration of professionals, students and faculty that provide analyses of the laws and regulatory measures that govern today's corporations.

*included the driver's $85,000 salary and bonus of $18,000, and*
*another $128,000 in overtime pay." The article noted that drivers*
*"of top executives are often paid about half that amount."*

*All of this is sensational enough in an era of incredible*
*hardship. But the issue isn't one spendthrift CEO (one imagines that*
*there are many other CEOs who did the same thing and are cringing*
*at the possibility of leaks to the press about their remodeling). It's the*
*entire system. We operate in a legal environment where this type of*
*information doesn't have to be reported to the board of directors.*

*Delaware courts have developed almost no standards*
*for what must be reported to the board and have in place a legal*
*system that encourages boards to remain uninformed. Even if by*
*some unexpected chance, the board learned of the remodeling, it*
*has no duty to act and, if directors want to retain their comfortable*
*sinecure, they have every incentive to ignore it. The only meaningful*
*way for directors to lose their sinecure is not to be re-nominated by*
*the board. The best way for that to occur is to irritate the CEO. Thus,*
*whether it's remodeling the office or allowing the CEO to make*
*personal use of the corporate aircraft, directors, under the standards*
*put in place by the Delaware courts, have little or no incentive to*
*deny the CEO these privileges.*

*And how much did the Merrill Lynch directors make in*
*the last year reported (for fiscal year 2007)? Between $250,000 and*
*$280,000, a very nice sinecure to be sure.[14]*

John Thain spent $1.22 million redecorating his office; I wonder
what percent of U.S. homes are even worth $1.22 million. After leading Mer-
rill Lynch to $15 billion in losses for the quarter—for the quarter—and putting
them in a position where acquisition by the Bank of America (BoA) was their
best viable option for survival, Thain rushed the payment of "a couple of billion bucks in bonuses before the BoA deal closed."[15]

Contrast this with Japanese Air Lines (JAL) President and CEO Haruka Nishimatsu, as told in this February 8, 2009, *CBS Sunday Morning* News
report, "Economy Class: CEO Of The People:"

*When Detroit's Big Three CEOs came to Congress beg-*
*ging for a bailout, they got a lecture for arriving in their private*

---

[14]  J. Robert Brown, "Executive Compensation and John Thain," *The Race to the Bottom.org*, January 26, 2009: http://www.theracetothebottom.org/home/executive-compensation-and-john-thain.html
[15]  Bill Saporito, "The Deeper Truth About Thain's Ouster from BofA," *TIME*, January 25, 2009: http://www.time.com/time/business/article/0,8599,1873835,00.html

*jets. There's a lot of resentment these days against executive com-*
*pensation and all their perks. Does any CEO anywhere set a good*
*example? Barry Petersen says maybe they could learn something*
*from the boss of Japan Airlines. When Haruka Nishimatsu had to*
*cut salaries at the world's 10th largest airline, he also cut his own,*
*to just $90,000. He also takes the bus to work, did away with his*
*private office, and even sorts out the newspapers for passengers on*
*flights.*[16]

The *CBS Sunday Morning* report went on to point out that Haruka Nishimatsu takes public transportation to and from the office (no personal limo and driver), and purchases his business suits at an everyday retailer. "When one wears an Armani suit," he said, "it puts distance between us." His explanation of his egalitarian philosophy was pretty simple, "We're all in the same boat."

It may be fairly argued that John Thain's situation is not representative of the norm. In his defense, Thain argued that the size of Merrill Lynch's 2008, $4 billion, discretionary bonus pool, the mix of cash and stock, and the timing of the payments, were all determined together with Bank of America. He also recognized his office redecoration as a mistake and has apologized for it, and he is no longer with the Bank of America. However, my experience tells me that while Thain's sins of executive excess may be among the more infamous, he is not a lone example. I cite him simply because his situation is so well-known. My experience tells me that there are many other leaders who have received handsome rewards that are not commensurate with their performance, and I challenge you to test this assertion against your own experience.

How does a board, how do leaders at any position, justify paying out bonuses and other incentives to people whose performance, or lack thereof, leads their company into the crapper? Frankly, I can think of no better icon to represent the excesses of executive aristocracy than Thain's $35,000 antique commode, which, by the way, is for decoration only and can't be used.

As reported by the *Associated Press* in a January 29, 2009, article in the *Los Angeles Times*, "John Thain Defends Merrill Lynch Bonuses Amid Bank of America Takeover," Thain defended Merrill Lynch's 2008, $4 billion, discretionary bonus pool saying, "if you don't pay your best people, you will destroy

---

[16] *CBS News Sunday Morning*, "Economy Class: CEO Of The People," *CBS News*, February 8, 2009, http://www.cbsnews.com/stories/1998/07/09/sunday/main13562.shtml

your franchise.[17]" I don't mean to keep picking on John Thain, but in this case I do believe his thinking is representative of current leadership norms. Perhaps I am naïve, but I humbly suggest that if you and your people led your firm to a $27 billion loss for the year, if you and your people led your franchise to the point where your acquisition by another firm was your best option for survival, then your franchise does not have the best people.

When they were young, I would tell my kids on Saturday that if they finished their household chores and school homework in time, we would go to a matinee movie on Sunday afternoon. They understood that if they didn't get their chores done, or didn't get their homework done, then we didn't go to the movies on Sunday afternoon. When they got older, I told my kids that if they got their household chores and their homework done, they could use the car for some special event. They understood that if they didn't get their chores done, or didn't get their homework done, then they didn't get to use the car. My kids understood this. How is it that worldly, well-educated executives can't understand this?

I've also heard other geniuses defend their undeserved bonuses with the argument that they worked very hard for that money. I must be really naïve. The way I was raised, I don't care how hard you worked, if you didn't produce the results, then you didn't get the bonus. My dad used to have a saying, "Every day you have to march twenty miles. Some days it will be sunny and the terrain will be downhill. Some days it will be cold with snow up to your belly button and the terrain uphill all the way. It doesn't matter. There may or may not be a prize if when you get there. There definitely will not be one if you don't. Every day you have to march twenty miles." This isn't that difficult a concept to grasp.

People think that professional athletes' salaries can be obscene, but at least there is some correlation between their performance and their incentives. A professional athlete's contract may include an obscene incentive if the team makes the playoffs. But no matter how hard the athlete works, if the team doesn't make the playoffs, the athlete understands that he or she isn't going to be awarded that particular incentive. Professional athletes understand this. How is it that worldly, well-educated executives can't understand this?

If these executives were to their organizations what Michael Jordan was to the business of basketball, or what Tiger Woods is to the business of golf, their compensation might make sense. However, with rare exception,

---

[17] *Associated Press*, "John Thain Defends Merrill Lynch Bonuses Amid Bank of America Takeover," *Los Angeles Times*, January 27, 2009: http://www.latimes.com/business/la-fi-thain27-2009jan27,0,476991.story

most of these guys are not that kind of impact player. Regardless of a person's level or rank, I don't mind paying "A-caliber" compensation to "A-caliber" talent, but I have a real problem paying "A-caliber" compensation to "B- and C-caliber" talent. Too many "B- and C-caliber" leaders are getting "A-caliber" pay.

I am not alone in my issue with people receiving excessive rewards linked more to their position in the organizational hierarchy than to their contribution and performance. In Ken Burns' film, *Baseball*, conservative American columnist and baseball fan George Will shared his perspective on the salaries major league baseball players have enjoyed since the death of the reserve clause.

> *Fifty-five to fifty-six million people pay to get into the ballparks each year; not one of them is buying a ticket to see an owner. I happen to be a semi-Marxist in this field; I believe in the labor theory of value. The players are the labor and create the economic value, so they ought to get the lion's share of the rewards.*[18]

How are other businesses different in this regard? When a customer buys a company's product or service, not one of them is handing over their hard earned money for anything the shareholders, the board, senior executives, or other members of management are doing. The people in the company that actually produce and deliver the product or service—the inventors, the product designers, those in manufacturing and sales, and those in service delivery—are the ones creating the economic value. Yet, on an individual basis, the lion's share of the rewards go to the executives and others who do the planning, the budgeting, the accounting and the other acts of administration, versus those who do the acts of value creation.

Again, I lay a lot of this at the feet of the leaders, like the boards of directors, because what gets rewarded is what gets done and it is the boards that ultimately decide what gets rewarded. In his July 18, 1996, Economics Discussion Paper #96-04, "Executive Compensation in Japan," written for Colgate University Economics Department's Institute for the Study of Labor, Takao Kato noted, "CEO compensation in Japan is structured to encourage young managers to develop long-term relationships with the company, whereas the reverse incentive exists in the U.S."[19]

[18] George Will, "Baseball: A Film by Ken Burns," The Baseball Film Project, Inc., 1994, Inning 9: Home, 1970 – 1994.
[19] Takao Kato, "Executive Compensation in Japan," *Social Science Research Network*, January 19, 1998: http://papers.ssrn.com/sol3/papers.cfm?abstract_id=8066

It's too bad that boards see their job only as one of working in the best interests of the shareholders, rather than working in the best interests of all stakeholders. I'd settle for them working in the best interests of the shareholders' grandchildren.

## SHARED SACRIFICE

Too many of these so-called tough bosses are brought into an organization, demand much sacrifice and inflict much hardship on others, while not taking a leadership share of that sacrifice and hardship for themselves. They reduce the work force, force fit performance ratings to a normal curve, put a cap on increases, cut middle management incentive plans, eliminate vacation accruals and restructure pensions. They inflict much sacrifice on those members of their organization who actually lay hands on product and deal with customers, and when this "let them eat cake" action produces immediate, albeit temporary, financial results, they themselves are richly rewarded. They do not take a leadership share of the sacrifice, nor do they make a durable dent in market share or market cap, yet they somehow earn seven- and eight-digit compensation packages.

Too many leaders are quick to ask others to sacrifice during times of adversity. Worse yet, too many leaders prosper from inflicting sacrifice upon others in their organization. Certainly, I can understand that an organization can get in such a bad way that it is necessary to cut wages and/or benefits, and reduce the workforce. What I can't understand is how a leader can personally prosper while throwing crewmates overboard, and/or while their remaining crew is enduring hardship. Leadership is about going first and setting an example, and this especially includes going first and taking a leadership share of the sacrifice during times of adversity.

It's such an iconic example, let's look again at the leadership shown by the U.S. financial industry leading to and following the $700 billion bailout, officially known as the "Emergency Economic Stabilization Act of 2008." After the American people, whose own investments and home values were beaten and battered, shared $350 billion of their own financial provisions to rescue the very industry that administered that beating, leading executives in that industry squandered those precious provisions on undeserved bonuses, frivolous retreats, jets and office renovations.

On Hornblower's ship, The Indefatigable, while patrolling off the coast of Spain, they learned that the ship that was to resupply their provisions

41

had been sunk by the French off the coast of Gibraltar. Consequently, it was necessary to conserve what provisions they had, and Captain Pellew ordered everyone's rations cut—including his own.

Imagine on Hornblower's ship, when provisions are being rationed, there is a crewmember who plays a role so critical in running the ship (like banks do in an economy), and that one crewmember is gravely ill. Even though this crewmember's illness is self-inflicted, what this ill crewmember does is so crucial to the ship's operation that we want to make a special effort to nurse him back to health. To do so, it means that other members of the crew are going to have to sacrifice even more of their already-limited rations because this ill, but vital, crewman needs them for his recovery (just like U.S. taxpayers, whose own investments and home values have been beaten and battered, did with the $350 billion bailout for the financial sector).

Now imagine that the other crewmembers on Hornblower's ship discover that the ill crewmember has been squandering the extra provisions that they so graciously shared with him to speed his recovery (perhaps he was trading them for personal entertainment or gain). What do you think the other crewmembers would have done to him even though his special skills are so important to the operation of the ship?

At what point does the toxic behavior of even an especially skilled crewmember, team member, or society member, become so detrimental to the chemistry of the crew, the team or the society, that the value of their special skills is outweighed by the toxic effect of their behavior?

You would have thought, after the public expression of outrage at the financial industry's belligerent bailout bacchanalia that some learning would have occurred and some humility might have enlightened those who were next in line with their hands out—the U.S. auto industry. Alas, the arrogance of a disconnected aristocracy knows no bounds.

Consider Ford CEO, Alan Mulally, whose own compensation package paid him about $22 million in 2008, when coming to the U.S. Congress in November 2008 to request yet another $25 billion of the U.S. public's own beaten and battered provisions to bailout the U.S. auto industry. When testifying before the House Financial Services Committee on November 19, 2008, Mulally, along with the CEOs of GM and Chrysler, was asked if he would consider cutting his own salary. His leadership response, "I think I'm okay where I am."[20] Congressional leaders sent the auto executives home after that

---

[20] *U.S. News & World Report*, "Auto Bailout: GM CEO May Work for $1 a Year," November 26, 2008: http://usnews.rankingsandreviews.com/cars-trucks/daily-news/081126-Auto-Bailout-GM-CEO-May-Work-for-1-a-Year/

contentious week of hearings on the bailout plan, asking them to draw up business plans explaining what they would do with federal money before the government will consider their plight any further. It wasn't until then that Ford Motor Company Chairman William Ford, Jr., said that he would review Mulally's pay.

Contrast these examples with that of Seagate Technology when faced with the need to cut nearly 3,000 workers, or six percent of their global staff, during that same time period. Yes, there were layoffs, but there were other big elements of their restructuring as well. First, William Watkins, Seagate CEO, and Dave Wickersham, Seagate president and COO, both abruptly left, and Stephen Luczo, who had been CEO prior to Watkins, returned to take the role again. Further, the entire C-suite saw their salaries chopped, as did some members of the rank-and-file. For the CEO and other top executives, their salaries were reduced by twenty-five percent; for senior vice presidents and vice presidents, their pay fell twenty percent and fifteen percent, respectively; and pay cuts of ten percent came for some members of Seagate's other management, sales, supervisory, and "professional" positions.[21]

As the numerator leader Bill George reminds us in his March 15, 2009, *Wall Street Journal* article, "Seven Lessons for Leading in Crisis:"

> *Before asking others to sacrifice, first volunteer yourself. If there are sacrifices to be made—and there will be—then the leaders should step up and make the greatest sacrifices themselves. Crises are the real tests of leaders' True North. Everyone is watching to see what the leaders do. Will they stay true to their values? Will they bow to external pressures, or confront the crisis in a straight-forward manner? Will they be seduced by short-term rewards, or will they make near-term sacrifices in order to fix the long-term situation?[22]*

I would have never imagined that it might be necessary to point out the obvious, but I am compelled to remind you that leadership is about leading. Leadership is about going first—especially in times of adversity.

---

[21] Jordan Robertson, *Associated Press*, "Seagate To Cut Nearly 3,000 Workers, 6 Pct Of Global Staff, As New CEO Takes Over," *StarTribune*, January 14, 2009: http://www.startribune.com/business/37589619.html?elr=KArksUUUU

[22] Bill George, "Seven lessons for Leading in Crisis," *Wall Street Journal*, March 15, 2009. http://online.wsj.com/article/SB123551729786163925.html

# ORGANIZATIONAL NICOTINE

A denominator leadership style is to an organizational body what nicotine is to a human body. Like the immediate satisfaction that comes with a hit of nicotine, so is there an immediate satisfaction and quite handsome rewards that come with hitting short-term revenue and EBIT targets. However, despite the immediate gratification, just as nicotine is harmful to the human body's long-term health, so is denominator management harmful to the long-term health of the organizational body.

When you inhale smoke, nicotine is carried deep into your lungs. There it is absorbed quickly into the bloodstream and carried throughout your body. Nicotine affects many parts of the body, including your heart and blood vessels, your hormones, your metabolism, and your brain. Similarly, when you adopt a pattern of denominator decision-making, that style is carried deep into the lungs of the organization. There it is absorbed quickly into the decision-making style throughout the organizational body. Carried by leadership-by-example and vicarious learning, denominator management becomes the preferred style, the rewarded style, the style to which up-and-coming leaders aspire, thus affecting the organization's heart, blood vessels, hormones, metabolism, and brain.

Nicotine produces pleasant feelings that make the smoker want to smoke more. But nicotine also acts as a kind of depressant by interfering with the flow of information between nerve cells. As the nervous system adapts to nicotine, smokers tend to increase the number of cigarettes they smoke. This, in turn, increases the amount of nicotine in the smoker's blood. After a while, the smoker develops a tolerance to the drug. Tolerance means that it takes more nicotine to get the same effect that the smoker used to get from smaller amounts. This leads to an increase in smoking over time. The smoker reaches a certain nicotine level and keeps smoking to maintain this level of nicotine.

Similarly, because it is much easier to cut costs than it is to add value, the immediate and tangible results produced by cost-cutting makes the denominator leader adopt cost-cutting as their primary answer whenever their organization's financial performance is lagging. And because the effectiveness of cost-cutting diminishes with the more cost-cutting you do, denominator leaders will begin playing accounting games to compensate for that diminished effectiveness, thus interfering with an honest depiction of the organization's true health.

When smokers try to cut back or quit, the lack of nicotine leads to withdrawal symptoms. Withdrawal is both physical and mental. Physically, the body reacts to the absence of nicotine. Mentally, the smoker is faced with giving up a habit, which calls for a major change in behavior. The physical and mental both must be addressed for the quitting process to work. And just as nicotine is addicting and creates a physical and psychological dependence in a human body, so is a denominator dominant leadership style addicting, and creates a physical and psychological dependence in the organizational body.

Those who have smoked regularly and suddenly stop using tobacco, or greatly reduce the amount smoked, will have withdrawal symptoms. Symptoms usually start within a few hours of the last cigarette and peak about two to three days later when most of the nicotine and its by-products are out of the body. Withdrawal symptoms can last for a few days to up to several weeks, and can include any of the following: dizziness; depression; feelings of frustration, impatience, and anger; anxiety; irritability; sleep disturbances, including having trouble falling asleep and staying asleep, and having bad dreams or even nightmares; trouble concentrating; restlessness; headaches; tiredness; and increased appetite. These symptoms can lead the smoker to start smoking cigarettes again to boost blood levels of nicotine back to a level where there are no symptoms.

An organization whose leadership has been dominated by denominator thinkers, but into which numerator leadership is now introduced, will have similar withdrawal symptoms. Symptoms usually start within a few hours of the new leaders' first planning session and/or capital investment decisions, and peak two or three quarters (or analyst calls) later when the new pattern of decision-making has become apparent. Withdrawal symptoms can last for a few quarters up to several years, and can include any of the following: organizational dizziness, organizational depression; organizational feelings of frustration, impatience, and anger; organizational anxiety; organizational irritability; and trouble maintaining organizational focus.

# 5

# Leadership, Rightly Understood

*Try not to become a man of success, but rather try to become a man of value.*
**Albert Einstein**
German-born theoretical physicist
1879 - 1955

## Based on my decades of observa-

tional research, one could reasonably conclude that leadership is about who can make the quickest decisions, and/or the most testosterone-induced decisions, and/or the most intellectually lazy, but cleverly cloaked in management-speak, decisions.

Power is the ability to transform your intentions into reality. Wisdom is the principle driven application of knowledge and experience. Leadership is the wise use of power. Leaders lead through: strength of vision and strength of values; commitment and loyalty; truth-telling; path-finding; creating safety to risk; and self-interest rightly understood

## Strength of Vision and Strength of Values

Leadership first necessarily requires strength of vision and strength of values. Leaders lead by articulating a positive view of the future for the group of people they seek to lead. Unfortunately, in too many organizations there is an excess of control, nearsighted vision, and situational values. Vision is looking into the future, not into the past—it is where you are going—your eyes are in the front of your head. Cultures that are growing and expanding have strong visions of where they are going. When they lose their vision, or lose faith in their vision, they begin to stagnate, decline, and decay.

Through strength of vision and strength of values leaders energize discretionary effort. Long ago, the nature of work was controllable effort. In Fredrick Taylor's factory, work was about the number of left-front fenders a person could hang on a chassis in an auto assembly line. Today, however, the important effort is not controllable. That effort which is important in today's fast paced, highly dynamic environment is not controllable effort; it is discretionary effort. It may occur on a Saturday afternoon when you're mowing the lawn and you choose to think about "the problem," and you come up with a better idea—that's the payoff effort.

Through strength of vision and strength of values leaders grow and acquire followers—followership is discretionary effort. As U.S. President John F. Kennedy reminded us, "Leaders cannot lead without the consent of the followers." In fact, voting is an excellent example of discretionary effort; but don't think for a second that voting is limited only to political elections. Employees vote every day. They vote when they decide to come early or stay late. They vote when they choose to think about "the problem." When an employee is staring at that computer screen you don't know if they're thinking about "the problem" or last night's ball game—you just won't know that. And customers vote every day. And stockholders vote every day.

Voting is a discretionary effort, and the degree to which you've created strength of vision and strength of values is the degree to which your stakeholders choose to engage in discretionary effort.

We know that we can hire a person's back and their hands, but if we want their minds, their hearts, and their soul, it takes more. You have to treat them like volunteers; you have to treat them like you want them to treat your finest customer. This requires strength of vision and strength of values. This is not a new leadership theory; this goes back to the cave. People will die for a noble cause, but not for $100,000 a year—no matter how materialistic the society. (This is a stolen line; the actual line comes from Jack London's *Martin Eden*, "God's own mad lover should do anything for the kiss, but not for thirty thousand dollars a year.") It has to do with the "mystery of sacrifice."

The mystery of sacrifice is not an intellectual concept; it is a spiritual one. When one sacrifices one's time, one's energy, to that which one believes to be noble and worthy, there is no sacrifice; there is an investment with a guaranteed return in that which is most precious to us—our own self-esteem. If you doubt this concept, just think about the last time you did something noble and worthy and ask yourself how you felt afterward. I guarantee you felt better; you felt more noble and worthy. No one's self esteem ever went down after sacrificing for something the person considered noble and worthy. Which is why there is no sacrifice; there is an investment with a guaranteed return.

In fact, we become like that unto which we sacrifice. Which is why, conversely, the person who sits around all day watching TV and eating junk food feels how? Low self-esteem. They'll go to the psychiatrist, and the psychiatrist will put them on the couch, but can't help them. Why? Because their patient isn't crazy; their patient is right. They have become like that unto which they have sacrificed. Their first best therapy is to get off their butt, go do something worthwhile, and presto, they'll start feeling more worthwhile.

What we have to do in our work organizations is create an environment where people feel there is some nobility about their work. This is one of the jobs of a leader, and they do it through strength of vision and strength of values—they create a sense of mission, a sense of purpose, which creates human energy. Leaders are not people who can make decisions quickly or loudly. Leaders are people who can create a common sense of mission and energize people about it.

## COMMITMENT AND LOYALTY

Leadership is not a title. John Quincy Adams, sixth president of the United States, makes this quite clear, "If your actions inspire others to dream more, learn more, do more and become more, you are a leader."

However one comes into a leadership role, once they earn the consent of their followers they must commit to their role or stand aside—and if they choose leadership, then he or she must be loyal to their choice. Of course, the leader and the followers' first loyalty must be to "the cause," the mission; next, however, they must be loyal to each other. In fact, stealing a page from eighteenth century philosopher John Locke, I would argue that whenever a leader or follower demonstrates a pattern of disloyalty—to the mission or to each other—then the other has the right, perhaps the duty, to throw them off.

Further, just like a seed grows roots below the surface before it blooms above, loyalty grows from the leader down to establish roots before it grows from the followers up causing the leader to bloom. That loyalty followers show for their leader is a function of the loyalty the leader has shown toward them.

Of course I have heard the argument that real business is not about all of this soft, feel-good stuff—real business is tough, it's about playing hard-ball and making money. Testosterone-fueled nonsense! Even General George S. Patton observed, "There is a great deal of talk about loyalty from the bottom to the top. Loyalty from the top down is even more necessary and is much less prevalent. One of the most frequently noted characteristics of great men who have remained great is loyalty to their subordinates."

One of the most common sins of leadership I have witnessed is a lack of loyalty in the leader toward his or her followers—the loss of the leader's commitment to the people they seek to lead—and it appears that this trend is increasing. Too many of our organizational leaders today are just passing through; like mercenaries they care more about their individual rewards than they do for the crew that earns it for them. If leaders don't display a genuine faith in their organization, its vision, its values, and dedicate themselves to it, then followers ask themselves, "Why should I?" And I'm not talking about that artificial, superficial, psych-up kind of dedication—the human capacity to detect insincerity is instantaneous and it just insults people's intelligence.

Today we are overpopulated with senior executives whose salaries have become more obscene than those of professional athletes (because there is less correlation with contribution and results), and who, with their rich golden parachutes, bounce from firm to firm with only transient loyalty. Because they assume that everyone else's motivations are the same as their own, they treat their followers like mercenaries, but will become seemingly puzzled and rankled when their followers actually begin to conduct themselves like mercenaries, too.

## TRUTH-TELLING

Hopefully, the concept of truth-telling is self-evident; however, to be clear, by "truth-telling" I mean unimpassioned, untainted, clinically objective honesty. In addition, by "truth-telling" I also mean authentic communication.

By "authentic communication" I do not mean that safe, sophisticated, academic language behind which so many people hide—and I especially do not mean that politically correct language that now dominates organizational dialogue. Such language only serves to camouflage meaning rather than reveal it. By "authentic communication" I mean civil, but clear and unambiguous language—respectful discourse—language that reveals your meaning. I want to elaborate on this point because I fear we—especially we Americans—are on a bad path in this regard.

In the spring of 2005 I had the opportunity to hear Mr. Marc Belton speak at a meeting of Medtronic's Black Employee Resource Group, MEC-CA. Mr. Belton was a senior vice president at General Mills at the time, and as cited in his introduction, Mr. Belton was recognized as "one of corporate America's most powerful African American executives." During his speech Mr. Belton caught my attention when he asserted, "Political correctness is the enemy of integrity." What a breath of fresh air! For so long we have confused political correctness with respectful discourse. Political correctness camouflages meaning; respectful discourse reveals it. Respectful discourse is our friend; political correctness is not.

## PATH-FINDING

Leaders don't work with roadmaps and driving directions; leaders work with a compass, reconnaissance, intelligence, and courage.

Too often I've seen managers dress up "best practices" and call it path-finding. For example, following the success of GE under Jack Welsh's leadership, how many of us in other companies had to endure our management's blind adoption of "GE best practices?" Certainly many of these were sensible ideas—those advancing a more quantitative approach to managing quality and making decisions, for example. And certainly, many of these were stupid ideas—like those around talent management that said you should deliberately churn the bottom "X percent" of a team's membership every year, or that you should force performance ratings to fit a particular statistical curve.

A similar effect can occur when a leader becomes infatuated with a particular book—"management by bestseller." For example, how many leaders were so smitten with Jim Collins' book, *Good to Great,* that they treated it like a biblical cookbook? You couldn't find a member of that leader's team that didn't have a copy on their desk—until the next book fad came along.

My point isn't whether a particular GE practice is a good or bad idea, or whether *Good to Great* or any other book contains good or bad ideas. My point is about the folly of emulation; it is the difference between being a carbon copy versus a genuine article. Whether it is the hero worship that occurs when another leader achieves celebrity status, or the management by bestseller that occurs when a particularly insightful book is published, too many leaders have become addicted to quick fixes, draw upon a narrow body of work, and have forgotten the ancient wisdom best expressed by the seventeenth century Japanese poet, Matsuo Bashō, "Do not follow in the footsteps of the master; rather, seek what the master sought."

By "path-finding" I mean more than setting a course; I also mean keeping oneself and one's organization aroused to challenge. In *Study of History*[1], Arnold J. Toynbee described parallel life cycles of growth, dissolution, a "time of troubles," a universal state, and a final collapse leading to a new genesis. His over-arching analysis cited moral and religious challenge, and response to such challenge, as the reasons for the robustness or decline of a civilization. He observed that it is leadership's arousal to challenge and creative response that provides the impetus for growth.

As illustrated in the Figure 2, a culture is stimulated by some challenge, requiring a new and creative response. But that response does not lead to a condition of ease; rather, it leads to a higher order challenge requiring a new and more creative response. And that response does not lead to a condition of ease but to a higher order challenge requiring a new and more creative response. Up the staircase of growth and development they go until leaders either become seduced by a condition of ease, or they lose their creativity.

*Figure 2 – Challenge and Response*

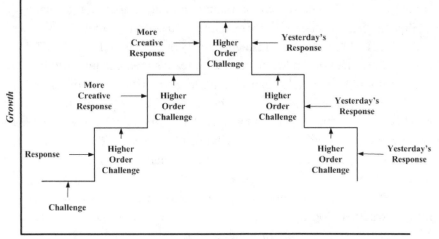

When leaders lose their creativity and respond to tomorrow's chal-

[1]  Arnold J. Toynbee, *A Study of History: Abridgement of Volumes I - VI by D.C. Somervell*, and *A Study of History: Abridgement of Volumes VII - X by D.C. Somervell*, (Oxford: Oxford University Press, 1946).

52

lenges with yesterday's solutions, then down the slope of decline and decay they go. Toynbee's observation is echoed in the sentiment of Albert Einstein's oft-cited observation, "We can't solve problems by using the same kind of thinking we used when we created them."

A condition of ease emerges with a tendency towards standardization and uniformity, and systems and structure become dominant to the spirit and substance of the mission. In fact, this is how I define a bureaucratic culture—one where systems and structure have become dominant to the spirit and substance of the mission. And as history teaches us, any time a bureaucrat meets a barbarian on the battlefield, the battle is over before it even starts because one is killing while the other is restructuring, or crafting their message to Wall Street, or updating their travel and expense policies or spending limits or conducting those highly value-adding Sarbanes Oxley reviews.

It's kind of a trick of life. Don't we all seek a condition of ease? Don't we all want to retire and sit on a sandy, sun-soaked beach drinking from hollowed out coconuts with little umbrellas in them? We have a form of genocide in the U.S.; it's called Palm Beach shuffleboard—people retire, turn their brains off, and they die. I remember reading about a study conducted of centenarians in an effort to learn what led to their longevity. The study looked at all of the normal lifestyle factors like diet and exercise, but found no correlation––health-food nuts and exercise fanatics, no correlation. What they did find is revealed in the story of their visit with a 105-year-old gentleman who was a topiary gardener. The gentleman described how he just shaped this one plant, and in five years he would reshape it another way; then there was this other plant that he would need to transplant a couple of times over the next fifteen years. This gentleman was 105 years old, but apparently had no concept of it. He kept himself aroused to challenge.

Challenge and response is what keeps people healthy—physically, intellectually, emotionally, and spiritually. Challenge and response leads to health—that is a law of life. And it is a law of life not only for people, but for organizations, too. Path-finding is more than just setting a course; it means keeping oneself and one's organization aroused to challenge.

It is also important to note that truth-telling and path-finding are interdependent; that is, truth-telling will compel you to acknowledge when you may be on the wrong path.

# SAFETY TO RISK

By "safety to risk" I am not necessarily talking about how conservative or aggressive the organization is relative to investment decisions. I am talking about the kind of culture where it is safe—where it is encouraged—for a person to speak their mind, and especially to "tell truth to power." I'm talking about the kind of culture where an unconventional idea is not viewed as heresy, or where disagreement is not viewed as disloyalty; but one where reasonable people can have legitimate differences of opinion and it's not taken personally, where issues and ideas may be attacked with passion, but people are treated with civility and respect.

You can't nurture truth-telling and path-finding without safety to risk. To give truth-telling, path-finding, and authentic communication air to breathe, the leader must cultivate a culture where it is safe to risk. Let me share a personal example.

In many families it is considered disrespectful for children to argue with their parents. In my family, however, if one of us disagreed with another—including my parents—they were being disrespectful if they didn't argue with that other person. If one of us disagreed with another, but didn't argue with them, they were essentially saying that the other person's opinion was so unimportant to them that they didn't even want to try to influence it. Our family argued about things ranging from history to politics, to work and money, to individual rights versus duty to family, to which movie we should see or where we should take our next vacation—debates that were spirited and passionate, but were respectful and not personal. In many cases these arguments took place at the dinner table, and two minutes after having had a knockdown, drag-out argument with someone, that person would be asking the other to help them with a favor. That dynamic could happen because we didn't take our disagreement personally, and we didn't take our disagreements personally because we didn't make them personal. In fact, the only way one was personally offended was if you knew another didn't agree with you and chose not to speak up.

This is an example of one of the ways in which my parents led our family. If you disagreed with someone, you said so—regardless of rank or station. You were expected to have competence enough so you knew what you were talking about, and you were also expected to have courage enough to tell truth to power. To voice honest disagreement is a sign of respect; to sit in quiet disagreement is a sign of disrespect.

It is important to understand that I am not talking about challenging a decision that has been made—that is insubordination. I am talking about one's duty to dissent during the decision-making process. I am talking about one's duty to voice their honest opinion during the after-the-fact debriefing that is hopefully done to assess the effectiveness of the decision-making process, the wisdom of the resulting decision, and the effectiveness with which the decision was carried out. I am talking about the spirit of "loyal opposition," which necessitates courage in followers to tell truth to those in power, and security in leaders to make it safe for followers to risk.

# SELF-INTEREST RIGHTLY UNDERSTOOD

Finally, and perhaps the most foreign and thus difficult of the leadership traits I believe to be essential to enduring organizational change, is the principle of "self-interest rightly understood." The principle of self-interest rightly understood is one of aligning individual interests with the greater good of the whole. A leader must possess, and must be able to cultivate in others, self-interest rightly understood.

I know there are those who will scoff at the concept of self-interest rightly understood, and will summarily dismiss my contention as naïve, unreasonably optimistic, and not realistic in a capitalistic world that plays political and economic "hardball." To this I can only say, "Nonsense!" Self-interest rightly understood requires more "testosterone" than the practice of "hardball." In fact, I would argue that self-interest rightly understood is essential to enduring organizational success—especially in a capitalistic, hardball world. I would argue that the natural consequences of its absence have already begun to manifest.

Herb Brooks, who is probably best remembered as coach of the 1980 U.S. Olympic hockey team, reminded his players—often with great vigor so they wouldn't be confused—that the name on the front of their jersey is more important than the name on the back. This illustrates the concept of self-interest rightly understood because to adopt this belief the players needed to know that working in the team's best interest also served their individual best interests—if they did well by the team, the team would do well by them. Unfortunately, in too many of today's organizations the players can't be so sure.

Earlier, I cited this observation made by Jared Diamond regarding societies that fail:

>*One blueprint for trouble, making collapse likely, is a conflict of interest between the short-term interests of the decision-making elites and the long-term interests of society as a whole—especially if the elites are able to insulate themselves from the consequences of their action. That is, when what is good in the short run for the elites is bad in the long run for the society as a whole, there's a real risk of the elites making decisions that will bring the society down in the long term.*[2]

Diamond's observation cites the natural consequences resulting when self-interest rightly understood is absent. You'll also recall my assertion that when you adopt a pattern of decision-making that creates benefit for one stakeholder group at the expense of another, you ultimately devalue the organization. Self-interest rightly understood is the principle underlying this assertion.

Self-interest rightly understood begins with the leader not only because it demonstrates leadership by example, but also because it prevents the leader from becoming insulated from the consequences of his or her decision-making to which Diamond refers. It is also the leader's job to cultivate self-interest rightly understood in those whom they seek to lead—to cultivate alignment among the interests of the individuals with that of the organization as a whole. Just as physical, intellectual, emotional, and spiritual exercise is essential to the growth and well-being of body, mind, heart, and conscience, so is self-interest rightly understood essential to organizational growth and well-being. Conversely, just as the absence of such exercise results in atrophy of the body, mind, heart, and conscience, so does the absence of self-interest rightly understood result in organizational atrophy.

The current state of capitalism presents an interesting study. With all of the ethical transgressions capitalism, in its current state, is not held in high esteem. As Lawrence M. Miller noted in his 1984 book, *American Spirit: Visions of a New Corporate Culture*, "The American corporation is not dearly loved by the populace. The corporation is viewed as an impersonal edifice of materialism. It neither inspires man to achieve his highest aspirations nor inspires the loyalty and devotion that would contribute to its own purpose."[3]

While self-interest rightly understood may be a scarce commodity today, it was once much more abundant. The essential property of self-interest

---

[2]  TED Ideas Worth Sharing, "Jared Diamond: Why Societies Collapse." February 2003: http://www.ted.com/index.php/talks/jared_diamond_on_why_societies_collapse.html

[3]  Lawrence M. Miller, *American Spirit: Visions of a New Corporate Culture,* (New York: William Morrow and Company, Inc, 1984), p18.

rightly understood proved itself in what may arguably be one of the most challenging, and at the time, unprecedented, organizational development undertakings in history—the creation of democracy and capitalism in America. The creation of America's system of democracy and capitalism was an undertaking with odds of success so long, and personal and organizational leadership so demanding, that it makes those things that we today characterize as "hardball" look like child's play in comparison.

With the publication of his 1776 work, *An Inquiry into the Nature and Causes of the Wealth of Nations*, the eighteenth century Scottish philosopher, Adam Smith, has come to be regarded by many as the father of capitalism. However, it would appear that the current state of capitalism has twisted 180 degrees from Smith's vision. In his 1989 Masters Forum lecture, "Excellence and Ethics: Management by Good Character,"[4] David Kirk Hart cited several excerpts from Adam Smith's 1759 book, *The Theory of Moral Sentiments*, which are pertinent here. In *Moral Sentiments* Adam Smith describes two societies based on two very different visions and values.

Smith describes the mercenary society—the lesser society—that organizes and conducts itself on the basis of quid-pro-quo transactions:

> *Society may subsist among different men, as among merchants, from a sense of its utility, without any love and affection; and though no man in it should owe any obligation, or be bound in gratitude to any other, it (the society) may still be upheld by a mercenary exchange of good offices according to an agreed valuation.*

Then Smith describes the sympathetic society—the greater society——that organizes and conducts itself on the basis of self-interest rightly understood:

> *All the members of human society stand in need of each other's assistance, and are likewise exposed to mutual injuries. Where the necessary assistance is reciprocally afforded from love, from gratitude, from friendship, and esteem, the society flourishes and is happy. All the different members of it are bound together by the agreeable bands of love and affection, and are, as it were, drawn to one common centre of mutual good offices.*

---

4   David Kirk Hart. "Excellence and Ethics: Management by Good Character," (Speech. The Masters of Executive Excellence. Minnetonka, MN, 18 Jul. 1989)

The Theory of Moral Sentiments, published in 1759, is important because it provides the philosophical context for understanding Adam Smith's later work, An Inquiry into the Nature and Causes of the Wealth of Nations, which he published in 1776, and in which he makes his renowned "invisible hand" analogy. As David Kirk Hart cited in his lecture[5], Adam Smith notes in Wealth of Nations that more public good is accomplished by individuals laboring in their own self-interest than is accomplished by the deliberate and arguably well-intentioned endeavors of government and society. Quoting from An Inquiry into the Nature and Causes of the Wealth of Nations, Book 4, Chapter 2. Hart noted:

> In his labours, the individual neither intends to promote the public interest, nor knows how much he is promoting it. He intends only his own security; and by directing his industry in such a manner as its produce may be of the greatest value, he intends only his own gain, and he is in this, as in many other cases, led by an invisible hand to promote an end which was no part of his intention. Nor is it always the worse for society that it was no part of it. By pursuing his own interest he frequently promotes that of the society more effectually than when he really intends to promote it.

With the theory of self-interest rightly understood firmly grounded in the work of the father of capitalism, the practice of this principle of self-interest rightly understood and its role in America's creation and subsequent growth—America's success—is well documented by Alexis de Tocqueville in his work, Democracy in America[6].

In May 1831, twenty-six-year-old French lawyer, Alexis de Tocqueville, was sent by the French government to the United States to examine the American prison system, and in 1833 he published The Penitentiary System in the United States and its Application in France. However, it was the wider subject of how American democracy worked which captured de Tocqueville's greater interest.

With his friend, Gustave de Beaumont, de Tocqueville travelled seven thousand miles in seven months—an amazing feat in those days before railroads. He traveled as far north as Sault Ste Marie, as far south as New Orleans, and as far west as Green Bay, Wisconsin. He visited seventeen of the

---

[5]  David Kirk Hart. "Excellence and Ethics: Management by Good Character," (Speech. The Masters of Executive Excellence , Minnetonka, MN, 18 Jul. 1989).

[6]  Alexis de Tocqueville, Democracy in America (Abridged), (Ware, Hertfordshire: Wordsworth Editions Limited, 1998).

twenty-four states and some of the territories. His primary concern was not America, nor even American democracy, but democracy in America—how the Americans had managed to make it work, while the French had failed to do so. Why did the French Revolution lead to the terror and counter-revolution, while the American Revolution brought forth liberal democracy? He interviewed hundreds of people and filled scores of notebooks, which resulted in the publication of Volume 1 of *Democracy in America* in 1835, with Volume 2 following in 1840. In Volume 2, Section 2, Chapter VIII, de Tocqueville addresses the question, "How Americans Combat Individualism by the Principle of Self-interest Rightly Understood."

> *I have already shown, in several parts of this work, by what means the inhabitants of the United States almost always manage to combine their own advantage with that of their fellow citizens; my present purpose is to point out the general rule that enables them to do so. In the United States hardly anybody talks of the beauty of virtue, but they maintain that virtue is useful and prove it every day. The American moralists do not profess that men ought to sacrifice themselves for their fellow creatures because it is noble to make such sacrifices, but they boldly aver that such sacrifices are as necessary to him who imposes them upon himself as to him for whose sake they are made.*
>
> *...They therefore do not deny that every man may follow his own interest, but they endeavour to prove that it is the interest of every man to be virtuous...*
>
> *Montaigne said long ago: 'Were I not to follow the straight road for its straightness, I should follow it for having found by experience that in the end it is commonly the happiest and most useful track.' The doctrine of interest rightly understood is not then new, but among the Americans of our time it finds universal acceptance; it has become popular there; you may trace it at the bottom of all their actions, you will remark it in all they say. It is as often asserted by the poor man as by the rich. In Europe the principle of interest is much grosser than it is in America, but it is also less common and especially it is less avowed; among us, men still constantly feign great abnegations which they no longer feel.*
>
> *The Americans, on the other hand, are fond of explaining almost all the actions of their lives by the principle of self-interest rightly understood; they show with complacency how an enlight-*

*ened regard for themselves constantly prompts them to assist one
another and inclines them willingly to sacrifice a portion of their
time and property to the welfare of the state. In this respect I think
they frequently fail to do themselves justice; for in the United States
as well as elsewhere people are sometimes seen to give way to those
disinterested and spontaneous impulses that are natural to man;
but the Americans seldom admit that they yield to emotions of this
kind; they are more anxious to do honour to their philosophy than
to themselves.* [7]

The ingredient necessary to Smith's greater society—the sympathetic society—is self-interest rightly understood. The quality necessary for
"we leadership" is self-interest rightly understood. A leader can possess all
of the other five leadership qualities—strength of vision and strength of values, commitment and loyalty, truth-telling, path-finding, and making it safe
to risk—but without self-interest rightly understood, they're just another "me
leader."

I would also argue that the quality of self-interest rightly understood
is not a Pollyannaish expectation. In fact, as de Tocqueville's writings teach
us, it is a virtue we Americans once possessed and held in high regard, earning us the admiration of others as a practitioner of capitalism in the context
of a sympathetic society. Unfortunately, we have clearly waivered from that
path, and have come to practice capitalism in the context of a mercenary society. Too many of our leaders have become like the nineteenth century European aristocracy to which de Tocqueville refers, and "feign great abnegations
which we no longer feel"—what the business schools call "cause marketing."
I would argue that we have impoverished ourselves as a result.

---

[7]  Alexis de Tocqueville, *Democracy in America (Abridged)*, (Ware, Hertfordshire: Wordsworth Editions Limited, 1998), p229-230.

# PART III:

# ORGANIZATIONAL ECOLOGY

# 6

# ORGANIZATIONS ARE ECOSYSTEMS

*The first problem for all of us, men and women, is not to learn, but to unlearn.*
**Gloria Steinem**
American feminist, journalist, social and political activist
b. 1934

# LEADING ORGANIZATIONAL CHANGE

is a problem as old as the Stone Age. After five million years of relatively little change, the first traces of formal organization appeared 35,000 years ago during the Upper Paleolithic, as part of the effort to build stable societies out of fallible individuals. The dominant organization for most of our history is that of the military; a command-and-control structure based on the goal of successful operations during a state of crisis. The second oldest organizational structure is the Catholic Church, which is patterned after the military's hierarchical model. The fact is that the interdependence needed by organizations of all kinds to be successful in this day and age is new for our genus.

The natural tendency, particularly men's, is to look at an organization as if it were a machine, like a car engine. If it is not running properly, you just need to adjust a few screws, or replace a few parts, then get it back on the road.

Experience has taught me that organizations are not mechanical systems made up of discreet interchangeable components; rather they are more like an ecosystem, holistic and highly interdependent. We may talk about an organization in terms of discreet components, but that is only to make it easier to talk about it, not because it really exists that way. How an organization may technically do its work—its processes—may be a matter of linear thinking, but how an organization socially governs the conduct of that work—its culture—is more a matter of nonlinear thinking. In fact, in her book, *Leadership and the New Science: Discovering Order in a Chaotic World*[1], Margaret Wheatley makes a compelling and convincing argument that organizational behavior, cultural cause and effect, has more to do with chaos theory than Newtonian physics.

I have found that an agrarian model—looking at an organization as if it were a crop or garden, rather than a machine—provides a better paradigm for thinking about an organization, and thus an organizational-change effort. Like a crop or garden, the results of any change are not immediate and may not be tangible. When you first plant a seed, it goes to work first building its root structure below ground (i.e., out of sight) before anything blooms above ground. Even after it does emerge from the ground, it continues to build its root structure—everything that is going on in full view above ground is dependent upon that which is going on underground, out of view. And as Stephen Covey reminds us, no good is done by pulling up the plant to see how the roots are doing.

Plant growth can also become stifled when its growth reaches the limits of its conditions. When you transplant a plant to new conditions, you know that it will suffer a period of no growth until it acclimates to those new conditions. Conversely, some plants can also become overgrown and choke off the water and light of their peers—like weeds do. I am not one of those who regard every employee as a delicate flower. When assuming leadership of new organizations, I have found them comprised of both flowers and weeds. While I might have had visions of a rose garden, what I inherited was a weed patch, and the first order of business was site clearance.

Like a crop or garden, you must pay the price of cultivating, planting, weeding, feeding, watering, fertilizing and dusting over a period of time. With the right combination of sun, water, and nutrients, along with proper control of weeds and pests, it may just bear fruit. But you have to pay the price; there is no quick fix. Again, as Stephen Covey has said on many occasions, you can't goof off all summer, finally get around to planting in September, and expect to bring in a crop in October.

---

[1]    Margaret J. Wheatley, *Leadership and the New Science: Learning about Organization from an Orderly Universe,* (San Francisco: Berrett-Koehler Publishers, 1992).

# SOCIOTECHNICAL ORGANIZATIONAL DESIGN

To better understand the organizational ecosystem, I found William Pasmore's book, *Designing Effective Organizations: The Sociotechnical Systems Perspective*[2], to be particularly instructive. It provides several important insights that apply to all organizations—no matter their size, type, or position in a larger organizational hierarchy.

As depicted in Figure 3, every organization takes inputs and through some chain of value-adding processes, it creates outputs. That chain of value-adding processes is a composite of the organization's technical systems and its social systems. In this context "technical system" does not mean technology; it means how the organization technically conducts its work (i.e., its processes). Similarly, "social system" means how the organization governs the conduct of its work (i.e., its culture). If the organization's customers find their outputs to be of value, then the organization prospers; if customers do not, then the organization suffers. The use of the dotted line to illustrate the organization's boundaries depicts that it is an ecosystem. That is, organizations are holistic in nature, their subsystems are interdependent, they can affect things outside themselves, and things from the outside can affect them.

*Figure 3 – Pasmore Sociotechnical Organizational Model*

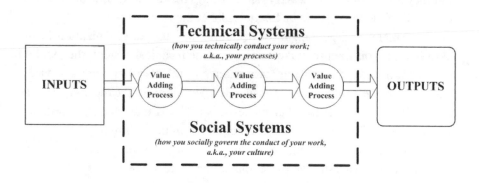

This model is a little deeper than it may initially appear. For example, it begs the question, "Who is your customer?" The way I answer this is to paraphrase Kaoru Ishikawa[3], "Anyone who depends on your work to do theirs is your customer." Whether your customer is a customer in the traditional sense,

[2]  William A. Pasmore, *Designing Effective Organizations: The Sociotechnical Systems Perspective. Organization Assessment and Change,* (New York: John Wiley & Sons, 1988).

or your customer is another department to whom your department provides some service, if your customers find your outputs to be of value, then you'll prosper; if they do not, then you will suffer (e.g., your customers will find a new supplier, or your function will be outsourced, etc.),

It also raises the question as to what "value-adding" means. Unfortunately, the term, "value-adding" has become so overused of late that it has lost its meaning. Of course, the traditional definition of value-adding is calculated as benefit divided by cost. However, when a customer buys something, there are often a number of things for which they are paying but of which they are not aware. So, I prefer to define something as "value-adding" if it is something the customer would be willing to pay for, were they aware they were paying for it. If a customer were made aware of a particular activity, task, feature or option that added cost to your product or service, and they weren't willing to pay for it, then that activity, task, feature or option is not value-adding. For example, value can be added as work moves horizontally through the organization; however, value is rarely added when work has to move vertically. Of course, there are some things, like regulatory compliance (e.g., Sarbanes-Oxley), that are not discretionary—that doesn't mean, however, that such things are necessarily value-adding. Therefore, organizations should take a hard look at all of those activities, tasks, features, and options that consume time and expense, but which their customers would not regard as value-adding, and make sure that they are absolutely necessary. Those things that are not value-adding but are not discretionary should be Spartan-like in their design.

Finally, and perhaps most insightful, because an organization is an ecosystem, if you want to make a change in the technical system, then you'll also need to make a complementary change in the social system; and vice-versa. Otherwise, the organization will reject your change like the body rejects a transplanted heart. And what makes this tricky is that technical systems require linear thinking; social systems require non-linear thinking.

For example, although it is now more often the punch line for a joke, there was a day when the word "empowerment" really meant something. It had to do with speed—reducing the actual cycle time of a process to as near its theoretical minimum as possible. Reducing process cycle time means re-engineering that process to be as free of interruptions as possible—changing the technical system. However, an objective evaluation of most processes will reveal that many interruptions are made in the name of managerial control. Eliminating process interruptions for purposes of managerial control necessarily requires changing the social system. Specifically, it means allowing, training, equipping, and trusting the person closest to that point in the process where the problem occurs to decide how best to solve the problem—it requires empowerment. In other words, actualizing speed as an organizational value requires changes in both the organization's technical system (i.e., interruption-free processes) and its social system (i.e., empowerment).

To better understand the interplay between an organization's linear technical systems, or processes, and its non-linear social system, or culture, let's compare and contrast battle operations on a naval gunship in the late eighteenth century with flight operations on a naval aircraft carrier in the late twentieth century.

## LIFE ABOARD A LATE EIGHTEENTH CENTURY GUNSHIP

First, let's look at the technical system (how they conducted their work) on board a late eighteenth century gunship. Everything was geared to battle. When they beat the drum to quarters, they cleared the decks, and the men took their positions on the guns (these are the workers). There were three men to each gun: one to load it; one with a slow burn match, or punk, to light the fuse; and one to ram it out. When the gun ports opened up, the men rolled the cannons out.

Meanwhile, the captain is standing on the poop deck—that's the high deck on the back of the ship. He is the one—the only one—with a perfect line of sight over the ocean. He is the one—the only one—who can see the enemy ships. He is the one—the only one—with all of the information. He represents the only computer on the ship. Also, there is a lieutenant standing on the companionway step—the step between the poop deck and the gun decks. The lieutenant can hear the captain's command, but he cannot see the enemy ships on the ocean.

The captain yells to the lieutenant, "Fire!"

When he hears the captain's command, the lieutenant yells, "Fire!" to the men on the gun decks.

When the men on the gun decks hear the lieutenant's command, the guy with the match lights the fuse, the fuse burns and the cannon fires. Each team pulls their cannon back in, rams it out, loads a new charge, maybe makes some adjustments, rolls the cannon out and fires it again.

Here's a real important point. When the captain gives the order to fire, that's not when the cannons actually go off. It is not an electronic or automated process; it's a totally manual process, so there may be a three-, four- or five-second delay. Now picture a ship on the ocean; it is rocking side to side due to the waves, the wind, and the way the ship rolled into battle formation. It matters a lot when these cannons go off—it is the difference between the cannon balls flying directly into the ocean and taking out a school of fish, or flying high over the enemy ship and not hitting a thing, or flying parallel to the ocean and ripping into the enemy ship.

They have practiced their firing over and over, but the whole roll of the ship will change with the weather conditions and how the ship comes about into battle. It is not such a simple problem. But the captain has the one and only computer on the ship. He is timing this thing, and if every thing works right, then the cannon balls will fire parallel to the ocean and rip into the enemy's ship.

Now let's look at their social system, their culture (how they socially governed the conduct of their work). We know that sailors in the late eighteenth century did not enlist to see the world or learn computer electronics. Many of these guys were knocked out while they were drunk on the docks and press ganged into service. If we are honest, these guys were the dregs of society. On Lord Nelson's ship, The Victory, half of his men weren't even British; some were Spanish and some were French (i.e., from the countries Britain was fighting). It didn't matter much because they weren't involved in the decision-making process. Meanwhile the captain knew celestial navigation. He spoke several languages. He was a diplomat and represented the Queen.

The whole socio-technical system made sense—the technical system and the social system were functionally related. The captain had the intelligence, the experience, and was the only one with a full line of sight over the ocean. The lieutenant was learning and building experience, but he couldn't see the enemy ships. And the guys on the lower gun decks, well, they were dummies doing what they were told.

Here's an interesting question. In today's business world, how much smarter is the plant manager than the workers, or how much smarter is the sales VP than the sales representative? Today, unlike the eighteenth century, we have workers with advanced degrees, they read best selling books and the *Wall Street Journal*, and they manage their family's investment portfolio.

# LIFE ABOARD A LATE TWENTIETH CENTURY AIRCRAFT CARRIER

Now let's look at life aboard a late twentieth century aircraft carrier. In "The

Secret of Life at the Limits: Cogs Become Big Wheels," by John Pfeiffer, appearing in the July 1989 issue of *Smithsonian,* Pfeiffer reports on a major research project that was launched by three professors at the University of California, Berkeley: political scientists Todd LaPorte and Gene Rochlin of the Institute of Governmental Studies (an ex-marine pilot and ex-physicist respectively), and Karlene Roberts, an industrial psychologist at the university's School of Business Administration. They studied examples of high-reliability, complex organizations, which, in the throes of adapting to fast-changing times, manage to achieve remarkably low failure rates. Flight operations on a naval aircraft carrier is one of several organizations that they studied and on which they report in their article —they spent 150 days aboard several carriers.

It is interesting to study what they learned about the socio-technical systems of carrier flight operations and think of it in contrast to battle operations aboard a late eighteenth-century gunship. For example, they found such flight operations to be a study in highly trained and drilled specialization, complexity with many "moving parts," breakneck process speed, flawless teamwork, continuous and unambiguous communications, a degree of interdependence heretofore unseen, with results held in higher regard than rank. "There are lessons to be learned from highly reliable systems. When working on the razor's edge of catastrophe, success demands constant training and easy communications from bottom-up as well as top-down—and that, in turn, demands leaders who are prepared to listen to and learn from their subordinates."[4]

Let's look at flight operations aboard an aircraft carrier, as described in excerpts below from Pfeiffer's article:

> *USS Carl Vinson: early morning mission in 400-fathom, choppy seas off San Diego... F14 Tomcat No. 104 is approaching, seven seconds away from a "controlled crash" landing, seven seconds of incredibly condensed action. This is the time of maximum stress for the ship's company as well as the pilot. (Pilot heart rates are significantly higher during carrier landings than they are in combat.)*
>
> *A man at the console calls "F14 Tomcat one-zero-four, five-four-zero" and pushes the F14 button. The "540" informs him that plane is coming in at a specified weight, 54,000 pounds, and that*

---

[4] John Pfeiffer, "The Secret Life at the Limits: Cogs Become Big Wheels," *Smithsonian*, Vol 20, No.4, July 1989, p41.

*determines the tension of the arresting wires. The figure is crucial. A wire too taut for the plane's slamming hook-on may snap, lashing across the deck at leg-severing level; too much slack could send plane and pilot skidding off into the ocean. Nearby in the arresting-gear room, four men hear the numbers, crank a dial to 540, and call, "Gear set! Gear set!"*

*"F14 Tomcat one-zero-four, five-four-zero." The same message sounds at the same time above the flight deck in the aircraft handler's office at the foot of the tower, where LaPorte is keeping tabs on a game played for real. The room houses a "Ouija board," a model of the six-acre deck scaled down to desktop dimensions. Every one of the 20-odd planes lined up outside is represented by a scaled-down plastic piece and one of them, the F14 No. 104 piece, is about to be placed in position when it lands and is moved off the miniature runway.*

*"F14 Tomcat one-zero-four, five-four-zero." Again, the same message, only uttered from on high in a different pitch—a woman's voice, the only woman among 5,800 men. Psychologist Roberts is standing seven stories above the flight deck in the ship's control tower, home of the air boss. "Scared spitless," but not show-ing it, she is playing the role of spotter-in-training, identifying each plane as it approaches under the watchful eye of an experienced spotter.*

*The talking never stops. An excerpt from LaPorte's field notes: "They talk to reduce ambiguity of information, to correct misinformation, often without a hint of blame or accusation." A network buzzing with signals repeated over and over again. It includes pilots in midair, Mercer [Captain Thomas Mercer, com-manding officer of the USS Carl Vinson, at that time] high on the bridge, men at green glowing radar scopes three decks below the flight deck in the library silence of the Carrier Air Traffic Control Center, monitoring the ship's airspace. The air boss is in touch with all of them over a score of channels, radios, sound-powered phones, TV monitors, squawk boxes, and a public address system powerful enough to out-decibel the racket on the flight deck. He has the last word, "Clear deck!"*

*It's a "hot spin" for F14 No. 104, being refueled for an im-mediate catapult launching with a new pilot. The arresting wire is sliding back into position, set for a new tension—all in a matter of seconds because attack bomber A6 Intruder No. 502 is descending fast at 36,000 pounds.*

*Just before launch, crewmen check for fuel leaks, make sure control surfaces respond to the pilot's actions and inspect everything in sight, and signal that what they have looked at appears to be normal. Another crewman flashes the gross weight of an F14, including fuel reported by the pilot, to the catapult officer in a "bubble" raised just a foot from the flight deck. Steam pressure must be set by weight and wind conditions for each launch. Information is given visually to avoid ambiguity.*

*One crewman dashes clear while another completes his check of hydraulic lines that operate the landing gear. Teamwork has to be perfect; during a mission a plane is rolled into position, checked from nose to tail, and launched every 50 seconds.*

*The black-visored pilot waits for the final hand signals that will tell him he is about to be fired into the air. The button will be pushed by a catapult officer he does not see, and the members of the launch crew run to safety.*

*And on and on, 21 planes in all, each requiring a different wire setting, landed without mishap at 50-second intervals.*[5]

These excerpts above tell us a lot about an aircraft carrier's technical system (how they technically do their work): the many functions involved, the coordination of those functions, the specialized skills required to perform them, and the process cycle time. They also provide some interesting insights to their social system (how they socially govern the conduct of their work): the constant communication to avoid ambiguity and to correct mistakes, the absence of blame or accusation, and the importance of knowledge and expertise over rank in the operation of their processes.

The sections that follow provide some additional excerpts that further inform us about a carrier's social system, and which I find even more fascinating.

# THE VARYING NATURE OF HIERARCHY AND RANK

The nature of rank and hierarchy is much different in organizations where

---

[5] Ibid, p42-43.

pushing the edge of the envelope is the norm and high reliability is key. Yes, there is still a hierarchical structure, and positions that vary in rank. But when the heat is on, it is expertise that matters more than rank.

> *Most organizations consist of people in separate catego-ries: big wheels, cogs, and specialists like accountants or chemical engineers. But the high-reliability version is a hybrid, a mix of these roles played by the same individuals under different circumstanc-es. The big wheels are there, but use their power rarely. The chain of command is much in evidence, orders may be barked out, and subordinates behave appropriately as spit-and-polish yes-men. But when tension is running high, all work together as specialists among specialists on equal footing in a more collegial atmosphere.[6]*
>
> *Now 150 officers and enlisted men are moving shoulder to shoulder across the full width of the flight deck, heads down. It's a FOD (Foreign Object Damage) walk-down. They're picking up every bit of debris that could be sucked up into jet engines and dam-age spinning turbine blades—scraps of wire, metal filings, nuts and screws—clearing the deck for the next mission already under way. Rochlin notes the competition to spot debris and the lack of defer-ence to hierarchy—the latter, he says, a signature of high-reliability organizations.[7]*

# THE IMPORTANCE OF MIDDLE MANAGEMENT

In many organizations middle management is under assault. In the case of high-reliability, complex organizations, which, in the throes of adapting to fast-changing times, manage to achieve remarkably low failure rates—such as flight operations on an aircraft carrier—middle management is essential organizational glue.

> *Carriers seem to run directly contrary to common sense. You'd expect that complex organizations engaged in hazardous ac-tivities would require experienced individuals, the more the better, and especially among the top brass. Yet the captain will be aboard for only three years, his 20 senior officers for about two and a half; most of the more than 5,000 enlisted men will leave the Navy or*

[6]  Ibid, p40
[7]  Ibid, p43.

*be transferred after their three-year carrier stints. Furthermore, the enlisted men are predominantly teenagers, so that the average age aboard a carrier comes to a callow 20.*

*The job of providing continuity falls to middle and lower management, a cadre of about 300 petty officers with long carrier service. According to LaPorte, "Their collective experience is the ship's memory; they run the show." They do much of the training and conduct the frequent drills, always emphasizing "redundancy"––non-stop repeating of messages.*

*Individuals at the top of today's organization have more to learn and less time to learn it; the higher they rise, the truer this becomes.*[8]

# OVER PROJECTING AUTHORITY

Creating safety to risk is an important element of leadership. A common sin of leadership is to over project authority because it creates an environment where people are afraid to speak up—the risk is too great to tell the emperor that he is wearing no clothes.

*Look back for a moment to November 2, 1985, time 5:45 p.m. The Enterprise is at sea, being evaluated for operational readiness. Bishop Rock, a shoal off the coast of Southern California, lies dead ahead. A number of men on the bridge see the shoal's big red light and assume their captain does, too. He doesn't. The result: millions of dollars in damage.*

*Roberts' report, to appear in the Naval Institute Proceedings, identifies this incredible accident as a classic case of "driving the bridge," projecting such authority that subordinates tend to keep their mouths shut. She reemphasizes a "not very startling" lesson: create an open, give-and-take atmosphere which encourages your men to speak up. Most captains do just that; the ones who don't rarely become admirals.*[9]

---

[8]  Ibid, p43-44.
[9]  Ibid.

# THE IMPORTANCE OF SYMBOLS

Symbols are important cultural glue. Too often they can be regarded as "fluff" and become targets during cost cutting binges or six sigma campaigns. Just understand that when you mess with symbols, you're messing with cultural bonding agents.

> *Parties serve to cement solidarity; "cake cuttings" com-memorate birthdays, holidays, jobs well done, practically any air-squadron anniversary. Carrier cooks had better be good bakers. Several years ago Vice Adm. John Fetterman issued a memorable "Cakes Forever" message. Someone in Washington had come up with a new rule: cakes were no longer to be baked in carrier kitchens, but purchased from commercial bakers, to be loaded aboard at inter-vals by naval supply ships. Fetterman would have none of it: "The cake at sea is a very important symbol. It's a way of honoring our men. You want it baked at home, inside the ship." That rule died fast.*[10]

# THE MYSTERY OF SACRIFICE

When one sacrifices one's time, one's energy, to that which one believes to be noble and worthy, there is no sacrifice; there is an investment with a guaran-teed return in that which is most precious to us—our own self-esteem.

> *What Mercer and his fellow officers work hard to main-tain is a quality rarely encountered in the civilian world—complete-ly unselfish devotion to the task at hand. A feeling for the team, the ship, the Navy, a feeling so intense that when someone else slips up, you feel as depressed as if it were your own failure. "This is the sort of thing that usually happens only in a family," Rochlin notes.*[11]

# THE GREAT UNNECESSARY DANGER: ORDERS FROM A REMOTELY INVOLVED PERSON OF HIGHER RANK

One of, if not the, greatest sins of leadership occurs when top executives, re-mote from frontline action, issue unrealistic orders to people down the line.

---

[10]  Ibid.
[11]  Ibid.

*The most striking and surprising role change occurs in the white heat of danger, when the entire system threatens to collapse. Then cogs can become big wheels. Whatever their status in the formal hierarchy, they are trained intensively every day so that—based on their expertise—they can take complete command, redirect operations or bring them to an abrupt halt. The system works. It comes under greatest strain when top executives remote from frontline action issue unrealistic orders to people down the line.[12]*

*The Enterprise had just completed a four-day, non-stop, 600-mission exercise near the "Bear Box," a region north of Guam within range of Soviet reconnaissance planes from Vladivostok. In the midst of the exercise, the fleet admiral had subjected carrier flight handlers to an extra strain: a sudden change of plans that disrupted tight schedules. The operators had to organize, on short notice, a 15-plane anti-submarine mission, without delaying other missions. They made it, with some pride in their achievement.*

*But the aftermath was deep resentment at what they'd been put through, unrealistic and unnecessary risk to life and limb––a clear cut case of overload, taskers having insufficient knowledge about the problems of operators. In complex organizations, taskers are almost necessarily less proficient at tasking than operators are at operating. LaPorte pinpoints the lack of, and the need for, an officially sanctioned way of "telling the Fleet they had fouled up," perhaps a board that would meet automatically after major exercises and give operators a chance to air grievances. As it is, carrier operators know that if they'd failed, a full-fledged investigation would have followed fast.[13]*

Just like the eighteenth century gunship, the whole socio-technical system on board a twentieth century aircraft carrier makes sense—the technical system and the social system are functionally related.

One of the biggest challenges in organizational leadership is aligning the technical and social organizational systems, and then tuning them in a way that tightens their alignment in order to boost their performance. Of course to do this, you must first realize that these two systems exist, then you must acknowledge their interdependence, then you must understand what makes them tick.

---

[12]   Ibid, p40.
[13]   Ibid, p44-45.

# 7

# ORGANIZATIONAL CULTURE AND HABITS

*If you want to truly understand something, try to change it.*
**Kurt Lewin**
German-born psychologist
1890 - 1947

IMAGINE YOU'RE THE LEADER OF A
competitive sculling team, and imagine that you have successfully recruited
the world's top rowers to staff your scull. Now imagine that the scull you've
given them in which to compete has a square bow. How successful do you
think they will be in competition? They may win a race or two on pure talent
and sheer will, but given a scull with a square bow they are not going to be perennial champions—your talent has to work against the poor design of your
scull. You need to put your talent in a boat designed for competitive sculling.

Your organization's culture is like that scull. You can populate your
organization with the world's greatest talent, but if your organization has a
square bow, they may win a race or two on pure talent and sheer will, but they
will not be perennial champions. You need to put them in an organization
whose socio-technical systems are designed to be competitive.

Unfortunately, cultures are exquisitely complex systems, made more
complex because they are more loyal to the laws of chaos theory than to
Newtonian physics. In his course, *Leadership & Mastery*[1], Peter Senge defined
system complexity as a function of the time and distance between cause and
effect—the greater the time and/or distance between a cause and its effect, the

---

[1] Dr. Peter Senge, "Leadership & Mastery," Seminar, Innovation Associates, Inc. Boston, MA, Jan. 1993.

more complex the system. For example, plumbing in a typical home is a pretty simple system; you turn on a faucet and you immediately get water. It gets a little more complicated when you add the need for hot water because now you must draw water from the water heater. In most cases there is a slight delay between when you turn your faucet toward "hot" and when hot water actually comes out because the hot water has to make its way from the heater to your faucet. My experience is that the human metabolic system is an incredibly complex system. For me, it seems like the time between when I improve my eating habits and when I see weight loss can be measured in weeks and months; meanwhile, the time between when I eat that chocolate bar and when it appears as fat seems to be almost instantaneous. An organization's technical system may or may not be complex. An organization's social system is most assuredly complex.

Most organizations have a good handle on their technical system––this is especially true in engineering, finance, IT, and manufacturing organizations—technical systems are linear systems served by quantitative thinking. Similarly, it is my experience that most organizations are clueless in regard to their social system—social systems are non-linear systems served better by qualitative thinking. Nor do most organizations realize the interdependence that exists between their technical system and their social system. Yet they wonder why their organizational change efforts require more energy than they expected and are far less successful than they hoped.

For these reasons, I'll spend no additional time on the topic of technical systems, but will dial our microscope down to examine the organizational social system, or organizational culture, in much greater detail.

# DEFINING "CULTURE"

I don't find any of the dictionary definitions of "culture" to be too useful when it comes to organizational change. Lawrence M. Miller provides a much more practical definition. He defines culture as "the sum of an organization's habits."[2]

Consider that there are at least these three types of behavior: emotional, intentional, and habitual. Emotional behavior is self-evident; it is behavior governed by the person's moods. Intentional behavior is the type of behavior that you plan and conduct very deliberately; it is behavior governed by the person's mind. The management by objective, or MBO, process is one

---

[2] Lawrence Miller. "Managing for Tomorrow: Visions of a New Corporate Culture." (Speech. The Masters of Executive Excellence. Minnetonka, MN, 22 Aug. 1989).

meant to drive intentional behavior: specific objectives are explicitly defined, plans are made to achieve those objectives, metrics are defined to measure progress against those objectives, rewards are provided to incent successful completion of those objectives, and so on. Finally, habitual behavior is the type of behavior that is "second nature"; it is learned but becomes almost involuntary, akin to breathing and blinking.

This is important: there is competitive advantage in habitual behavior. There is competitive advantage in habitual behavior because it is highly reliable and requires little management. For example, when I arrive at my office, I hang up my coat, turn on my computer, check for voicemail messages, and get myself some caffeine. I do not make plans to do these things, I don't make a to-do list for them, and no one has to remind me or incent me to do them—yet, you can count on me doing these things, because they are habitual. There is competitive advantage in habitual behavior because it is highly reliable and requires little management. In fact, I would argue that the intentional behavior embodied in MBOs is largely wasted effort if the habitual behavior is dysfunctional—working on MBOs in the presence of dysfunctional habitual behavior is akin to putting on a production of *Aida* with a cast that doesn't know how to sing.

So, if we define culture as the sum of an organization's habits, and there is competitive advantage in habitual behavior, then we must also define "habit."

# DEFINING "HABIT"

To define "habit" I turn to Stephen Covey. He describes habit as the intersection of knowledge, skill, and attitude as shown in Figure 4.

*Figure 4 – Covey Habit Model*

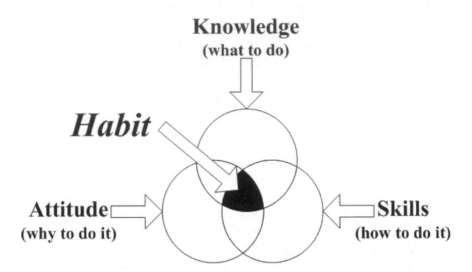

Source: Stephen R. Covey. *The 7 Habits of Highly Effective People* (New York: Simon and Schuster, 1989), p48.

"Knowledge" means knowing what to do. "Skills" means knowing how to do it. "Attitude" means knowing why to do it. When there is an intersection among these three things, you have habit—the greater the intersection, the stronger the habit. Consider the case of a person working at a help desk, constantly dealing with displaced anger from disgruntled callers. They may know what to do to help a particular caller, they may know how to do it, but they just don't care anymore—you don't have habit. Similarly, you may be the parent of a child with a substance-abuse problem. You may know that you must intervene, you may desperately want to do it, but you don't know how to conduct a constructive intervention—you don't have habit.

## ORGANIZATIONAL HABITS

We've defined culture as the sum of an organization's habits, and we've defined habit. So, if culture is the key to competitive advantage, then the next questions you have to ask yourself is, "What are the habitual behaviors that will lead to the success of my organization, and how do I cultivate them?"

First, you can't create enduring success for the organization without also creating success for the individuals in that organization—this is the sympathetic society, the invisible hand, and self-interest rightly understood. For example, just as Adam Smith argues in his "invisible hand" analogy that by pursuing his or her own interest the individual frequently promotes that of the society more effectually than when he really intends to promote it, so it is with individuals in any organization when the leader has instilled the practice of self-interest rightly understood. That is, more organizational good can be accomplished by individuals laboring in their own self-interest than can be accomplished by the deliberate and arguably well-intentioned endeavors of headquarters, given self-interest rightly understood is well inculcated in the culture.

Further, while intellect may drive the technical system, emotion and passion drive the social system. For example, individuals are often told to focus—focus their attention, focus their energy. I contend that focus is an emotion—the ability to focus on something is a function of the individual's passion for it.

So, better put, and in the context of self-interest rightly understood, the question we need to ask is "What are the habitual behaviors that will lead to the success of the individual and the success of our organization?"

You know your organization best and will need all of your truth-telling and path-finding powers to determine those behaviors, if made habitual, will lead to competitive advantage. However, let me prime your intellectual pump by offering those habitual behaviors that I have found to best serve the interests of high-performing organizations, and those that I have found to best serve the interests of individuals. I think you'll find the alignment between these two lists to be self-evident. (You may have a different set of behaviors that you believe will lead to the success of your organization, and the success of the individuals in it, if they could be made habitual. That's okay. It's not important that yours agree with mine; it's important that yours are the product of your best truth-telling and path-finding, and that they are in alignment.)

# HABITS LEADING TO THE SUCCESS OF THE ORGANIZATION

There is a difference between playing to win and playing not to lose. High-performing organizations play to win, and below are the four habits that I believe characterize a high-performing organization.

# Quality

The traditional definition of quality is conformance to customer requirements; some will argue that it is exceeding customer requirements. They are all lightweights. True leaders in quality create customer requirements to which competitors must respond.

# Speed

Speed is realized when actual process cycle time is reduced to as near the theoretical minimum cycle time as possible. Speed is important for three reasons.

First, speed is essential for quality. Customers are fickle and good competitors are fast. You know that opportunities are becoming less predictable, not more. You know that they are coming with shorter lead times, not longer. And you know that their windows of opportunity are shrinking, not growing. If quality is truly a value you wish to actualize, then you also need to value speed.

Second, speed is essential for the development of skill and capability. There is only one way to get better at anything: practice. If your concept-to-commercialization process takes four years, and your competitor's takes two, then your competitor gets twice the practice that you do.

Finally, speed is essential for cost effectiveness. I guarantee you that a process that can be properly done in two years will be less expensive than one that takes four.

# Cost Effectiveness

Notice I did not say "cost reduction." Cost effectiveness is the elimination of waste, with waste being defined as the difference between the way things actually are and the way things theoretically could be. Waste can exist in many areas. Certainly money can be wasted, as can any kind of resource, but so can opportunity. And most important is time. In fact, in today's world, I would argue that the single greatest sin one person can commit against another is to waste their time. Regardless of race, gender, class or rank, time is the one thing of which we all have the same amount—everybody has only twenty-four hours in their day.

Speed and cost effectiveness drive productivity, but I deliberately list quality before either speed or cost effectiveness because I value quality before productivity. If you chase quality you'll get productivity; but if you chase productivity, you don't necessarily get quality—producing crap faster and cheaper than you did before serves no useful purpose. Similarly, customer service comes before administrative efficiency for the same reason. If you chase customer service, you'll get administrative efficiency; but if you chase administrative efficiency, you don't necessarily get customer service—abusing customers faster and cheaper than you did before serves no useful purpose.

## Continuous Improvement

Continuous improvement goes beyond Walter Shewhart's[3] PDCA cycle. One of the most critical abilities that an organization needs to develop is the ability to sense and respond—to be attuned to what the hell is going on around you, have the wisdom to put it in proper context, and have the courage to act on it. Hopefully, it is self-evident that the one who learns and applies their learning fastest, wins.

## Habits Leading to the Success of the Individual

In his book, *A Great Place to Work,*[4] Robert Levering clearly depicts the positive correlation between a healthy culture and a healthy bottom line. In doing so, he observes that there are really very few habitual behaviors that are required in order to make any place a great place to work; he cites four, which I have paraphrased below, and I have added a fifth.

First, **people have to do valuable work.** Nobody likes a job that is routine drudgery, or "make work." While most people understand that there is some of that in every job, it needs to be a small percentage. People need to see how the work they are doing contributes to the organization's mission.

Second, **people have to be valued when they do their work well.** No one likes his or her work to be taken for granted. Everyone likes to have their work recognized and appreciated—especially when they do it well or overcome adverse conditions to get it done at all.

Third, **there must be trust among co-workers.** This is especially true

---

[3] Walter Andrew Shewhart was an American physicist, engineer and statistician, sometimes known as the father of statistical quality control.

[4] Robert Levering, *A Great Place To Work: What Makes Some Employers So Good (And Most So Bad)* (New York: Random House, 1988).

between management and staff.

Fourth, **people need to be friendly.** This doesn't mean that everyone needs to be drinking buddies. It just means that people must be pleasant with each other and treat each other with respect and civility. At the very least, people don't want to work with jerks, as is most deftly pointed out by Robert I. Sutton in his book, *The No Asshole Rule.*[5]

Finally, I add that **people need to be allowed to practice their craft in a way that gives them pride.** I'm not talking about striving for perfection; that would be neurotic. I am talking about striving for excellence. The true meaning of excellence may have been lost in the toxic waste of management fads, but people still want to be proud of what they produce—no one wants to be associated with crap.

## CHANGING AN ORGANIZATION'S HABITUAL BEHAVIORS

It is important to understand that you don't work on habits directly; you work on them indirectly. Just like you don't strengthen your heart by exercising it directly, but by exercising your large muscles, which in turn exercise your heart, so it is with organizational habits. So, what are the things that influence organizational habits—what are the organizational analogs to the body's large muscle groups? These are the things that are represented in something called "The 10S Model," which we will review in detail in the chapters that follow.

---

[5]  Robert I. Sutton, Ph.D., *The No Asshole Rule: Building a Civilized Workplace and Surviving One that Isn't,* (New York: Warner Business Books, 2007).

# PART IV:

# CULTURAL FORCES, FROM STEM TO STERN

# 8

# THE 10S MODEL

*I like to see a man proud of the place in which he lives. I like to see a man live so that his place will be proud of him.*
**Abraham Lincoln**
Sixteenth president of the United States
1809—1865

# HOW DO YOU CULTIVATE THE HABIT-

ual behaviors that will lead to the success of the individual and the success of your organization? As mentioned previously, you don't work on habits directly; you have to work on them indirectly. Just like growing a plant or a garden, once you plant a seed you don't work directly on the plant; you work on those things that influence the health and growth of the plant—things like preparing the soil, watering, weeding, feeding, dusting, and pruning. So what are the things that influence habitual behavior?

For this, I turn to something called the "10S Model;" it is a model I use for understanding and remodeling an organization's culture—the place in which you live. Your organization is your ship, and as the leader you need to know your ship from stem to stern—this is especially true if you are going to lead organizational change.

Just like a building's blueprint with its various components (e.g., the floor plans, the electrical plan, the heating/ventilation/air conditioning, or HVAC, plan, the exterior elevations, etc.) help a remodeler understand what they are working with (e.g., which walls are load-bearing, which carry electrical, which carry mechanical, etc.), so has the 10S Model helped me understand the culture of the organizations I sought to remodel. Applying She-

87

whart's PDCA cycle for the purposes of leading organizational change, I have found the 10S Model to be extremely useful in understanding an organization's culture, analyzing it, planning and making changes to it, understanding cause and effect and making adjustments.

My first exposure to the 10S Model was in *The Art of Japanese Management*, by Dick Pascale and Tony Athos, where they cite a framework of seven levers developed by McKinsey & Company.[1] This 7S Framework consists of: Subordinate Goals at the center, with Strategy, Structure, Systems, Style, Staff, and Skills circling about it. Over the years, it appears that different folks have put their own fingerprints on this model. For example, Stephen Covey taught the "9S Model,[2]" which is a derivative of the 7S Model. Covey changed the center from "Subordinate Goals" to "Shared Vision & Values," hung "Self" off of "Staff," put the whole thing inside a dotted-line box, and added Streams outside the box but connected to Strategy. I took Covey's 9S Model, added Symbols, which I learned from Lawrence M. Miller[3], and, *voilà!,* we have the 10S Model, as depicted in Figure 5.

[1]   Richard Tanner Pascale and Anthony G. Athos, *The Art of Japanese Management: Applications for American Executives*, (Warner Books ed. New York: Warner Books, 1981), p326.

[2]   Dr. Stephen R. Covey, "Advanced Leadership," (Seminar, Stephen R Covey & Associates, Sundance, UT, Sep. 1988).

[3]   Lawrence Miller. "Managing for Tomorrow: Visions of a New Corporate Culture." (Speech. The Masters of Executive Excellence, Minnetonka, MN, 22 Aug. 1989).

*Figure 5 – The 10S Model*

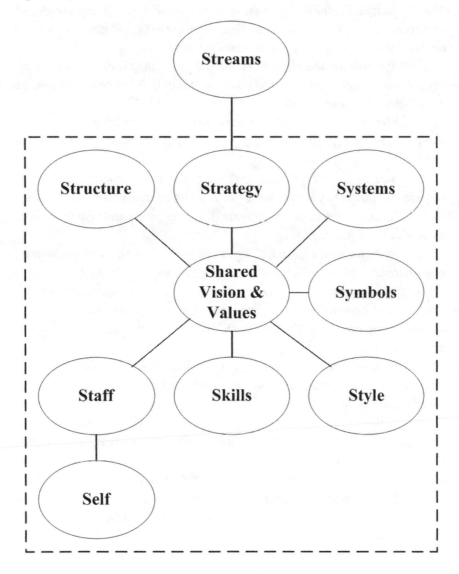

## Quick Tour

In the chapters that follow we'll take a detailed tour of the 10S Model—we will visit each "S." I will provide its definition; share some philosophy about it; and give some practical examples and advice in regard to it. First, let's take a quick tour of the 10S Model so you have a picture of the whole before we dive into the parts.

**Shared Vision and Values:** At the heart of every culture are shared vision and values. These talk about <u>what</u> you want to be and <u>how</u> you want to be. Shared vision and values are essentially changeless.

**Symbols** are the physical manifestation of the vision and values being practiced—not necessarily the vision or values that are espoused, but the ones that are being practiced.

**Streams** are external forces outside of your control (e.g., market forces, economic forces, political forces, or other exogenous factors). Streams are constantly changing.

**Strategy** is how you deal with the constantly changing Streams in a way that is faithful to your essentially changeless Shared Vision and Values.

**Structure** includes how you are organized, roles and responsibilities, span of control, and the like.

**Systems** means management systems—all of the various systems used to make your organization operate (e.g., decision-making systems, communication systems, measurement systems, performance-management systems, reward systems, etc.). Do not infer anything having to do with technology; in the context of the 10S Model, it is irrelevant whether a system is automated or not.

**Style** means management style, and there are fundamentally two kinds: an autocratic-style based on command and control, and a release-style based on consensus and commitment.

**Skills** means just that—skills. There are two broad categories of skills: generalist and specialist. Generalist skills are the skills that everyone needs in order to be a good citizen in your organization. Specialist skills are those skills required to perform a particular role or discipline.

**Staff** represents the people in your organization; not only employees, but also those members of your talent pool that you choose to rent or lease (i.e., contractors and consultants).

**Self** is you as a member of the staff—your personal leadership.

# WHAT THE 10S MODEL IS AND WHAT IT IS NOT

Please understand that my purpose is not to promote a particular model. Every academician, consultant, expert, author, and speaker has their own model. Some are round, some are square, some are layered, and some are fancy three-dimensional ones. The model is not the point; the point is to give you a way to think about your culture. The person who is crazy is the one who says that their model is <u>the</u> model. Perhaps you already have a model by which you think about your organization's culture. If so, fine; if not, now you do. That said, before we dive into the detail in the chapters that follow, there are several important things to know about the 10S Model.

First, the 10S Model is a people model. Nowhere will you see things like capital, land, or technology. Such things may be important in understanding your organization's technical system. However, the purpose of the 10S Model is to understand your organization's social system, or culture.

Second, just like Pasmore's Socio-Technical Organizational Model, the 10S Model can also be applied to any and all types of organizations. It can be applied to a political or commercial organization, a company or a union, a business unit within a company or a local within a union, a function within a business unit or union, a department within a function, a team within a department, public or private, profit or non-profit.

Third, referring back to Figure 5, the dotted-line box represents your organization's boundaries. That which is within the box is within your organization's sphere of control. That which is outside of the box is outside your organization, within your sphere of influence perhaps, but outside your sphere of control. The use of a dotted line is intended to connote that your organization is an ecosystem—it is holistic; everything is interdependent with everything else. Not only do the things within the box affect each other, but also things outside the box can affect those inside, and those things inside the box can affect those that are outside.

Finally, and perhaps most important of all, please remember that although the model is defined in terms of ten discreet components, cultures do not really exist in discreet components. As discussed earlier, cultures are part of the organizational ecosystem. The only reason we'll talk about culture in terms of discreet components is because it's easier to talk about it in that way, not because it really exists that way.

# 9

# SHARED VISION AND VALUES

*Seven Traits Perilous to Humanity:*
*Wealth without Work,*
*Pleasure without Conscience,*
*Science without Humanity,*
*Knowledge without Character,*
*Politics without Principle,*
*Commerce without Morality,*
*Worship without Sacrifice.*
**Mohandas Karamachand Gandhi**
Political and spiritual leader of India
1869 - 1948

VISION AND VALUES have become the butt of office jokes and cartoons. To be honest, given most of the vision and values fluff I've seen organizations come up with—this mom, God, and apple pie stuff—they deserve the ridicule. Unfortunately, shared vision and values are central to your culture, and you can't get away from them. You'll have them by design, or you'll have them by default—but you will have them. So, if the thought of vision and values still triggers an adverse biological reaction for you, take whatever time and space you need to get past it, but get past it.

Vision is <u>what</u> you want to be; values are <u>how</u> you want to be. Shared vision and values are more than just a mission statement—a mission statement is a subset of shared vision and values. Shared vision and values are a body of work, a superset of all of the formal and informal, written and unwritten bits that guide what you want to be and how you want to be. This includes your mission statement, which is usually explicitly stated; it also includes other things that may or may not be explicitly stated, like cultural norms. For example, in the USA we have the Constitution, but citizens also know that their state has a constitution, and their city may also have a charter. In addition, there are cultural norms that seem to vary by geographic region and heritage. So it is with all organizations. By design or default, a company will have its shared vision and values; each business unit within the company will have its derivative; and cultural norms will vary from site to site, from department to department, and team to team.

So, when I talk about "Shared Vision and Values," do not think of any single document—do not think solely of a mission statement. Rather, think of a body of work, and remember that this body of work will exist even if it is not articulated—whether by design or by default, it exists. In fact, the more common problem isn't that an organization hasn't bothered to articulate them, it's that the shared vision and values they have articulated are different from the ones that they actually practice.

## CHOOSING BETWEEN COMPETING VALUES

By articulating your organization's values, you provide practical guidance when situations arise where people have to choose between competing values. While it may be cause for debate among some ethical theorists, pragmatically, most people can make a decision when faced with choosing between a good thing and a bad thing. For example, I think it safe to speculate that nearly everyone will agree that respecting the property of others is good and stealing is bad. In fact, I believe most people can even make the more complicated choice for a bad thing when the harm done is outweighed by the good that comes of it. For example, imagine a person was found ready to throw him or herself off a fifty-story building because their spouse told them they were leaving them. Now imagine that a passerby persuaded that person to step back and come down by telling them the lie that their spouse had changed their mind. I think it safe to say that it would be okay for that passerby to lie to the would-be jumper because, in this case, the good of the life saved outweighs the bad of the lie told.

There are also times when most people will even approve of civil disobedience. For example, if a man is stopped for exceeding the speed limit,

94

but the officer discovers that the man is doing so because his wife has gone into labor so he is rushing her to the hospital, I suspect that the officer will not only excuse the man's speeding, but will perhaps even escort the couple to the hospital if duty permits.

Those are the easy decisions. The tough decisions involve choosing between two good, but competing values—decisions where a meritorious argument can be made for either choice, where there is no clear "right decision." Here's a purely hypothetical example. Imagine that you and your family are going to a wedding. You'll be giving your mother-in-law a ride to the wedding and you stop at her home to pick her up. She's not ready when you arrive, so you go inside and wait for her. She announces that she is finally ready, and emerges wearing the ugliest dress you have ever seen—it has colors next to each other that are not found together anywhere else in nature. Whereby she turns to your five year-old daughter and asks, "How does Grandma look?" You hold your breath. You have taught your daughter the values of both honesty and compassion. Which is the higher order value? Is there a right and a wrong answer? How do you hope she responds?

Here is a political example. Democracies have a similar dilemma involving public security and individual privacy. Both are good, and a meritorious argument can be made in favor of each. However, there is a tension between the two, and that tension increases as the preference for one over the other increases. The debate over this societal tradeoff was well underway with personal computers, the Internet, and e-business providing the catalyst; then September 11, 2001, happened, and, at least in the U.S., the public debate was blasted into an even higher orbit. There is no right or wrong answer. Both privacy and security are good things, but they are also at odds with each other. Which is the higher order value? Good, well-intentioned people, will honestly reason to different conclusions on how to make this tradeoff. In the U.S., the ultimate arbitrator in such dilemmas is the Supreme Court. Nine individuals, selected for just such purposes in accordance with the Constitution, according to a process specified in the Constitution, will apply their interpretation of our shared vision and values as expressed in our mission statement, the Constitution, along with the complimentary body of constitutional work that our country has crafted since.

We face similar, albeit not as weighty, dilemmas in organizations every day. Consider these tradeoffs that a business organization must make, and decide which is the higher order value:

- Quality or productivity? Is it better to hit your production schedule, even though it may be at the expense of quality; or is it better to ensure high quality, even though it may mean you miss your production schedule?

- Customer service or administrative efficiency? Is it better to provide good service to a customer, even though you will have to deviate from the established administrative process or protocol to do so; or is it better to stick to the process, even if you know it will result in substandard customer service?

- Value for customers or value for shareholders? Is it better to drive value for customers, even though it may have an adverse affect on this quarter's results; or is it better to drive value for shareholders, even though it may have an adverse effect on customer value over time?

Do your shared vision and values help your people make such tradeoff decisions? Interestingly, when faced with making such tradeoffs, the decision maker will likely choose based not on the stated shared vision and values, but on the operating shared vision and values as manifest in the reward system. As the old adage says, "What gets rewarded, gets done." The fact that an organization's reward systems may be out of alignment with their stated shared vision and values is a very common organizational alignment problem.

In addition to ethical dilemmas such as those above, there are decisions that Harry Truman, thirty-third president of the U.S., called "51/49s;" fifty-one percent of the data argues one way, forty-nine percent argues the other. Based solely on the data, allowing the necessary margin of error given the known human fallibilities, and without any external point of reference, such decisions are a toss-up. (Truman would complain that his staff always brought him the 51/49s, and never brought him the 90/10s. Of course, he would also admit that if a staff member ever did bring him a 90/10, then he had chosen the wrong person for that job.)

Shared vision and values, well-inculcated in the culture, can help everyone in an organization choose between competing values. For example, in May 2002 I was able to participate in an educational program that Walt Disney World offers guests called, "Keys to the Kingdom."[1] These "keys" represent four key values, in this order:

- Safety.
- Courtesy.
- Show.
- Efficiency.

---

[1] "Disney's Keys to the Kingdom Tour," (Seminar, Walt Disney World, Orlando, FL, May 2002).

The sequence is important because in addition to telling Disney employees, (a.k.a., cast members) that safety, courtesy, show, and efficiency are important, it also tells them that safety is the most important, courtesy is next, show is after that, and efficiency is last. It is for reasons of safety and courtesy to guests, whose hands may be full with packages, that the doors on the shops on Main Street are propped open even though it is inefficient for the air conditioners in the midday Orlando heat.

## COMMON PITFALLS

Of course the most obvious problem regarding an organization's shared vision and values is that they fail to articulate them. Another common problem is that an organization's stated shared vision and values are so generic and/or so sickeningly sweet that they'll make your tongue snap off its roller. As if there were some formula, or some standard template, most of the statements of shared vision and values that I have seen will contain something about customer service/satisfaction, continuous improvement, empowerment, quality, and workforce diversity. But, they are rendered meaningless because they are so generic.

Worse yet, they can become the victim of one-upmanship. Typically, it is decided that "customer satisfaction," or "meeting customer requirements," isn't aggressive enough. So, the rhetoric is dialed up; now you want to exceed customer requirements. No! Wait! You want to delight your customers. I am willing to bet there is a mission statement out there that talks about customer ecstasy. And continuous improvement, empowerment, total quality, and diversity fall victim to this same irrational exuberance. It's enough to make you sick. It's all just fluff, and it's just one more reason why statements of shared vision and values have fallen into such disrepute.

Perhaps the most serious problem that many organizations have isn't that they don't have a formal statement of shared vision and values; it's that they have two: the one that's printed on the wallet cards and displayed on the fancy plaque in the reception area, and the one by which they really operate. This is a problem of organizational integrity, and it's probably the chief reason why statements of shared vision and values are not taken seriously and often ridiculed.

# CHARACTERISTICS OF A GOOD MISSION STATEMENT

There is little disagreement on the importance of a well-crafted and well-in-culcated mission statement. The challenge is deciding what a well-crafted, well-inculcated mission statement looks like. I have learned that there are five characteristics common to good mission statements; a good mission state-ment:

- Is essentially changeless.
- Articulates a distinctive value proposition.
- Has something for all stakeholders.
- Embodies values based on sound principles.
- Is specific, and doesn't strive for total buy-in.

These characteristics are described more fully in the sections that fol-low; examples that exhibit these characteristics are also provided.

## ESSENTIALLY CHANGELESS

A well-crafted mission statement is essentially changeless. The U.S. Constitu-tion is an example with which there is broad familiarity. The U.S. is the oldest standing government in the world—it is not the longest lived of those that have ever existed, but it is the oldest of those currently in existence. The U.S. Constitution was drafted by the members of the Constitutional Convention held from May 25, 1787, to September 17, 1787. In June 1788, New Hamp-shire became the ninth state to ratify the Constitution, making it the law of the land. However, the Constitution's ratification was conditional on the addition of certain amendments, and by December 15, 1791, three fourths of the states had ratified the first ten amendments, which are commonly referred to as the "Bill of Rights."

In its two hundred-plus year history, there have been a total of twen-ty-seven amendments to the U.S. Constitution. However, the first ten are the Bill of Rights that were ratified less than four years following the ratification of the Constitution itself. In addition, Amendment 18, which abolished liquor on January 6, 1919, was repealed with Amendment 21 on December 5, 1933. So, there have really been only fifteen amendments to the Constitution in its two hundred-plus year history—it is essentially changeless.

# DISTINCTIVE VALUE PROPOSITION

Every organization needs to have a distinctive value proposition. Otherwise, why is that organization necessary? If you're leading a company, your value proposition addresses the question as to why customers should do business with you. If you're leading an organization within a company, your value proposition answers the question as to why your company shouldn't out-source or abolish your function. Your distinctive value proposition articulates your license to exist.

The best thinking I've found in this regard comes from Michael Treacy and Fred Wiersema's book, *The Discipline of Market Leaders: Choose Your Customers, Narrow Your Focus, Dominate Your Market*[2]. In this work, they define three dimensions on which all companies compete. The three value dimensions defined by Treacy and Wiersema are depicted in Figure 6; they are:

- The distinctive competency of "operational excellence" begets a "low cost" value proposition.
- The distinctive competency of "customer intimacy" begets a "high service" value proposition.
- The distinctive competency of "innovation" begets a "product leadership" value proposition.

---

[2]   Michael Treacy and Fred Wiersema, *The Discipline of Market Leaders: Choose Your Customers, Narrow Your Focus, Dominate Your Market*. (Reading, MA: Addison-Wesley Publishing Company, 1995).

*Figure 6 – Competitive Dimensions*

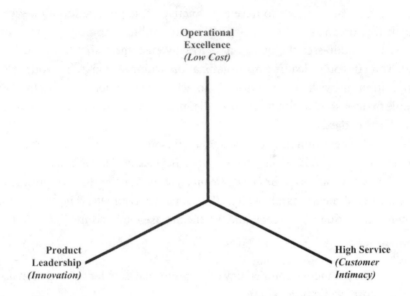

Source: Michael Treacy, "Sustaining Value Leadership," (Speech. The Masters Forum, Orpheum Theatre, St. Paul, MN, 11 Apr. 1995).

However, just as important as the definition of these three dimensions is Treacy and Wiersema's assertion that while every organization must certainly be competent on all three dimensions, organizations that earn enduring success choose one dimension on which to excel (i.e., choose your customers, narrow your focus, and dominate your market). Perennially successful organizations do not try to excel on all three. In fact, that's not possible because there is a tension among these three dimensions, and at a certain point they begin competing with each other. An organization cannot be the leader in operational effectiveness (low cost), and the leader in customer intimacy (high service), and the leader in product leadership (innovation), because the three are mutually exclusive at their extremes. There may be a dimension on which an organization wants to place secondary emphasis, but it is just that––secondary. Only one dimension can be primary, and it is the one on which they choose to excel. Let's look at an admittedly over-simplified example: public transportation; more specifically, let's look at mass transit versus taxis and limousine services.

The distinctive value proposition of a mass transit system is operational excellence—they are selling low cost. Certainly they must offer a minimally acceptable level of customer service, and they must also be competent innovators so they evolve at a pace commensurate with the evolution of the people and markets they serve. However, the distinctive value proposition of mass transit is operational excellence—low cost. In fact, public mass transit gets into trouble when it is not operationally excellent—when it is not low cost—and increasing taxpayer subsidies are needed to maintain the appearance of low cost.

To keep their costs low, they deal in rider volume and standard routes with fixed pick-up and drop-off points. Imagine what would happen if the public bus system decided to focus on customer intimacy (i.e., high service) and began picking riders up at their doors. Their costs would sky rocket because of the tension between operational excellence and customer intimacy. You can't excel at both—as you advance each along its continuum, you reach a point where they become competing values and one must give way to the other.

The distinctive value proposition of taxi and limousine services is customer intimacy—they are selling high service. Unlike mass transit, a taxi or a limo will take you door to door; they do not have fixed routes. However, taxis and limos diverge in their secondary values. In the case of taxis, their secondary value is operational excellence (i.e., low cost)—they're not as low cost as mass transit, but they are lower cost than a limo. In the case of limos, their secondary value is product leadership (i.e., innovation). Their vehicles are appointed with luxury, and they have become innovative in offering choices beyond the traditional limo, or even the stretch limo. Now they offer stretch Hummers, stretch 1957 Chevys; and some even offer a luxury appointed van or bus that gives their customers more room and amenities for "socializing."

Imagine what would happen to a taxi or limo company if they decided to focus equally on customer intimacy (i.e., high service) and operational excellence (i.e., low cost) in an effort to compete with mass transit. They could never match the low-cost structure of a mass transit system while maintaining their high level of customer service—at some point one gives way to the other.

Another example is an organization's "help desk" or "customer support" function. A common practice among many companies recently is to outsource their help desk, or customer support. What does it tell you about a company when they turn over a point of customer contact to people who are not employees? Well, it doesn't tell you that they are a bad company. It just tells you that customer intimacy (i.e., high service) is not their distinctive value proposition. Their outsourced help desk or customer support function may be quite competent, but it is not competitively distinctive.

Organizations get into trouble when they try to be all things to all people—neither fish nor foul. Listed below and depicted in Figures 7-9, which follow, are a few further examples that I use to help people understand this notion of a distinctive value proposition.

In retailing, Walmart's value proposition is clearly operational excellence—delivering low cost for their customers, as depicted in Figure 7. Innovation in retailing may be second, but their higher order value is operational excellence.

*Figure 7 – Walmart Excels at Operational Excellence*

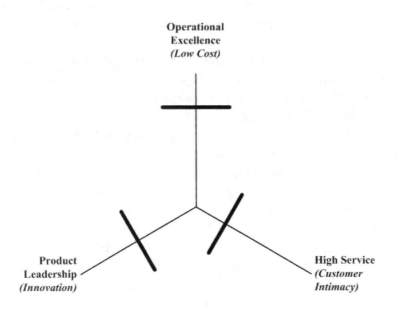

In auto manufacturing, Lexus' value proposition is clearly customer intimacy—delivering high service to their clientele, as depicted in Figure 8. Innovation in automobile features may be second, but their higher order value is customer intimacy.

*Figure 8 – Lexus Excels at High Service*

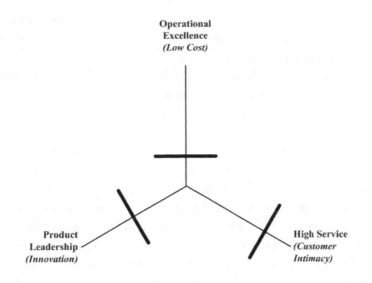

Finally, in consumer electronics, Apple's value proposition is clearly innovation—delivering cutting-edge products to their customers, as depicted in Figure 9. Customer intimacy may be their second, but their higher order value is innovation.

*Figure 9 – Apple Excels at Product Leadership*

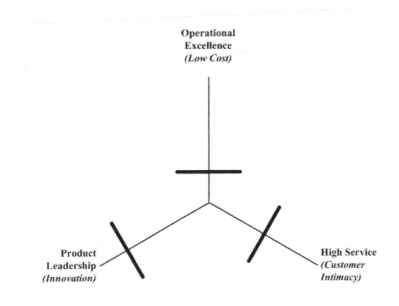

## SOMETHING FOR ALL STAKEHOLDERS

Another characteristic of a well-crafted mission statement is that it has something in it for all stakeholders: customers, employees, owners, suppliers, and the various communities to which it belongs. This is consistent with my assertion that if leadership adopts a pattern of decision-making that creates benefit for one stakeholder at the expense of another, then they will devalue the organization over time. So, a well-crafted mission statement has something for each stakeholder.

Further, that something is the cause for which members of the organization would be willing to die. The mission statement has to articulate the noble and worthy cause I spoke about when describing the mystery of sacrifice. Take these two insurance company examples: "We will be the insurance company with whom it is easiest to do business," versus "We help our customers restore normalcy to their lives in the event of an accident or natural disaster." Of course it can't be just a tag line, it has to be a legitimate expression of your cause, but which one do you find more noble and worthy? For which insurance company would you rather work?

## VALUES BASED ON SOUND PRINCIPLES

Durable mission statements talk about improving the economic wellbeing and quality of life for all of its stakeholders. A mission statement—be it the formal one that hangs on the wall, or the informal one by which people really operate—that focuses only on profit, or EPS, can only produce a mercenary society. Besides being culturally disabling, it is also stupid—to focus on profits or EPS in business is, as I've asserted before, no different than trying to play tennis by watching the scoreboard. There is a similar problem with expediency. When your guiding value is expediency, then you will only breed cynicism and contempt.

The values represented in the well-crafted mission statement will be based on sound principles. Imagine a busy city sidewalk. A man brushes by a lady, grabs her purse and starts running with it down the sidewalk. As he is running, he passes the purse to a buddy, who passes it to another buddy, who passes it to another until they disappear in the cityscape. Did these thieves not value planning, speed, and teamwork? Certainly, but their values were not based on sound principles, such as respect for other people and their property. Did Enron not value creativity, speed, and rewards for hard work? Certainly,

104

but their values were not based on sound principles.

In this book, *American Spirit: Visions of a new Corporate Culture,*[3] Lawrence M. Miller identifies eight key principles that lead to a more vibrant American economy, and suggests that a return to these core principles is still a basis for sound management and leadership. The excerpts below summarize those eight principles. As you read them, see if you also sense congruence with Adam Smith's sympathetic society, and de Tocqueville's self-interest rightly understood.

> *American managers have a tradition of pragmatism which is a traditional source of strength. However, this pragmatism may require the balance of new values that are lofty, that do inspire the imagination, engage the loyalty and devotion of the common man.*
>
> *These eight values are labeled "primary values" because they are applicable to the management of all organizations, and indeed many successful companies are already acting on them. I have selected these eight because my colleagues and I have observed they are the ones most related to high innovation, loyalty, and productivity. In brief, here they are:*
>
> ***The Purpose Principle.*** *We all have a need to confirm our self-worth. Self-worth cannot be achieved in the absence of a sense of contribution to some higher purpose. Leaders fulfill this need. They communicate purpose to those who follow. The ability to communicate a valued purpose is a rare art among corporate managers. Achieving return on equity does not, as a goal, mobilize the most noble forces in our souls. The most successful companies have defined their aims in terms of product or service and benefits to customers in a manner that can inspire and motivate their employees. Most corporations do serve a worthy purpose. Individuals seek to identify with it. The competitive leader will make the connection between our souls and our work, and will benefit from the energies released.*
>
> ***The Excellence Principle.*** *Our culture values comfort, both material and psychological. We feel we should achieve personal satisfaction and fulfillment. We not only value this comfort, but feel that it is our due. We do not welcome personal tests and trials,*

---

[3]   Lawrence M. Miller, *American Spirit: Visions of a New Corporate Culture,* (New York: William Morrow and Company, Inc, 1984).

*we seek to avoid them and view them as contrary to satisfaction. Satisfaction and excellence are inherently in conflict. Satisfaction implies acceptance of things as they are. Dissatisfaction is the source of motivation. It leads to actions to change that which is the source of discomfort. The achievement of excellence can occur only if the organization promotes a culture of creative dissatisfaction.*

*     **The Consensus Principle.** Managers are stuck in the culture of command. They feel an excitement and exhilaration when they are able to command. Unfortunately, command behavior is what was successful in the crisis climate of battle. The leader of old marched ahead of his troops because he was the strongest and the most brave. He exemplified the values that were important to that organization. The future corporation will not march into battle. It will succeed by its ability to bring ideas together, to stimulate the employees and managers to think creatively. The employee will not be asked to risk life and limb for his superior. He will be asked to risk sharing his thoughts and feelings. He will be asked to focus not his physical energies, but his mental energies. This change in task necessitates a change from command to consensus.*

*     **The Unity Principle.** Our corporations maintain the traditions of a class society. We maintain the distinctions of management-labor, salary-hourly wage, exempt-nonexempt, thinker-doer. They are all false distinctions, the old, useless baggage of a deceased society, carried forward into a new world. We live in an age of unity, of integration, when distinctions that disunite and limit people are inherently counterproductive. There are other traditions from our past to which management must return. There was a time when ownership and identity with the job were a source of pride. The industrial age, with the anonymity of mass production, swung the pendulum from ownership to alienation. The electronic age, with its emphasis on information, the flexibility of information technologies, and the psychological needs for community, identity, and a source of personal worth, will swing the pendulum back toward ownership. The competitive corporation will accept the value of fully involving the individual in his workings and decision-making so that he or she again feels in unity with and ownership for his work.*

*     **The Performance Principle.** In Western society the corporation is the agency that metes out more rewards and punishments*

*than any other. The prevalent principle by which it distributes its re-wards is power. Those who organize, those who are in short supply, those who can control have power and are rewarded in proportion to that power. The distribution of rewards according to power is as old as our civilization. However, this system contains within itself the seeds of its own destruction. When rewards are granted with-out regard to performance, productivity suffers. When they are tied to performance, individual and corporate performances improve. If the corporation is to succeed in the new era we are entering, it must reevaluate the values by which it distributes its rewards. In the future rewards must be granted according to the value of the performance, a value not currently exhibited at the level of the chief executive or the union apprentice.*

*__The Empiricism Principle.__ We are not skilled thinkers. Much of the explanation for the poor performance of American in-dustry in recent years can be found in the sloppy mental habits at every level of our organizations. It is a myth that American manag-ers manage by the numbers. Most of them have little understanding of data, statistical methods, the use of empirical analysis. However, this is only a reflection of the larger culture. We are a nation of sloppy thinkers. In the school, in the supermarket, and in the execu-tive suite we make decisions based on gut reactions that are often easily manipulated. Intuition is most useful when it is founded on a sound knowledge of the facts. Intuition in the corporate culture is more often an excuse for lazy and undisciplined analysis. If we are going to improve our corporate performance, we must begin to teach the value of statistics and their appropriate use at all levels of the corporation.*

*__The Intimacy Principle.__ The military model of man-agement was necessarily impersonal. In battle the cost of personal involvement in the psychological world of another individual pre-sented too great a risk to the emotional well being of the leader. This is our tradition. Strength is represented as a detached, masculine absence of emotion and intimacy with fellow human beings. Man-agement style will inevitably change because the future corporation is faced with a different challenge. The new challenge will be to tap not only the physical labor of the individual, but also his inner thoughts, his emotional and spiritual energies. This will require an intimate culture. Tasks will be accomplished when individuals are* *able to share openly without risk of emotional punishment, when managers have intimate knowledge of their subordinates' thoughts, feelings, and needs. But intimacy requires a strength and security that are not promoted in most American corporate cultures.*

***The Integrity Principle.*** *Decision-making in our organizations has become dominated by a concern for legalisms, regulations, and precedents. Integrity is the foundation upon which must be built all other values, and upon which rest the trust and relationship between individual and corporation. The ability to discriminate between what is honest and what lacks honesty is a skill that is critical to the establishment of the new corporate culture. We live in a society of law and legalism in which the lawyer has become the corporate high priest of right and wrong. That which is honest has become confused with that which is permissible by law. Our managers and corporations generally adhere to what is legal. However, the law does not specify what is right, and it is a poor guide for making the decisions that will establish trust and unity between individuals and organizations, between customers and suppliers. These relationships have deteriorated to the point where they represent a drag not only on productivity within major corporations but also on their ability to market their products in this country. When managers are able to discern and act on that which is honest in spirit, trustful business relationships will be reestablished.*[4]

# Specificity and Buy-In

A generic, or saccharin-sweet mission statement—a "fluffy" mission statement—is not good for much more than a laugh. A well-crafted mission statement will be specific; to be useful a mission statement needs to be specific enough so that a reasonable person could honorably disagree with it.

All too often, otherwise competent people's brains seem to turn to mush when they work on their mission statement. They meet, they talk, and they wordsmith it to death, but it's all where the rubber meets the sky.

"Customer satisfaction!"

"That's too mild. How about customer delight!? No! Wait! How about total customer delight!"

"How about total, ecstatic, orgasmic customer delight!"

4  Lawrence M. Miller, *American Spirit: Visions of a New Corporate Culture*, (New York: William Morrow and Company, Inc, 1984), p15-18.

This is what they do. In the unlikely event they ever declare completion, their next major task will be to decide if they should shrink and laminate that sucker so people can keep one in their wallet, or should they put it on banners or brass plaques that hang on walls everywhere, or should they do both.

Of course, a high-level, generic mission statement is about all you can expect to achieve if you're also expecting to achieve total buy-in. However, if you're trying to lead transformational change and you're renovating your mission statement, and if you achieve total buy-in, then you should know that you are on a bad path. Most people think that you're supposed to strive for total buy-in. But how can you be talking about doing something revolutionary, yet achieve total buy-in? A customer service revolution, a quality revolution, how do you have a revolution without someone getting upset? Go back to your history books. Can you cite one revolution where nobody got pissed off in opposition to it? If you're having a good revolution it ought to make some people cranky and upset.

Do you know what it means when you get total buy-in? It means that no one intends to change their behavior in a substantive way. The language is so high-level that people can interpret it to mean that other people may need to change, but not them, because everything they're doing is mission consistent. You have a phony kind of buy-in—it's an illusion. Nobody's planning on changing; nobody intends to change how they help the business. People are just in love with the words.

If your mission is not stated with enough specificity that reasonable people cannot voice honorable opposition to it, then it's not interesting, it's not useful, it's just fluff.

"Continuous improvement" instead of what? "occasional improvement?" or "continuous decay?"

"Customer satisfaction." Instead of what?"Customer disgruntlement?"

"Total quality." Instead of what? "partial quality?"

Of course you're going to get buy-in, who would be against these things? Yet, this is what people do. They just keep wordsmithing their mission statement and it's crazy; it's nuts; it's a sickness; it's a pathology.

# CRAFTING A MISSION STATEMENT

*Miracle at Philadelphia: The Story of the Constitutional Convention May--September*

*1787,*[5] by Catherine Drinker Bowen, tells the story of the crafting of the U.S. Constitution. I have found the process used by America's founding fathers provides an excellent template for crafting mission statements in general. Let's look at some key attributes of their process.

First, the states assigned their best people as their delegates—the delegates were not necessarily the ones in power in their home state, but they were people who were well-educated in the domain (i.e., democracies and republics) and gave quality mental time to its study; they were also influential people who were held in high regard (largely) by both the people of their state and their colleagues at the convention.

Second, a number of the delegates knew and had worked together before. They had laughed together, cried together, suffered defeat together, fought with each other, overcame obstacles together and celebrated victories together—they had a prior and successful working relationship.

Third, they conducted the convention's business behind closed doors. This way delegates could be as open to persuasion as they were ready to persuade, and they could permit themselves a change in heart without the fear of public loss of face. Their environment was every bit as political and neurotic as ours is today—perhaps not as time starved as we are today, but every bit as political and neurotic.

Fourth, there was individual pre-work done prior to convening (e.g., the Virginia Resolves). Delegates came prepared and they didn't start from a blank sheet of paper.

Fifth, they navigated through the process under George Washington's strong leadership, James Madison's faithful chronicles, a common devotion to the cause, and each individual's strength of character.

Lastly, they utilized a three-committee process as described below.

The main committee was called the "Committee of the Whole." The Committee of the Whole was chaired by George Washington and consisted, as its name suggests, of the entire convention. It was in the Committee of the Whole that the guiding principles were debated and established.

A subcommittee, the "Committee of Detail," was commissioned to work out the details of how the guiding principles, as adopted by the Committee of the Whole, would be put into operational practice. The Committee of Detail's job was to move the work from a philosophical context through the pragmatic issues into operational practices. The Committee of Detail's work products were brought back to the Committee of the Whole for review, re-

---

[5] Catherine D. Bowen, *Miracle at Philadelphia: The Story of the Constitutional Convention May to September 1787*, (Boston: Little, Brown and Company, 1986).

work and eventual approval. Once approved, the Committee of Detail's work products were turned over to the Committee of Style.

The Committee of Style's job was to put the Committee of Detail's work in terms and conditions that would be understood by (and marketable to) those people who did not participate in the convention. Like the Committee of Detail, the Committee of Style's work products were brought back to the Committee of the Whole for review, rework and eventual approval. (The Constitution ultimately had to be ratified by three-fourths of the states. This was achieved, but only on the condition that amendments would be developed immediately to safeguard individual rights—hence the first ten amendments, which we know as the Bill of Rights.)

I have used an adaptation of this process to develop the mission statement equivalents for my areas of responsibility. However, whenever I assumed leadership of a new area of responsibility, developing a new mission statement was not the first thing I would do. It wouldn't have worked because I was missing two important things: understanding of their current state, and relationships with key stakeholders and opinion leaders. The first thing I would do is get the current state working as well as I could. I was hired to renovate an under-performing organization, or revitalize a neglected one. I was not so ignorant or naive not to know that those who hired me wanted to see results, and they didn't want to wait a long time to see them. But those results also needed to be durable. As we got the current state operating more effectively, as relationships were built, as values took root, as learning occurred, a vision of future state possibilities evolved.

As I learned and the vision evolved, I began sharing it casually and informally—no pomp or circumstance—as W. Edwards Deming[6] coaches us in the tenth of his fourteen points, "Eliminate slogans and exhortations…"[7] I would make modest changes to advance the current state in the direction of the future state, and a shared sense of direction eventually emerged. This process took time, but in that time, shared vision and values were inculcated, and in the process I put that shared vision and values in writing, ala the Virginia

---

[6] William Edwards Deming was an American statistician, professor, author, lecturer and consultant, widely credited with improving production in the U.S. during WWII, although he is perhaps best known for his work in Japan. There, from 1950 onward he taught top management how to improve design (and thus service), product quality, testing and sales (the last through global markets) through various methods, including the application of statistical methods. Deming made a significant contribution to Japan's later renown for innovative high-quality products and its economic power. He is regarded as having had more impact upon Japanese manufacturing and business than any other individual not of Japanese heritage. Despite being considered something of a hero in Japan, he was only beginning to win widespread recognition in the U.S. at the time of his death in 1993.

[7] W. Edwards Deming, *Out of the Crisis*, (Cambridge: Massachusetts Institute of Technology, Center for Advanced Engineering Study, 199 0). p24.

Resolves. I then engaged my leadership team and selected others in the three-committee process of formally articulating the shared vision and values that, by this time, had already become our mode of operation. In other words, we officially codified the operating principles that we were already practicing.

# CORPORATE MISSION STATEMENT EXAMPLES

One of the select companies that I have followed with professional interest over the course of my career is Honda. My interest has not been out of any particular fascination with Japanese management; rather my interest has been in their culture and love of engineering. I don't think Honda is a very good example of Japanese management, anyway. Mr. Honda almost seemed to have an American spirit of individualism. When Mr. Honda expressed an interest in getting into the automobile business, Japan's central planning agency, MITI (Ministry of International Trade and Industry), told him to stick to motorcycles. Mr. Honda chose to get into automobiles, and now Honda seems to be manufacturing just about every product that runs on an internal combustion engine. Honda was also the first Japanese company to establish an offshore manufacturing facility and ship cars back to Japan, which they did when they built their plant in Marysville, Ohio. Honda's management style flows from Mr. Honda's philosophy, the "Racing Spirit:"

> *The first president of Honda America was Shoichiro Irimajiri, known as Mr. Iri by the associates. Earlier in his career Mr. Iri was responsible for managing Honda's successful racing efforts, designing engines and managing production facilities in Japan. He frequently spoke of the "Racing Spirit." The Racing Spirit includes five principles:*

- *Seek the challenge.*
- *Be ready on time.*
- *Teamwork.*
- *Quick response.*
- *Winner takes all.*[8]

In another, and admittedly biased, example, I believe that one of the best examples of a corporate mission statement is that of one of my former

[8] Lawrence M. Miller, "The Honda Way: A Visit to Marysville—A Model for the Future," (paper presented at The Masters of Executive Excellence, Minnetonka, MN, 22 Aug. 1989), p2

employers, Medtronic, Inc. Medtronic was founded in 1949, but their mission statement wasn't crafted until 1960. The company's performance was headed south, and somewhere near Tierra del Fuego Earl Bakken, one of the co-founders, was told by the board that before they would take any rescuing action, he had to focus the business. Sitting at his kitchen table, facing the demise of his company, he came up with the six objectives shown below. (Today, they are referred to collectively as the Medtronic Mission. At that time they were referred to as the six corporate objectives, as the term "mission statement" was not yet in vogue.)

### Medtronic Mission

- *To contribute to human welfare by application of biomedical engineering in the research, design, manufacture, and sale of instruments or appliances that alleviate pain, restore health, and extend life.*
- *To direct our growth in the areas of biomedical engineering where we display maximum strength and ability; to gather people and facilities that tend to augment these areas; to continuously build on these areas through education and knowledge assimilation; to avoid participation in areas where we cannot make unique and worthy contributions.*
- *To strive without reserve for the greatest possible reliability and quality in our products; to be the unsurpassed standard of comparison and to be recognized as a company of dedication, honesty, integrity, and service.*
- *To make a fair profit on current operations to meet our obligations, sustain our growth, and reach our goals.*
- *To recognize the personal worth of employees by providing an employment framework that allows personal satisfaction in work accomplished, security, advancement opportunity, and means to share in the company's success.*
- *To maintain good citizenship as a company.*[9]

Just as sequence is important in Disney's keys to the Kingdom, so was the sequence of these six objectives important to Earl. When I started my first tour of duty with Medtronic in April 1980, one element of their new employee orientation was lunch with Earl. A group of ten new employees along with Earl and his assistant went to lunch at a local restaurant where we

---

[9]  Medtronic, http://www.medtronic.com/about-medtronic/our-mission/index.htm

sat around a large table and listened as Earl told the story of the company's history and the six corporate objectives. As Earl shared the heritage of the company, the genesis of the six objectives, and their importance to the company's soul, I was struck that he emphasized not only the importance of each of the individual objectives, but also the importance of their sequence.

The first objective defines what they did and why they did it, "To contribute to human welfare by application of biomedical engineering in the research, design, manufacture and sale of instruments or appliances that alleviate pain, restore health and extend life."

The second objective talks about the competencies and discipline vital to growing the business, "To direct our growth in the areas of biomedical engineering where we display maximum strength and ability; to gather people and facilities that tend to augment these areas; to continuously build on these areas through education and knowledge assimilation; to avoid participation in areas where we cannot make unique and worthy contributions."

The third objective establishes the unequivocal importance of quality—the one thing which, in the medical device industry, may not distinguish the company by its presence, but will certainly kill the company by its absence, "To strive without reserve for the greatest possible reliability and quality in our products; to be the unsurpassed standard of comparison and to be recognized as a company of dedication, honesty, integrity, and service."

The first mention of money does not come until the fourth objective, and nothing is said about EPS. The fourth objective recognizes that if there is no margin, then there is no mission. However, this objective is deliberately fourth because it will be the inevitable result if they do well on the first three objectives, "To make a fair profit on current operations to meet our obligations, sustain our growth, and reach our goals."

So, the first three objectives talk about what they do and how they do it; and the fourth objective talks about the financial prize they win if they do the first three objectives well. With that, the fifth and sixth objectives talk about how they want to share the fruits of their success.

The fifth objective talks about sharing their success with their employees, "To recognize the personal worth of employees by providing an employment framework that allows personal satisfaction in work accomplished, security, advancement opportunity, and means to share in the company's success."

Finally, the sixth objective talks about sharing their success with the many communities in which they belong, "To maintain good citizenship as a company."

# DEPARTMENTAL MISSION STATEMENT EXAMPLE

Every organization has its own shared vision and values, even organizations that are contained within a larger organization. The only question is whether it is articulated or not, and whether what's articulated matches what's practiced. As an example of departmental vision and values let me offer that which we developed for an organization I once led. The organization was the 300+ person IT group that was comprised of teams located around the world, and which served a large business unit within the company.

The company's corporate mission statement provided our purpose. The business unit had long had its own mission statement—a specialized derivative of the corporate mission statement. Adding further to the body of work comprising their shared vision and values, the business unit was also explicit about its cultural norms and strategic goals.

As members of the company our organization was, of course, bound by the company's mission; and as members of a particular business unit we were similarly bound by that business unit's mission, cultural norms, and strategic goals. In addition, however, there were certain operating principles that our IT organization adopted to guide not only how we conducted our work, but also how we governed the conduct of our work. These became our *IT Operating Principles*, and they are provided in full detail in Appendix A.

In summary, our *IT Operating Principles* addressed our license to exist, our purpose, our market(s), our value proposition and alignment in the company's larger IT community, our clients and how we define good client service, our distinctive competencies, our work and work products, our culture, and our jobs.

# A FAMILY EXAMPLE

If you're a parent, you have probably struggled with allowances for your children—I certainly did. I have two daughters, the oldest is Rebecca, and three years younger is Jessica. When they were in pre- and lower school, it was pretty easy. Their allowances were based on how well they behaved in three categories: taking care of themselves, taking care of their things, and helping others. We even had a simple scorecard posted on the refrigerator (i.e., the family communication center) to remind them, in little kid's language, of what was involved in each of those categories; it even had little boxes they could check to track how well they were doing.

As they progressed through lower school this approach lost its effectiveness, and by the time they entered middle school they found the approach insultingly childish. So we tried something different. Leveraging the Management 101 training I had received from my employer at the time, I came up with a new approach that I though was really cool; it itemized the chores they were expected to do, and it provided penalties and incentives (financial and otherwise) for doing those chores poorly or for doing them exceptionally well. I was quite proud of it.

Unfortunately, I was completely out of tune with my "followers" and it was totally ineffective. One evening when my daughters were doing the dishes—one washing and one drying—they began arguing over whose turn it was to wash and whose turn it was to dry (I guess that washing is the preferable job). Hearing this argument and seeing the dishes not getting done, I intervened, "Jessica, you wash. Rebecca, you dry."

Of course, Jessica proceeded to taunt Rebecca, but I just smiled because my Solomon-like intervention was only partially implemented. When they finished, but before they put the dishes away, I intervened again. I took the dishes from the drying side of the sink, put them back on the washing side of the sink, and said, "Okay, now Rebecca you wash, and Jessica, you dry." They stared at me with disbelief. With them now realizing the full grandeur of my Solomon-like solution, I seized that teachable moment and beamed with pride over the pearls of wisdom I had just handed down.

I was still swollen with pride over my fatherly savoir-faire when I returned to the kitchen and saw the incredibly poor job they were doing washing the dishes. (As Rebecca would later tell me, "Dad, a job not worth doing, is not worth doing well.") I absolutely lost it. I told them both that they required way too much supervisory attention and the quality of their work sucked. In fact, I fired them—I literally told them that they were fired. I told them they should step away from the sink, that their mother and I would do the dishes along with the rest of their chores from this day forward, and that they would no longer receive any allowance—I would pay them for the week up to that day but, after that, nothing.

"But how will we pay for our movies, or CDs and other stuff?"

"I have no idea. You should have thought of that before you decided to suck at your chores. Maybe you can find someone else to hire you and pay you for doing a crappy job while requiring excessive supervision!"

It was a complete meltdown. A bad outcome for me—I didn't want to be stuck with their chores. A bad outcome for them—they needed money. And a bad outcome for the family—the main idea was to teach them something about family citizenship and about managing money.

This troubled me—a lot. I spoke with friends and colleagues to see how they handled their kids' allowance. I read books to see what the experts said. In the end, I decided that paying the kids to do chores was wrong and the two had to be de-coupled—doing chores is something you do because you are part of the family, not because you are paid to do them. However, I did want them to learn how to manage their money, and they weren't old enough to get a "real job," so they had to receive an allowance. Ultimately, I concluded, we needed to have an understanding as to what "good family citizenship" means.

To organize my own thoughts, I set about putting my thoughts regarding "good family citizenship" on paper, and I began outlining what I thought to be the important elements of an allowance agreement. This took about two weeks. By that time I was pretty sick of doing their chores, and they were pretty sick of not having any money to do the stuff kids their ages do. The environment was pretty conducive to having an open, honest, and quite grown-up conversation.

I showed the girls the two documents I drafted: one described what I meant by "good family citizenship," and the second outlined the terms by which they would receive an allowance. At first, of course, my two beloved teenagers crossed their arms, shifted their weight to one foot, tilted their heads down, rolled their eyes up and stared at me with a look that said they have never seen so much dumbness stacked in one pile before—they couldn't believe that I had actually written these up. I was a professional, and their initial response was not unexpected. So, I explained to them that these documents were just vehicles for me to organize my thoughts, that I just wanted to use them for the purposes of our discussion, that I wanted them to be comfortable with them, too, and at the end of the day the important thing was that we know and understand what to expect of each other.

In the end, we kept the documents. In fact, we actually signed the *Allowance Agreement*. Later, when they came of driving age, I crafted a *Driving Contract,* which we also signed—again, so we would know and understand what to expect of each other.

I don't know who learned more from whom. I am particularly proud of how it turned out, and I certainly learned more from this experience than I ever did from any company Management 101 training. The *Good Family Citizenship* document became akin to our family mission statement, and maintaining good family citizenship became a condition upon which both the allowance agreement and the driving contract were based.

All three documents—*Good Family Citizenship*, *Allowance Agreement*, and *Driving Contract*—are provided in Appendix B.

# 10

# SYMBOLS

*Being powerful is like being a lady. If you have to tell people you are, you aren't.*
**Margaret Thatcher**
Leader of the Conservative Party and prime minister of the United Kingdom
b. 1925

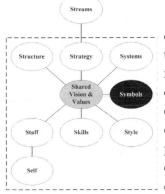

# SYMBOLS ARE THE PHYSI-

cal manifestation of the shared vision and values that the organization practices; these may be different than the shared vision and values that the organization cspouses. This is the primary value of symbols; they give you visual clues as to the organization's <u>real</u> vision and values. They also provide a lever for initiating cultural change because one way to start changing a culture is by changing the symbols.

The symbols that come to mind for most people are things like their organization's logo, or certain awards. For example, one of Medtronic's important symbols is a medallion that is given to each new employee during a part of his or her orientation known as the "Mission & Medallion Ceremony." On one side of the medallion is the first of the company's six objectives—the one which defines Medtronic's purpose. On the other side of the medallion is a series of figures showing a man rising from a prone to a standing position. This "rising man" symbolizes the Medtronic Mission to "alleviate pain, restore health, and extend life." Displaying the medallion on their desk, it becomes a constant reminder of the company's heritage and mission.

## CULTURAL INSIGHTS

In addition to things like logos and medallions, there are more subtle symbols that provide even more powerful insights into the culture. Think of your own organization. Are there different cubicle/office sizes and different calibers of office furniture for people of different ranks? Is there executive parking? Are supervisors, managers, directors, and/or VPs located with their teams, with their peers, or with their superiors? Is there a "mahogany row?" Are there different rules for hourly workers and salaried workers? Is there a dress code? Are people allowed to personalize their cubicles and offices, or is that prohibited? Are programs launched with a lot of pomp and circumstance; are there a lot of banners in your hallways? Is organizational and/or process performance data continuously projected for all to see? Does your organization's stated vision and values suggest an egalitarian ethic, yet executives have reserved parking spots?

Again, symbols are important for two reasons: they provide powerful insights about the culture, and they provide a lever for initiating cultural change. One of my favorite symbols to pick on is dress code. Some of you may remember the days of IBM under the leadership of Tom Watson, when dark suits and white shirts were the uniform. Conversely, there are the well-known examples of Silicon Valley firms where jeans, T-shirts, shorts, and sandals are the norm. Walt Disney theme parks have a strict dress code for their cast members. They provide the costume for many of their cast members, but there is a strict dress code for those for whom a costume is not provided. In addition they have specific and strict guidelines pertaining to personal grooming to which everyone must adhere. A graduated scheme of dress has also emerged in business akin to that in the military. The military has its Class A, B, and C uniforms, and business has business formal, business casual, and casual.

Some symbols are carriers of fabricated social value. People in financial services, attorneys, and accountants tend toward business formal, sometimes permitting business casual on Fridays. People in manufacturing and engineering tend toward business casual, sometimes permitting casual on Fridays. And, of course, in the world of consulting, there has always been an unwritten rule for consultants to dress commensurate with their client, and some marquis firms require their consultants to dress one notch higher than their client.

Some symbols are carriers of legitimate social value. In the medical world, you can tell someone's status by the length of their lab coat—while still attending classes, medical students wear shorter lab coats; once they've completed their academic coursework they graduate to a longer lab coat. At Disney, the Imagineers are at the top of the food chain and have their own style nametag; theirs has Sorcerer Mickey on it. Then there is the military approach where the symbols of social value are deliberately and proudly displayed in the form of symbols of rank and badges of accomplishments. Let's take a closer look at dress code and privileges of rank.

I personally don't like wearing a business suit—I am a business casual guy (khakis and collars). If I had my way, I would wear blue jeans, T-shirts, and Nikes. I'm okay wearing a suit (my Class A uniform) when meeting with customers, interviewing for a job, and attending a wedding or a funeral. However, even though the ladies in my life prefer how I look in a suit, I don't like wearing one around the office. I don't like suits for three reasons.

First, I find business suits physically uncomfortable and silly. What percent of the time do people in suits actually keep their coat on? Even the people who wear suits will take off their coat, roll up their sleeves and maybe even loosen their ties when they want to look like a workin' man. And what is the purpose of a tie, except decoration? As a strong believer that form follows function, I have a hard time tying a nonfunctional piece of cloth around my neck.

My second reason is an economic one. I find suits to be incredibly expensive—or to be more blunt, a waste of money.

My final reason is cultural: I find suits to be elitist. At their worst they create a caste system; at best they create social and emotional distance between people. Someday in the future archeologists will dig us up and conclude that our society had two classes of people: the decision makers who wore brightly colored strips of cloth around their necks, and the workers who did not. Of course, having already concluded that we were intelligent and rational beings, they wouldn't suppose that we had no idea why the decision makers would wear these strips of cloth. They will reason that those brightly colored strips of cloth certainly must have served a useful purpose; they will surmise that because it was the decision makers who wore them, those strips of neck cloth must have had something to do with the decision-making process. Perhaps they were used in voting—those who voted one way would toss the strip of cloth over their right shoulder, those who voted the other way would toss it over their left shoulder, and those who abstained or were indecisive would do nothing.

I know businessmen who wear suits because they genuinely prefer to; their preference is authentic. On the other hand, I also know businessmen who wear suits because they are image-conscious aristocrats who perceive social value in doing so. Worse, I know companies that seem to be schizophrenic about dress code. Dress at every other building will be business casual; however, dress at their "world headquarters" will be business formal—regardless of rank—except on Fridays and all days between Memorial Day and Labor Day when business casual is permitted. If you work at another building, and have to visit world headquarters on a day other than Friday or between Labor Day and Memorial Day, then you are expected to dress in business formal attire. What a waste of cultural energy.

I think some of the most interesting and telling symbols involve "privileges of rank." For example, I've noticed that a caste system has emerged at some companies around personal digital assistants, or PDAs (e.g., iPhones, Blackberries, Windows Mobile devices, etc.). The device you get will be a function, not of your responsibilities, but of your rank. Executives will get a company-paid Blackberry, the rest of management might get a company-paid Windows Mobile device, others may get only a company-paid phone, others will get nothing at all, and nobody gets an iPhone because then everyone will want a cool iPhone, and God forbid businesses provision workers with anything "cool." So, while an executive who never puts hand to product or interacts with a customer may get a Blackberry because of their rank, the poor person responsible for the 24/7 support of a critical system gets nothing because they lack sufficient rank.

The most dysfunctional of these situations involves administrative assistants, some of the hardest working people in many offices, and often the one person upon which so many others depend. Unless you are an executive assistant, administrative assistants are usually in a low pay grade; in fact, it is not uncommon to have an administrative assistant's pay grade unfairly constrained by the pay grade of their boss. If the company views gadgets such as a PDA as a privilege of rank, rather than a tool necessary to do business in a global, 24/7 world, these administrative assistants who are quarterbacking meeting schedules and travel schedules, who become a hub of communications especially in times of crisis, and who do all of this at all hours of the day and night, may not even get a company paid phone let alone a company-paid PDA. It is nuts.

There are two symbols of which I am particularly fond because they are congruent with a culture of meritocracy, which is my personal preference.

122

The first is establishing a policy declaring that sunlight is part of the public domain. Therefore, no offices or cubicles, only aisle ways, may be built along outside windows. The other involves travel policy. Whether you fly business class or coach is not a function of your rank, but is a function of the duration of your flight. If a flight is over four hours in duration, then the individual--regardless of their rank—may travel in business class. If the duration of the flight is four hours or less, then the individual—regardless of their rank—must travel in coach.

Editorial aside, the point is not that one symbol is good and another is bad; symbols are neither good nor bad. The point is that symbols give you powerful insights into the values actually practiced in the culture, regardless of what might be on the brass plaque in the lobby or on the laminated wallet cards. In fact, symbols can reveal an organizational integrity problem. If there is a difference between the espoused shared vision and values (which you can find on the brass plaque or wallet cards), and those that are practiced (which you can see by reading the symbols), then there is an organizational integrity problem.

## LEVERS FOR CHANGE

Symbols also provide a powerful lever for initiating cultural change—if you choose to pull that lever. Working with clients on organizational change efforts during my days as a management consultant, I came across executives who could talk with clinical objectivity about eliminating a whole layer of middle management. However, if you raised the idea of eliminating executive parking, it was as if you had lost your mind. Or propose a rule that declares sunlight to be public domain, so there will be no cubicles or offices—including executive offices—along outside windows, and it is if you were speaking in tongues. Of course, this just goes to show how important symbols really are; which I say is all the more reason they may need to be changed.

# 11

## STREAMS

*What we call chaos is just patterns we haven't recognized. What we call random is just patterns we can't decipher. What we can't understand we call nonsense. What we can't read we call gibberish.*

**Chuck Palahniuk**

American freelance journalist, satirist, and novelist

b. 1961

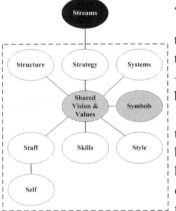

# THERE IS NOT MUCH

to say about streams because streams represent those things over which you have no control––you may be within your sphere of influence, but they are outside your sphere of control.

Streams are those external forces that affect your organization (they might also be called market forces or exogenous factors, but neither of those begin with an "S"). For a company, streams include things like actions taken by competitors, government regulators, and Wall Street analysts. For a department within a company, for example, streams include those things that other departments do to you, such as unfunded mandates from corporate headquarters. Where a hallmark of shared vision and values is that they are essentially changeless, a hallmark of streams is that they are constantly changing.

# 12

# STRATEGIES

*Young riders pick a destination and go. Old riders pick a direction and go.*
**Anonymous motorcycle wisdom**

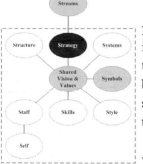

STRATEGIES ARE HOW your organization deals with the constantly changing streams in a way that is faithful to your essentially changeless shared vision and values. The combination of shared vision and values, streams, and strategies is also sometimes referred to as the "Strategic Path."

I took an executive course from Harvard in 1981, "Strategic Planning for Information Systems."[1] What they taught me then is wrong today. I was taught strategic planning in the context of ends, ways and means, but that's not the part that is now wrong.

I was taught that you first determine your desired end, then you choose the best from among the various ways of achieving that end, and finally you gather the various means you will need to execute the chosen way. This was noted thus: ends➜ways➜means. For example, say your desired end is to go to the North Pole. There are various ways you can get there: by foot, snowshoe, cross-country skis, dog sled, snowmobile, plane, or submarine.

---

[1]    Allen H. Schmidt, "Strategic Planning for Information Systems," (Seminar, Harvard University. Cambridge, MA. Jun. 1981).

You choose to go by snowmobile. So what are the means you will need to go to the North Pole by snowmobile? For one thing, you'll need a snowmobile along with all of the things required to keep a snowmobile going (e.g., fuel, oil, grease, repair tools, and parts, etc.). You'll also need food, cold-weather gear, and navigation equipment. You may not need, but you will want, communications equipment. And you will want all of the intelligence you can get on the Arctic (e.g., weather, wildlife, etc.). This is the part that may have been right then but is wrong today. The ends➔ways➔means approach to strategic planning was well-suited for a static, evenly paced world of yesteryear, but not for the fast-paced, dynamic world of today.

Opportunities are becoming less predictable, not more; they are coming with shorter lead times, not longer; and windows of opportunity are shrinking, not growing. A better approach is ends➔means➔ways. That is, you still begin by determining your desired end. But then you gather all of the means you can afford to carry, and every time a way presents itself to take a step toward your desired end—every time you have an opportunity to take a step north—you take it.

The difference between these two approaches to strategic planning is like the difference between an American football game plan and a basketball or hockey game plan.

The old way of strategic planning is akin to an American football game plan. In American football, action stops while the team huddles to decide and communicate which play it is going to run; that play is almost always sent in from someone not on the field, but on the sideline or up in a box. Every player in each position knows what they are supposed to do for that particular play; the linemen know their blocking pattern, the receivers know their pass routes and/or blocking assignments, the running backs know their rushing routes and/or blocking assignments. The team lines up. One person, the quarterback, calls the cadence, and the play goes into action on his signal. Play continues until some independent third party blows a whistle, at which time action stops and the team huddles to call their next play.

In hockey and basketball, play is much more fluid and stops a lot less often. While it may not be as apparent as in American football, there are plays in basketball and hockey. However, the plays are not as rigidly structured, and how a team gets the ball or puck from point A to point B is a function of the players' speed, strength, skill, and most importantly, their "attunedness" to what is going on around them.

Our current environment is much more like hockey or basketball than it is like American football. No longer can you have a roadmap to your strategic goals—a plan that tells you exactly how far to go in a particular direction, when to change direction, and how far to go in that new direction before changing again. You will need a compass and a full backpack. Most importantly of all, you need people who are comfortable without a roadmap and only a compass, people who know how to improvise when faced with an uncharted river to forge or terrain to cross, and can do so in unexpected weather conditions.

# 13

# STRUCTURE

*Most organizational restructuring has about the same effect
as rotating a car's tires to fix a flat.*
**Scott Adams**
Author and creator of the Dilbert comic strip
b. 1957

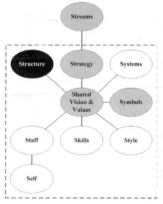

# STRUCTURE MEANS NOT

only who reports to whom, but also roles and responsibilities, span of control, and other such elements.

# BUILDING BLOCKS

The building block of society—all societies—is the family. It may vary as to how extended versus nuclear, but the family is the building block for all civilizations. In a work organization there is a building block, too; it's the team. Teams are the natural work group. Let's look at three stages in business history.

In stage one there were the family-owned craft shops and farms. In the case of a print shop, for example, the father was the master craftsman, and when the son became old enough he would work in the shop as an apprentice. In the case of a quilt shop, the mother may have been the master craftsman, with the daughter working as an apprentice. And the apprentices who weren't sons or daughters were often treated like sons and daughters. The same was

131

true of family farms. Economic life was built on family craft shops and family farms.

Can you imagine a politician saying that the family farm is not important? I'll say it; in today's economy the family farm is not important. At the beginning of the twentieth century, fifty-five to sixty percent of Americans worked on a family farm. Today it is one-and-one-half percent and shrinking. But we have this tremendous emotional reaction when we hear someone say that the family farm is not important. Do you know what you don't like about someone saying that the family farm is not important? It's not the "farm" part; it's the "family" part.

This is not new management theory; this goes back to the cave—it's primordial. Since the beginning of time, people have gathered in small groups for protection—physical and psychological. It is in our genetic code, and we have a strong psychological connection to it no matter how hard we try to ignore, deny, or destroy it.

Stage two came along with the industrial revolution; its Henry Ford's assembly line and Fredrick Taylor's factory. It was the manager's job to design "the best way" of doing something, and it was the worker's job to "just do it." If a worker had a problem with their job, they didn't see a co-worker, they saw their manager.

If you remember your Psychology 101, there is a condition called marasmus. There was a time when a high percentage of orphaned infants would die in the hospital even though their physical needs, such as feeding and diapering, were taken care of. This changed when nurses and doctors learned that the babies also needed to be picked up, cuddled, and played with. Now we even have surrogate mothers who will provide such care to orphaned infants. We discovered that a bonding needs to occur, or infants will literally roll over and die.

Similarly, during the Korean War, North Koreans attempted to psychologically isolate American prisoners of war (POWs). The North Vietnamese attempted to do the same thing to American POWs during the Vietnam War. In his book, *Beyond Survival: Building on the Hard Times—A POW's Inspiring Story,*[1] Navy pilot, and ex-POW Captain Gerald Coffee tells the story of his seven years in North Vietnamese POW camps. He emphasizes how absolutely essential their "tap code" was for maintaining lines of communications among the POWs to keep everyone connected, and keeping the North Vietnamese from psychologically isolating them.

---

[1] Captain Gerald Coffee. *Beyond Survival: Building on the Hard Times-A POW's Inspiring Story*, (New York: G. P. Putnam's Sons, 1990).

There is a basic psychological need to be part of a group of people who care about each other. This is nothing new; it is not new management theory; this is in our genetic code.

In neighborhoods when the family unit breaks down, what do kids form? "Hey buddy, join our gang. This is our territory…" What's going here? Are these kids crazy? They may be bad, but they're not crazy. They're just taking care of that basic psychological need. They have to belong to something. They have to have something they can call their family. They have to belong to a group of people that care for and take care of each other. The gangs aren't the problem; the gangs are the kids' solution to another problem.

In Fredrick Taylor's factory, when people were told, "You just do your job, and don't worry about the other guy," what did the workers do? They formed unions. They called each other brother and sister. They went down to the union hall and drank beer together, played cards together and shot pool together. They were just taking care of that basic psychological need.

Even today, if you look at the kinds of things people will do in their spare time, it is really kind of ridiculous. People will actually get together and wander around a field all day hitting a little white ball into a series of holes. They'll roll a ball across a narrow hardwood alley to knock down a bunch of pins at the other end, knowing full well that the pins will just be setup again. You have to be some sort of loon to want to do stuff like this. Imagine if there were jobs like this, and how much you would have to pay people to do work as dumb as this. Yet people choose to do this. Why? A bunch of buddies get together, they keep score together, they get excited together, laugh together, cry together, celebrate victory together and bear defeat together—they do it *together*.

Today they do it together at the speed of light because the Internet has brought this basic psychological need—this need for bonding and connection—into even greater focus. In their book, *The Cluetrain Manifesto: The End of Business As Usual*, authors Rick Levine, Christopher Locke, Doc Searls, and David Weinberger proclaim:

> *People of Earth: A powerful, global conversation has begun. Through the Internet, people are discovering and inventing new ways to share relevant knowledge with blinding speed…*[2]
>
> *What if the real attraction of the Internet is not its cutting-edge bells and whistles, its jazzy interface, or any of the advanced*

---

[2]  Rick Levine, Christopher Locke, Doc Searls, and David Weinberger, *The Cluetrain Manifesto*, (Cambridge: Perseus Publishing, 2000), pxi

*technology that underlies its pipes and wires? What if, instead, the attraction is an atavistic throw back to the prehistoric human fascination with telling tales? Five thousand years ago, the marketplace was the hub of civilization, a place to which traders returned from remote lands with exotic spices, silks, monkeys, parrots, jewels——and fabulous stories.*

*In many ways, the Internet more resembles an ancient bazaar than it fits the business models companies try to impose upon it. Millions have flocked to the Net in an incredibly short time, not because it was user-friendly—it wasn't—but because it seemed to offer some intangible quality long missing in action from modern life. In sharp contrast to the alienation wrought by homogenized broadcast media, sterilized mass "culture," and the enforced anonymity of bureaucratic organizations, the Internet connected people to each other and provided a space in which the human voice would be rapidly rediscovered.*[3]

Today, in stage three of business, we need to recognize this basic psychological need. That one way or another it is going to get met, and there is absolutely, positively no reason why it can't get met within the work organization, as opposed to some outside extra-curricular activity. It was met in the family craft shop and on the family farm, and it can be met on the work team, on the third shift, in the corner of the factory—if you design it into the culture.

This is the main reason I take issue with a practice that has come into vogue of deliberately shaking up teams each year by moving out the individuals representing the bottom ten percent of that team, regardless of how well those individuals may have performed. The point of the exercise is to keep the team aroused to challenge, and, apparently, the performance level of the bottom ten percent is irrelevant. To keep teams in such a state of agitation runs contrary to their basic psychological need. And to do so as a deliberate management practice can only promote dysfunctional internal competition to the detriment of teamwork.

In the factory and in the office, we still need to create all of the same dynamics that cause people to bond together, to be cared for and to care about each other and each other's performance. We can have that same sense of bonding—that same sense of ownership—as was present on the family farm and in the family craft shop, and is present on the golf course and on the

---

3    Ibid., pxxi.

bowling alley. We can create a place where people will work hard, and where they'll have fun at the game of business. That is how teams work.

## TEAMS AND PROCESS

Jobs need to be designed so people and teams have responsibility for as much of a whole process as possible. I have a friend who does woodworking as a hobby; he makes furniture. One of the pieces of furniture he made is a table. The important thing is that he makes a whole table. What would we think about somebody who just made table legs? Imagine someone saying, "I am going to make the neatest table legs," and all they make is table legs? We'd think they're crazy. We don't think they're crazy if they make a whole table, but we think they're crazy if all they make is just the legs. Why? The work is the same; there's measuring, and sawing, and sanding and finishing. Why don't we think they're crazy if they make a whole table, but we think they're crazy if all they make is just legs? The reason is that there is a customer for a whole table, but there's no customer for just table legs.

How do we design work? Do we have people making whole tables or just table legs? If you have people who are just making legs, you shouldn't wonder why they're not motivated—it's ridiculous work.

I know that some products are so complex that teams cannot reasonably be organized around final-end items. In these cases teams need to be organized around lower-level sub-assemblies. However, the point is that jobs need to be organized so people and teams have responsibility for as whole of a process as possible, so the product of their work is something in which they can take pride.

## JOB DESCRIPTIONS AND ROLES

I hate most job descriptions; I find them unnecessarily complicated and overly sophisticated. In any organization that is growing and expanding, they are meaningless anyway because they can't keep up with the rate of change. If you have a job description that says what you actually do, then you are probably part of a nice little bureaucracy that isn't going anywhere. I know that human resources (HR) departments require job descriptions so they can benchmark positions in your organization against positions in other organizations. So, I am okay with job descriptions as long as we are clear that they serve the purposes of HR and not the purpose of the people responsible for the work.

If I were HR king-for-a-day, everyone's job would be defined in the context of five roles, with each role defined in terms of its desired results. Defined more fully below, these roles are: producer, resource manager, innovator and entrepreneur, personal and team developer, and citizen.

# PRODUCER

This role represents the value-adding work products or services that are specific to the position. For example, this describes the database products and services that a database analyst is expected to deliver; or the manufacturing process products or services that a manufacturing engineer is expected to produce; or the order processing products or services that a customer service representative is expected to deliver.

# RESOURCE MANAGER

This role represents the responsibility every position has for managing those resources that the organization has entrusted to them—even if the only resource they are managing is themselves.

# INNOVATOR AND ENTREPRENEUR

This role represents the responsibility every position has for the improvement of processes, products, and services.

# PERSONAL AND TEAM DEVELOPER

This role represents the responsibility every position has for the improvement of themselves and their team—not just themselves, and not just their team; both themselves *and* their team.

# CITIZEN

This role represents the responsibility every position has to give something back to one or more of the many communities to which they belong. For example, this could include internal efforts outside of the individual's normal producer responsibilities (e.g., participation on the company's fund-raising team for a particular charity, participation on a company wide, cross-functional team to study and make recommendations regarding the competitive state of the company's benefits program, etc.); or it could include external efforts such as playing a leadership role in a pertinent professional society.

## VERTICAL HIERARCHY

In addition to defining every position in the context of the above five roles, I would also place limitations on vertical hierarchy. I think most organizations currently have too many levels of vertical distinction. Looking at non-management positions there are associates, seniors, principals, senior principals, and so on.

Again, if I were HR king-for-a-day, I would define just three levels for non-management positions: apprentice (i.e., still learning); journeyman (i.e., self-sufficient); and master craftsman (i.e., teaches others). The expectations for each role will vary depending on the position and its level. For example, the producer role will be a higher percentage for a journeyman than it would be for a master craftsman or an apprentice, because the master craftsman is spending a larger percent in their personal and team developer role teaching apprentices, as are the apprentices who are being trained.

I will argue for fewer management layers, too. In fact, the mother lode of cost reduction opportunity lies in removing layers of management—especially senior management. For a single-facility company, I would strive for no more than three levels from top to bottom: the CEO, the functional leaders, and the first-line supervisors. For a company with facilities in multiple geographies, I would strive for no more than five levels: the CEO, the geography leaders, perhaps two tiers of functional leaders, and the first-line supervisors. For a multi-business, multi-geography business, I would strive for no more than six to seven levels: the CEO, the business unit leaders, the geography leaders, perhaps three tiers of functional leaders, and the first-line supervisors.

The reason I argue for fewer organizational layers is because increasing layers has an increasingly toxic effect on the five characteristics of the high-performing culture that I presented earlier: quality, speed, cost effectiveness, continuous improvement, and wealth creation. Another argument against increasing organizational layers is what I call the "reduction gear theory of management." Take any organization and imagine each layer is like a gear, the higher the level, the bigger the gear, and these gears are stacked one on top of the other. This is depicted in Figure 10, which represents an organization with nine layers of management.

*Figure 10 – Reduction Gear Theory of Management*

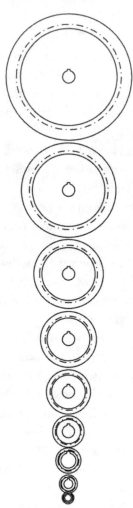

Now imagine that the CEO—the gear at the top, the biggest gear––has a modest idea, perhaps he or she is merely thinking out loud, thus turning their gear just one click. What happens to the gears at the lower levels? Because they are of decreasing size, they make a greater revolution with each layer. The turn of just a single click by the top gear may result in multiple, head-spinning revolutions by the bottom gear. Conversely, imagine that the bottom gear has an idea they want to advance. How many revolutions will be required by the bottom gear in order to produce any action at the top? Finally, if one gear turns clockwise, in which direction will the gears above and below it turn?

The point is that in addition to increasing economic costs, organizational layers also waste precious cultural energy. The fewer the layers in an organization, the more efficient and effective the organization can be.

## ORGANIZING COLLECTIONS OF ORGANIZATIONS

Discussions about organizational structures are often limited to the best way to structure a single organization. I'll close this chapter by presenting ways of organizing a collection of similar organizations. For example, Darwinian organizational forces have led to IT organizations emerging in three domains within many large companies. Often there is a corporate IT organization. Business units will also often have their own IT organizations, too. Finally, non-IT organizations, such as engineering, finance, HR, manufacturing, and sales will develop their own IT capability—I refer to these as embedded IT organizations. This same organizational phenomenon can occur with other functions, too.

There are three different models for structuring collections of similar organizations: hierarchy, hub and spoke, and peer-to-peer network. Since I have spent a large part of my career leading IT organizations, I will use the example of a company with multiple IT domains, as described above, to illustrate these various models in the sections that follow.

## HIERARCHICAL MODEL

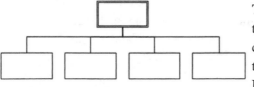

The first method of organization is the traditional hierarchical model, which supports a centralized organizational structure. Under this model there is a single superior function and the other functions are subordinate to it. As its name implies, a hierarchical model is based on a strong, centralized command and control system, and is most often used in companies that are centralized or in decentralized companies for functions where conformity is paramount.

In some cases, the subordinate functions may have what is affectionately referred to as a "dotted line" reporting relationship to some other superior function. This is common with functions that are traditionally considered "staff," such as Finance, HR, IT, and other internal service providers; as opposed to those that are considered "line" functions, such as product development, manufacturing, and sales. For example, all of the business unit IT functions may report on a solid-line basis (i.e., directly) to the company CIO and on a dotted-line basis (i.e., indirectly) to the head of the business unit they serve. Or it could be the other way around where they may report directly to their business unit head, and indirectly to the CIO. My experience tells me that these dotted-line reporting relationships can work as long as all parties understand that the direct superior is primary and the indirect superior is secondary. This doesn't work when both superiors think they are equal, or when the secondary superior thinks they are (or should be) primary.

## HUB-AND-SPOKE MODEL

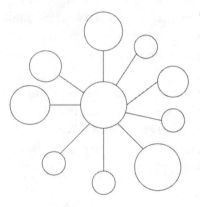

The second method of structuring a collection of similar organizations is a hub-and-spoke model. The business unit IT organizations, for example, would report directly to their business unit head and indirectly to the CIO. However, the nature of this secondary reporting relationship is much stronger. Unlike the hierarchical model, the hub-and-spoke model is based more on centralized coordination than centralized control; for example, business unit IT activities would go through Corporate so they could be centrally coordinated. This sort of structure is often used in companies that are decentralized. They want the functions to focus primarily on the needs of the business unit they serve, but they also want to maintain a level of standardization and consistency.

# PEER-TO-PEER MODEL

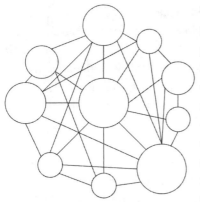

The third method of structuring a collection of similar organizations is a peer-to-peer model, which supports a decentralized organizational structure. All of the company's formal IT functions—corporate, business unit, and embedded alike––would be peers and work directly with each other rather than up and down a hierarchy or through a central hub. In this model corporate IT would report directly to the CIO. The business-unit IT organizations would report directly to their respective business units and have a dotted-line reporting relationship to the CIO.

Driving work through a monolithic, hierarchical model, or even a hub-and-spoke model, may be appropriate for a mature, static, casually and evenly paced business, or a business whose distinctive value proposition is operational excellence (i.e., low cost). However, these models are a poor fit for a high growth, fast paced, highly dynamic business—it is these cases for which the peer-to-peer model is much better suited.

What makes a peer-to-peer model challenging, however, is that it requires much stronger leadership and more talented management in order to operate properly. The peer-to-peer model will stretch lesser leaders and managers beyond the limits of their capability; at which point they will assert that this model doesn't work, and they will revert to a more traditional hierarchical or hub-and-spoke model.

However, because it does not demand that work be forced through a monolithic organization, a peer-to-peer model can enable the speed, flexibility, and responsiveness required by high growth, dynamic, fast-paced businesses, as well as businesses whose distinctive value propositions are customer intimacy (i.e., high service) or product leadership (i.e., innovation)—if the peer-to-peer model is properly led and managed.

Three aspects important to the effectiveness of a peer-to-peer organizational model are worthy of further discussion: harmonizing the model, clarifying roles in the model, and governing the model.

# HARMONIZING A PEER-TO-PEER MODEL

What gives the peer-to-peer model its speed, flexibility, and responsiveness is that it permits an environment where multiple parties can develop solutions, concurrently, and even unbeknownst to each other, yet be assured that their results will be interoperable. To the casual observer, this would appear to be a daunting challenge. How do you keep the various organizations comprising a peer-to-peer model harmonized? Fortunately, other areas of society have already figured out how to do this, and they provide us with a workable approach.

You manage organizations in a peer-to-peer model the same way we manage cities. Cities have zoning plans and building codes. There are residential zones and commercial zones. There are infrastructure design rules specifying where roads will be, the side of the road on which people are to drive, and the protocol to be followed at each intersection. There are infrastructure design rules as to where water, sewer, and power utilities will run and how individuals will hook up to them. Also, there is a building code governing construction: studs in homes must be sixteen inches on-center; copper, not aluminum, wiring must be used, and so on.

With these architectural rules in place, different developers may come into a city, build their developments concurrently and unbeknownst to each other. And as long as homes are built in the residential zones and factories are built in the commercial zones; and as long as everyone drives on the same side of the road no matter what development they're in; and as long as everyone hooks up to sewer, power, and water the same way; and as long as the studs in homes are sixteen inches on-center, and they use copper wiring not aluminum; then everything generally interoperates in an acceptable way.

Finally, recognizing that no human is privy to divine wisdom, cities also have a process by which a developer can petition for a variance when the zoning plan or building code doesn't make sense in a particular situation.

This same approach can be used to harmonize organizations in a peer-to-peer model. In IT, for example, there are commercial-like zones where systems are of such a caliber that their development and support should be left to the IT professionals; the transaction processing systems that maintain the company's business records are a good example of this. There are also residential-like zones where systems are of such a caliber that they can be, and probably should be, developed by the do-it-yourselfer; typically, these are decision support systems. Just as cities have architectural rules governing civil infrastructure (e.g., roads, sewer, water, power, etc.), so should there be architectural rules governing IT infrastructure (e.g., network standards, platform standards, etc.). And, because no human is privy to divine wisdom, IT should have a process by which an organization can petition for a variance when a standard doesn't make sense in their particular situation.

The key is that you don't harmonize around an individual or a function, or through command and control; you harmonize through common architectural rules.

## ROLE CLARIFICATION IN A PEER-TO-PEER MODEL

A typical concern in a peer-to-peer model is that resources and/or opportunities are wasted because the organizations involved will perform redundant efforts and/or will not leverage greater benefit via collaboration. Unfortunately, in order to avoid organizations performing redundant work and to ensure they collaborate when mutually beneficial, many companies will regress and create a "shared services" function; typically, this is a corporate function. Under this approach, if a solution will be (or can be) utilized by multiple business units, the work to develop that solution will be directed to the corporate shared services organization to perform. I say "unfortunately" because this is a very primitive and inefficient way to direct work. There are several reasons for this.

First, it creates a bottleneck by driving all such work through a single organization. The corporate shared services function morphs into a monolith which then neutralizes the speed, responsiveness and other advantages gained by creating an environment where multiple parties can develop solutions, concurrently, and even unbeknownst to each other, yet be assured that their results will be interoperable.

Second, it drives up hidden costs because corporate monoliths cannot move at business unit speed, and business units, who have revenue and EBIT (earnings before interest and taxes) targets to hit, will never wait for the monolith. Business units will quietly go about developing their own solutions "under the radar."

Third, it underutilizes the capacity and capability that exists in the business unit organizations. Corporate or headquarter functions typically are not merchants of speed or agility. In addition, while they may be a fount of creativity, innovation, and genius in ways that reduce costs for the company, they typically are not a similar fount of creativity, innovation, and genius in ways that add value for the customer because they are usually just too far re-

143

moved from the customers.

So, how do you get all of the organizations to play together and play their position?

A better approach, albeit one that demands greater strength of leadership, is to distribute work throughout the peer-to-peer model. In addition to harmonizing the model as described earlier, a peer-to-peer model also requires clarity around the roles and expectations of each organization. For example, it is important that each of the organizations in a peer-to-peer model develop their work products so they can be leveraged by their peer organizations. In other words, each organization in the peer-to-peer model needs to behave with a shared services perspective.

Further, it is crucial that each organization in a peer-to-peer model be clear about their distinctive value proposition, and stick to it. For some it may be operational excellence and low cost, for others it may be customer intimacy and high service, and for others it may be innovation and product leadership. It doesn't matter; what matters is that each organization have a distinctive value proposition and that they focus on that work which is best suited to it. Just like any sports team, each player needs to know their position and then play it.

Staying with the IT example, in large corporations it is not unusual for IT capability to emerge in three domains: corporate IT, business unit IT, and embedded IT. This may seem like an intolerable situation to less capable leaders who believe that the only way to achieve coordination is through formal command-and-control, and they will call for all of IT to be consolidated and centralized—a form of organizational imperialism. However, as cited earlier, having this decentralized and distributed kind of IT capability is really well suited for a high growth, dynamic, fast paced business—as long as each domain understands their unique value proposition and sticks to it.

The traditional way to direct IT work among the three domains is often to base it on the number of business units served by that work. If an IT project serves a single business unit, traditional thinking says such work should be performed by that business unit's IT organization. If an IT project serves multiple business units, then traditional thinking says such work should be directed to the corporate IT or shared services organization. As asserted before, this approach is primitive, albeit less demanding of leadership—it does not enable quality, speed, and cost-effectiveness (cost-reduction, perhaps; cost-effectiveness, no), which are key habits of a high-performing organization.

A more productive approach is to distribute work to that organization whose distinctive value proposition is best suited to that work. Applying the Treacy and Wiersema model to our IT example, the distinctive value proposition of the corporate IT organization is usually operational excellence (i.e., low cost) via economies of scale. Therefore, the IT work that would be best served by a low cost value proposition should be directed to the corporate IT organization—regardless of how many business units will be served by it. The distinctive value proposition of the business unit IT organizations is usually customer intimacy (i.e., high service). Therefore, the IT work that would be best served by a high-service-value proposition should be directed to the IT organization of the business unit sponsoring that work—again, regardless of how many other business units might be served by it. Finally, the distinctive-value proposition of embedded IT organizations is often product leadership (i.e., innovation); these are the mad scientists who have little legacy baggage to care for, and who can experiment with less fear of screwing up essential infrastructure. Therefore, they should continue to focus on innovating IT solutions for their functional areas.

An important clarification is required here. If you have a function existing at three levels, such as the IT function used in this example, and their value propositions are not distinctive, then you should consider consolidating those organizations around the value propositions that are distinctive. Conversely, if you have a function existing at only one level (e.g., corporate), and it is trying to make more than one distinctive value proposition primary (i.e., be all things to all people), then you should consider distributing its responsibilities so no one organization is asked to make more than one distinctive value proposition its primary.

Further, it may be entirely appropriate to transfer a product produced by one domain to another domain depending on which life cycle stage that product is in. An embedded IT organization in engineering, whose value proposition is typically innovation, may experiment and find that the applications on which they perform their product design simulations will run twice as fast on a non-standard operating system (perhaps Linux) than it does on the standard operating system (typically Unix or Windows). The engineers discover this dramatic improvement in product design simulation cycle time through their own experimentation.

If the relationship between the embedded IT folks in engineering and their peers in their business unit IT organization is healthy, the engineers should seek to move their solution "out of their lab" and into "production"––off the server under their desk and onto a server in the business unit's secure, environmentally controlled, fire-protected data center. (It wouldn't make sense to move it to the corporate IT data center because their distinctive value proposition is operational excellence and low cost via cookie-cutter solutions and economies of scale, and this "one-off" server would screw that up.) If the peer relationship is not healthy, the embedded IT folks in engineering will just keep things "under the radar"—they'll keep their solution on that server under their desk.

Unfortunately, the typical response should the embedded IT folks in engineering ever approach one of their peer IT organizations with such a request is for the IT organization to argue that the engineers shouldn't be allowed to develop anything on a non-standard operating system. This is what happens when an organization cares more about standards and structure than they care about the spirit and substance of the larger organization's mission. The fact is that improving speed-to-market is probably one of the business' strategic objectives, and if running on a non-standard operating system advances that objective, then that trumps IT's standards regarding operating systems.

At a later point in the life cycle, should instances of the non-standard operating system propagate to the point where economies of scale can be achieved, it may be entirely appropriate to transfer that design simulation system from the business unit IT organization to the corporate IT organization. And at an even later point in the life cycle, when a technology is in its retirement stages, and fewer business units have use for it, it would make perfect sense to transfer that technology from corporate IT to the IT organization of one of the business units that still depend on it.

The point is that in a harmonized peer-to-peer model, organizations need to establish their distinctive value proposition, and work should be directed to that organization whose distinctive value proposition is best suited to the work. Every player needs to know their position, and play it.

## GOVERNING IN A PEER-TO-PEER MODEL

In a city, the zoning plan and building code are the responsibility of the mayor and the city council. They are aided in formulating and maintaining that zoning plan and building code, and in vetting petitions for variance, by city staff and a planning commission comprised of volunteer citizens with expertise in civil engineering, commercial and residential construction. The mayor and city council are aided in the licensing of builders, contractors, and sub-contractors, and in the enforcement of the zoning plan and building code by the city staff. A company could take a similar approach to governance in a peer-to-peer model.

Staying with the IT example, the CIO would be equivalent to the mayor, and the leaders of the various business unit IT organizations would be equivalent to the city council. They could be aided in formulating and maintaining the equivalent of a zoning plan and building code, and in vetting petitions for a variance, by a team equivalent to a city's planning commission––a cross-organizational team comprised of employees expert in the area of IT architecture and respected by their peers.

To "license" system analysts, programmers, database analysts and the other equivalents of builders, contractors and the various subcontractors, the company could employ a certification program. The company could even extend this certification program to the non-IT professionals, the do-it-your-selfers, who develop decision support systems. This way there is some tangible assurance that the spreadsheet built by the wizard in mergers and acquisitions is a reliable one.

Inspecting information systems for their compliance with the established zoning plan and building code could be done in one of several ways. Positions could be established with the responsibility to sample information system projects and review them for compliance. Another way would be to include such compliance reviews in the company's internal audit program. A better way might be to build the compliance reviews into the company's systems development life cycle, and have it conducted via peer-review.

# 14

# SYSTEMS

*Ninety percent of what we call management consists of making it difficult for people to get things done.*
**Peter Drucker**
Writer, management consultant, and "social ecologist"
1909 – 2005

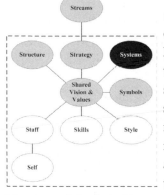

# SYSTEMS, IN THE CONTEXT

of the 10S Model, is not meant to connote things like technology or automation. In the context of the 10S Model, systems means things like decision-making systems, budgeting and planning systems, communication systems, performance management systems, reward systems, measurement systems, and so on—whether those systems are automated or not. Further, systems includes those that are formal, informal, and/or a combination of the two. For example, your organization's reward system is most certainly comprised of both formal and informal systems of incentives and disincentives.

Systems arguably represent the largest body of work in the 10S Model. For our purposes I will focus on those systems I believe to be most critical in aligning individuals with the organization's shared vision and values.

# Scorekeeping

If you say you want people to be a team, you have to tell them how the process for which their team is responsible will be measured, and you have to give them regular feedback as to how their process is doing. It is very much like sports. Where I grew up, the only people who played basketball were those too lazy to learn how to skate, so let's use hockey as an example.

Can you imagine a hockey game where the players aren't privy to the score? The official scorekeeper is keeping the score, the coaches and owners have the score, but the players … we'll tell them the score at the end of the periods. When a hockey team brings the puck up ice, you watch the passing. When one of the players takes a shot your eyes follow the puck from the player's stick to the net. If the puck gets past the goalie and goes into the net, your eyes then go from the net to see the red light behind the net go on thus signaling that a point has been scored. From there, your eyes go immediately to the scoreboard, and when your eyes get to the scoreboard, you want to see something happen. Hockey is big in Minnesota and I am a big fan of University of Minnesota's hockey team, the Gophers. There was one Gopher game when a new guy was working the scoreboard, and he was a little slow. I figured he had about three seconds—if more than three seconds elapsed between the red light going on and a point being added to the Gopher's score, the crowd of about 15,000 fans would start to yell at this guy to update the scoreboard. In that moment, this scoreboard operator was the best-managed guy on the planet.

Isn't this interesting? Everyone in the stands knew there was an official scorekeeper who was keeping the official score in the official scorebook. But we couldn't wait three seconds. We weren't on the ice—we weren't playing—but were we involved? Absolutely! Involvement is an emotional construct—involvement is caring and going home worried at night. What if the fans weren't told the score until the end of the period? Each period is only twenty minutes long, and the fans know someone is keeping the official score. Do you think you'd lose any involvement? Of course you would. Actually, some fans would take it upon themselves to keep their own scorebook and use that record to keep themselves and those around them informed.

Sports fans can't wait three seconds. How long do the people in your organization wait to hear the score? How many of them keep their own scorebooks in the absence of anything "official?" Not informing the players of the score in real time is ridiculous—this is as true in business as it is in sports. Unfortunately, informing players in the game of business of their score only at the end of the fiscal period is common practice. The degree of involvement, the degree of commitment, and the degree of self-management are directly related to the immediacy, specificity, and frequency of feedback. If you want teams and you want self-management, then there must be a scorekeeping system that provides immediate, specific, and frequent feedback.

However, it can't be just any scorekeeping system. It has to be one that the people involved will accept—it has to be one to which they will play. In fact, their acceptance of the scorekeeping system is perhaps more important than the accuracy of that scorekeeping system. Take American football for example. In American football, we keep track of all kinds of statistics that measure a team's performance: yards gained on offense, yards gained rushing, and yards gained passing. We keep track of first downs. We keep track of third-down conversions. We keep track of penalties and turnovers. Yet the correlation between who played the best game according to these statistics and who played the best game according to the scoreboard is only forty to sixty percent. You might as well add the numbers on the players' jerseys and divide the sum into the population of the teams' hometowns. The official scorekeeping system in American football does not tell you who played the better game—yet, people play to it.

Let's look at another example: golf. I'm not a golfer myself (I lose balls in the washer), but I understand lots of other people play golf and will part with much money for the pleasure, so let's buy the game of golf. I do have a concern, however; I have noticed one flaw in the game that we will have to correct. I've noticed that people actually keep track of their own score. Worse yet, some people even cheat—I know, I found it surprising, too. So, one of the first things we need to do once we buy the game of golf is change the scorekeeping system. Ideally we can automate it somehow; employ technology so people's scores are calculated automatically rather than relying on them to keep them themselves.

What do you think of this idea? Do you think any people will lose interest in the game? Certainly, you will. Those for whom golf is a religion may be okay with it. However, for the majority of those who play golf, golf has very little to do with it-golf is about socializing and communing with nature (in this way it is much like fishing). For these folks, self-scorekeeping is central to much of that socialization, and a lot of them will lose interest in the game. For the majority of those who play golf, automating the scorekeeping system, even though it would be more accurate, is a pretty stupid idea.

In baseball, technology has long existed that will determine balls and strikes more accurately than a human umpire. However, it hasn't been employed to call balls and strikes and relegate the home plate umpire to calling balks, illegal pitches, and plays at the plate. The role of the umpires, and the human biases and fallibility they bring to their roles, is such an important part of the game that replacing them with technology just wouldn't be allowed.

I would much rather have a scorekeeping system to which people will play, albeit less accurate, than one that is highly accurate but causes players to lose interest in the game. The acceptance of the scorekeeping system is every bit as important, perhaps more important, than its accuracy.

## Reward Systems, Measurement Systems and Desired Behavior

Performance problems often show up late, so you will often think you have a reward-system problem. If you have a change initiative like "diversity" or "empowerment," you might even say that you can't reward those things. That's not true, and rewards are pretty easy—the problem is counter-intuitive. Organizations will often want to start a change effort by changing their reward systems. My friendly advice to you is that reward systems are not the place to start; in fact, they're the third thing at which you should look. If you do rewards first you're likely to get into trouble. Rewards can look like the problem, but when you think you have a reward-system problem, you often really have a measurement problem. If you don't know what to measure, you won't know what to reward. And if you measure the wrong things, you'll reward the wrong things. Unfortunately, while working on reward systems can be kind of fun, working on measurement systems is not.

If your organization is typical, you've already changed your appraisal system more than once in the last two years, and if you're organization is typical, your people hate the new system about as much as the hated the old one. When people don't like a measurement system—a signal—they tend to ignore it. Many systems have bad measurements and it doesn't hurt the organization because they also have a bad reward system—it's a nice kind of synergy. In an odd way, this is true. Imagine that you're driving your car and you have an indicator light that keeps saying, "low fuel." You check the fuel level, and it's not low. What do you do after a while if the low fuel indicator keeps coming on? You ignore it; or if it's really distracting, you disconnect it. That's the same thing people do if they have a measurement system they don't trust. The measurement system gives off false signals, but they ignore them and keep driving. Meanwhile, you hand out rewards unrelated to the measurement system or you disconnect it.

By the way, this is not a bad way to handle an inept measurement system. And as long as the rewards aren't interesting, it doesn't hurt you very much. In a world where the superstar gets a three-percent increase and the airhead gets a two-percent increase—where the difference between a superstar and an airhead isn't much more than $500 per month after taxes—who cares about the measurement systems? But if you begin at the wrong end, if you start making the rewards sexy and powerful, and you have weaknesses in the measurement system, then those weaknesses are really going to light up because people will get mighty interested in who's getting what rewards and what they have to do to get more.

Think of the measurement system as the base holding up the weight of the reward system. The more meaty and hefty you make the rewards, the more weight and strain you are asking the measurement system to bear. If you start at the wrong end and make your reward systems really attractive, but you don't have a good measurement system, then it's all going to crumble under the weight, and you're going to get killed.

So rewards are something that you address after measurements. However, measurements are only the second thing you do, because in the same way people will say you can't reward some things, they will also say that you can't measure some things. If your initiative is around something rigorous—usually an aspect of the technical system, like cycle time or cash flow management--you probably feel comfortable with your metrics. Although you probably feel more comfortable than you should, you probably don't need to worry. But if you're working on a softer issue—usually an aspect of the social system, like diversity or empowerment—you will hear people say that you can't measure those things. "Oh, you can't measure diversity." Nonsense! Everything can be measured. Not everything can be counted, but everything can be measured.

If you believe something can't be measured, there are only two reasons you believe that, and they're both wrong.

The first reason you may think you can't measure something is because you haven't defined it. People say they can't measure diversity. That's because they haven't defined it—they don't know what they want. If they knew what they wanted they could measure it. It just shows up as a measurement problem. You have to define what you want in terms of behavior.

The other reason you think you can't measure something is because you have been brainwashed into believing that measurements have to be super-rigorous algorithms. Don't let the quantoids brainwash you. Quantoids are half-human and half-finance. I'm not saying that all people in finance are quantoids. I'm just saying that when you find a quantoid you usually find them in finance. They look lifelike, unless you look real close—then you'll find the eyes of a codfish and a heart of pure feldspar. Quantoids mess with people's minds; they convince you that you need a super-rigorous, super-quantitative, verifiable, replicable algorithm to measure everything.

The result is that we spend our time picking aesthetic measurements rather than ones we need to help the organization. It's like the person who loses their car keys in a dark alley but looks for them on the corner under a street lamp because the light is better there. This is what we do, and of course anything worth doing is worth doing to excess. So, we develop volumes of these aesthetic measurement systems that have little or nothing to do with the phenomenon we really want to measure. That territory under the street lamp is mapped within an inch of its life. Unfortunately, our car keys are still lost in the dark alley. And because our competitors tend to travel in the same alleys—especially when we adopt each other's best practices—a competitor will sometimes find our keys before we do. Let me tell you that a sloppy measurement gives you most of the same goodness as a rigorous one.

So when people say they can't measure something, either they don't know what they want, or they've been brainwashed into thinking that they need some super-rigorous algorithm to do so.

If reward systems are the third thing you do, and measurement systems are only the second, then where then do we start? We start by defining what it is we want in terms of desired behavior.

## DEFINING DESIRED BEHAVIORS

Very often the reason someone can't conceive how he or she would measure an objective is because they haven't defined it. You have to define your objective in terms of desired behavior--especially in the case of social system processes. Steven Kerr provided a useful way to think about this. Imagine an onion consisting of three layers, as depicted in Figure 11: vision and values are the outer layer, thoughts and feelings are the middle layer, and behavior is at the core. The key is to drive people to the center; define the success of your change initiative in terms of changed behavior. Which behaviors there will be more of, and which behaviors there will be less of?

154

*Figure 11 – Defining Change in Terms of Desired Behaviors*

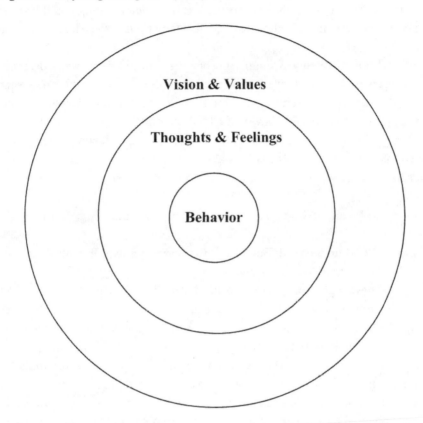

Source: Steven Kerr, "Reality-Based Re-engineering and GE's 'Workout'," (Speech, The Masters Forum. Minnetonka, MN, 2 Mar. 1993)

If you want to change the organization, then you have to hit the center. If you're having a revolution, someone, somewhere in your organization ought to have to behave differently. If no one changes his or her behavior, then what kind of revolution are you having? You have to drive people to the center, to the inner circle. There are hundreds of techniques for driving people to the center. My favorite is one called "backward imaging," or "forward hindsight." I'm not saying this is the way. If you've got a technique that works for you, great; but if not, then in five minutes you'll have one.

Imagine its several years from now and your change initiative (whatever it is) has been wildly successful. You've hit a homerun; it went better than ever expected. A journalist will be reporting on how the people say they are behaving differently as a result of the change initiative's success. Specifically, what behaviors are people reporting they are seeing more of, and what behaviors are people reporting they are seeing less of? The first thing you'll learn is if people have any ideas in their head at all—sometimes people just fall in love with love.

I think diversity is important, but it is fun to watch many diversity groups at work because they often have no idea of what they want. They want diversity, they love diversity—great, but they don't know how to define diversity in terms of changed behavior. So I ask them, "It's been five years; your diversity initiative is wildly successful. How are people behaving differently?" Most of the time what I get is a look akin to a deer trapped in the headlights--it's like a house where the lights are on, but nobody's home—there's nothing there.

So I wait, and eventually they respond, "People will be acting more diversely."

"Yes, I understand. But what will they be doing differently?"

"Well, they'll be more diverse."

They've got nothing in their head, and later they'll tell you that you can't reward diversity, you can't measure it.

Of course you can't measure that stuff. If you can't hit the center, if you can't define it in terms of changed behavior, then you can't measure it or reward it. If you can't hit the center, then you can't use any of the tools for leading and managing change: you can't communicate it, you can't train it, you can't coach it, and you can't mentor it. You can't do anything if you can't hit the inner circle. You can blame it on measurement, but it has nothing to do with measurement until you define the change in terms of behavior.

When I force folks to talk about diversity, when I push them toward the center, the next thing I usually get is ethnicity statistics—the least interesting aspect of diversity. They don't know what they want. Whereas in a healthy diversity environment, people can tell you how they are behaving differently. They'll tell you about changes ranging from diverse modes of dress and divergent office/cubicle decorations, to more substantive changes like more different points of view being voiced, different ways of listening and gathering input, and different ways of making decisions. But people often fall in love with the idea of the initiative, so the first thing you have to do is see if they have anything in their heads about what they actually want or expect from the initiative.

If people do have something in their head, then get them to share those ideas. But be prepared, because I guarantee that once you get them to the inner circle you won't have total buy-in. During the first Gulf War, CNN interviewed a pilot who had just completed his mission but had taken a load of anti-aircraft fire. He wasn't hit, but he was pretty shook up. The reporter asked him how he felt and the kid's answer was great. He said, "The way I look at it, if you're not taking flak then you're not over the target." The kid knew that nobody wastes anti-aircraft fire defending worthless desert. When you've got a lot of flak coming at you, you know you're over something interesting.

This is why most mission/vision/values teams achieve total buy-in——they're never over any target. Total quality, total customer satisfaction—who is going to object to these things? And when you start pushing people toward the center circle—over the target—you'll find they start getting cranky. That's great. Yes, groups tend to run from conflict, so as the leader you have to minister to that—this is where strength of leadership comes in. But when you eventually get over the target, you will start taking flak because now you're actually threatening to change the way people behave. That's great because that's what change initiatives ought to do. Maybe you will get true agreement; I'm not wishing conflict on you. But be wary of top-circle agreement; it's just fluff, there's nothing there. If you're not taking flak, then you're not over anything interesting—get to the center. Whatever change you're working on, do people agree on the stuff you'll have more of and the stuff you'll have less of when you're done? It's a great conversation.

I've worked with a lot of senior executives. Most are competent; few get up there the wrong way. They're very competent people, yet they often disappoint and sometimes break people's hearts. My belief as to why this happens is because they don't go through this exercise. They give each other a target described in motherhood terms. So people will often start at the outer circle and, as the leader, your objective is to get them to the inner circle.

You may be wondering about the middle "thoughts and feelings" circle. I can't give you any theory to account for this, but I've done this work with a lot of groups and when you drive people from the outer to the inner circle, they often don't go there directly—apparently they need to make an interim stop in the middle circle. Take customer satisfaction—what's there going to be more of and what's there going to be less of? A common answer is something like, "There will be more respect for our products and services." Good answer, and probably accurate. On the other hand, respect is a thought word; it's not a behavior. I wouldn't know how to measure respect, or coach respect, or reward respect.

So people often won't go directly to the center circle; for some reason they need to make an interim stop in the middle. That's all right; just keep them moving. "Okay, if people would have more respect for your products or services, then what would they do that they're not doing now because they don't have respect?" If you frame it that way, people will come crashing right into the center. It's not hard, but it takes discipline. Here's another example: empowerment. "There'll be less fear." Good answer, but fear is an emotion word, another one of those words I can't measure or reward. "So, if people had less fear, what would they be doing that they're not doing now because they have more fear?"     Last example: "There'll be less parochialism." Fine. "If there were less parochialism what would you be doing more of than you are now because there's more parochialism?"

Once you get the definitions done, then you can move on to measurement.

## MEASUREMENT SYSTEMS

The scorekeeping systems—the measurement systems—are one of the most important, if not the most important, systems in a culture. Age-old maxims remind us, "What gets inspected gets respected," and "What gets measured gets treasured."

Measurements can be the single biggest drag on a change effort—you can have everything else right, but if you haven't recalibrated your measurement system to encourage the behaviors you want and discourage the behaviors you don't want, then your whole change effort will tank. It happens all of the time. If you're trying to do something different, but you don't change what you measure, you're toast. Unfortunately, too often there is a disconnect between what is desired and what is inspected/measured. For example, a factory is striving to improve quality (i.e., reduce process variability), but they only measure aspects of productivity (i.e., yield and meeting schedule). Some measures have no connection with what is desired—stuff is measured simply because it can be. It's like a doctor trying to judge the health of a patient by taking his or her own blood pressure.

So, there are several aspects of measurement systems that we need to explore further. First, as mentioned previously, a common lament is that not all things can be measured. This is nonsense—everything can be measured. Second, a common problem with measurement data—especially highly quantitative data—is that it creates a false sense of objectivity. This is dangerous——all data is subjective. Finally, I will outline the characteristics of a good measurement system and a process you can use to assess the health of your measurement system.

# EVERYTHING CAN BE MEASURED

I am a devout and unapologetic believer in statistical process control (SPC) for measuring processes in any system. I think SPC is applicable beyond its traditional domain of manufacturing, and can be applied to other processes in the organization's technical systems (e.g., sales processes, product development processes, financial processes, etc.). In his book, *Understanding Variation: The Key To Managing Chaos*, Donald Wheeler shows us that the traditional measures of a management process, ala the "monthly report," are dangerously misleading; he cites this quote from Myron Tribus[1], "Managing a company by means of the monthly report is like trying to drive a car by watching the yellow line in the rear-view mirror."[2] He goes on to teach us how SPC concepts and methods can be applied to management processes and replace the traditional monthly report.

The common lament that a particular thing can't be measured just isn't so. It is true that not everything that can be measured can be counted; however, just because something can't be counted, doesn't mean it can't be measured. Never overlook the power of the signaling function—the signaling function of even a sloppy measurement system will often give you most of the sweet stuff you need.

Simply telling people that something is going to be measured is, in itself, a powerful reason for compliance. Count the number of intersections between your home and your office. There's a traffic protocol at each intersection: if there's not a light, there's a stop sign; if there's not a stop sign, there's a yield sign; if there's no sign then there is still a protocol based on who arrived at the intersection first; and if there are no signs and more than one vehicle arrives at the intersection at the same time, then there is still a protocol defining who goes first (i.e., the vehicle to the right). On average, how many police officers do you encounter in your drive between your home and your office? None, maybe one—it's a small number. This is no different than products. You can't afford to look at every one, so you sample and look at one in every

---

[1] Myron T. Tribus is perhaps best known as former director of the Center for Advanced Engineering Study at MIT. He headed the center when it published W. Edwards Deming's book, *Out of the Crisis*, and became a leading supporter and interpreter of W. Edwards Deming. He is also known in the 1970s for an insightful book called *Rational descriptions, decisions and designs,* which popularized Bayesian methods with examples. In the 1960s, Tribus coined the term "thermoeconomics."

[2] Donald J. Wheeler, *Understanding Variation: The Key to Managing Chaos*, (Knoxville: SPC Press, Inc, 1993), p4.

fifty. The police want your compliance on fifty blocks. They've got only one officer patrolling them. That's a sloppy measurement system, but it is capable of being measured because it is eligible to be sampled, so most drivers comply with the protocol at each intersection. Imagine the police saying, "Effective next week, we're going to cease all surveillance between 1st and 50th Streets, but we sure hope you continue to comply with the law." What do you get between 1st and 50th Streets? You get a speedway, a demolition derby.

Whether or not you measure something is often far more important than how elegantly you measure it. Take commissions. Typically commissions are based on sales. You want your sales people to sell—it's the most important thing they do. But don't you want other stuff done? Don't you want consignment inventory stocked? Don't you want the place kept clean? Don't you want the paperwork kept up to date? Don't you want the mentoring? Don't you want all of the other stuff you expect a good sales person to do? If you don't build those things into the measurement system, you might as well hang up a sign that says there'll be no surveillance of any kind between 1st and 50th Streets, and hope drivers obey all of the rules.

Then there is the "soft stuff." For example, I know that you can't measure mentoring as thoroughly as you measure sales. I know you can't measure keeping the paperwork up to date as completely as you measure sales. You don't need to. All you need to do is tell people, "I care about these things (that's definition), and I've got a way to tell (that's measurement). It's a sloppy way—I can't do it often and I can't do it rigorously—but I've got a way to tell. I'll reward you if you do it, and I'll ding you if you don't." That's infinitely more powerful than hanging up a sign saying there's going to be no surveillance on these dimensions, but, golly, I sure hope you do them.

On the flip side, it is also important to note that not everything that can be counted should be measured. Even Albert Einstein observed, "Not everything that can be counted counts, and not everything that counts can be counted." The worst situation is when we choose to measure something because we can do so quantitatively, even though it sheds no light on the objective we've defined—again, this is the same as looking for your lost car keys under the corner streetlamp because the light is better, even though you lost your keys in a dark alley.

## ALL DATA IS SUBJECTIVE

I cannot emphasize this point strongly enough: all data is subjective and requires interpretation prior to use—even quantitative data, often disguised as objective, is subjective. People in the decision support system, or DSS, discipline of IT have a long-held understanding:

$$Data + Interpretation = Information$$
$$Information + Judgment = Decisions$$

For example, "8318675309" is data; whereas "831-867-5309" is information. The point is, all data is subjective, and requires context for proper interpretation—content without context is pretext. Let me drive this home with some baseball examples.

Baseball is a game where a couple of hundred grown adults generate statistics for a couple of million grown adults to analyze. One of the crown jewels of baseball statistics is the Triple Crown. The Triple Crown is "awarded" (no physical award exists) to the hitter who leads his own league in all three of these hitting statistics: batting average, home runs, and runs batted in, or RBIs. It is a rare season when any player wins their league's Triple Crown. Let's look at each of these three highly quantitative statistical components of the Triple Crown.

Batting average is one of the most simple, yet elegant, measures in the world—successes divided by opportunities (i.e., the number of times you hit safely divided by your number of at-bats). The number of home runs is a pretty straightforward statistic as well. However, it is not expressed as a percentage; it is simply the raw number of times you hit a home run regardless of your number of at-bats.

Both batting average and home runs are quantitative and have the appearance of being objective; however, their subjectivity is revealed with context. For example, I am old enough to remember the Mickey Mantle and Roger Maris summer of 1961—one of the best summers in the history of baseball. Throughout the '61 season, these two Yankees—the M&M boys, as they came to be called—were battling at the plate. However, Maris batted third and Mantle batted fourth. This means that Maris got one-ninth more at-bats than Mantle. And because he batted before Mantle, Maris always got better pitches because the other team never tried to pitch around him—they'd only have to face Mantle. Meanwhile, Mantle got fewer good pitches because the other team wasn't as afraid to pitch around him and face Yogi Berra instead. All data is subjective.

Mickey Mantle and Roger Maris were also engaged in a great home-run race that year. They kept pushing each other closer to Babe Ruth's thirty-

161

year-old record of sixty home runs in a single season. At the time, The Babe's single season home run record was the holiest of holy records in baseball (to many it still is), so this was a big deal. Late in the season Mantle had to drop out due to an illness that ultimately landed him in the hospital. But Maris went on to hit sixty-one home runs; the sixty-first coming on October 1, 1961, in the last game, the 162$^{nd}$ game of that regular season. However, while the baseball season in 1961 consisted of 162 regular season games (just as it does today), in 1927, when The Babe set the record of sixty-one home runs, the baseball season consisted of only 154 regular season games. So, even though Maris hit sixty-one home runs in the 1961 season, it took him eight more games to hit those sixty-one home runs than it took Ruth to hit his sixty home runs in 1927. Citing this as his reason, Ford Frick, the Commissioner of Baseball, decided that separate records should be kept, and that Maris' home-run record should be noted in the record books with the dreaded asterisk, thus: 61*.

At first blush, this seems reasonable. However, upon deeper investigation we find that, like Maris, Ruth also took more games than his predecessor when he broke the previous home-run record, but Ruth's record was never noted with an asterisk. It is also relevant that Ruth didn't have to play any night games, or fly across country to play teams three time zones away. It should also be noted that Frick had previously been a ghostwriter for Ruth. Fortunately, sanity returned thirty years later, on September 4, 1991, when the "Committee for Statistical Accuracy," chaired by then Commissioner Fay Vincent, removed the dasterdly asterisk from Maris's record. With that, Maris became the sole owner of the single season home-run record with sixty-one—until he was eclipsed by Mark McGwire when McGwire hit seventy home runs in 1998; a record that was later eclipsed by Barry Bonds when Bonds hit seventy-three in 2001. Of course, now there is controversy about McGwire's and Bond's records because of the accusations that they used performance-enhancing drugs. All data is subjective.

The last statistic in the beloved Triple Crown is also one of the most deceptive: runs batted in, or RBIs. Interestingly, the statistic that has the highest correlation to a player's RBI total has nothing to do with the player that earns the RBI. The statistic that has the highest correlation to a player's RBI total is the batting average of the players hitting ahead of him. All data is subjective.

Let me share one last baseball example, just to drive my point home. Imagine you are the manager of a baseball team. You have a player who can't field and can't throw, but he has thunder in his wrists and can hit the ball a ton. His bat is too valuable to leave on the bench, and you're in the National League where there is no designated hitter. At what position do you play him? The first blush answer most people give is right field, because that is where you usually put your weakest fielder on your neighborhood softball team. However, because we're talking about the major leagues where there are a lot of left-handed batters, and because it is a longer throw from right field to bases where a runner would be in scoring position, I'd put him in left field. But this is not all I'd do. I'd also get myself a terrific center fielder and tell him, "Cheat towards left and go for everything; we have nothing to lose."

At the end of the season, what do the fielding statistics for your left fielder and center fielder look like? Your left fielder's statistics look great, because his glove rarely touched the ball. Meanwhile, your center fielder's statistics look abysmal because he spent the season diving after balls, making lunging catches and off-balance throws. Yet, you know that the center fielder saved your season, so you award him a greater bonus. At which point, your left fielder complains, citing his superior fielding statistics. About all you can tell the arbitrator is, "Listen, if you knew these two guys for just ten minutes you would have done the same thing." Not a winning defense. All data is subjective.

To bring us back to a business example, what's the more important determinant of sales success: the skill of the sales person, or the fertility of the territory? One person sells $100,000 in Beverly Hills; the other sells $75,000 in south LA. Who's the better salesperson? You have to interpret this stuff because all data is subjective.

## CHARACTERISTICS OF A GOOD MEASUREMENT SYSTEM

There are eight characteristics of a good measurement system that I learned from Steven Kerr[3]. Described in greater detail below, they are: completeness, timeliness, visibility, cost, interpretability, importance, time balance, and motivational balance.

## COMPLETENESS

"Completeness" means the extent to which a measurement adequately mea-

---

[3] Steven Kerr, "Reality-Based Re-engineering and GE's 'Workout'," (Speech, The Masters Forum. Minnetonka, MN, 2 Mar. 1993)

sures the phenomenon rather than only some aspect of the phenomenon. During one of the U.S. wars in the Middle East, there was a news conference following a mission where food supplies were supposed to be air-dropped to a group of civilians. A military spokesperson reported that the mission was successful, no planes were lost—but he didn't say anything about whether or not the food got into the hands of the people they intended. Certainly, losing no planes is absolutely good news, but that doesn't tell me about the success of the mission. The mission was to put food in the hands of friends on the ground. The most successful outcome of their mission would be if the friends got the food and no planes were lost. A less successful mission would be if the friends got the food, but some planes were lost. The mission would be a failure if no friends got the food, or if foes got the food, even if no planes were lost. And the mission would be a disaster if no friends got the food, or foes got the food, and planes were also lost.

# TIMELINESS

Timeliness represents the extent to which a measurement can be taken soon after the need to measure, rather than being held to an arbitrary date (e.g., an employee's anniversary date, or the fiscal year end), or performed as an "autopsy" (e.g., an exit interview, or a returned-product analysis). Physicians have known about this for a long time. Measurements such as vital signs and blood test results that are captured with your annual physical, or when you are otherwise well, provide informative data, with the trends over time being even more useful. However, once you become ill, or if a disturbing trend is observed, this data—even more detailed data—is captured more frequently, with some measures being taken real time. Imagine that your physician suspects you have come down with a debilitating disease, and says to you, "Well, you are scheduled for your next physical in only three months. Let's wait and see what those results tell us." Similarly, imagine a manager who suspects that an employee has come down with a debilitating performance problem, and says to that employee, "Well, you are scheduled for your next performance review in only three months. Let's wait until then to gather 360° feedback." Or worse yet, what about the manager who waits until an exit interview to learn exciting new things about the health of his organization's culture.

# VISIBILITY

Visibility is the extent to which a measurement can be openly tracked by those being measured. Remember my earlier example of an imaginary hockey game where the officials have the score, the coaches have the score, maybe even the fans have the score, but we'll give the score to the players at the end of each period. Now imagine a manufacturing organization where the managers have the process-control charts and the production volume and yield data, but the operators have to wait until the end of their shift or the end of their work week. Imagine a sales organization where the managers have the unit volume and revenue data, but the sales representatives have to wait until the end of the fiscal period.

# COST

When we talk about cost, we are talking about whether the measure is inexpensive, making use of data easily obtained, or perhaps already being collected for some other purpose. During times of wellness, physicians will rely on a select set of "vital signs"—measures that are quick, easy, and relatively inexpensive to capture (many of which a patient can gather on their own at home). However, during times of illness, or when those vital signs suggest a concerning trend, the physician will invoke more involved and costly tests.

# INTERPRETABILITY

Interpretability means the degree to which a measurement is easy to understand and produces data that is readily comparable to other organizations and/or time periods. Remember, all data is subjective and requires context for meaning—content without context is pretext. Also, not all measures need be quantitative. The signaling function of a sloppy measure can give you most of the sweet stuff you need—the trend of the data, rather than the data itself, may be what is most important.

# IMPORTANCE

Importance asks if the measurement is connected to salient business objectives, rather than being measured merely because it is easy to measure.

165

# TIME BALANCE

Time balance is how well the measurement system reflects the desired balance between long- and short-term objectives.

# MOTIVATIONAL BALANCE

Motivational balance refers to how well the measurement system reflects the desired balance between competitive invigoration and collaborative teamwork. For example, are your sales measures such that only the highest performer "wins," or are they such that everyone who achieves a certain level of performance "wins?" The former can cause dysfunctional competition among your sales folks. The latter will cause sales folks to compete against the specified goal rather than against each other, and may even promote collaboration amongst colleagues so more can earn that trip to Maui.

# ASSESSING THE HEALTH OF YOUR MEASUREMENT SYSTEM

Here's an interesting exercise that you can do on your own, but might be more fun to do with a team of folks over an extended lunch hour:

- Do a memory dump of existing measures; you'll get ninety percent of them, don't worry about getting them all.
- Next, ask how well your existing measures test against the characteristics of a good measurement system. For example, look at each measure and ask if it's a lead indicator or an autopsy. Are they timely? Are they interpretable? Are they important? And so on.
- Identify which existing measures provide little or no information about any of the desired behaviors? For example, list your desired behaviors in a column on the left, then list your existing measures on the right. Now draw lines from each desired behavior to the existing measures of that behavior.
- Also, identify which of your desired behaviors cannot be readily measured by one of the existing measures. How could you measure those desired behaviors not now being measured?
- Finally, if you achieve your desired behaviors, which existing measures are going to emit false signals? For example, you want to be

more aggressive with innovation, however, you still measure people based not on their number of innovative ideas, but on their percent of "failed" ideas. Existing measures that emit false signals are a huge inhibitor of change. They are wonderful things to nuke.

# REWARD SYSTEMS

If you do definitions well, and you tie your measurements to those definitions, rewards are pretty easy. You've got two kinds of rewards. You have financial stuff, and you have non-financial stuff. Money can come in the form of base compensation, incentives, profit sharing, commissions, lightening awards—you know what it takes. There are also non-financial awards like prestige awards, trips, plaques, and job content where you give the better performers more training and sexier assignments. It isn't hard; if you've got the other stuff lined up, rewards are pretty easy. Unfortunately, in practice there is more often a disconnect between desired results and rewarded results, and most companies are elitist.

# DISCONNECTED RESULTS

Some have called it the greatest management principle in the world, "What gets rewarded gets done." Unfortunately, it is too often the case that what is desired is not what gets rewarded—it is an old problem. In his classic 1975 article, "On the Folly of Rewarding A, While Hoping for B", Steven Kerr talks about the disconnect between desired results and rewarded results; he cites these examples.

| We hope for... | But we often reward... |
|---|---|
| Long Term growth, environmental responsibility | Quarterly earnings |
| Team Work | Individual effort |
| Setting challenging, "stretch objectives" | Achieving goals, "making the numbers" |
| Downsizing, rightsizing, de-layering, restructuring | Adding staff, adding budget, adding "Hay points"[4] |
| Commitment to total quality | Shipping on schedule even with defects |
| Candor, surfacing bad news early | Reporting good news, whether true or not, agreeing with the boss, whether he/she is right or not |

Source: Steven Kerr, "On the Folly of Rewarding A, While Hoping for B," *(Academy of Management Journal*, Vol. 18, 1975), p 769-783.

Twenty years later, Kerr updated his original article at the request of Academy of Management Executives. In those twenty years, things hadn't changed much; they found that the fundamentals of "Kerr's Folly" were still intact. This updated article was published by the Academy of Management Executives, "An Academy Classic: On the Folly of Rewarding A, While Hoping for B.[5]" Prompted by Kerr's update, the Academy of Management Executives conducted an informal poll of their executive advisory panel to see, based on their own experience, how much progress corporate America had made in addressing "Kerr's Folly." Here are a few examples that were reported in their poll:

---

[4]  "Hay points" are a function of the Hay Group Guide Chart-Profile Method, a proprietary point-factor job evaluation methodology developed by the Hay Group.

[5]  Steven Kerr, "An Academy Classic: On the Folly of Rewarding A, While Hoping for B," (*Academy of Management Executive*, 1995 Vol. 9 No. 1).

| We hope for... | But we often reward... |
|---|---|
| Teamwork and collaboration | The best team members |
| Innovative thinking and risk-taking | Proven methods and not making mistakes |
| Development of people skills | Technical achievements and accomplishments |
| Employee involvement and empowerment | Tight control over operations and resources |
| High achievement | Another year's effort |

Source: Poll conducted by Kathy Dechant and Veiga in November 1994: http://reliablesurveys.com/rewardinga.html

On May 2, 2007, Bill George, former Medtronic CEO, now author and professor, and a person for whom I have much respect, spoke at a book-signing event at Medtronic World Headquarters following the release of his book, *True North: Discover Your Authentic Leadership*. In his talk, Bill spoke of the death of the "great man" theory of leadership. This theory says that you need one great person to head an organization, and that person's leadership will drive performance. He contended that this "great man" theory is obsolete and has been replaced with the theory of "distributed leadership," which says that today's organizations need leaders sprinkled throughout.

I agree with him that the "great man" theory of leadership is obsolete, and that organizations require leaders sprinkled throughout. However, while distributed leadership may indeed be what we hope for, the "great man" is still what gets rewarded. Not only is the "great man" theory not dead—it is alive and kicking. A tremendous disparity often exists between a CEO's individual compensation and that of the other leaders sprinkled throughout the rest of the organization. Also, the financial crisis of 2008 revealed CEOs who efficiently led their companies right off the cliff and into the sea but were still handsomely rewarded by their boards of directors. We may hope for distributed leadership, but we reward "great man" leadership.

From the time Steven Kerr first wrote about this in 1975, to the AME update twenty years later in 1995, to today, no learning has occurred.

I also wonder what keeps us from carrying into our professional, organizational lives that which we have already learned and practice in our personal, home lives. For example, what parent doesn't know that the best way to evenly split a piece of cake between two children is to explain to both children that one of them will cut the piece into two slices and the other will choose which slice they would like? And what couple hasn't learned to inform their dear, but free-spending, friends before a meal that separate checks will be brought at the end? And what homeowner hasn't learned to tell the neighbor's boy that he will be paid for cutting the lawn after they inspect the lawn? In these cases, we are making use of prospective rewards and punishments to cause other people to care about our objectives. What is it that keeps us from carrying forward into our organizations what we already know to be true through our personal experience? Organizational life may seem to be more complex, but the principles are the same.

# ORGANIZATIONS ARE ELITIST

Organizations are elitist. They like to make people eligible for stuff, but they especially like to make people ineligible for stuff. The reason I know that they like the second better is because they make most of the people ineligible for most of the good stuff.

In a 1993 Masters Forum lecture, Steven Kerr noted that the percentage of American workers who are eligible for so-called bonuses and stock options is two to three percent, depending on what you count[6]. I don't think the numbers have gotten any better since. In a more recent example, Merrill Lynch's 2008, $4 billion discretionary bonus pool was awarded to just 700 of Merrill Lynch's 39,000 employees—that's less than two percent. Here's how it was reported by the *New York Times* in their February 11, 2009, article, "Nearly 700 at Merrill in Million-Dollar Club:"

> *For nearly 700 lucky Merrill Lynch employees, 2008 was a million-dollar year, even though the brokerage firm lost $27 billion.*
>
> *On a day the chief executives of eight large banks were*

---

[6]   Steven Kerr, "Reality-Based Re-engineering and GE's 'Workout'," (Speech, The Masters Forum. Minnetonka, MN, 2 Mar. 1993)

*questioned about their industry's excesses on Capitol Hill, Andrew M. Cuomo, the attorney general of New York State, raised hackles by disclosing how Merrill Lynch distributed its 2008 bonus pool. The payments, made just before Merrill Lynch was sold to Bank of America in December, have already stirred anger for being paid earlier than usual. And Mr. Cuomo made it clear that the bulk of the bonuses were paid to a small portion of Merrill Lynch's 39,000 employees.[7]*

Although, at $1 million per person, the size of Merrill Lynch's 2008 bonuses may be unusual, and although it may be unusual that these bonuses were awarded during a year in which the firm lost $27 billion, it is not unusual that less than two percent of the employees received a discretionary bonus. Even at companies whose discretionary rewards aren't as rich or frivolous as Merrill Lynch's, who gets them? Every year, in just about every large organization, the top-level executives will go on a retreat to some five-star resort, enjoy exceptional food and wines, and between rounds of golf or tennis, while enjoying each other's company in plush chairs by the fireplace or the pool, they talk in genuine earnest about the need to economize. Meanwhile, everyone else is having their off-site meetings at the Days Inn by the airport. Who gets the reserved parking? Who gets to fly in the company jet? Who gets to fly in first class rather than coach? These are rewards given based on level, not on performance—they are elitist.

One of the biggest changes one can make when cultivating a new culture is to challenge rank as a basis for distributing rewards. This is true not only in businesses, but elsewhere as well. In universities, people starve while they're graduate students, then they get their Ph.D.s and begin to live a little better, then they get tenure and live very well. In medicine, when you're a resident or intern your life is horrible. In accounting and law firms, you are treated like an indentured servant until you make partner. Distributing rewards based on rank might have made sense at one time, but no more.

Most companies have, are, and will engage in downsizing and de-layering in reaction to the cost and competitive pressures of their markets. (Although I have seen companies that do the downsizing without doing the de-layering, and their management-to-staff ratio gets further out of whack than it was before. Yet, everyone knows that cutting management is where

---

7   Michael J. de la Merced and Louise Story, "Nearly 700 at Merrill in Million-Dollar Club," New York Times, February 11, 2009: http://www.nytimes.com/2009/02/12/business/12merrill.html?_r=1&th&emc=th

the mother lode of cost savings lies.) We also have slower market growth rates predicted for many industries. The demographers will add the fact that people had a lot more kids after WWII, and this baby boom generation is not retiring at the early ages of their predecessors—especially now that their 401ks and the value of their homes have been beaten and battered. Add it all together and one observation that's kind of interesting is that every time corporate America makes a new officer, there will be thirty qualified candidates for that job. Even if you use rigorous criteria, you'll still have five or six well-qualified candidates. So, when you say "yes" to one corporate appointment, you may very well be saying "no" to four or five other, very competent people.

There is no indication that we are going to run out of money, or trips to Maui, or private parking spaces. But as long as we hold to the notion of rewards based on hierarchical advancement, and then in our downsized and de-layered environment, we don't have hierarchies in which people can advance, we are creating succeeding generations of what are called, "the POPOs"––passed over and pissed off. So, my friendly suggestion is that you begin to dismantle the relationship between rewards and hierarchical advancement. We need to give people the realistic sense that they can have a meaningful career without having to zoom up some hierarchical structure when there simply aren't going to be the hierarchies up which to zoom.

Toward this end, many companies have defined dual ladders, although most are token dual ladders, not meaningful ones where competent individual contributors can realistically earn rewards on par with managers and senior executives. On sports teams, there are only two levels: players and coaches, and players often earn more than the coaches. Yes, there are minor league sports teams and major league sports teams (just like there are small local companies and large global companies). In almost all cases, the rewards dispensed by the larger organizations are greater than those dispensed by the smaller ones. However, within a sports team—be it a minor or major league sports team—most of the good things that happen to a player have nothing to do with them being promoted.

So, it's not fiction; it can be done, and we just have to do away with this notion of classifying people according to hierarchies. You could be the most powerful contributor among individual contributors, but unless you're among the management ranks, you're never going to the annual retreat in Maui. Conversely, you can be the biggest slug they've got in the officer ranks, and you'll go every year. Nobody asks if you're doing your job, nobody asks if you have a need to be there, nobody asks if you're any good. They just ask, "What's your level? Okay, you go and you don't."

Pretend the Powerball lottery is at $55 million. Here's some mathematics for you: the difference between 1:195,249,054 and zero is zero—there's no difference; graph it for yourself if you like. If you don't like the math, then here's a real life look at it: if you don't enter the lottery, there's a zero chance that you're going to win; if you do enter, there's a 1:195,249,054 chance you're going to win—I've got news for you; you're still not going to win. But do people play? Yes, people play—that's how it got up to $55 million.

Imagine that the lottery folks introduce a new rule to save money: all people whose last name begins with the letter "S" will be ineligible. They will still be permitted to enter, but will be prohibited from winning. If a matching ticket belongs to a person whose last name begins with "S," then they're just going to throw those numbers back and redraw new ones. Is Mr. Smith going to buy a ticket next week? We didn't change his odds—he wasn't going to win anyway. But what did we do? We told people at the beginning, people whose last name begins with "S," that no matter how good they are, no matter how well they do, they're not eligible to receive the reward. What a surprise; now Smith doesn't buy a ticket.

This is the same thing that happens when people know that you have all of these goodies for which they're ineligible. Again, allocate rewards based on rank if you have to, but this old notion of having people work hard at the lower levels to lust after the higher level rewards doesn't work in a downsized, de-layered world. You won't have people lusting after levels that aren't there anymore. I'm particularly worried about MBA students—especially those that companies pursue as if they were franchise players in a major league draft. These "chosen ones" seem to come with a note from their dean pinned to their suit coat saying that they should expect their first promotion in well under one year, their second promotion in a little over one year, and should be at the director level in less than three years. The schools are still cranking out these MBA grads, and they're all headed your way.

# Characteristics of a Good Reward System

In Psychology 101, we learned that what makes feedback—positive or negative—effective is its immediacy, frequency, and specificity. Without meeting these prerequisites, other attributes such as the size of reward or the severity of punishment have little effect. (In my humble opinion, this is one reason why capital punishment will not be an effective deterrent as long as justice is not administered in a way that is swift and sure.) In addition, we all know that rewards include a lot more than just monetary ones. In fact, as organizations become flatter, and money becomes scarcer, non-monetary awards will increase in importance. Accordingly, there are eight characteristics of a good reward system that I also learned from Steven Kerr[8]. Described more fully below, they are: availability, eligibility, visibility, performance contingency, timeliness, flexibility, reversibility, and perquisites.

# AVAILABILITY

Availability refers to the extent to which a particular reward is available for distribution within the organization. Is it broadly available, or only available to persons of a certain pay grade and above? If you tie rewards to hierarchical position, people will lust after those positions; this is particularly problematic when the Darwinian effect of cost and competitive pressures is to flatten the organization.

# ELIGIBILITY

Eligibility refers to whether classes of employees (e.g., hourly, non-exempt, executive, non-executive, etc.) are eligible to receive a particular reward. What kind of incentive affect on Jimmy Olson's performance should you expect a bonus to have if all employees whose last name begins with "O" are ineligible to receive the bonus? Also, is your reward given to the one employee who comes in first or highest, or is it given to all employees who meet or exceed a specific target? Giving an award to the employee who comes in first or highest on a particular metric tends to stimulate dysfunctional competition. Whereas giving a reward to all employees who meet or exceed a specific target tends to promote collaboration.

# VISIBILITY

Visibility is the degree to which a reward is visible to the recipient and to other organization members. More direct and vicarious learning occurs the more visible a reward is.

---

[8]   Steven Kerr, "Reality-Based Re-engineering and GE's 'Workout'," (Speech, The Masters Forum. Minnetonka, MN, 2 Mar. 1993)

# PERFORMANCE CONTINGENCY

Performance contingency refers to the extent to which the receipt and size of a reward is based upon the recipient's performance. Again, too often rewards are tied to rank or class, rather than performance. Who gets the premium parking spaces: the better performers, or the higher-ranking employees? Who's holding their meetings at the airport hotel, and who's holding theirs at the five-star resorts: the better performing team or the higher-ranking team?

# TIMELINESS

Timeliness refers to whether a reward can be distributed soon after the decision is made to award it, versus being delayed by calendar dates, employee anniversary dates, or one-over-one approvals. A lot of rewards are tied to calendar dates, anniversary dates, fiscal closings, etc. No blaming; in the old days it cost a lot of money and took a lot of time to close the books, and it was appropriate to tie the performance-review cycle and the reward cycle to the fiscal cycle. But today, it is not necessary, so it makes sense to do something about the timeliness of rewards. If a rat pulls a lever and eight months later, on his anniversary date, a lump of sugar comes out, no learning occurs. The same is true with people. We'd like to believe that people track better than rats, but there's surprisingly little evidence of that. Even if you're able to give the reward anytime in the year, we're back to our old friend, approvals—you can give the reward, but so many approvals are needed that by the time it comes back down nobody can remember what it was for.

# FLEXIBILITY

Flexibility means the extent to which a reward can be tailored to the needs of individual employees. The type of reward that will excite one employee is going to be different than what will excite another. One employee may prefer dinner with the CEO; another employee may prefer beers and a ballgame with his or her teammates; and another employee may prefer dinner and a play with his or her significant other.

# REVERSIBILITY

Reversibility refers to whether the reward, once given, can be reclaimed; or whether the decision to give the reward can be reversed so that the reward need not be given again. Can the reward be reclaimed if it is later found to be undeserved, like an athlete being stripped of his or her medal if tested positive for prohibited drugs? Similarly, is the reward perpetual or finite; does the employee win the premium parking spot for a year or for life? Increases to base pay are perpetual; bonuses are finite. Also, can the reward program be terminated when it has lost its usefulness, or is there a social commitment to carry it on in perpetuity? Similarly, will the reward be given no matter what, like the Academy Awards, or will it only be given if someone is qualified to receive it?

# Perquisites

Perks are typically elitist rewards, but I caution against placing them under assault. The issue isn't the perks; the issue is how they're handed out. Do they pass the tests of a good reward as outlined above? Are the perks awarded based on performance or based on rank? Take a private parking place. Who typically gets the private parking place? Some senior VP. When did he get it? 1911. Look at the tests. Is it performance contingent? Not since 1911. Is it reversible? Yeah, you try to take it away. Eligibility? Nope, you're not eligible unless you're a VP. It's a bad reward and a lot of companies are doing away with them.

But in a lean money world, I wouldn't be so quick to throw out interesting rewards. Frankly, I think you barely have enough to get the job done ,and I wouldn't be throwing any away. I think a better answer is to recast perks so they pass the tests.

# Assessing the Health of Your Reward System

You can assess the health of your reward system with an exercise similar to the one I described for assessing the health of your measurement system. Again, you can do this on your own, but might have more fun doing it with a team of folks over an extended lunch hour:

- First, do a memory dump of existing rewards; again, you'll get ninety percent of them, don't worry about getting them all.
- Next, ask how well your existing rewards test against the characteris-

tics of a good reward system. Are they timely? Are they performance contingent? Are they reversible? And so on.

- Listing your same desired behaviors in a column on the left, and your existing rewards on the right, draw lines from each desired behavior to the existing rewards for that behavior.

- Also, which of your desired behaviors is not readily rewarded by one of the existing rewards? How could you reward those desired behaviors not now being rewarded?

- Finally, if you achieve your desired behaviors, which existing rewards are going to hurt you? These are the crossover items. Crossover items are behaviors that you want more of, but where people say that they'll get punished or ignored if they do them; or they are behaviors that you want less of, but where people say that they'll get rewarded if they do them. A fun way to identify these is with an anonymous survey. Show people the list of desired behaviors, without indicating which ones you want more of and which one you want less of. Ask them, "If you did this particular behavior, would you be rewarded, ignored, or punished?" For example, you want to more aggressively address product quality, but you still reward your manufacturing people based only on meeting their production schedule. Crossover items are another huge inhibitor of change. They, too, are wonderful things to nuke.

## PERFORMANCE MANAGEMENT SYSTEMS

One of the most hated systems in many organizations is the performance-review system. Every few years the griping will rise to a level where the HR folks develop a new performance-review system, which folks seem to hate about as much as they hated the old system. It is important to understand that most performance reviews have nothing to do with managing performance. The primary objective of most performance review systems is to establish a legal paper trail in the event of future litigation. Performance management is a secondary objective.

Sports teams are way ahead of business teams when it comes to performance management, In baseball, when a pitcher is struggling on the mound, a co-worker, usually the catcher, will be the first to talk to him—players (peers) are the first to tend to an individual's performance problem. If the troubles persist, but aren't too serious, the pitcher will be visited next by the pitching coach. If the problem is serious or the struggles continue, then the pitcher will be visited by the team manager. None of these people—the co-worker catcher, the first-line supervisor pitching coach, or the big-boss manager—will necessarily wait until an inning ends to talk to the pitcher. If the pitcher is struggling, they intervene right away—they can't afford to wait. They'll stop the action to visit the pitcher in the middle of an inning, and, if necessary, the manager will pull the pitcher right off of the mound and out of the game. What the manager doesn't do is wait until the end of the season to ask the pitcher what he was thinking, in the forty-third game of their 162-game season, when he threw that hanging curve ball to the other team's number nine hitter, who had a one-and-two count in the eighth inning of a one-run game, when there was one out with runners on first and third.

Other sports are no different. In American football, a coach cannot go out onto the field, but he can call a timeout and have a player come to him. There are assistant coaches sitting in skyboxes at the stadium, recording the game and critiquing theirs and the opposing team's performance in real time. Between possessions, when the offense or defense is off the field, the coaches in the skyboxes transmit photos to the bench and talk to a player about something they saw in their previous series of plays. Feedback in sports is effective because it is immediate, specific, and frequent.

We need to remember that the annual performance review is all about documentation and has little to do with good performance management. Good performance management with employees at work (and children at home) is governed by the same principles as in sports—what makes feedback effective is its immediacy, specificity, and frequency. The key, therefore, is to provide feedback in as near real time as possible, and again at the completion of a project or assignment—certainly more frequently than at the end of the fiscal year or on the employee's service anniversary. This is not just a managerial obligation—I expect the senior team members to play a leadership role and provide their peers with feedback just like the catcher does with the pitcher.

That feedback needs to include not only coaching, but also rewards, and those rewards can't come only at the end of the fiscal year or on the employee's anniversary date either. What is your equivalent of the game balls that many sports teams award to players following a game? Why don't we pay out profit sharing and/or bonuses to employees at the end of the quarter, at the same time we reward stockholders with their dividends, rather than waiting until the end of the year?

Of course, we do have to bring all of the performance feedback together once a year and document it in the individual's annual performance review. If you've been giving feedback all along, and have kept notes when that feedback was given, pulling it all together for the purpose of creating an annual performance review is a relatively easy process. Unfortunately, it has been my experience that HR folks turn this process into an unnecessarily complex and overly sophisticated managerial burden.

If I were HR king-for-a-day, performance reviews would begin with the job description that is comprised of those five roles I described earlier: producer, resource manager, innovator and entrepreneur, personal and team developer, and citizen. The expectations for each role will vary depending on the position and its level: apprentice (i.e., still learning), journeyman (i.e., self sufficient), and master craftsman (i.e., teaches others). Performance review periods would be defined around projects or assignments, not fiscal periods or anniversary dates. Prior to each project or assignment, the employee and the manager would come to agreement as to what one thing the employee could do to advance in each role—one objective per role. This discussion would necessarily include those things the manager will do to help the employee achieve their objectives (e.g., task assignments to develop a particular skill, training classes, mentoring assignments, etc.). When it comes time to write the performance review, I would ask each employee to comment—principally in prose—on his or her own performance in each role.

When it comes to assigning actual performance ratings, I would simplify the ratings and employ a triangulation process. First, although companies may differ in their use of ratings—some use numeric values (e.g., zero to four, one to five, one to ten, etc.), others use category labels (e.g., effective, exceeds expectations, far exceeds, etc.)—almost all companies try to delineate performance at a level of granularity that is too fine. Again, if I were HR king-for-a-day, I would have only three, self-explanatory rating categories: needs coaching, doing just fine, and superstar. I think you could take a random poll of team members, customers, and suppliers, and just about everyone would agree on who the superstars are and who are the people who need coaching; everyone else is doing just fine. I just don't see the value in trying to parse the "doing just fine" group into smaller subsets. Performance ratings are inherently subjective and to attempt a finer level of granularity creates a false sense of precision; it just doesn't add any useful value.

While assigning ratings is, like the rest of the process, inherently subjective, ratings are particularly important because they usually drive merit increases and promotions. The best way that I know for bringing objectivity to an inherently subjective process is through triangulation—spotting the person's position based on multiple points of view. By this I don't necessarily mean soliciting 360° feedback.

My experience with 360° feedback is that if you use it on an exception basis it can be a valuable management tool. However, if you use it as a normal part of your process, then it's not worth the trouble. This is especially true if your company has the policy of performing all performance reviews at the same time (e.g., Q1), because people are inundated with requests for 360° feedback, and what might otherwise be a useful managerial tool is turned into a managerial burden. The times I have solicited 360° feedback as a regular part of the performance-review process, the feedback I received was of little value—frankly, it was mostly crap, shallow in substance, done with obvious haste by people probably overwhelmed with requests to provide 360° feedback on others. However, I would call for 360° feedback on an exception basis: whenever I sensed or discovered that my appraisal of their performance and their self-appraisal were at odds.

I used a different kind of triangulation process with my leadership team to assign performance ratings to their employees:

- I would call a meeting of my directors, their managers, and our HR representative. These meetings were organized by location, and would usually last a full day (sometimes two days at the locations with larger organizations).
- At these meetings, each manager would walk through each of their employees stating the performance rating they thought that employee had earned (obviously, this required advance preparation by the managers). The manager did not have to elaborate on any employee they were rating as "doing just fine," or its equivalent. However, if the manager anticipated rating an employee anything other than this—whether it was on the low side or the high side of "doing just fine"— that manager also had to provide concrete examples of the employee's performance that warranted that rating.
- At any point in a manager's presentation of their employees, other managers could (and were expected to) speak up if they had experience with the employee that either supported or challenged the rating the employee's manager had planned. It went both ways. Often another manager presented examples that challenged the employee's manager's rating as too high. Just as often, other managers presented examples that challenged the employee's manager's rating as too low.

- An important ground rule was that, because an employee's manager is the one ultimately responsible for their employees, the employees' manager is the one who made the final decision regarding their employees' rating. The group could not usurp the employees' manager's decision.

The discussion that ensued was rich and healthy. The directors, the HR representative, and I were there not only to participate in the process and keep it on track, but to ensure consistent calibration among the managers across the entire organization. I do not subscribe to the practice of force-fitting ratings to a normal curve. I certainly believe that when you have a population of sufficient size the ratings distribution should approximate a normal curve. However, the practice of force-fitting the distribution of performance ratings to any kind of curve is ridiculous. First, force-fitting a result is not a statistically valid thing to do. Second, it is a win/lose methodology; in order to give someone an "A" you have to give another person an "F," and it just doesn't always work out that way. Finally, and most importantly, it is unfair—people should be given the rating they earn, not the rating you need to fit your distribution to a curve. I understand that some companies adopted this practice because they saw performance ratings creep up over time. If this is the case, then the correct answer is to train, coach, measure, and reward/punish managers on their measurement of their employees' performance. But to address ratings creep by enacting a broad policy that force-fits ratings to a normal curve is just managerial laziness.

At the end, when we had gone through this rating process for all employees at all locations and consolidated the results to create a population sufficient in size, the final ratings did generally fit a normal distribution without having to be forced. There were some exceptions, of course, but given the rigor of the process, they were defensible.

# BENCHMARKING

Benchmarking against other companies—even those companies touting best practices—does not produce competitive advantage. The absence of a best practice may represent a competitive disadvantage, but the presence of a best practice does not represent a competitive advantage. Adopting a best practice may provide you with the best solution to yesterday's problem, but it does not produce competitive advantage. So if you're talking about a generic business process, then benchmarking your process against industry best practices might be a good thing to do. But, if you're talking about a process that is a competitive differentiator, then benchmarking against industry best practices is pretty much an academic exercise.

On the other hand, benchmarking against your customers can result in competitive advantage—but only if you benchmark against your toughest customers. Easygoing customers don't help you. You may like them in the short run because they make you feel good, but in the long run they make you sloppy; they give you an outlet for your crappy work. It is amazing how powerful a tough customers' help can be. They're thinking you don't understand them, or worse yet, that you don't give a damn. They don't have any idea of how hard it is for you to produce and deliver for them because your processes aren't integrated or are bureaucratic, and your messed up processes are reflected in your messed up information systems. Your tough customers can help you fix a lot of this stuff. They also become a lot more tolerant of the stuff they can't help you fix because they understand that you are honestly trying to do a good job while dealing with all kinds of crazy restraints.

There is also a theory to which I subscribe that says: if you help a customer be more productive, then there will be more money to go around and more of it will come your way. So, when you benchmark with your toughest customers, you want to do so with this perspective: If you two were one system rather than two, what would you do differently? If doing something one way would cost you five dollars but save them eight dollars, then you should do it. You can get into a lot of interesting stuff when you treat your boundaries as imaginary and just go where the data takes you. There is a lot of gold to be mined if you're willing to work outside the boundaries of your organization and in the world where your customer lives.

Finally, you may also learn that ninety percent of the junk you find is junk you are doing to yourself—it is self-inflicted and can be self-corrected and prevented. Only about ten percent, or less, of the junk you'll find is inflicted upon you by someone outside your organization, and will require their cooperation and/or approval to correct and prevent. Yes, I know organizations are political and parochial, but it is amazing what you can accomplish with the attitude, "I don't care about your politics; I'm simply here trying to help the business."

# 15

# STYLE

*You can always tell the people with real authority because they rarely have to use it. Authority is like a bar of soap; the more you use it the less you have.*
**Bill Ruprecht**
Engineer, jazz musician, and author's father
1922 – 1997

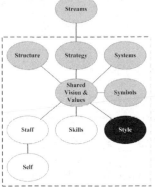

# "STYLE" REFERS TO MANAGE-

ment style, and there are two basic types: command-and-control, and consensus-and-commitment.

# NO ONE RIGHT STYLE

One style is not right, and one style is not wrong. They are different and each serves a different purpose. A command-and-control style promotes conformity, which is useful in times of true crisis, whereas a consensus-and-commitment style promotes creativity, which is useful in times of growth and expansion. A good leader's repertoire includes both.

Throughout most of history, the military has been the dominant organization—built with the goal of successful operation in times of crisis. If consensus and commitment were a better style during times of crisis, some army in history would have figured it out. They would have gotten their soldiers to gather in small groups, brainstormed alternative battle plans and talked about how they felt about them. Through Darwinian selection, consensus and commitment would have emerged as the preferred style in times of crisis. But it hasn't, because it isn't. Recall the eighteenth century gunship I described earlier. Imagine what would have happened in a battle if, when given the command to fire, the lieutenant or one of the guys on the guns asked, "Captain, why do you think now would be a good time to fire?"

Or, imagine you're in a large meeting and the fire alarm goes off. The person in charge could certainly have the attendees gather into small groups and brainstorm different evacuation plans for the larger group then to discuss and debate. That is an obviously stupid idea. Better that a person who knows, stands up and, in a loud commanding voice, orders everyone to proceed double-time to the specified exits. And everyone better move at double-time speed—no walking or running—or you'll trip the people behind or ahead of you. Command decision-making produces conformity, which is what you want in times of true crisis.

Command and control, as a default style, may have led to competitive advantage in the past. However, given the speed, dynamism, and interdependencies of our world today, what leads to competitive advantage is something very different. It is not the manager who makes the quickest, loudest, or most testosterone induced decision. It is the manager who creates collective wisdom and commitment, and energizes it.

## Growing a Culture of Consensus

I do not define consensus as unanimity, but neither do I define consensus as majority rule. My operational definition of a consensus decision is when everyone can genuinely state, "I can live with it." The decision may not be their personal favorite, but they can live with it.

To grow a culture of consensus you need two things. First, a consensus-and-commitment style of management means you control your processes—maintain your processes in a state of statistical control—whereas a command-and-control style means you control your people. (This relationship between method of control in how you conduct your work and management style with which you govern the conduct of that work illustrates one of those interdependencies between an organization's technical system and its social system.)

Second, a consensus-and-commitment style of management is based on the belief that the world's greatest experts are the people who are "on the spot"—the people on the front lines doing the work, not the people remote from the frontline activity, even though they may be of higher rank. This particular concept is quite evident at Honda, and is revealed in this vignette told by Shocichiro Irimajiri, Mr. Iri, first president of Honda of America:

> *It was 1965 and I was working on Honda's Formula 1 racing engines. In the British Grand Prix of that year, the engine failed and it was torn down and examined by Mr. Honda himself. Examining the failed piston he turned to me and demanded, "Who designed this piston?!"*
>
> *"I did," I acknowledged.*
>
> *After examining the engineering drawing Mr. Honda roared out, "You! Stupid! No wonder the piston gets burned. You have changed the thickness here." As a young engineer, I attempted to defend my design change with some data from previous engines. Mr. Honda roared again, "I hate college graduates! They use only their heads. Do you really think you can use such obsolete data obtained from old, low-performance engines? I have been making and touching pistons for several tens of years. I am fully aware of how critical half a millimeter is here. A company does not need people like you who use only their heads. Before you laid out this design, why didn't you listen to the opinions of those experienced people in the shop? If you think academic study in college is everything, you are totally wrong. You will be useless in Honda unless you spend more time on the spot for many years to come."*
>
> *"You will go to the machining shop," Mr. Honda ordered, "and you will apologize to every person there, for you have wasted their efforts."*
>
> *Mr. Honda followed me down the hall to make sure I did as directed. I was only glad that I had no ambition of becoming president of the company. I wasn't even sure I would succeed as an engineer. I learned my lesson.[1]*

Honda's culture stresses that you must be "on the spot" in the plant and see the problem, touch the part, and gain experience in the actual job, in order to effectively solve a problem. Engineers and management spend most of their time in the factory, in touch with their associates, the product, and

---

[1]   Lawrence M. Miller, "The Honda Way: A Visit to Marysville—A Model for the Future," (paper presented at The Masters of Executive Excellence, Minnetonka, MN, 22 Aug. 1989), p2.

the processes. This kind of philosophy flies right in the face of the cultural mythology with which most of us were raised—at least with which I was raised. When I was a kid, one of my favorite TV shows was *The Lone Ranger*[2]. *The Lone Ranger* provided lesson number one in problem solving and decision making.

Every half-hour there was a problem and it got solved. You never saw the Lone Ranger ride into town and leave scratching his head, "Boy, I sure hope they figure that one out." You also never saw him ride into town and say, "Well, there's nothing going on here; I guess I'll leave." Baloney! There was always a problem and he always solved it. We learned from this, and let no one kid themselves that we didn't learn from this. When the Lone Ranger rode out of town, to the top of the hill to the sound of the William Tell Overture, and a mighty, "Hi Ho, Silver!" there was this emotional rush—truth, justice, and the American way! Vicarious learning did occur. What did we learn? How did the problem get solved?

There were stereotypical characters every half hour. The helpless victim was the old, gray-haired rancher. He was the guy that always had the problem. It was the deed to his ranch, or his cattle, or his water rights that were being threatened; or the railroad was going to run through his living room. That was about it; it was usually one of those four things. You liked this guy; he was a sweet old man. Sweet, but stupid, because every half hour he would get himself into trouble, but not once did he ever get himself out of it. Always living with him was his knockout granddaughter. The knockout granddaughter was never the one who fixed the problem either. She was cute, she cooed a lot, but she never fixed anything—she was a potted plant. So, if these people never solved the problem, who did?

Riding for days across the West Texas range came the original white tornado. Have you ever been on the West Texas range—in August? This guy's clothes were perfectly white, and perfectly pressed, with no sweat stains under the arms. Obviously, this guy can perform miracles, and so he does. In a half hour he diagnoses the problem, finds out who the bad guys are and takes care of everything. How does he do this? Riding with him, with the darker-colored skin, the darker-colored horse, and riding the right number of steps behind him, is the Lone Ranger's faithful sidekick, Tonto. Clearly, Tonto was not the brains of the outfit. The Lone Ranger would send Tonto into town. Tonto would go, get beat up, and come back to report, "Kemosabe, there are bad

---

[2]   *The Lone Ranger* is an American, long-running, old-time radio and early television show. The eponymous character is a masked Texas Ranger in the American Old West who, on his white horse, Silver, galloped about righting injustices with the aid of his clever, laconic Potawatomi Native American sidekick, Tonto.

guys in town."

"Yes, Tonto, I suspected so. It's the Dalton Gang." (At which point I always wondered why Tonto didn't just deck the Lone Ranger, "What do you mean you suspected so?")

Tonto, being the faithful and forgiving sidekick that he is, rode back into town with the Lone Ranger, and through clever deception and bold confrontation they solved the poor rancher's problem.

What is the first thing the Lone Ranger and Tonto did after solving the problem? They hightailed it out of town. Consultants have understood this process for years. At first everything looks great, but after a couple of weeks you learn that the accused was never read their Miranda Rights, they didn't have the right search warrants, evidence becomes inadmissible at trial and the whole case starts falling apart.

What else do we know about the Lone Ranger? Not much. You never get too intimate with this guy. You never learn his real name. You never see his face. But the guy comes in, solves the problem and quickly gets out. You can't get too intimate; it would destroy the consultant magic.

Now, nobody rides into work these days and says that they're going to use the Lone Ranger method of problem solving; but we do have these maps in our head, and American organizations tend to emulate those maps. We do have consultants—internal and external—and corporate staff groups that come riding into town, shoot things up, and then leave. After all, the town folk aren't going to solve the problem. They created the problem, or allowed it to be created; how the hell are they going to solve it?

But this is all cultural mythology. In truth, when the townspeople had a problem, what did they really do? They formed a posse—they formed a team. They got their fellow ranchers together, and they went out and got the bad guys. They solved the problem themselves. And that knockout granddaughter probably wasn't all that pretty because she was working all day; she probably had a face toughened by sun and wind and calluses on her hands from fixing fences and plowing fields.

This Lone Ranger mentality is cultural mythology and we have to break out of it. You can't have a culture of consensus without believing that the world's greatest experts are the people "on the spot"—the people who work on the ranch.

# SELF-MANAGEMENT

Early in my career, I was lucky to be invited to my company's Management 101 training, which I'm sure was much like the Management 101 training at your company. At the same time my daughters were entering their teens, and I knew theirs were performances I wanted to manage closely. So, I brought all of my new-found management training to bear. We went through the objective setting process:

"How many courses do you have this semester?"

"Seven."

"Good! And how many A's and how many B's do you think would make a reasonable goal?" [See how I solicited her opinion first? Just like I was taught good managers do!]

"How about four A's and three B's?"

"Good!" [Notice that positive reinforcement? Just like I was taught good managers do!]

Then there was the day-to-day execution:

"What do you have for homework tonight?"

"Math and Spanish."

"Good! And how long do you feel it will take for you to do your math and Spanish homework?"

"A couple of hours."

"Good! When do you feel you should do your homework?"

"Dinner is at six, so how about seven to nine?"

"Good!"

Of course I'm concerned about quality so I would wander by her bedroom at eight o'clock and just listen to make sure I heard the sound of her doing homework and not the sounds of her stereo, video game, or a telephone conversation. I may have also peek in just to make sure she's not texting or instant-messaging. Then I would wander by again around nine; this time I'd stop in.

"How's it going?"

"I'm all done."

"Good!" But I want to show interest, so I'd say, "May I see your work?"

To which she responded by showing me her Spanish. Of course, she knew that I didn't understand Spanish, and I knew that she knew that I didn't understand Spanish, but I wanted to look interested and what was my role there anyway.

188

While the theory is cute, we need to judge the process by its results––by how well she did. The results were good; she got A's and B's. If it wasn't broke, I wasn't going to fix it. I was going to do this each and every day until the day she graduated from high school. I was a dedicated father! However, what's going to happen when she goes off to college? Am I going to go with her? How many kids do you know who went out of control when they went to college? One reason why a kid may go out of control when they go to college is because they were never in control—they were always under control. The violence of the breakaway when a child goes away from home for the first time is a function of how controlling the parents were.

What good parents do, of course, is teach their children to care more about how they do in school than the parents do. You teach them to self-manage. You may begin with a controlling style when they are young, but you want to move them to commitment and ultimately to self-management. Certainly there are times when you need to ask, "How much homework do you have tonight?" But you don't want to stay in that mode. The good parent, the good coach, the good manager, the good leader does not have a single style and expect their children, players, or employees to adapt to his or her one style. The good parent, the good coach, the good manager, the good leader is sensitive—they sense and respond—and they draw upon a repertoire of styles as the situation may warrant.

## STEWARDSHIP DELEGATION

How many employees can one person manage using a command and control style of management? The answer is seven. You're familiar with the rule of seven—you can command and control about seven people. But in a culture of consensus and commitment, you can achieve much broader spans of control––one-to-fifteen and even one-to-thirty. Because your processes are in control, you can manage people differently. As a result, you can eliminate multiple layers of expensive management, and de-layering management is the mother lode of cost reduction.

Unfortunately, while many companies have gone through downsizing—many more than once, and some on a regular basis—they don't de-layer. The command-and-control style common to most numerator managers does not lend itself to a de-layered environment. There are others that de-layer, and as they do, they increase their management-to-staff ratio from an average of one-to-seven to a new average of one-to-fifteen. Unfortunately, they still try to manage via command and control, and it doesn't work—it burns people out. De-layering management requires that the span of control be expanded, and increasing the span of control beyond the traditional ratio of one-to-seven requires a consensus and commitment management style.

A key to a consensus-and-commitment style is effective delegation. In Habit Three (Put First Things First) of *7 Habits of Highly Effective People*[3], Stephen Covey talks about "go-fer" delegation vs. "stewardship" delegation. Go-fer delegation is little more than telling people what to do—go for this, go for that. Sometimes it even means telling people how to do something. Go-fer delegation focuses on actions and methods, and is well-suited for close, command-and-control managerial attention—the kind that prevents a manager's span of control from expanding beyond one-to-seven.

Where go-fer delegation is about ordering people, stewardship delegation is more about enrolling people. A stewardship is a trust. Stewardship delegation creates results by building people, by encouraging them to be responsible for their actions and results, and to use their initiative and ingenuity. The goal is to gain their willing consent as partners in a common effort, to move them to volunteer their hearts and minds in a cause that they themselves have come to share. Stewardship delegation creates both results and good working relationships; whereas go-fer delegation produces only results—results that are often inadequate and more costly. They are often inadequate because people learn to do only as they are told—no more, no less. They are often more costly because of the extra managerial attention required. Stewardship delegation is suited for a consensus-and-commitment style and is necessary to enable broader spans of control.

The constructs of good stewardship delegation also make good constructs for things like project charters, too. Paraphrased below, these constructs are: desired results, guidelines, resources, accountability, and consequences.

# Desired Results

Stewardship delegation focuses on results, not methods. In fact, if you dictate methods, then you automatically take responsibility for the results. Instead, you want to specify the quantity and quality of the desired results, outline the budget and schedule, commit people to getting results and then let them determine the best methods and means within the guidelines that you'll establish next.

---

[3] Stephen R. Covey, *The 7 Habits of Highly Effective People*, (New York: Simon and Schuster, 1989), p173-174

190

# Guidelines

Guidelines represent correct principles, often summarized in the form of standardized procedures. It is best to have as few of these as possible; otherwise you get too much into methods delegation. Of course, if your industry is highly regulated, you're subject to those regulations imposed upon you (i.e., they're one of your streams). These regulations may be voluminous and complex; however, because they are imposed upon you, there is little you can do about them. On the other hand, your organization's own policies and procedures should be only a few pages long, not volumes, and focus as much on the philosophy and reasoning behind a policy or procedure as on the policy or procedure itself. By specifying guidelines, rather than methods, people can use their own initiative and good judgment, as the situation changes, and do what's necessary to accomplish the desired results. Guidelines should also specify what not to do—the "no-no's"—what concepts, methods, and/or tools simply will not work. "Sacred cows" should also be identified.

# Resources

Identify the various resources (e.g., human, financial, technical, organizational, etc.) that the steward may draw upon to accomplish the desired results within the specified guidelines. You may want to identify yourself as a resource and indicate ways in which you could help. Of course, you wouldn't want to give unlimited access to your budget or time, but you will want to share your experience so that the person can decide whether you would be a valuable source of help or not.

# Accountability

Specify when progress reports are to be made, together with what criteria or standards of performance that will be used in evaluating results. These criteria are the essence of the accountability process. Accountability means that the steward accounts for his or her performance based upon the criteria he or she helped develop. It does not involve evaluation by the boss because their evaluation has already been built into the desired results section of the agreement. Accountability is the key to stewardship delegation. When people know that they are responsible to get results and give progress reports, they are set free and feel a sense of responsibility to do whatever is necessary to accomplish

191

those results within the guidelines, drawing upon the resources identified. Accountability follows responsibility. If there is no accountability, little by little people will lose their sense of responsibility and start blaming circumstances or others for their poor performance.

## CONSEQUENCES

Consequences should be stated in terms of financial and non-financial rewards (e.g., recognition, appreciation, advancement, new assignments, new training opportunities, etc.). Consequences have positive and negative sides, and both sides should be stated and understood up front. People can then evaluate themselves.

## MANAGING BY COMMITMENT VS. THE CLOCK

Unfortunately, too many managers still judge an employee's contribution by their on-site presence during normal office hours—if they're in the office, at their desk, good; if they're not, bad. How quaint! If you have the type of job where you can only serve your customer by being leashed to your desk, then this is fine. However, if this is not the case, then one of the biggest things a leader can do to ease the challenge every employee has in balancing their home and work life is to move past this quaint notion that employees need to be at their desks, or even in the office, during "normal hours."

While there may be "normal office hours," there is no such thing as "normal working hours." Telecommuting, laptops, remote access, home offices, ubiquitous Wi-Fi, PDAs, mobile email, mobile Internet access, and other such technologies have successfully rendered the concept of "normal working hours" moot. Work time and home time are no longer discrete, contiguous blocks, and we need to adjust our management style accordingly.

Rather than managing by the clock, we need to manage by commitments. If an employee is celebrating their wedding anniversary tonight, and they have not yet purchased a gift for their spouse, then they need to get their mangy butt out of the office and to the store. If their child's band concert is at 3:00 pm, then they need to be at their school. However, if it's Monday, and an employee has promised to complete something by Friday, and it will take them eighty hours of work to complete it, then I expect to see them with their sleeping bag. I don't care if employees use the company's computer and Internet connection at the office to order birthday presents online, because I also expect them to use their own computer and home Internet connection so they can join that video conference with a customer on the other side of the globe, when it's the customer's day but their night.

The idea is to give employees a little more latitude in addressing their increasingly difficult challenge of balancing home and work—as long as they honor their commitments. Where and when they do their work is negotiable, honoring their commitments is not. It is just a matter of shifting our managerial focus from the clock to commitments.

# 16

# Skills

*I have been impressed with the urgency of doing.*
*Knowing is not enough; we must apply.*
*Being willing is not enough; we must do.*

**Leonardo da Vinci**

Italian scientist, mathematician, engineer, inventor, anatomist, painter,
sculptor, architect, botanist, musician, and writer.

1452 – 1519

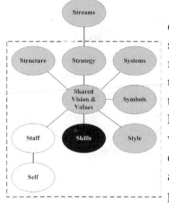

# There are two basic

categories of skills. One category is generalist skills. Generalist skills are those that everyone needs to know in order to be a good, fully functioning citizen in the organization. For example, this might include skills such as how to use email, how to arrange and conduct a meeting, how and with whom to request and report time off. The other category is specialist skills. Specialist skills are those skills that one needs in order to do their particular job. For example, finance people need to know how to calculate an ROI (return on investment) and IRR (internal rate of return); sourcing people need to know how to conduct a reverse auction; and manufacturing process engineers need to know SPC.

## Possession v. Application of Skill

I don't believe in paying someone based on the skills they possess; I prefer to pay people based on their application of the skills they possess. A hiring practice I find disturbing is one where organizations place more weight on a candidate's degree or the school from which it was earned (i.e., their credentials), than on the candidate's prior performance (i.e., their track record). I regard a person's degree as evidence of the skills they possess, and their track record as evidence of their ability to apply the skills they possess. (If the candidate is a recent graduate, with no track record, then that is a different matter.)

For example, the compensation paid to teachers in many U.S. primary and secondary public schools is based on the degree the teacher possesses and their time in service. I am also aware that there is a strong push among some to institute a system for compensating teachers based more on their performance. Another approach is one taken by a private school with which I am familiar, Mounds Park Academy,[1] or MPA.

MPA is an independent, K-12, coeducational, college preparatory, day school located in St. Paul, MN. It was founded in 1982 by Robert and Lois Kreischer—visionaries and entrepreneurs in the field of primary and secondary education. MPA's approach to teacher compensation reflects their values. Essentially, all teachers, regardless of the subject(s) and/or grade(s) they teach are paid the same. Part-time teachers are paid in proportion to fulltime equivalence, and those teachers that also coach an extra-curricular activity will receive an additional stipend for that work. However, there are only two steps in the pay structure based on years of experience—one after three years of teaching experience, the other after fifteen years. Also, there is no distinction in pay based on the degree a teacher may possess. A fulltime middle-school mathematics teacher with their masters degree and seven years of teaching experience, and a fulltime first grade teacher with their Ph.D. and eleven years of teaching experience, will earn the same annual salary because there is no difference in the school's expectations of them as faculty members—the school does not expect more of the teacher with the Ph.D., or less of the teacher with the masters.

My point is that a person's mere possession of skill is not as important as their ability to successfully apply the skills they possess.

## SPECIALIST SYNDROME

In the words of my friend and colleague, Scott Nintzel, "If you don't have a specialist skill, you need to get one. If you have one, you should get another." The point, of course, is that one has to be very deliberate in keeping their skills fresh and relevant. This means committing to life-long learning. It also means

[1] Mounds Park Academy: http://www.moundsparkacademy.org

not marrying your career to a specific technology because when that technology becomes obsolete or irrelevant, so will you.

I worry about people becoming too specialized—developing deeper but narrower knowledge in their field of expertise. I worry because as they become more specialized they also become more prone to losing their customer focus. What they are doing and how they are doing it becomes more important than the reason they are doing it and the people for whom they are doing it.

It's like what happened in the universities. In the beginning there was simply the Humanities Department, which encompassed everything dealing with people. Then, Humanities split into Sociology and Psychology. Psychology then split into Animal and Human. Within Human Psychology, we got Freudian and Behavioral. Within Behavioral Psychology, we got Organizational Behavioral, Abnormal Behavioral, Adolescent Behavioral, and so on. As the specialization gets deeper, it also gets narrower, until you become the world's greatest expert on absolutely nothing.

The Greeks and Romans had a word to describe this. The word was used to describe, not people of low intelligence, but extremely smart people who had become so narrow that their knowledge lacked practical applicability— it had become useless. The word "idiot" derives from the Latin "idiota," which is a transliteration of the Greek "idiotis," which means useless. I spent most of my career in the IT field and I can tell you that the IT profession is particularly prone to this. IT professionals can become so specialized, so technically expert, that they lose their customer focus and become useless—they may be very, very smart, but they become idiots.

Every team has customers and every team member should know who their customers are. By this, I do not mean who their customer organizations are, I mean their customers—the people. Organizations don't become unhappy; people become unhappy. Too often organizations are structured so that people don't have to look their customer in the eye. So, instead of worrying about pleasing the customer, people worry more about pleasing their boss. Don't try to please your boss; please your customer. If your boss has his or her head on straight, they'll be pleased when you please the customer—as long as you do so in a way that is faithful to your organization's shared vision and values. Every team member should be able to answer these three questions: Who is your customer? How would they say you are doing? How do you know?

# EDUCATION AND DEVELOPMENT ARE SACRED

When you make the commitment to hire an employee, you are making a complementary commitment to help that employee with their ongoing education and development. Each employee needs to take responsibility for their own education and development, but the organization needs to commit to supporting their employees' education and development plans. When an organization hires a person, there is a concomitant to that person's personal development plans.

You may not think much of the idea of personal development plans. Frankly, if you've had to endure the formalized individual development planning processes that many companies force upon you, then I can see how you would harbor such feelings. That aside, you are responsible for your own development. It will happen by design or default—it is better that it happen by design. If you do not plan and make careful choices for yourself, others will do so for you. I don't care if your approach to your personal development (or your team's development, for that matter) is formal or informal; I just care that it be done with deliberate, serious thinking.

We've all heard the maxim, "If you think training is expensive, consider the cost of ignorance." No one will argue this; the wisdom is self-evident. Yet, too often, especially during times of cost pressure and budget reductions, the training, education, and development budgets are among the first to go. These things should be the last to go. Imagine a baseball team in trouble, and the owner or coach says to the players, "I've got the answer to get us back on a winning track. I've sold off the weightlifting equipment and we're cutting back on batting practice." Yet this is what we do in organizations and it's just nuts. Do it if you have to, but make sure you have to.

# KEY CORE COMPETENCIES

If I asked you to create a list of those competencies that should be considered "core," I'm sure you could produce that list in short order. I'll also bet that if you compared different people's lists there would be strong congruence. However, there are two particular competencies that are often overlooked, and need to be on everyone's list: facilitation and project management.

# FACILITATION

Being able to get work done in groups is a required skill for anyone who aspires to lead, and facilitation skills are how you get things done in groups. Therefore, facilitator training is an essential element in leadership training. If you want to be a leader, you better know how to run a group and get things done through a group. Effective leaders are also effective facilitators.

Being a good facilitator is like being a good umpire in a baseball game. If you do it well, the next day no one will remember that you were even there. The umpire certainly meets with the team managers before the game to review the ground rules. But you'll never see an umpire swing a bat, throw a pitch, catch a ball or run a base. So it should be with a good facilitator. They may lead the discussion when going over the ground rules, but they should never pick up the chalk or the magic marker. Just like an umpire may throw a coach or player out of the game for inappropriate behavior (e.g., a pitcher deliberately throwing at a batter, or a manager or player physically touching the umpire, etc.) so should a facilitator wrestle any person to the ground if they try to dominate the proceedings, and eject any one who loses their ability for respectful discourse.

## PROJECT MANAGEMENT

The difference between a wish and a goal is that a wish is simply a desired result; whereas a goal is a desired result supported by a plan that accurately estimates the achievable. Project management is about achieving a goal.

A project, as compared to a process, is a temporary endeavor undertaken to create a unique product or service. "Temporary" meaning that every project is discrete with a definitive start and end. "Endeavor" meaning that there is a measurable level of effort associated with it. And "unique" means that the completion of the project results in something new. Project management is the skill of organizing people, resources, and work to accomplish a goal. Project management is how stuff gets done. Competency in managing projects, programs and portfolios, and aligning them with strategic goals is essential to the success of any organization. More specifically, project management is indispensable for organizational results. Project management should be a core competency required in all personnel.

Project management and project-management methodology is a body of work unto itself, and the profession is well served by the Project Management Institute, or PMI[2]. There are, however, several very simple project management practices that I have adopted over the years and highly recommend.

---

[2] Project Management Institute: http://www.pmi.org

# CHANGE CONTROL

Define a change control process and allocate a change control budget to every project. When budget time rolls around and a project is being considered, you will hear this dreaded request, "Give me an estimate for Project X." You'll protest because the project's requirements at this point are usually sketchy at best, and you fear that any estimate you give now will be carved into stone forever. To which you will hear, "I'm just looking for a ballpark estimate; it's just for planning purposes." Unfortunately, your instincts are usually right--too often the estimate that you thought you were providing "just for planning purposes" will become the budget for your project.

Estimating projects whose definition is sketchy is risky business. We may be good at estimating those things of which we are aware, but we all suck at estimating those things of which we are not aware. The more you can define something, the more accurately you can estimate it. The less you know about something, the more you should use ranges rather than specific figures to express an estimate; this way you won't imply a false sense of precision. Everyone understands that if you ask a homebuilder how much it would cost to build a house, and all you tell them is that it should be a four-bedroom two-story, the estimate the builder will give you will be a pretty broad range. However, when you present that same homebuilder with a set of blueprints, they can give you an estimate good enough to take to the bank. So it is with estimating business projects.

The way you mitigate the risk associated with sketchy requirement is the change-control process, and a change-control budget. Engineering and finance folks are usually pretty good at thinking through the details of what they want; so for their project requests I would add ten percent for change control. On the other hand, I would add a thirty percent change control budget to those project requests brought forward by sales or marketing folks. For everyone else, I used something in-between.

# REQUIREMENTS COME IN FOUR FLAVORS

In an adaptation of the Kano model[3], I have learned that customer requirements come in four categories:

- **Expected** requirements are ones that people just expect will be there, and they won't bother to articulate.
- **Expressed** requirements are the ones that are articulated.

---

[3]  A theory of product development and customer satisfaction developed in the 1980s by Professor Noriaki Kano.

- **Emerging** requirement are those that emerge as the project progresses and people give it more thought.
- **Exciting** requirements are those that the customer didn't ask for, but which you add because "you get it"; these are the requirements that cause customers to want to come back and do business with you again.

While we estimate the first two categories pretty well, we suck at estimating the other two categories, even though we know they will occur. We may not be able to anticipate the requirements that will reveal themselves in these last two categories, but we can anticipate that un-anticipatable requirements will occur.

# THE IMPORTANCE OF THE WBS

Project plans should be developed to a level of detail granular enough so that each project team member has at least one deliverable (i.e., a milestone or task completion) each week; no fewer than one deliverable every two weeks. This way, your project can never wander off course more than one or two weeks without knowing about it. The secret to doing this is in the quality of the work breakdown structure, or WBS. In other words, the quality of the WBS has a direct affect on the quality of the project plan.

# DUE DATES

All deliverable due dates should be Mondays, not Fridays. This gives the individual or team the weekend as capacity in reserve in the event of problems. Also, the consequences for missing a due date without advance notice should be more severe than the consequences for missing a due date but with advance notice.

# WEEKLY HUDDLES AND STATUS REPORTS

Project teams should huddle weekly to mutually checkpoint progress, plans, and issues, and to manage project change within the change control budget (using version control to manage changes to the project plan). With weekly huddles you can abandon the practice of generating weekly status reports. Weekly status reports are more for management's benefit than the project teams; if management wants to know how a project is doing on a frequency less than monthly they should feel free to sit in on the weekly huddles. Otherwise, the project team should create and maintain a website where they post the project plan, their monthly progress reports, and any material items that might arise during weekly huddles.

## Monthly Progress Reports

Among other things, monthly progress reports should show the actual amount of calendar time elapsed versus plan, the actual amount of resources consumed versus plan, and the actual number of milestones completed versus plan. The relationship among these three "vital signs" allows people to assess the general health of the project. For example, if ninety percent of the allotted calendar time has elapsed, but only twenty-five percent of the milestones have been completed and fifty percent of the resources have been consumed, then you know you have a project that may be in serious trouble, and deserves a closer look.

## Refresh the Project Plan Monthly

In conjunction with the monthly progress reports, project plans should also be refreshed monthly. Milestones may need to be added or deleted or modified. Estimates to complete open tasks should be reforecast, and they should not default to the mathematical difference between the original plan and the actual to-date—they should be reforecast. The WBS may need to be revised.

## Estimating Project Phases

All projects are conducted in phases, such as: feasibility study, requirements definition, design, construction, testing, implementation, and post-implementation support. Different organizations may define different phases, and may manage a project's transition from one phase to the next differently, but all projects are conducted in phases. When refreshing a project plan, the estimates for the project's current phase should be specific and regarded as "firm;" the estimates for the subsequent phases should be expressed in ranges, so as not to suggest a false sense of precision, and should be regarded as "soft."

# 17

## STAFF

*I'm not looking for the best players; I'm looking for the right ones.*
**Coach Herb Brooks (explaining his player selection philosophy**
**for the 1980 U.S. Olympic Hockey Team)**
American ice-hockey coach and hockey Hall of Famer
1937 – 2003

## "STAFF" MEANS JUST THAT–

–staff—the people in your organization. When I say "the people" I mean all of the people: management and staff, exempt and non-exempt, employees and contractors/consultants.

## DIVERSITY

I've picked on diversity quite a bit. It's not that I believe that diversity is unimportant; I believe it is essential. I've just found that most organizations either only pay it lip service, or have it all wrong. In the U.S., we seem to have chosen not to celebrate diversity, but to squelch it. Unlike my experience in Singapore where they seem to celebrate the holidays of most religions (except Judaism, for unfortunate reasons), many U.S. companies choose not to celebrate any religious holidays for fear of offending those whose religion doesn't honor that particular holiday. In 2005, there was even a serious debate about whether a Christmas tree should be called a "Christmas tree" or a "holiday tree."[1] This is nuts—it's a Christmas tree; just like it's a Menorah and not a holiday candelabrum.

How can we say that we value diversity, while we simultaneously and deliberately make decisions and take actions that steer us toward universal blandness? Certainly, it would be wrong to celebrate the events of only one or a select few; certainly it would be wrong to allow one religion, ethnic heritage, or other tradition to impose itself on others; and certainly it would be wrong to embrace traditions whose practice requires human sacrifice or anything else illegal. But with those caveats understood, if we truly value diversity, we should be celebrating each other's heritage and traditions, not ignoring them. And, if you are an individual who is offended by the celebration of a heritage or tradition other than your own, you are destined for irrelevance.

In the U.S., while many organizations talk about diversity in grand and noble terms, it boils down to ethnicity metrics in practice. Too often diversity in race and gender are valued more highly than diversity in thinking, which may not be valued at all, or may actually be persecuted and expunged. There are some who will argue that race and gender are primary determinants of an individual's values, thus yielding diversity in thinking. That may have been true at one time, but it is less and less the case with each passing day. If diversity in values is the motivation for focusing on race and gender, then we should be lobbying hard to overturn the regulations that prevent us from tracking the spiritual tradition of candidates and employees, because a person's religion or faith tradition is often a stronger driver of their values than their race or gender.

Many U.S. companies have adopted the practice of targeting certain colleges and universities for the purpose of recruiting diverse candidates. However, their primary interest appears to be to merely boost their ethnicity metrics, because all they look at is grade point average (GPA) and degrees earned. Some companies even limit their recruiting efforts to marquis colleges and universities. If they look only at highly selective schools, if they look only at the candidate's GPA and degree(s) earned, and you ignore or marginalize life experience, then they are ensuring sameness in thinking. Because many colleges and universities tend to use the same textbooks, examine the same case studies, and employ professors who've been taught by the same professors, when you look only at GPA, degree earned, and perhaps the selectivity of the school, you are just on another path toward universal blandness. Stu-

---

[1]    *ABC News*, "At Christmas, What's In a Name: Effort to Rename Christmas Trees 'Holiday Trees' Sparks Debate," November 29, 2005: http://abcnews.go.com/WNT/ChristmasCountdown/story?id=1356566

dents so prepared—regardless of their race and gender—will have a clear and convincing command of the problems of the past, but be ill-prepared to deal with problems for which a case study does not yet exist.

On the other hand, if you show me a single parent—any single parent, regardless of race or gender—who has figured out how to put themselves through college—any college—while working and raising one or more children, and I'll show you someone who looks at things differently and knows how to solve problems they haven't seen before. I'll show you diversity in thinking.

A diverse workforce is not a melting pot, where different races and genders blend together; that is universal blandness. A diverse workforce is more like a mosaic. The value in workforce diversity lies in diversity of thought, diversity in perspective, diversity in problem solving, diversity in solution approaches, diversity in listening, diversity in decision-making approaches, and it can be seen in the diversity of dress, and diversity with which workers decorate their offices and cubicles, and so on. Achieving difference in race and gender, but sameness in thinking, does not make for a diverse workforce; it is universal blandness with different coats of paint.

# CHARACTER IS SACRED; COLLEGE DEGREES ARE NOT

As I was going through college, my father who, besides being a trumpet player, guitar player, and bandleader, was also an engineer for 3M for over forty years, told me, "There's a big difference between an education and book learning." I've yet to find anyone who will disagree with this; yet, a growing number of companies—especially large corporations—have made the possession of a college degree a condition of employment. Some have even made the possession of a post-graduate degree a condition of promotion into management. I think this is wrong. I am not saying that a college degree should not bear weight in a hiring or promotion decision, but I am saying that its presence or absence should not be a deciding factor.

The best predictor of future success is past success. Having had successfully completed the gauntlet of college life and earned their degree does say something about a person's ability to persevere and achieve, and that is important. However, to me, a college degree is a credential, and if a candidate has work experience or has overcome adversity in their life experience, I am far more interested in their track record in that experience. A college degree certifies the possession of certain skills, but I don't pay for the <u>possession</u> of skill; I pay for the <u>application</u> of skill. I would rather have a person who possesses "C" caliber skills, but an "A" caliber ability to apply them, than vice-versa. I have seen too many people with advanced degrees who couldn't hit the floor with their hats if they had three tries. Conversely, I have seen people who, despite not having earned a college degree, have successfully navigated life and overcome adversities in ways that demonstrate a huge heart, a huge talent, and a huge capacity to sense and respond, learn and adapt.

If a person has no track record, then their credentials are important to me. However, if a person has a track record, but does not possess a college degree, or does not possess "the right" college degree, I think it is criminal to summarily eliminate them and not let them compete for an opportunity. Further, as the cost of college continues to rocket skyward, and as the cost of college loans follows close behind, this requirement that a person possess a college degree is going to marginalize a greater and greater portion of the talent pool, and there is just no good reason for it.

Again, I am not saying that a college degree is a bad thing. I think a person's formal education absolutely cannot stop with high school; they must attend some form of post-secondary school, whether it is a vocational-technical school to learn a trade, or a college or university to earn their degree and/or post graduate degree(s). The possession of a formal degree is an admirable thing. Further, a person's formal learning cannot stop with the end of their formal education; everyone—I don't care who you are or what you do—must commit to life-long learning.

What I am saying is that the absence of a degree should not eliminate an otherwise qualified candidate from consideration. More important to me than a degree certifying a person's possession of skills is their track record demonstrating successful application of skills. More important to me than a person's possession of a degree is the person's possession of character. The possession of a degree should bear weight in a hiring decision, but it should not be a deciding factor. A person's heart is more important than their degree.

# THE IMPORTANCE OF "HEART"

A consensus-and-commitment style of management requires individuals and teams with "heart." Of course, you need people who are smart, talented, and have a seasoned sense of judgment (they may or may not have graduate or post-graduate college degrees, but they must have expertise). However, I want people with expertise who also have the right heart; as Coach Herb Brooks pointed out, "You don't win with talent alone. You win with heart." Put another way by General George S. Patton, "Give me an army of West Point graduates and I'll win a battle. Give me a handful of Texas Aggies, and I'll win the war."

By "heart," I mean a person's strength of character and their drive: heart = passion + honor. This can embrace all numbers of traits, but chief among them are their trustworthiness as demonstrated by their honesty and integrity; their courage; their attunedness and curiosity; their initiative; and their track record of getting things done.

Let's take a closer look at initiative in particular. In his 1988 "Advanced Leadership," seminar,[2] Stephen Covey theorized that people develop initiative through five levels or stages. Stewardship delegation allows people to move through the five stages. A command-and-control style of management can arrest their development at level one. However, a consensus-and-commitment style of management requires staff that operates at level five.

The lowest level of initiative is **waiting for instruction.** These people require "go-fer delegation." Go-fer delegation can be part of the stewardship process if it represents the person's true level of initiative, and is a step toward a higher level. It becomes damaging primarily when people have initiative that we're not willing to acknowledge.

The second level is comprised of those who **ask what to do.** Here the person begins to take initiative by asking. He or she expresses interest and awareness, but still has no notion of what to do.

The third level of initiative represents those who **recommend.** Now the person begins to see the job clearly and creates ideas for doing it.

People at the fourth level **act independently, but report immediately.** Here the person acts on his or her own initiative, but reports quickly to ensure that his or her actions are correct, and what he or she has done correlates with everything else.

Finally, people at the fifth and highest level **act independently, and report routinely.** Now we trust the person to act on his or her own, with confidence that periodic review will be enough to keep things on track.

---

[2] Stephen R. Covey, "Advanced Leadership," (Seminar, Stephen R Covey & Associates, Sundance, UT, Sep. 1988).

# LOCUS OF CONTROL

A psychological concept developed in 1954 by Julian Rotter[3], locus of control refers to a person's belief about what causes the good or bad results in his or her life. The locus of control can either be internal, meaning the person believes that they control their life, or external, meaning they believe that their environment, some higher power, or other people control their decisions and their life. For example, a student with an internal locus of control who does poorly on a test will explain the poor performance with comments such as, "I should have studied harder for the test. I should have re-read Chapter 9. I should have gone over my class notes more thoroughly." Whereas a student with an external locus of control who does poorly on a test will explain the poor performance with comments such as, "The teacher never liked me. It was a trick test."

The concept of locus of control embodies the concept of personal responsibility. In the U.S., there seems to be an erosion of personal responsibility and a growth of a victim mentality—I have no data to support this, it is just my sense after more than thirty years of observational research. Over the course of my career, I have encountered many people who, for example, missed commitments, without advance notice, citing many reasons outside their control (some more creative than others). I recall that in most cases the explanations given were quite reasonable; rarely was I given a reason that was lame. However, unless the circumstances are extenuating, my posture in such situations is that, while their reasons may make the individual's behavior more understandable, it does not make them any less responsible.

I have found that people with an internal locus of control, a stronger sense of personal responsibility, will tend to perform with greater effectiveness, while those with an external locus of control, a victim mentality, will realize less effectiveness. The folks I want on my staff are those who demonstrate an internal locus of control.

# EMPLOYEES VS. CONTRACTORS OR CONSULTANTS

I know there are reasons to use contractors or consultants versus employees at times. A contractor/consultant may possess a skill that you need only in the short term. Or, a contractor/consultant may possess a very specialized skill

---

[3] Julian Rotter is an American psychologist known for developing influential theories, including social learning theory and locus of control.

208

that you want the person to bring aboard and teach to your employees over the course of the engagement. Or, you may forecast or be experiencing a spike in demand that requires supplemental resources for a finite period. There also is the school of thought that prefers contractors/consultants to employees because, in the U.S. at least, you can legally treat them differently. For example, you don't have to give contractors exquisite performance reviews or create a lengthy paper trail to terminate them. Of course, contractors/consultants typically cost more than employees, but they are more akin to a variable cost, whereas employees are more akin to a fixed cost. Contractors/consultants just impose far less managerial burden than employees, and they are easier to terminate.

There are also times when using contractors/consultants is entirely inappropriate. For example, if the value proposition on which you compete is customer intimacy, then I can't imagine putting anyone other than an employee in a position that interacts with your customers.

I am opposed to treating contractors/consultants like a commodity for a variety of reasons. I have been with firms that buy contract and consulting services strictly on their hourly rate. Certainly, the consultant proposed by the consulting firm must meet the job specifications. However, when I was in the consulting business, I knew that when I received a spec from a company, and I knew that company buys only on price, I did not propose one of my superstars, because I could easily get serious money for their services elsewhere. I would propose Larry, Moe, or Curly—they met the job spec, they've been riding the pines, and any hourly rate is better than zero.

More importantly, buying talent strictly on price is just plain stupid because these are people not machines. Individuals not only have to be able to operate successfully in the organization's technical system, they also must be able to successfully operate in the organization's social system. Contractors and consultants are not commodities; they just represent that portion of your talent pool that you have chosen to lease or rent rather than buy.

# 18

## SELF

*This above all: to thine own self be true, and it must follow, as the night the day, thou canst not then be false to any man.*
**William Shakespeare (Polonius to Laertes, Hamlet, Scene I, Act III)**
English poet and playwright
1564 – 1616

**"SELF" MEANS YOU; MORE** specifically, it means personal leadership. How does one become comfortable with change—with change and change's faithful sidekick, ambiguity? The key to being comfortable with change and ambiguity is to be grounded in sound principles. When people are properly grounded, they can survive and even prosper, not only when the sun is shining, but also when the unpredictable storms of life descend upon them.

Adopting a principle-centered leadership approach, be it a matter of personal leadership or organizational leadership, is not something that just happens; it requires deliberate effort and great discipline. It must become an integral part of your personal vision and values. As someone trained by Covey to facilitate the training of others, I can tell you that *Principle Centered Leadership*[1] and *7 Habits of Highly Effective People* are a great place to begin. However, I want to share a different but complementary perspective with you. It is the work of Dr. Roger Rosenblatt, an award winning journalist, essayist, author, and playwright.

---

[1]   Stephen R. Covey, *Principle-Centered Leadership: Teaching People How to Fish*, (Provo, UT: Executive Excellence, 1989).

Rosenblatt offers a different look on the same topic of personal leadership, and it brings a creative tension that I think is very helpful. He has developed seven rules about discovering and leading one's self. To capture our attention, he calls them "non-rules" and he gives them provocative names; they are:

1. Be out of things.
2. Be slow.
3. Go to hell.
4. Distrust rational thought.
5. Be beside the point.
6. Avoid the company of people.
7. Do not understand it.

Earlier, I defined leadership as: strength in vision and strength in values, choice and loyalty, truth-telling, path-finding, creating safety to risk, and self-interest rightly understood. Rosenblatt's seven "non-rules" represent mental and emotional disciplines necessary to cultivate these leadership traits. What follows is a recap of what I learned from Rosenblatt's 1995 Masters Forum lecture[2], combined with my own interpretation, comments, perspectives, and adaptation resulting from my experience incorporating them into my own life.

# NON-RULE #1: BE OUT OF THINGS

Do not pursue the narrow quest. Position yourself in relation to experience so you look off to the side of the normal world. This means going against the normal tendency of modern times to stay on the point. Stay off the point; stay to the side. The real question, as we all discover sometimes too painfully in life, is often the question that is *not* asked, not the question that *is* asked.

In his classic 1941 film, *Citizen Kane*, Orson Wells portrays publishing tycoon Charles Foster Kane; a character inspired by the life of William Randolph Hearst. When the enormously wealthy Kane dies, he utters his last word, "Rosebud," while holding a glass snow globe, which he drops causing it to smash on the floor. An obituary newsreel follows, which documents the events in Kane's public life. After its preview, the producer of the newsreel feels that it lacks something and asks a reporter, Jerry Thompson, to find out

---

[2]  Roger Rosenblatt, "A Perspective on Leadership," (Speech, The Masters Forum, Minneapolis, MN, 28 Jan. 1992).

about Kane's private life and personality. In particular, he instructs him to discover the meaning behind Kane's last word, "Rosebud." His belief being that if they discover the underlying meaning of "Rosebud" they will come to know Charles Foster Kane.

The reporter, Thompson, is deliberately anonymous, and he goes around interviewing Kane's friends and associates. Kane's story unfolds as a series of flashbacks, some of which present the same incidents but from different recollections. Of course, we learn at the end of the movie that Rosebud was the name of the sled that represented Kane's innocent youth, and we see his sled, Rosebud, being burned in the furnace along with all of the other debris Kane had collected over his life—all without the reporter ever discovering what Rosebud meant. We are meant to conclude that the reporter believed that because he never discovered the meaning of Rosebud he never got to understand Charles Foster Kane.

But for us, the audience, the reporter did get the answer to his questions. The answer to the question of who Charles Foster Kane is had nothing to do with Rosebud. It had to do with the people to whom the reporter talked, and the answers, not about Rosebud, but the other answers—the "off point" answers. The whole life of the man was acquired by us, the audience, and not by the reporter, because we were not on a narrow quest; we were "out of things."

The interesting thing about pursuing the narrow quest, as Rosebud exemplifies, is "so what?" So what if the reporter discovered Rosebud? What if the reporter had discovered Rosebud on its way to the furnace, yanked it away, and made the connection with Kane's innocent youth? Would that have explained Charles Foster Kane? Certainly not.

The narrow quest often disappoints us because it will only yield the narrow answer. We see this all around us, and this is why the first rule is to be out of things, to look aside or in another direction.

Companies that are in trouble will often hire consultants, or boards will bring in new CEOs, to figure out why they're in trouble. I'm not talking about high-risk companies; I'm talking about otherwise sound and solid companies that were running well, but suddenly and inexplicitly find themselves in trouble—their business is heading south and they don't know why. So they bring in the consultants or hire the new CEO, and ninety-nine times out of one hundred, they bring in denominator thinkers who focus immediately on expenses. "I've got it! It's the travel and entertainment expenses! (Or the cell phone expenses, or some other such nonsense.) I'm sure that if we got these expenses under control then we could turn this company around."

It's the usual nonsense of the narrow quest. Very rarely do the problems of a good-company-gone-bad have much to do with expenses, the number of lunches, the number of dinners, the number of trips, the number of cell phones, or the amount of supplies being used in the printers. If you want to find out what's going wrong at a company where things had previously been going right, just ask the people. Ask them what has changed in the company's attitude toward them, and in their attitude toward the company. Ask what has begun to pollute their pride in their work; more importantly, ask them about the sense of meaning that their work has in their lives.

Freud was very simple and very correct about this. He said that all we really live for is love and work. What people forget is that we live for them equally; that work has a lot to do with our love because it has a lot to do with our self-respect. What we do with all of those hours during the day, and the sacrifices we make for it, matters. I think of the bravery of American working people—of working people everywhere—as something truly astonishing. Watching the courage with which people go to work in the morning, even when something is wrong with their family, or with themselves, or they're weary or unappreciated. But they still put on that dress, put on that suit, straighten that hem, straighten that tie, and they show up.

That courage is not to be underestimated, nor is it to be violated, by the people who employ them. It is a real act of trust, but it is a trust that has been called into question more and more as the fabricated pressure for quarterly EPS results mounts, and as we move through the real pressure of hard economic times. It is a trust that is called into question when partnerships that we previously took for granted, and assumed were an odd mixture of friendship and business, suddenly turn out only to be business only and people are left out in the cold. What then? What do you have but yourself—and you better have some sense of self, some center. If you want to find out what's wrong with a company that once used to be right, find out what happened to the people and their attitudes toward their work, and thus toward themselves.

This is especially true in mergers. Say a small company, Company A, is bought by a larger company, Company B. It's okay that Company A's business now represents only twenty percent of the merged companies' total. But what you can't live with is when the people at Company A are treated as if they are worth only twenty percent of what they were formerly worth, and what they do is worth only twenty percent of what formerly counted. This is what happens in mergers when you discount the minds and souls of the people doing the work.

When I worked for my former boss and lifelong mentor, Pat Irestone, hardly a day went by when we didn't disagree about something. Often his comments on a report I had drafted or an idea I had submitted were along these lines, "This is very interesting, Jim; of course, I disagree with every word." One time Pat sent back a lengthy strategy paper that I drafted at his request. I had worked hard on this. It was a hot topic and there was no easy solution. I was proud of the result, how I built consensus around issues that crossed organizational boundaries. This was in the days when everything was still done in hard copy, so I put the whole thing in a nice three-ring binder complete with tabs so as to organize it in a way that would lead Pat to reason to our same conclusions. When he returned it to me, he had massacred it with his infamous red pen, and on the front of the binder was a lonely note that simply read, "Nice tabs." Pat and I went back and forth, there was give and take (but not much), and it was great. It was great because I knew I was working for someone who cared about what I was doing.

We all know this experience. We'd much rather tussle with someone who takes us seriously, than be given a free ride by someone who thinks we're absolutely expendable. Unfortunately, there's not much you can do about it because this is the nature of business today (unless you have the personal wealth to buy the company). So where do you turn? I suggest turning inward.

Be out of things; look the other way. In fact, there are a number of things we can do to cultivate the ability to "be out of things:" be a generalist, don't rely on the news for news, connect with nature, live in the past, cultivate a state of repose, and reserve your hate for those things that really deserve hating.

## BE A GENERALIST

There is a tendency in organizations toward specialization. Certainly, it is not wrong to assume that people like to pursue individual interests. What is wrong is the extreme assumption that people are the accretion of their individual interests; that we are all specialists in our interests. When you begin to think of an organization as an amalgam of specialties, you are headed for trouble. There are many more areas that connect us than divide us, many more generalizations than there are specializations. It is these things and it is the tension among these things that keeps a culture moving up the curve. How we survive depends on a series of delicate balances based on the tension between the individual and the community—who we are as people and what we can do for one another. This is Adam Smith's sympathetic vs. mercenary societies; this is Alexis de Tocqueville's self-interest rightly understood.

The whole balance of power in the U.S. entails a deliberate effort to create and ensure an ongoing tension among the three branches of government. When we see one branch become too powerful, the others pull it back into place before it gets too far out of whack. And we live in a world—a social world—where these tensions are required. They are the reason "We the people" works.

So, being out of things, also means being a generalist—not in lieu of, but in addition to, your specialized interests. Specialized interests divide us; whereas there are many more interests that we have in common and thus connect us.

# DON'T RELY ON THE NEWS FOR NEWS

I enjoyed eight years at the StarTribune newspaper, and now I suggest that you not rely on the news for your news--especially cable news shows and most news blogs. Cable news shows are to journalism what professional wrestling is to athletics, and most news blogs are to journalism what the Etch-A-Sketch® is to art. If you want, you can get the news in five minutes through most media organizations now—you can get all of the things that would satisfy you about the facts of the news in the world via the Internet (again, you must exercise great caution because too much of what is purported to be news today is really opinion disguised as news, or entertainment disguised as news). Just don't rely on the news for knowledge. Be out of things.

Instead, I recommend you read history, fiction, poetry, or anything else, but in some way get out of it. This will teach you more about things than you would otherwise learn by staying on the nose, by pursuing Rosebud.

I remember tennis pro John McEnroe's comeback in 1987 after a brief sabbatical. He struggled, and every tennis expert in the country was telling us that his backhand wasn't what it used to be, his forehand wasn't what it used to be, his serve wasn't what it once was. And that was the conventional analysis of John McEnroe. I don't think that had anything to do with John McEnroe. If you read Bernard Malamud's, *The Natural*,[3] I think you will understand McEnroe. McEnroe thought he was and he was, in fact, a natural. We see athletes like this all the time. We see students like this all the time; we see students who ace courses without any hard study at all. McEnroe didn't

---

[3] Bernard Malamud, *The Natural*, (New York: Farrar, Strauss and Cudahy, 1952).

need to rehearse; he didn't need to practice; he didn't need to study. He was born with these gifts and he won championship after championship doing things that you're not supposed to be able to do in tennis. He was able to do those things because he was a virtuoso; he was a natural.

What is interesting about naturals like McEnroe is what happens when they begin to fail. During his comeback, when McEnroe missed a shot, you could see his palpable confusion on the court: "That was there before. Why isn't it there now?" How many times have we seen a natural athlete at the end of his or her playing career attempt a new career as a coach only to fail disappointingly? This is because it is hard to teach that which you never had to study and learn yourself—it is hard to teach what comes to you naturally. Meanwhile, the player who was not a natural, who had to study and work his or her butt off and perhaps didn't even make it to the major leagues, will become a very successful coach.

To understand "the natural," to understand the news, you deliberately have to take a position off to the side. Just like you have to do in birdwatching, be irrelevant to the center of the action, and you will thus understand the center of the action. By that understanding you will understand a bit more about yourself. Be out of it.

## CONNECT WITH NATURE

It is so hard to connect with nature these days. Beginning in the twentieth century we have been moving away from nature, and we have suffered penalties for it—penalties that are very subtle. My parents, their parents, and certainly their parents, had whole references in their lives that we now inherit without their meanings--terms such as horsepower, for example. These terms were connected to things in nature and they have no such meaning in our lives now. What have we lost by losing that connection? We have lost a sense of the cyclical natures of our lives, of the combination of being in control of things and not ever being in control of things, of the great power we have and of our absolute powerlessness. All of which our forbearers had, but we have lost because we have pursued another way of life. We could not help this, but there is a way to reclaim it.

Hunting, fishing, camping, canoeing, and hiking, are all pursuits to commune with nature. The environmental movement itself is a reflection of our connection to nature. Interest in the ozone layer, rainforests, coral reefs, or the polar ice-caps indicates that people have recognized the absence of nature in their lives--almost a biological absence that causes a certain rising of the spirit when we do find it, like the feeling we have spending time in the countryside.

How much time do your feet actually spend touching Mother Earth versus concrete and asphalt? Many years ago French farmers were protesting something in the European Common Market. They wanted to make their point to the people in Paris, so they cut slabs of wheat fields, transported them to Paris and put them right in the center of the Champs Elysées. They brought in horses, cows, goats, and sheep to graze in the field. They created this countryside in the middle of the city. You can just imagine what this looked like, this scene—a wheat field in the middle of Paris.

The gendarmes came out ready for a fight. This was a protest movement, so they naturally expected that there would be a lot of trouble—and a lot of mess with all of the farm animals. But there wasn't a fight; in fact, the people loved it. The policemen themselves enjoyed the field. Lovers took hands and walked among the fields. The countryside, suddenly imposed upon the people's lives, produced a visceral reaction in which they found themselves in identification with something real—the real world—and something out of their control. Modernity is ordinarily defined by making more things in our control that are not ordinarily so. Now here was nature that was not in our control and it was wonderful. For a moment they felt it—a connection with nature.

## LIVE IN THE PAST

People will tell you not to live in the past, but that is preposterous. We have no choice but to live in the past—we can't live in the future, and we don't understand the present, so we live in the past anyway. In Thornton Wilder's, *The Skin of Our Teeth,*[4] a fortuneteller says, "I tell your future. Nothing easier. Everyone's future is in their face. Nothing easier. But who can tell your past— eh? Nobody!" The past is where we live. That's where we discover ourselves. So take to it, seize it eagerly even though it is sometimes painful and even dangerous. They say you can't go home again, but we go home again all of the time—sometimes reluctantly, or with a lot of fear. Live in the past. Discover yourself there and you'll find your way back to the present because you'll know who you are.

---

[4] Thornton Wilder, *The Skin of Our Teeth: A Play in Three Acts*, (French's Standard Library Edition, New York: Samuel French, Inc., 1999), Act II, p60.

# CULTIVATE A STATE OF REPOSE

We are told not to daydream, "Don't be out of it. Why are you daydreaming?" People are always admonished for daydreaming or digressions. In J. D. Salinger's, *Catcher In the Rye,*[5] you may remember that Holden Caulfield's speech class was taught to yell out the word "digression" every time somebody makes a digression in their speech. Of course, all Holden Caulfield does is digress––that's the meaning of his story. Similarly, we are told not to dream. Interestingly, one of the more common complaints among workers—especially professionals—is that there is little to no time for creative thinking. The higher you rise up the organizational ranks the less time you will have for creative thought, and it will become dangerous just to think out loud. You need to make the time for creative thinking. Find yourself in repose—cultivate a state of repose. Take long walks, read books, sit back, know who you are.

You've probably heard that people reveal their true selves in crises––that however you behave in a crisis reveals how you are as a person. I don't believe it for a minute. I think it is just as likely that people don't behave like themselves in a crisis, but that they behave as aberrations of themselves. I think it is more likely that people behave more like themselves when they are in a state of repose—in the quiet moments when they are alone with themselves, and they don't have to live a public life at that moment. They're not on stage; they can just be calm and cultivate that stillness and be themselves. The wonderful thing about finding such a state is that a lot of things leave you that result in welcome changes. In my experience this happens—all envy leaves, most ambition leaves, hatred and enmity leave.

# RESERVE YOUR HATE FOR THOSE THINGS THAT REALLY DESERVE HATING

It's not that we shouldn't hate things, but we should reserve our hatred for the abstractions that really deserve hating, and not for the small or petty things. Rosenblatt's book, *Children of War,*[6] won the 1983 Robert F. Kennedy Book Prize, and for good reason; it is compelling, it will give you pause. The book's genesis was a story he had done on children in war zones. He talked with children in Northern Ireland, Israel, Lebanon, Cambodian children living on the Thailand border (the Khemer Rouge were still running Cambodia at the time), and to Vietnamese children living in a refugee camp in Hong Kong. He

---

[5] J.D. Salinger, *The Catcher in the Rye*, (New York: Little, Brown and Company, 1951).
[6] Roger Rosenblatt, *Children of War*, (New York: Doubleday, 1992).

chose these children because their countries had been at war all of their lives, and he was interested in the mentality this creates. Wanting to "stay out of it" he didn't ask them the usual questions; he wanted to know who they were and what they thought. As he moved east the stories got worse and worse, and in Cambodia they were truly dreadful indeed. I'll share one with you[7], and it will be unpleasant to read.

A twelve-year-old girl, Peov, had been, like a lot of other Cambodian children, captured by the Khemer Rouge. The Khemer Rouge frequently murdered the parents, but kept the children, enlisting them in a kind of Nazi-youth organization. It was a fiercely murderous, anti-intellectual movement—people who wore glasses were murdered on the assumption that they could and wanted to read. It was a murderous madness in the jungles of Cambodia. The kids captured by the Khemer Rouge were enlisted to do work, and Peov was one of those kids; but she was fortunate enough to escape with her life into Thailand.

For the first year after her escape, when she lived in Khao I Dang, a refugee camp in Thailand, Peov did not say a word—to anyone. Eventually, she drew a picture, a crudely drawn picture of some Khemer Rouge soldiers with their rifles trained on several children. Off to the side in the picture was what looked like an odd wagon wheel—a large circle with what looked like spokes leading to a smaller circle, or hub, in the center. There were also a couple of lines trailing away from the outside of the wheel. Working with a psychiatrist attached to the camp, Peov finally explained the meaning of her drawing.

The soldiers had rounded up children who had escaped. The device that looked like a wagon wheel was actually a portable guillotine. What looked like the inner circle of the wheel, the hub, was, in fact, the area that was placed over the child's head. What looked like the wheel's spokes were actually the lines of demarcation among the steel blades. The two lines trailing away from the outside of the wheel were ropes that triggered the blades. The device worked like a camera lens. It was placed over a child's head, the ropes were pulled, the lens closed and the child was decapitated—this as an object lesson to the other children. However, it wasn't the soldiers who pulled the ropes; the Khemer Rouge soldiers made another child pull the ropes.

When you learn of something like that, not that there is anything else like that, you realize the depravity of which the human mind is capable, and you may be tempted to dwell on it. Yet when Rosenblatt talked to the children to find out how they thought, which you'll remember was his purpose,

[7] Ibid., p135-136.

he found that their thinking went the other way. This happened in Northern Ireland, in Israel, in Lebanon, with the Vietnamese children, and with the Cambodian children, too.

When Rosenblatt asked the Cambodian children what they would like to do when they grew up, many said that they wanted to go back to Cambodia and seek revenge. Revenge—now there's something we can understand! But when he clarified by asking if they meant that they wanted to go back with others and destroy the Khemer Rouge, they corrected him, "Revenge is to make a bad man better than before," said Nop Narith.[8] The children believed that both good and evil spirits live among us, but the two cannot exist in the same person—they are in separate places and the good must defeat the bad. This makes sense because anyone who committed deeds as terrible as the Khemer Rouge could not possibly have any good within them:

> *Could their idea of revenge thus be a way of dealing with the fear of evil in themselves? If they could see how dangerous a good and gentle people can become, was it not possible that the only form of revenge to which they might be susceptible would be the reassertion of greater goodness and mercy? Revenge, conventionally defined, cannot be taken against oneself. If hate destroys the hater, it does so doubly when the enemy is within… What the children meant by revenge might be that revenge is a self-healing act, a purification into compassion and wisdom, as Buddhism itself prescribes. Revenge is to be taken against fate, against a whole world of incomprehensible evil. Living well, in a moral sense, is the best revenge.*[9]

And this was said by all of the children who also had horrific experiences. There is Cherokee wisdom that is remarkably similar as demonstrated in this legend, Two Wolves:

> *An old Cherokee is teaching his grandson about life. "A fight is going on inside me," he said to the boy. "It is a terrible fight and it is between two wolves. One is evil—he is anger, envy, sorrow, regret, greed, arrogance, self-pity, guilt, resentment, inferiority, lies, false pride, superiority, and ego." He continued, "The other is good—he is joy, peace, love, hope, serenity, humility, kindness, benevolence, empathy, generosity, truth, compassion, and faith. The*

[8]  Ibid., p134.
[9]  Ibid., p134.

*same fight is going on inside you - and inside every other person, too."*

> *The grandson thought about it for a minute and then asked his grandfather, "Which wolf will win?"*
> *The old Cherokee simply replied, "The one you feed."*[10]

These children had, through their pain, learned to live with themselves because the outside world was so menacing that they had no other place to go to discover themselves but within themselves. Through that privacy they discovered something astonishingly generous, something the rest of us could not discover, except, perhaps, by going through an analogous experience. Hating is a wearying business, and those kids had had enough of it.

Be out of it. Stand to the side. Ask the different question. Do not pursue the narrow quest.

# NON-RULE #2: BE SLOW

Be very slow in understanding things. I have no trouble being slow in understanding things—it takes me a while.

Look at the former Soviet Union. That whole thing was baffling to me. I don't mean the economics or the politics of it; I mean the inner questions. For seventy-plus years the Soviet Union—the people of the Soviet Union—lived a lie. They were lied to by a philosophy, they were lied to by their government—they lived a lie. But that was the easier lie to live with. The harder lies to live with were the lies they told one another. The times they told on one another, reported the infractions of one another. The lie they told when they put signs in their windows that said, "Workers of the world unite!" The whole lie of pretending to live a normally progressive life in a system that was repressive. The lies they told themselves and their children. The art they didn't teach, the books they didn't read—all lies.

Then suddenly, after meeting all weekend at the Kremlin, the Politburo comes out and addresses the hundreds of thousands of people gathered in Red Square, looking as if children toward their father. These leaders who, along with their predecessors, represented seventy years of denial, seventy years of executions, seventy years of gulags and imprisonments, seventy years of fear, seventy years of reports, seventy years of no telephones, seventy years of snitching and spying, these leaders emerged from that weekend meeting at

---

[10] First People—The Legends: Two Wolves—Cherokee Legend: http://www.firstpeople.us/FP-Html-Legends/TwoWolves-Cherokee.html

the Kremlin, and they said to the hundreds of thousands of people representing the hundreds of millions of people in this vast place of eleven time zones, "Just kidding. We didn't mean it. Now you can vote for another party, now you can have a capitalistic economy, because now we're headed in a different direction."

Then the people of the Soviet Union—leaders and workers alike––had to look inside themselves. They had to learn what it means to find some inner truth and discover who they really are. They had to learn to trust themselves and to trust one another.

Such experience is not limited to whole governments that find the philosophy on which they are based is flawed. This can happen to businesses, too. There are businesses that have found the whole premise on which they are founded is flawed. I give you Enron as a case in point.

This same phenomenon can also occur at other levels, too—it doesn't have to be a whole government or a whole business. It can happen within a government when the premise on which a particular policy is based is flawed. The U.S. decision to invade Iraq, based on the premise that Iraq possessed weapons of mass destruction, is a case in point. It can happen within a business, too, when they find that the premise on which a whole strategy or line of business is based is flawed. I give you the sub-prime loan situation in the U.S. financial industry as a case in this point. It can happen anytime we drink the Kool-Aid and elevate a premise, a theory, a hypothesis, to the premature stature of a truth.

The problem is that after the theory and premise are preached long enough and hard enough, after all of the systems and structure necessary to support and reinforce the premise are built, people come to believe the premise, the theory, as truth rather than the hypothesis that it is. It is only after the gap between the truth of reality and the flaw of the theory becomes so big and so apparent that it can no longer be denied, that it all implodes—not unlike what happened in the Soviet Union, not unlike what happened in the George W. Bush administration, not unlike what happened at Enron, not unlike what happened to the financial industry.

*In a primitive political system, power is transmitted through violence, or the threat of violence: military coups, private militias, and so on. In a less primitive system more typical of emerging markets, power is transmitted via money: bribes, kickbacks, and offshore bank accounts. Although lobbying and political campaign contributions certainly play major roles in the American political*

*system, old-fashioned corruption—envelopes stuffed with $100
bills—is probably a sideshow today, Jack Abramoff notwithstand-
ing.*

*Instead, the American financial industry gained politi-
cal power by amassing a kind of cultural capital—a belief system.
Once, perhaps, what was good for General Motors was good for the
country. Over the past decade, the attitude took hold that what was
good for Wall Street was good for the country.*

*...As more and more of the rich made their money in fi-
nance, the cult of finance seeped into the culture at large.* [11]

A story going around sometime ago about these two high school
boys, I'll call Smith and Jones, provides another example. Smith and Jones
both applied to Harvard; Smith got accepted, but Jones did not. Unfortunately, Jones' parents had been ruthless and relentless in pushing him to accomplish this stretch goal of getting into Harvard (as parents and stockholders
and boards mistakenly sometimes will do).

Smith was also accepted at Yale, decided to go there and wrote to
Harvard to inform them of his decision to go to Yale. Learning that Smith
decided to go to Yale, desperate and distraught, Jones wrote to Harvard under
Smith's name and said that he had changed his mind and was coming to Harvard after all.

So Jones enrolled as Smith at Harvard and navigated college life so
he didn't have to live in a freshman dorm, or do many of the other things that
might have resulted in him being recognized. He lived under the name of
Smith for most of the first term. Unfortunately for Jones (a.k.a., Smith), colleges have the habit of reporting back to parents whenever a first year student
is earning a "C," or below, in any of their courses. And as it turned out, Jones
(a.k.a., Smith), while doing well in most subjects, was earning a "C" in one.
So Harvard sent a note to the parents.

Of course it wasn't Jones' parents to whom they sent the note, it was
the real Smith's parents to whom they sent the note informing them that their
son was getting a "C" in one of his courses. To which Smith's parents were
somewhat surprised and replied with a note to Harvard saying that they were
sorry that their son wasn't doing well at Harvard, but they were very pleased
with how he was doing at Yale. Whereupon Jones was discovered, thrown out
of Harvard and his name expunged from the record. There's a minor irony

---

[11]   Simon Johnson, "The Quiet Coup," *The Atlantic*, May 2009, http://www.theatlantic.com/doc/
print/200905/imf-advice

here in that it wasn't Jones' name that was expunged, but Smith's.

To many, that would be the end of the story. But what if Jones hadn't gotten the "C?" What if he had lived as Smith as a freshman, sophomore, junior, and senior? What if he had gone on to graduate school? What if he had become a lawyer under the name of Smith? What if he married under the name of Smith? What if he raised his kids as Smith? What if he went through all of the joys, penalties, envies, triumphs, and all of the self-inspections of any man—except his name was now Smith, and then he dies and on his gravestone is written: "Smith?"

What happens to someone in the process of starting with a small lie that accumulates upon itself and becomes a large lie, and then the large lie becomes the whole life? What happens to a government, like the Soviet Union, that begins with a philosophy, not yet recognized as flawed, and invests so heavily in that philosophy—financially and emotionally—that it begins living it as if it were an unassailable truth? Or what happens to any government that adopts policy, not yet recognized as flawed, and invests so heavily in that policy—financially and emotionally—that it begins living it as if it were an unassailable truth? This happens sometimes. What happens to a business that starts with a premise, not yet recognized as flawed, and invests so heavily—financially and emotionally—in that premise that it begins living as if it were an unassailable truth? Or what happens to a business that starts with a strategy, not yet recognized as flawed, and invests so heavily—financially and emotionally—in that strategy that it begins living it as if it were an unassailable truth? This happens sometimes, too.

You have to be slow about some things because very often the first thing you see is not the truth. I don't mean this in just a professional context; I mean this as a stance in life—of taking it slow, of waiting, of the kind of private patience that one can only cultivate when they are slow with things.

Be slow with things. Nothing is ever finished; no story is ever dead. The mind lives in its aftereffects—we know this from our experience; it is where we discover ourselves. Be slow and you begin to understand both yourself and your circumstances more deeply.

# NON-RULE #3: GO TO HELL

When I say, "Go to hell," I do not mean to attack you—just the reverse. I mean: discover the chaos within you. Literally, I mean, go to the hell of your mind. It is where you will find things that surprise and frighten you, but ultimately lead you to something better. Nietzsche said, "You must have chaos within you to give birth to a dancing star." Think of that. You must have chaos within you to give birth to a dancing star. A dancing star doesn't need to be a work of literature, or art; it can be a child, spouse, friend, business, colleague, community, or neighbor. But touch that chaos within you, go to your hell, and discover what feelings are engendered there—not what certainties, but what feelings, what frights—and you will move out from it. I offer this not as a psychologist; I have no knowledge of psychology. I'm only talking about experiences I have observed in friends, others, and in myself—experiences that I'll bet you have observed as well.

Perhaps one of the best journeys to the hell of one's mind comes from Mark Twain's, *Adventures of Huckleberry Finn*. There's a passage where he really goes to hell; he talks about it. It is the passage where Huck has to decide about turning in Jim, the runaway slave. He's been harboring Jim, he's been breaking the law, and he's convinced he will go to hell for it. However, if he turns Jim in, he'll absolve himself, so he decides to do so, and he writes a letter to Mrs. Watson, Jim's owner, to tell her where Jim is. But then he sets the letter aside, and thinks:

> *I felt good and all washed clean of sin for the first time I had ever felt so in my life, and I knowed I could pray now. But I didn't do it straight off, but laid the paper down and set there thinking—thinking how good it was all this happened so, and how near I came to being lost and going to hell. And I went on thinking. And I got to thinking about our trip down the river; and I see Jim before me, all the time, in the day, and in the night-time, sometimes moonlight, sometimes storms, and we a-floating along, talking, and singing, and laughing. But somehow I couldn't seem to strike no places to harden me against him, but only the other kind. I'd see him standing my watch on top of his'n, 'stead of calling me, so I could go on sleeping; and see him how glad he was when I come back out of the fog; and when I came to him again in the swamp, up there where the feud was; and such-like times; and would always call me honey, and pet me, and do everything he could think of for me, and how good he always was; and at last I struck the time I saved him by telling the men we had smallpox aboard, and he was so grateful, and said I was the best friend old Jim ever had in the world, and the only one he's got now; and then I happened to look around and see that paper.*

*It was a close place. I took it up and held it in my hand.*
*I was a-trembling, because I'd got to decide, forever, betwixt two*
*things, and I knowed it. I studied a minute sort of holding my*
*breath, and then says to myself:*
*'All right, then, I'll go to hell'—and tore it up.*[12]

We love that passage, as we love that book, not only for the idea
of equality it insists upon, but because we see a person discovering who he
is—discovering his center, discovering it through language, through his own
words. Huck becomes himself by going to hell. It is the necessary journey.
He disobeys. He finds trouble. He takes a risk. He goes back to where the
pain was, and he is carried forward to do what's right, because he now knows
what's right.

We go to hell to create ourselves and, by so doing, we change the
world around us. You have to have chaos within you to give birth to a dancing
star.

# NON-RULE #4: DISTRUST RATIONAL THOUGHT

We know the value of rational thought—that's drummed into us all of the
time—we see its product and we're proud that we can create it. Now, I say,
distrust it and start trusting your irrational thought; start trusting your intuition.

I started trusting my intuition because I don't know as much as other
people. I think we all have this intuition, this instinct, but we just haven't
learned to trust it because we don't understand it, we can't explain it. Yet, how
many times have we ignored our intuition, our instincts, and followed our rational thought only to have it go badly and find ourselves saying to ourselves,
"I should have trusted my instincts. I should have gone with my gut." I'm not
talking about placing bets in Las Vegas; I'm talking about making normal,
ordinary, everyday decisions.

Public figures lead these lives that almost prevent us from seeing
them as real people. But we, too, lead public lives—perhaps not as publicized,
but certainly just as public—which disallows us from seeing one another as
people. We present ourselves and see each other gleaming, smiling and saying, "Okay, no problem; you bet." But it has nothing to do with how we really
live, and we know it—it is not as if we do not know it.

---

[12] Mark Twain, *The Adventures of Huckleberry Finn*, (New York: Penguin Classics, Penguin Putnam,
Inc., 1994), p283.

When intuition undercuts what you see, learn to trust it; moderate it with facts, of course, but trust it. We need to learn to trust our instincts and intuition much more than we do; we need to trust in the mystery of it.

# NON-RULE # 5: BE BESIDE THE POINT

This is a variation on Non-rule #1: Be Out of Things, but there is a difference you will detect.

There was a kid on a high school basketball team that wasn't getting much game time. He wanted to play better so he could get more game time. When he talked to the coach, the coach asked him what he does when he practices. The kid told him that he dribbles and shoots just like everyone else. The coach told the kid to watch a couple of games—real games or scrimmages—and keep track of the amount of time that any one player's hands are actually on the ball. The kid did that and came back to the coach astonished. He said that over the course of a forty-minute game, a player's hands touched the ball—as in dribbling, passing, and shooting—fewer than three minutes. So the coach asked him, "Three minutes out of forty. What does that teach you?" It teaches us that most of the game of basketball is played away from the ball. The same is true in other games, too; it is true in hockey and it is true in football. It is also true in chess, because you must look at the whole board and not to fixate on just a few pieces.

The same is also true in life, as well. The fact is that most of the game of everything is played away from the ball. For example, all natural disasters are typically explained in terms of the fiscal damage that they cause—this many dollars in homes lost, this many acres of farmland destroyed, this much in federal assistance spent, and so on. That is not what such an event is about at all. What that event is about is human helplessness in an age in which we are, again, helpless to control our own lives—when nature can, with one swat, take away our home, a loved one, or our self. Nobody talks about that, but that is the thing that is the terror of it—not the dollars lost. Yet we fixate on the thing that we're not thinking about, the story that is not the story.

If you want to know a person or a group of people, don't look where the noise is, where the ball is. You can't come to know a person or a group of people by the episodic moments in their life, just as our own lives are not to be learned by others by our cataclysmic moments. You come to learn others, and others come to learn you, by our ordinary moments, the quiet moments, the moments away from the ball. Be beside the point; study your soul, and the soul of others, in repose, not in crises.

Another pearl of my father's wisdom is that you learn more about a person in a day of play than you will in a year of work. I have found this to be true, and I'll bet you have, too. Perhaps you've had the experience where you go on a weeklong business trip with a colleague with whom you have worked for many years, but with whom you've never traveled. As a result of traveling together—just being together during a week of ordinary moments—did you not develop a collegial bond in that one week that was stronger than the one you had developed over the years before?

Being beside the point also means being comfortable with being uncomfortable with ambiguity. I am really going to go out on a limb and cite the issue of abortion to illustrate my point. I am not going to advocate for it or against it; rather, my purpose here is to give you a different way of thinking about it—a way that has to do with the normal confliction that most people have with it.

Both those who are for and those who are against abortion treat it as a rights issue; those favoring abortion argue for a woman's right to choose, those opposing abortion argue for the fetus' right to life. The whole issue is treated as a rights issue. But it isn't purely a rights issue; it is a deeply emotional, painful, and confusing issue. It has less to do with rights, in fact, than with what is right. When *Roe v. Wade* was decided, there was a great liberal thinking in the majority of the country. Later, however, those people found themselves in political trouble when the country started to rise up against it as if to say, "Oh, no you don't. This is much more complicated than that, and I'm against it!"

If such issues were decided by majority rule—which they should not be—we in the U.S. wouldn't know what to do, because polling data tells us that we struggle with the issue of abortion—as we should. In his 1992 Masters Forum lecture, Rosenblatt cited that while seventy-three percent of the country thinks abortion should be permitted, seventy-seven percent of the country also thinks that abortion is a form of killing.[13] Since then, we have seen a shift—sort of. A Gallop Poll taken in May 2009 indicates that forty-two percent of the country is "pro-choice," while fifty-one percent is "pro-life."[14] Yet a CNN/Opinion Research Corporation Poll taken that same month revealed that only thirty percent of the country is in favor of over-turning Roe v. Wade,

---

[13]  Roger Rosenblatt, "A Perspective on Leadership," (Speech, The Masters Forum, Minnetonka, MN, 28 Jan. 1992)

[14]  Gallup Poll. May 7-10, 2009. (N=1,015 adults nationwide. MoE ± 3). //http:www.pollingreport.com/abortion

while sixty-eight percent said it should not be overturned.[15]

That is all you need to know to understand how much trouble this issue ought to give us—<u>ought</u> to give us. We are dealing with essential matters of life and death, matters we do not understand. We ought to live in ambiguity, but we live in a climate of social science thinking that makes every thought a potential lobby in Washington. Consequently, we do not dwell where we really live—in the natural, understandable, useful, and sometimes quite beautiful confusions of our minds. We should learn to live uncomfortably with the abortion issue because it is impossible to live comfortably with it.

We need to learn how to live uncomfortably with other issues, too. Take capital punishment. How many times have those who are against capital punishment said in a flash reaction to a heinous crime, "Kill the bastard!" Or, vice versa, depending on your point of view. Free speech is another example. We can be all for free speech, but that magazine... The same is true for hate speech.

Why shouldn't these things be confusing? These are issues not to be settled by lobbies or polar arguments or by the social sciences that work towards the definite. They are, if anything, subject to an old-fashioned kind of thinking, a humanistic thinking that certainly has its own troubles, but at least has the virtue of acknowledging that life is layered. You can live with two conflicting thoughts simultaneously—and sometimes you should.

We need to learn to live with these confusions, and become comfortable with ambiguity. It is productive stuff. I'm not talking about ignoring or denying these issues and sticking your intellect in the sand like an ostrich. I'm saying to keep your mind in a state of friction and know it; it will be more honest that way, more true. I also think you will be a better leader by acknowledging the complex truth rather than trying to force-fit such things into a bumper-sticker truth.

# NON-RULE #6: AVOID THE COMPANY OF PEOPLE

I don't mean it, of course, because you can't avoid the company of people. I'm suggesting that you work at it; cultivate your privacy. This is important because it is very difficult to cultivate privacy in a public age. We seem to have moved from an era of conspicuous consumption to an era of conspicuous introspection. Now everybody is talking about their grief, and everybody's talking about their fears, and everybody's talking about their worries. Men

---

[15]  CNN/Opinion Research Corporation Poll. May 14-17, 2009. (N=1,010 adults nationwide. MoE ± 3). //http:www.pollingreport.com/abortion

now will sit around in a circle and share their woes.

Fine, if you have to do it, if it helps you, then do it. What I suggest, however, is that if you have to engage in conspicuous introspection, don't forget to also learn where you really live because it has nothing to do with the public face you put on things. We are not conspicuously introspective when we are introspective; we are introspective when we are introspective. There is a very quiet place, a very private room where we know ourselves. It is the place where we do not have false language.

I come back to this again and again, but that safe, sophisticated, academic language—that politically correct language—that many have adopted in their public lives is not our friend. Such language seems to be at its worst in an organization's headquarters, whether that is the capital of some government or the corporate headquarters of a business; and matters are made worse because it is emulated by those who seek to curry the favor of the headquarters' big shots.

We Americans have a particular problem with euphemisms—that language we use to soften an issue and dress it up a bit. To illustrate my point, let me share some excerpts from George Carlin's speech to the National Press Club (NPC) on May 13, 1999, in which he shared some of his language complaints.

> *There's a well-known condition resulting from combat where a fighting man's nerves have been stretched to the breaking point, or have indeed snapped. In WWI this condition was called, "shell shock;" two syllables, and it even sounds like what it is—shell shock. That was almost ninety years ago.*
>
> *In WWII this very same combat condition was called, "battle fatigue." We're at four syllables now, it takes a little longer to say, and it doesn't seem to hurt as much when we say it.*
>
> *In the Korean War this very same battle condition was called, "operational exhaustion." We're up to eight syllables now, and the humanity has been almost totally squeezed from the phrase——it sounds more like something that might happen to your car.*
>
> *Then, of course, there was the Vietnam war, and given all of the lies surrounding that war, I guess it should be no surprise that the vary same battle condition was called, "post-traumatic stress disorder." We still have eight syllables, but we have added a hyphen, and the pain is now completely buried under jargon. It's also more difficult to say, it doesn't just roll off the tongue, so we have begun*

*to refer to it by its initials, PSD, or PTSD.*[16]

We also have that false language fabricated by Madison Avenue wise guys, fashionistas, or other aspiring elitists who invent new words as a way of asserting their coolness, or making us more comfortable with a questionable purchase or decision. Even the simplest words are misused nowadays. Have you noticed how the word "fun" is being used now? Everything is now "fun," even if it isn't fun. Some years ago there was an ad on late-night TV for an unusual product called, "Safe Ears." A woman steps forward to advertise gold-looking earrings that have secret compartments that contain condoms. Condoms secreted inside of earrings—most inventive—they've sure come a long way from the Lone Ranger bullet ring that I had as a kid. It had a secret compartment, too, but it contained nothing like a condom, I can assure you. The product was called "Safe Ears," but even that was an imprecise use of language as it's not the ears' safety it offers to protect (at least I hope not). And even more interesting was the fact that they sold these earrings in sets of three. You would think that if your date were so constructed as to wear three of these big dangly earrings, then safe sex would be the least of their worries. But the woman who was advertising them said, "Safe Ears are fabulous and fun!"

Quoting from George Carlin's speech to the NPC again:

> *Sometime during the last forty years, toilet paper became bathroom tissue. Sneakers became running shoes. Loafers became slip-ons. Motels became motor lodges. Trailers became mobile homes, which became manufactured housing. Truck stops became travel plazas. Used cars became previously owned transportation. Manicurists became nail technicians. Store clerks became product specialists. Employees became associates. Uniforms became career apparel. Stewardesses became flight attendants. Maids became room attendants. Room service became guest room dining. Medicine became medication. The dump became the landfill. Gambling joints became gaming resorts. Shacking up became living together. Reruns became encore presentations. Monkey bars became pipe frame exercise units. Wife beating became intermittent explosive disorder. Constipation became occasional irregularity. And we got rain forests and wet lands when the environmentalists discovered that people were unwilling to give money to save jungles and swamps.*

[16] George Carlin, "Language Complaints," (Speech, National Press Club, Washington, DC, 13 May 1999)

*When I was a kid, a person who got sick would go to the doctor or hospital, who would then bill their insurance. Now, the health maintenance organization sends them to the wellness center where they consult with a healthcare delivery professional. Poor people used to live in slums. Now, the economically disadvantaged occupy substandard housing in the inner city.*

*It's enough to make you want to throw up. Well… engage in an involuntary protein spill.*[17]

This is the problem with euphemisms and politically correct speech; it's the language that takes the life out of life. And it just keeps getting worse. As time goes on, it seems that people find new ways of shading the truth, and camouflaging meaning, rather than revealing it. We must all strive to use authentic language and respectful discourse and civility—if not with others, then at least with ourselves. The use of language is so important in our lives. If you have to use the "in" word, the jargon, the cliché, at least know and recognize it as a cliché. Do it as a social gesture the same way you would ask a person who you don't care about, "How are you doing?" Treat it like that. "The suspect exited the vehicle;" apparently no one just gets out of a car anymore. If you mean "dysfunction," say "dysfunction." If you mean "self-actualization," say "self-actualization." If you mean "synergy," say "synergy;" of course what you probably mean is political collaboration with ulterior motives, but say "synergy."

Do this for yourself. If you have to compromise, call it "compromise;" don't call it "prudence," don't call it "sound, practical, common sense." We have to learn to call things what they are. If an idea is crazy, don't call it "interesting." If an act is treason, don't call it "a shift in priorities." If it's a death, don't call it "a casualty." If it's love, don't call it "a relationship." If a person is a pianist, don't call them a "keyboard artist." If a person's a liar, don't call him "confused." If a person's a prick, don't call him "eccentric."

You have to find the right words—especially when you are in the privacy of your own thoughts. And the right words are usually the simple words—they're the words that say what we actually mean. You can play games with your language in public, but you've got to say what you mean, mean what you say, and don't be mean when you say it.

Find the language. Find the real words. When you learn your own language, when you have the real words, then and only then can you go public. And then you do something good because people hear how you speak.

---

[17] Ibid.

From that, they can learn how you honestly think. And from that, they can know who you are. Others will know you as a leader of yourself, and most of the world appreciates that.

# NON-RULE #7: DO NOT UNDERSTAND IT

I do not mean this coyly; I really mean do not understand it, do not become so sophisticated that you avoid being puzzled. In this day and age when you think you have something figured out—especially something involving people—you are in trouble. We all need to doubt a little more—perhaps a lot more—of our own infallibility. If you do, if you begin with the assumption that you do not understand something, you'll find that most things are better that way. Retain the mystery, the necessary ambiguity. The truth is that we hardly understand anything deliberately. In fact, I think there are both a peace and a motivation to be derived from the admission and comfort, knowing that our understanding is never complete nor totally accurate.

The play and movie, *Inherit the Wind*, was about the Scopes Monkey Trial. William Jennings Bryant represented the State of Tennessee in the prosecution of John Scopes, a high school science teacher who taught evolution in his class, which was against state law. Clarence Darrow defended Scopes, and H. L. Menken was a reporter covering the trial. William Jennings Bryant could easily represent the state and prosecute Scopes because he, himself, was a creationist, a fundamentalist who believed in the absolute truth of the stories in the Bible. The verdict, as we know, came out against Darrow, against the teacher, and against the evolutionists. So, technically, Darrow and Scopes lost. However, so powerful and forceful was Darrow's intellectual argument that everyone knew they had really won.

So forceful was it, in fact, that in the play William Jennings Bryant had a stroke following the trial. In the play the reporter, H. L. Menken, a wise guy and an atheist—some would say an arrogant and intolerant atheist—went to Clarence Darrow and said, "You did it. You made mince meat out of that Bible-beating bastard!"

Where upon Darrow turned on the reporter and replied, "What could you possibly know about a man like that? What could you possibly know?"

That is the question that we should all be asking, because we cannot know. In fact, the more we learn the more we discover that we don't know. We want to avoid becoming too sophisticated to be puzzled and we should all doubt a little of our own infallibility. Do not understand it.

# LEADERSHIP DISCIPLINES

As I mentioned in this chapter's introduction, I believe that Rosenblatt's Seven Rules, or "Non-rules," are intellectual and emotional disciplines worth cultivating in order to develop the traits by which I define leadership. I don't know how you can be a faithful reporter of the truth without having the ability to be out of it, be slow, or be beside the point. I don't know how you can path-find if you don't have the ability to go to hell, distrust rational thought, or if you believe you understand it. I don't know how you make it safe for others to risk, if you don't first make it safe for yourself to risk. And I don't know how you come by the security and self-confidence to do any of these things if you don't first have strength in your personal vision and values.

The last child Rosenblatt saw when he was working on *Children of War*[18] was a fifteen-year-old boy named Khu. His parents were dead, and he had only a second grade education. He had sailed up the South China Sea on a boat commanded by a murderous captain. They had run out of food and water. They turned to cannibalism and decided to have Khu as their first victim. One night when Khu was sleeping, they pulled a cloth over his head, and the man chosen to do the killing hit Khu with a sharp instrument. But the blow did not kill him, and when they removed the cloth they discovered that he wasn't dead but that he was crying—tears were streaming down his face. They said to him, "Khu, do you want to live?" Khu, of course, said that he did, and for reasons unknown they let him live. Eventually they made it to shore and Khu went his own way winding up in a refugee camp in Hong Kong where Roger met him.

Interviewing Khu in that camp along the water in Hong Kong, Rosenblatt asked Khu if he understood what those men were trying to do to him. Khu said that he did understand what they were doing and why they did it—they were starving and were so desperate that they turned to eating one another. At which Rosenblatt asked Khu if he would have done the same thing being in their position. Khu said, "No, we go together in life in one boat. I would not kill in order to live."

Staring at the Hong Kong Island with all of its lights in the night's air, the boats in the harbor with all of their lights, and the reflection of it all in the water, Rosenblatt asked Khu:

"What do you think about when you look at Hong Kong?"

"I see lots of lights which are beautiful. And boats."

"What do you think when you see all the boats?"

---

[18] Roger Rosenblatt, *Children of War*, (New York: Doubleday, 1992), p162-167.

"The boats have lights too, which are also beautiful."

"What else is beautiful, Khu?"

"Everything is beautiful."[19]

Khu knew who he was. I know who I am. You know who you are. And it is only from here that we can begin to lead.

---

[19]   Roger Rosenblatt, *Children of War*, (New York: Doubleday, 1992), p167.

# 19

# Important Properties of the 10S Model

*I dream of a day when my children will live in a world without the shackles of cause and effect.*
**Stephen Colbert**
American comedian, satirist, actor, and writer
b. 1964

## Over the past eleven chapters

we have examined 10S Model (shown again in Figure 12) in great detail—element by element. In addition to describing each element, I have also shared the lessons I've learned and the opinions I've formed as to what makes for good practice and what makes for bad practice based on my personal and professional experience.

*Figure 12 – The 10S Model*

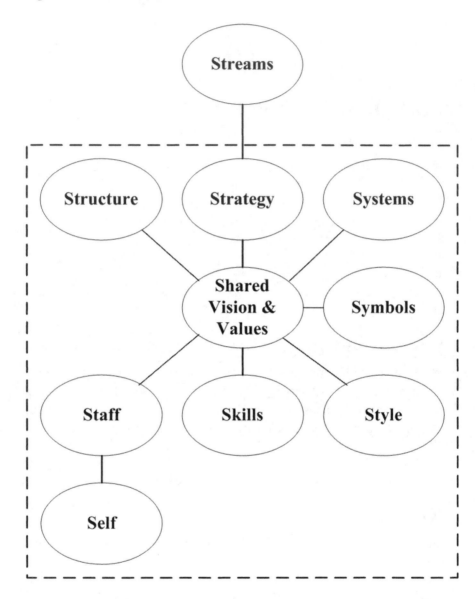

To close my discussion of the 10S Model, I'll share four properties of the 10S Model that I think make it an even more powerful tool in the Shewhart PDCA cycle of leading cultural change: it is a people model; it is an ecosystem; it is a holistic model; and it is a developmental model.

# PEOPLE MODEL

First and foremost, the 10S Model is a people paradigm--nowhere do you see land, capital, or technology. This is the kind of model you want for a social system, or culture.

# ECOSYSTEM MODEL

Second, the dotted line around the 10S Model reminds us that the organization is an ecosystem. Streams external to the organization will affect things inside the organization, and things inside your organization can also affect the streams. Where does your company really end and the outside environment really begin? It is becoming more and more the case that you can't tell. You have customers forming strategic alliances with your company. You have vendors in partnerships. You may be in an industry that involves outside regulators. And you even have cases where you collaborate with competitors.

An international love fest for GE grew under Jack Welch's leadership such that many other companies emulated some of the practices employed by GE. This is an example of the practices of one company affecting the practices of many other companies. If your organization is one within a larger one (a department within a company, for example), then those streams affecting you often arise in conversation as, "what that other department is doing to us."

So, when you are planning cultural change, or analyzing the cause and effect of a change that has occurred—whether that change originated inside or outside of your organization—you'll do well to remember that your outside walls are not impervious; they are porous.

# HOLISTIC MODEL

Third, the 10S Model is a holistic model. Although this model depicts a culture as if it were ten discreet components, remember that your culture doesn't really exist this way—we just depict it this way to make it easier to talk about. The cultural components it depicts are interdependent—if you touch one, you touch them all.

The fact that your culture is holistic, that these elements are interdependent, reminds us of the importance of alignment. In fact, one of the major reasons achieving organizational performance improvements is more difficult than it ought to be, and one of the biggest reasons why organizational change will be less successful than it ought to be, is due to alignment problems. If your vision and values promote creativity and innovation, yet your decision-making process is risk-averse, then you have an alignment problem. If your vision and values promote quality, yet the most important number on production's scorecard is meeting schedule, then you have an alignment problem. If your vision and values promote customer service, yet the most important number on your help center's scorecard measures administrative efficiency, then you have an alignment problem. If your organizational structure is a matrix (vs. hierarchical), but your management style is command and control, then you have an alignment problem.

The reward system for most sales people is called "commission," and most often it is based on sales (it could be, but usually isn't, based on profit or margin on sales, or percentage of intelligent sales). So what do we know about sales people? They sell stuff you don't make. They promise delivery schedules no one could meet. They sell a lot of customized features because bells and whistles are what the customers like and it's a lot easier stuff to sell, although it is often the more difficult stuff to engineer and manufacture. This is because they're rewarded on sales. Meanwhile, how are you measuring production? You're measuring them on yield, scrap, cost, and operating efficiency. What volume of production guarantees no scrap? As production volume approaches zero, scrap approaches zero. So you look for uninterrupted flows, minimum set up times, minimum switchovers––all of which represents products that are usually the toughest to sell.

So, you're measuring sales on things that make life tough on production, and you're measuring production on things that make life tough for sales. Ask production people what they think of sales people. How do they describe them––in terms that are flattering or derogatory? Ask sales people to describe production people. Are they flattering or derogatory?

This is an excellent example of an alignment problem. You've created different systems; they're not integrated, they're not calibrated, and everyone's banging on everyone else. Under these measurement systems, the school of hard knocks teaches them that cooperation gets them killed while hoarding information gets them rewarded—probably the exact opposite of what you say you value in your shared vision and values. You have an alignment problem.

# DEVELOPMENTAL MODEL

Finally, and perhaps most powerful of all, the 10S Model is a developmental model with a hierarchical relationship between the different levels of development: personal development, interpersonal development, managerial development, and organizational development.

# LEVEL I: PERSONAL DEVELOPMENT

The first level, which encompasses "self," as depicted in Figure 13, represents the world of personal development—developing your personal leadership, matters pertaining to your individual character and personality. This level is the sweet spot of Steven Covey's Habits 1—Be proactive, 2—Begin with the end in mind, 3—Put first things first, and 7—Sharpen the saw.

*Figure 13 – Level I: Personal Development*

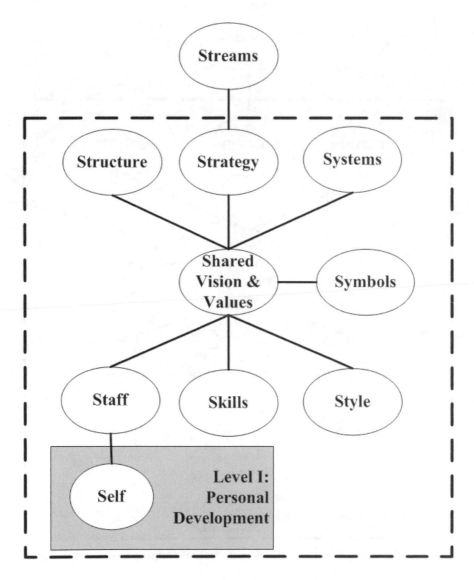

# LEVEL II: INTERPERSONAL DEVELOPMENT

The second level, which encompasses staff, self, and skills, as depicted in Figure 14, represents the world of interpersonal development. This level is the sweet spot of Stephen Covey's Habits 4—Think win/win, 5—Seek first to understand, then to be understood, 6—Synergize, and, again, Habit 7—Sharpen the saw.

*Figure 14 – Level II: Interpersonal Development*

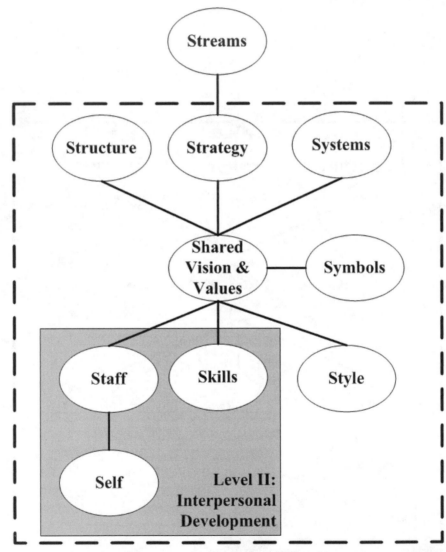

I have found that a good interpersonal relationship requires two things.

One is confidence in each other's competence, which is a function of skill. The other is trust, whose self-evident root is trustworthiness, which is a function of self. However, both are required; one without the other won't work. An individual may be the world's greatest web designer—they may be able to make your website sing—but if you can't trust them, it's no good. Conversely, another individual may be unconditionally trustworthy, but they don't know what they're doing; again, it's no good. Sound and solid working relationships require both competency and trust.

# LEVEL III: MANAGERIAL DEVELOPMENT

The third level, which encompasses skills and style, as depicted in Figure 15, represents the world of managerial development. As mentioned before, there are two fundamental management styles: command-and-control, and consensus-and-commitment. While some skills are the same, there are other skills required by a command-and-control management style that are fundamentally different than the skills required by a consensus-and-commitment management style.

*Figure 15 – Level III: Managerial Development*

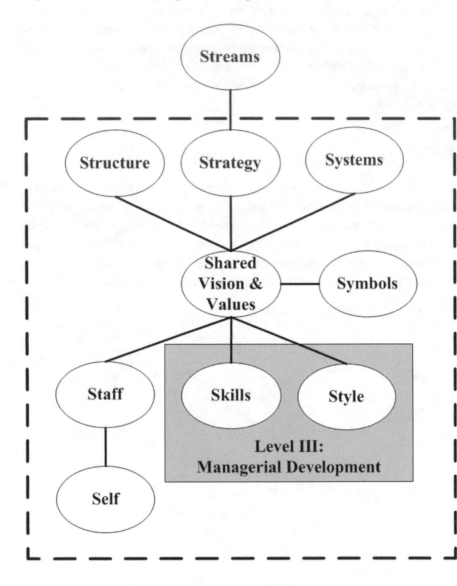

# LEVEL IV: ORGANIZATIONAL DEVELOPMENT

Finally, the fourth level, which encompasses shared vision and values, symbols, structure, strategy, and systems, as depicted in Figure 16, represents the world of organizational development.

*Figure 16 – Level IV: Organizational Development*

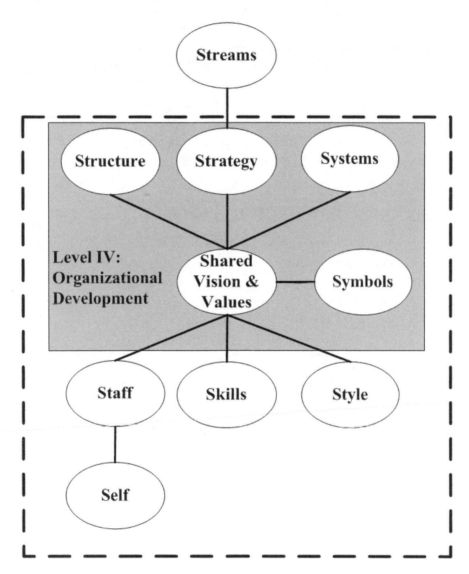

By design or default your organization has shared vision and values—better by design than by default. Unfortunately, the problem many organizations have is not that they haven't articulated some kind of shared vision and values––usually they have. The problem is that the shared vision and values that they have articulated is different from the shared vision and values that they practice–

245

–they have an organizational integrity problem. This is where symbols come in handy. Symbols tell you what the real shared vision and values are because they represent the physical manifestation of the shared vision and values that are being practiced—regardless of what might be on the bronze plaque or the laminated wallet cards. And streams, well, they are outside your control anyway.

It is self-evident that structure includes how you organize roles and re- sponsibilities, span of control, etc. Strategies represent your plans for dealing with the constantly changing streams in ways that are congruent with your essentially changeless shared vision and values. And systems represent your various manage- ment systems (e.g., decision-making systems, communication systems, systems for measuring and rewarding performance, etc.).

# HIERARCHICAL RELATIONSHIP

Now, here's the really powerful part. A hierarchical relationship exists between these four levels of development:

- You can work as hard as you want on Level IV (organizational devel- opment), but you will never be any stronger than you are on Level III (managerial development). I don't care how great your structure is, how great your strategy is, or how great your systems are, if you can't ex- ecute, it just doesn't matter.
- And you can work as hard as you want on Level III (managerial develop- ment), but you'll never be any stronger than you are on Level II (inter- personal development). I don't care how skilled you are as a manager; if your team is incompetent and/or doesn't trust each other, you're going nowhere.
- And you can work as hard as you want on Level II (interpersonal de- velopment), but you'll never be any stronger than you are on Level I (personal development). As I have mentioned earlier, healthy working relationships require individuals of character—people who are trustwor- thy—otherwise it's no good.

Therefore, when you are seeking to change an organization's culture, where should you start? You should start with you—self. Like it or not, you lead with the example of your character, and you should look to the other leaders in your organization to do the same. Then start working on teamwork, then manage- rial discipline, then structure, strategy and systems. I don't mean to imply that you work on these things serially; certainly you work on them concurrently. However, personal development must lead interpersonal development, interpersonal development must lead managerial development, and managerial development must lead organizational development.

Unfortunately, what is the first thing a denominator manager does when he or she takes over an under-performing or neglected organization? They make a token effort to get to know the people, and then they reorganize, develop a new strategic plan, tinker with the performance management system and probably cut benefits and restructure the compensation plan. Meanwhile Bill and Susan, two critical members of the organization, trust each other about as far as they can throw a grand piano, and the denominator manager can't figure out why his or her change effort is going nowhere—the environment is toxic, their change effort dies birthing.

# Part V:

# The Organizational Lifecycle

# 20

# THE RISE AND FALL

*The people will save their government,*
*if the government itself will allow them.*
**Abraham Lincoln**
Sixteenth president of the United States
1809 - 1865

# WE'VE SPENT THE PAST SEVERAL

chapters talking about organizational culture, its composition, important properties of it, and the influences on it. Now, I must add one more level of complexity, because as they move through time, cultures also go through various lifecycle stages, and their 10S elements take on different characteristics during the different lifecycle stages.

Change agent, author, and consultant, Lawrence M. Miller has done illuminating work in this area. He took the work of historians like Arnold Toynbee and Oswald Spengler, in which they chronicle the rise and fall of various civilizations, and correlated that with the rise and fall of corporations. My own experience corroborates Miller's work—it is insightful stuff—and in this and the subsequent chapters is a recap of what I learned from, combined with my own interpretation and adaptation resulting from my experience incorporating them in my career.

Previously, I introduced two curves important in understanding the life cycle of a civilization or a corporation. As illustrated again in Figure 17, the asset curve depicts the civilization's/organization's accumulation of wealth, whereas the culture curve depicts the civilization's/corporation's power to produce wealth.

*Figure 17 – The Culture and Asset Curves*

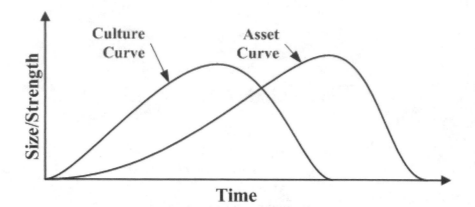

So what do "up" and "down" look like on the culture curve? Going up the curve, when the organization is growing and conquering, there is social unity and cultural energy mobilized around common purpose. It is a period of unity, cohesion, growth, conquest, and expansion. The down slope is a process of decline, disintegration and decay, families and teams fall apart, and social institutions breakdown.

During the days of the Republic, when Rome was growing and conquering, the conquered people became Roman citizens, they could serve in the senate and they paid taxes equivalent to other Roman citizens—there were feelings of affiliation. Whereas, during the days of the Empire, when Rome was in a state of decline and decay, the conquered people were subjugated and paid taxes higher than the people in Rome—there were feelings of alienation, aversion, and outright aggression.

During the days of the Empire, when Rome was in decline, it was normal for Roman citizens to go through ten marriages, as marriages often stemmed from political motives. People lost faith in their leaders, and didn't want to serve in the military or other public institutions. People lost faith in their religion. There were severe alcohol and drug abuse problems. There was excess leisure time with public monies spent on leisure related infrastructure (like stadiums) versus essential infrastructure (like roads and bridges). There were also high deficit and debt problems.

On the up-slope, the spirit is strong. On the down-slope, the spirit is weak. General George S. Patton is quoted as saying, "It is the unconquerable nature of man, and not the nature of the weapon he uses, that ensures victory." Patton also observed, "Wars may be fought with weapons, but they are won by men. It is the spirit of men who follow, and of the man who leads, that gains the victory." In effect, he was observing that every war is the same; the tools may change, but you win by defeating the soul of your enemy.

At the end of the Empire, Rome was strong in assets, but weak in spirit. They had plentiful resources; they had a well-ordered society; they had buildings, libraries, and stadiums. Their asset curve was still riding high on sheer momentum, but their culture curve had long since headed south. Conversely, the Huns had little in the way of assets, but their spirit was strong. The Romans fiddled while Huns ran through their streets, and Rome burned. The Huns conquered because every war is the same—the tools may change, but you win by defeating the soul of your enemy. A task made much easier if your enemy's culture is already weak.

As an American baby-boomer, it is natural for me to compare and contrast WWII and Vietnam (I will deliberately stay away from current geopolitical conflicts because they are too emotionally charged). In WWII, we knew why we were there and we became unified around the cause. With all of the various forms of rationing, the pain of sacrifice for the war effort was broadly shared. We knew how to define progress and victory, and our commitment to the effort was clear. In Vietnam, we debated why we were there; we were not unified around the cause. There was no rationing and, before the draft lottery, the pain of sacrifice was narrowly shared. We didn't know how to define progress and victory, and our commitment to the effort was not at all clear. There was much anxiety about the war in Vietnam, and you can't fight a war anxious.

On the other side, Ho Chi Minh (who had been our ally in WWII against the Japanese and who had hoped for our support in dealing with the French in Vietnam after WWII) told us, "You may kill ten of my men for every one I kill of yours, but it is you who will tire of it first." Ho Chi Minh understood what General Patton understood—that every war is the same; the tools may change, but you win by defeating the soul of your enemy.

I am not asserting that war and business are the same—they are not; no matter how much some testosterone, turbocharged, career warrior may claim they are; they are not. However, if you can keep them in perspective, there are many useful analogies between a civilization's culture and an organization's culture, and between conflict among countries and competition among businesses. For example, when I want to learn about the health of a company's culture, I ask people at that company who their heroes are. Cultures that are emerging, growing and conquering have heroes of the present. Cultures that are in decline and decay have heroes of the past. Why? Because a hero is someone who responds to a challenge in a new and creative way––heroes are risk takers. If you don't want to take any risks, you won't have any heroes––you may still have celebrities, but you won't have any heroes.

In business competition, too, the tools may change, but you win by defeating the soul of your competitor. What does it mean to defeat the soul of your competitor? It means staggering their confidence in their cause, in their leaders, in their strategies. It means that as you slug it out in the market place it is they who tire of it first. It means to win the battle for the hearts and minds of the customers––a task made easier if your competitor's culture is already weak. Companies on the down-slope of the culture curve, although they may be wealthier, do poorly against companies on the up-slope, although they may be less wealthy.

Toynbee observed that civilizations in decline are consistently characterized by a tendency towards standardization and uniformity––they die from suicide, not by murder. The same can be said of companies. A now-legendary example of corporate death by suicide––where their culture fell into ethical bankruptcy well before the company fell into financial bankruptcy––is Enron[1]. There is also the 2008 meltdown of the entire U.S. financial industry due to the flawed, but widespread practice of extending mortgages with high-risk terms to borrowers with sub-prime credit. And let us not forget the fall of U.S. automakers. For different reasons, and manifest in different ways, GM's, Chrysler's, and Ford's cultures began to decline and decay––their arousal to challenge, their inability to respond to the day's problems with anything more creative than yesterday's solutions, their focus turned from the ball to the scoreboard––decades before they began to lose market share.

There are even examples of business units within corporations suffering a similar fate. A case in point is Disney Animation Studios following Walt's death. In this case, it is not a matter of a culture becoming corrupt, as was the case for Enron. Rather, Disney Animation is a case of a culture losing its creative spirit, and their focus shifting to making money from making animated movies––they, too, turned their focus from the ball to the scoreboard. While Disney Animation Studios had fallen into a state of decay and decline, Pixar Animation Studios, under the creative leadership of John Lasseter, was growing and conquering. Ultimately, unable to renovate its own creative engine, Disney decided to kill off their own animation studios and enter into an agreement with Pixar. However, even this agreement came about only after the internal warfare within Disney ran its course and came to an end with Mi-

---

[1] Bethany McLean and Peter Elkind, *The Smartest Guys in the Room: The Amazing Rise and Scandalous Fall of Enron*, (New York, NY: Penguin Group, 2003).

chael Eisner's departure, as chronicled in, *Disney War*, by James B. Stewart.

So what are the lifecycle stages through which a culture can go? There are six ages: the prophet, the barbarian, the builder/explorer, the administrator, the bureaucrat, and the aristocrat.

# 21

# THE AGE OF THE PROPHET

*I only hope that we don't lose sight of one thing—*
*that it was all started by a mouse.*
**Walt Disney**
Academy Award-winning American film producer, director, screenwriter,
voice actor, animator, entrepreneur, and philanthropist
1901 – 1966

# IN THE BEGINNING IS "THE WORD;"

in the beginning is the creative act. Every culture—every civilization, religion, company, union, and organization—begins not with money, but with an idea and a person who champions that idea.

We call such people, "prophets." Prophets are never good administrators. They don't keep records or filing cabinets. They tend to wander around in the world of ideas. It is their idea, through which they channel their energy and passion, that becomes the cause—and they would die for the cause. It is the prophet and their idea that provide the rocket blast. It gives other people a reason to die. It is this energy that creates the culture, and propels them up the curve creating social unity and cultural energy mobilized around common purpose.

*Figure 18 – The Age of the Prophet*

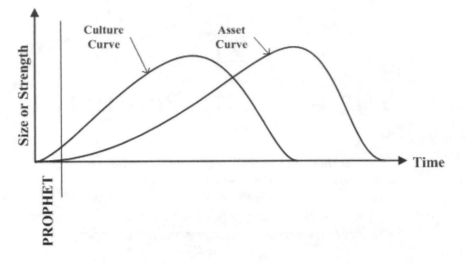

Religions have prophets. Governments and societies have prophets. For-profits and non-profits have prophets, too. Take Thomas Edison. Would you hire this guy? He went bankrupt eleven times and was a slob. He chewed tobacco and spit on the floor. His wife bought him a spittoon, but he never used it. When asked why, he explained that the spittoon was hard to hit, but the floor was not. But, he also earned over a thousand patents including the locomotive, the mimeograph machine, the phonograph, and the light bulb. So, would you hire him? Better yet, would GE hire him? He is the father of General Electric, but would they hire him today—would he be hired by that which he is the father of?

Nicola Tesla, Henry Ford, Walt Disney, Earl Bakken, Steve Jobs, and Steve Wozniak—would you hire these guys? Steve Jobs gets a lot of attention, as well he should, as he continues to rewrite the rules for whichever space in which he chooses to compete—a poster boy for numerator leaders. But his partner, Steve Wozniak, was also a real prophet. At Apple, Woz said that he didn't want to get into politics, which means he didn't want to be in management. He hadn't finished college when he and Jobs started Apple, and didn't go back to get his electrical engineering degree until after Apple was a huge success.

The point is that prophets tend to live in the world of ideas. But, you can't build a great civilization, or a great company, on ideas alone. You have to go to the next stage, and that is the Age of the Barbarian.

# 22

# THE AGE OF THE BARBARIAN

*Burn the ships!*
**Hernán Cortéz**
Spanish conquistador
1485 – 1547

# BY BARBARIAN, I DO MEAN GENGHIS

Kahn and Attila the Hun. The barbarian is a very important character; read *The Mask of Command*, by John Keegan, and you will see the personality of the barbarian.

*Figure 19 – The Age of the Barbarian*

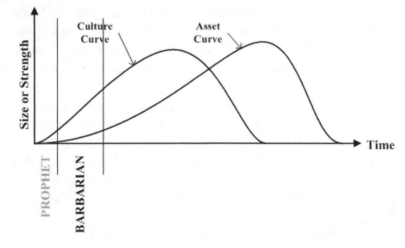

259

Barbarians are not participative managers. These are managers of crises. They are the Lord Nelson's, and the Oliver North's: "I was ordered to do what I did, and I didn't ask any questions."[1] If you are going to be in a battle or crisis, you better have people like this.

One barbarian especially worthy of note is Hernán Cortéz. Cortéz landed on the shores of Mexico in 1519 with 500 soldiers, 100 sailors, and 17 horses—600 Spaniards against 600,000 Aztecs. The Aztecs had a great empire. They had tall buildings, a specialized social structure with sixty categories of priests—one for each craft. The Aztecs were well organized. What was the first decision Cortéz made? It's one of the most important decisions in the history of the Western Hemisphere. He ordered his ships to be burned! (Where was the controller on that expedition?) This is pretty simple stuff if you're a soldier—the absence of alternatives does wonders to focus the mind––and the 600 defeated the 600,000.

My favorite historical character and favorite barbarian is Alexander the Great. In fact, I will go so far to say that if you want to understand leadership, at least in the context of Western Civilization, you must know Alexander because he created the archetype, and it is worthwhile to study the original article.

# ALEXANDER

Alexander was born in 356 BCE, the son of Prince Phillip of Macedonia, who had unified the various city-states of Greece. Alexander studied under Aristotle at the Lyceum in Greece. He was leading one of his father's legions at age sixteen. In 336 BCE, when his father was assassinated, Alexander took over his army and became Alexander III, King of Macedon. Over the next sixteen years, he had to re-unify Greece two more times, and went on to conquer most of the known world by the time he was thirty. He died in 320 BCE when wounds he suffered in battle became infected.

Alexander was a military genius and innovator. His best known exploits were in his conquest of the Persian Empire and the defeat of their leaders, first King Darius III, then Bessus, then Spitamenes—all of whom were murdered by their own men (in 330, 329, and 328 BCE respectively), in futile attempts to quell Alexander's aggression against them. In the west, we know him as Alexander "the Great." But, the name by which you know him

---

[1]  Lt. Colonel Oliver North is best known for his involvement in the Iran-Contra Affair that erupted when President Reagan and Attorney General Edwin Meese revealed that profits from secret arms sales to Iran had been diverted to Nicaraguan rebels.

depends on which end of his sword you stood. To the Persians, Alexander is known as "The Accursed Alexander," or "Alexander the Destroyer." However, because it is the victors who write history, the world knows him as "Alexander the Great."

Alexander's troops were well trained and highly disciplined. They cared deeply for him because he had demonstrated that he cared deeply for them. He would personally lead them in battle—not from a rear position, but from a position on the field, usually riding on a flank with his elite cavalry, his "companions." After a conquest, he would share the spoils of victory with his men. He also went to great lengths to incorporate some of the customs of the people he conquered. For example, traditional Greek dress consisted of a toga-like garment, whereas the Persians wore pants. Alexander introduced pants into western civilization. To promote stability in conquered regions, he would keep in place those local rulers and systems whom he trusted. After conquering the Persian capital and capturing King Darius' family, Alexander ensured that Darius' family continued to be treated as royalty; he allowed them to remain at the palace and retain their royal privileges. He also condoned marriages between Greek soldiers and women of conquered regions to promote social stability. He himself took the Persian princess Stateira, the daughter of Darius III, as one of his wives (he had two).

The Battle at Gaugamela was arguably Alexander's most impressive victory. Although the Greeks were severely out numbered by Darius and the Persians, they won the day through Alexander's innovative battle tactics, his highly trained and disciplined troops, the trust, confidence, and familiarity among Alexander's leaders, Alexander's front-line leadership, and the troops' and leaders' loyalty to and confidence in him. This battle has much to teach us and has been well chronicled. However, there are two other great battles also worthy of note because of what they teach us about Alexander's leadership. One took place on the Plains of Issus, the other at the River Granicus.

## THE PLAINS OF ISSUS

On the Plains of Issus in 333 BCE, Alexander's army faced King Darius III of Persia and his army. The 60,000 Greeks were outnumbered ten to one. As was their custom, the night before the battle Alexander's senior officers came to his tent. They ate together, drank together, sang together, and exchanged notes with each other to be given to their loved ones should they fall in battle.

When the battle began, the Greeks were so fierce in their march on

Darius that the Persian troops broke ranks and ran. In that era, this is when the killing would begin in earnest—the advancing troops would slaughter the retreating enemy. Darius was forced to flee, leaving not only the battle, but also leaving behind his wife, two daughters, his mother Sisygambis, and much of his personal treasure. After the battle, Alexander went to the tents of his wounded soldiers. He congratulated them on their victory, had them tell him the story of how they received their wounds in battle, and he prayed to their gods with them.

What is the difference between a business leader having breakfast or lunch on a regular basis with the hourly employees and Alexander going to the tents of wounded soldiers? Loyalty for the leader comes from the leader's genuine affection for and affiliation with his or her followers. Alexander showed affection and affiliation for his troops. This is not complicated stuff; it's simple stuff. It's not easy stuff, but it's not complicated.

## THE RIVER GRANICUS

If you study Alexander, you'll also learn something about theater. Alexander was a student of Aristotle, he studied at the Lyceum, he knew Greek theater; he was an orator.

In 334 BCE, the Greeks met the Persian line encamped on the opposite bank of the River Granicus. Alexander, on his horse, Bucephalus, rode up and down the river bank for several hours examining the Persian fortifications on the other bank. With the Persian soldiers watching, Alexander turned to his troops and spoke to them in groups moving down the line from one group to the next. It is estimated that he gave over fifty speeches (there are thousands of men and no electronics). He spoke of their past battles and victories, of their families, and of Greece. He would call out to his soldiers, and they would respond in an escalating crescendo. He fired them up—and not that superfical psych-up stuff that you see at most sales meetings; this was genuine—and he did it all in full view and earshot of the enemy. The Persian troops on the other bank could hear and see everything. Then, finding the strongest point in the Persian fortifications, Alexander uncharacteristically dismounted his horse and led his men in the attack. Whether due to their own fear of the now highly energized Greek troops and Alexander's unpredictable action, or due to Alexander's own boldness and personal leadership, the Persian line broke and retreated. Alexander understood theater!

Why is theater important? What is theater about? Theater is not about intellectual processes—it's not about counting, recording, and planning. Theater is about affecting the heart and the human spirit—raising those of your team and deflating those of your enemy. Every successful barbarian understands what General Patton understood: that every war is the same; the tools may change, but you win by defeating the soul of your enemy. Tell me that business competition is any different.

# GEORGE WASHINGTON, THE INDISPENSIBLE MAN

What happened to Alexander's empire upon his death? There was no empire; there was only the personality of Alexander. He had named no successor; there was no structure, no systems, no checks and balances. There was just the personality of Alexander, and upon his death, his empire began to crumble.

Which, by the way, is why George Washington is the indispensible man in America's history. It's 1783, the war had been won, and the Continental Congress owed the troops back pay, but refused to pay them. These guys had given their blood, many lost their farms and their businesses, their families were under enormous hardship, but the Continental Congress refused to pay what they had promised to pay them. Outrage grew among the troops, and there were whispers of revolt. One of Washington's colonels, Lewis Nicola, even wrote him a letter, urging him to accept the responsibility of becoming king of the United States. The whispers of revolt grew into calls for such action. Unsigned papers urging revolt began circulating at the camp at Newburgh, and Washington himself was so moved by an anonymous author's emotional description of the soldier's plight he said he felt that the "force of expression has rarely been equaled in the English language."

When Washington learned that an illegal meeting of those advocating insurrection had been called, he summoned a meeting of his own for the following Saturday, March 15, 1783. As James Thomas Flexner reports in his book, *Washington: The Indispensible Man*:

> *This was probably the most important single gathering ever held in the United States. Supposing, as seemed only too possible, Washington should fail to prevent military intervention in civil government?*
>
> *The Commander In Chief hinted that he would not appear personally, and thus when he strode on the stage, it was a*

*surprise. And the faces of his gathered officers made it clear that the surprise was not a pleasant one. For the first time since he had won the love of the army, he saw facing him resentment and anger.*

*As Washington began to speak, he was "sensibly agitated." He talked first of his own early and devoted service, of his love for his solders. The faces before him did not soften. He pointed out that the country which the anonymous exhorter wished them to tyrannize over or abandon was their own: "our wives, our children, our farms and other property." As for the exhorter's advice that they should refuse to listen to words of moderation, this would mean, "reason is of no use to us. The freedom of speech may be taken away, and, dumb and silent, we may be led, like sheep, to the slaughter." By now, the audience seemed perturbed, but the anger and resentment had not been dispelled.*

*Washington then stated that he believed the government would, "despite the slowness inherent in deliberative bodies," in the end act justly. He urged the officers not "to open the flood gates of civil discord, and deluge our rising empire in blood." They should "afford occasion for posterity to say, when speaking of the glorious example you have exhibited to mankind, 'had this day been wanting, the world had never seen the last stage of perfection to which human nature is capable of attaining.'"*

*Washington had come to the end of his prepared speech but his audience did not seem truly moved. He clearly had not achieved his end. He remembered he had brought with him a reassuring letter from a congressman. He would read it. He pulled the paper from his pocket, and then something seemed to go wrong. The General seemed confused; he stared at the paper helplessly. The officers leaned forward, their hearts contracting with anxiety. Washington pulled from his pocket something only his intimates had seen him wear: a pair of eyeglasses. "Gentlemen," he said, "you will permit me to put on my spectacles, for I have not only grown gray but almost blind in the service of my country."*

*This homely act and simple statement did what all Washington's arguments had failed to do. The hardened soldiers wept. Washington had saved the United States from tyranny and civil discord. As Jefferson was later to comment, "The moderation and virtue of a single character probably prevented this Revolution from being closed, as most others have been, by a subversion of that liberty it was intended to establish.'*[2]

Again, as we saw in Alexander, and as this vignette reveals about Washington, leadership is not about intellectual processes—it's not about counting, recording, and planning. Leadership is about affecting the heart and the human spirit. By Washington's action, the United States established itself as a nation of laws, rather than a nation of men. This is why Washington is the indispensible man in America's history, and this is the story of the transition into the next stage—the Age of Builders and Explorers.

---

[2]  James Thomas Flexner, *Washington: The Indispensible Man*, (Collectors ed. Norwalk, CT, The Easton Press, 2002), p174-175.

# 23

# THE AGE OF BUILDERS AND EXPLORERS

*That's one small step for a man, one giant leap for mankind.*
**Neil Armstrong**
U.S. Naval aviator, test pilot, astronaut, university professor,
and first man on the moon
b. 1930

## IN THE BUILDER AND EXPLORER

stage we begin to see differentiation in structure and specialization in skills.

*Figure 20 – The Age of the Builder / Explorer*

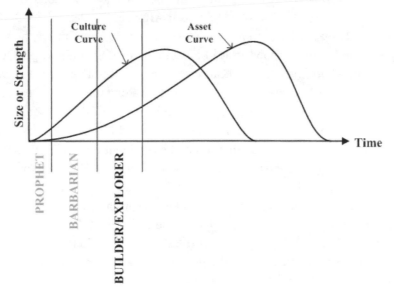

Imagine we're marching across the plains; we've been winning and conquering, and we've become weighted down with the spoils of our victories. But, we look at our army's chariots, and their wheels are beat to hell—they're more square than they are round. Consequently, our troops are exhausted before they even get into battle—except this one guy; he has the nicest, roundest wheels, but he's not so hot with a sword. So, we have him stay back and make wheels, and now our army is cruising, again, into battle.

In the blink of a historic eye, do you know what our wheel maker is going to have? He's going to have a hub department, a spoke department, and a rim department. It's the beginning of horizontal structure, and it is good because it leads to efficiency. Now he's sending out the nicest, roundest wheels like never before. As he establishes the hub department, the spoke department, and the rim department, vertical structure also emerges. Now we have junior hub makers, lead hub makers, senior hub makers, and hub maker supervisors. Pretty soon we will even have an administrative building.

With the differentiation in structure and the specialization in skills, the style of decision-making must shift from command (are you going to argue with a barbarian?) to a more participative, consensus-oriented style. If you are in the hub department, and have an idea for a new hub, you better talk to the folks in the spoke and rim departments. (By the way, when your culture descends back down the curve, the decision-making style will necessarily switch back to command because crises will become more prevalent.)

A quick story illustrating how competitive advantage is now gained by something different—by differentiation, specialization, and collaboration––can be found in the defeat of the Spanish Armada. The year is 1588. King Philip II of Spain, the last emperor of the Holy Roman Empire, appoints the duke of Medina Sedona to lead an armada to England and get Queen Elizabeth back for the Church because she'd gone Protestant, and that was a problem. The duke wrote to the king something along the lines, "Dear King, I love you, I serve you, but there are two problems that I think disqualify me from this mission: I've never been to sea before, and I have no money. Either one of these should disqualify me; surely the combination of the two does."

The king wrote back something like, "Tough luck; I said you're going, so you're going!"

The king also appointed the duke of Parma, who had a standing army in Holland, to go to England with the duke of Medina Sedona. The duke of Medina Sedona was to build the ships, sail to Holland, pick up the duke of Parma and his army, and together they were to sail to England and get the queen back for the Church.

Interestingly, King Philip II and the duke of Medina Sedona never met face to face. Nor did King Philip II and the duke of Parma ever meet face to face. Nor did the duke of Medina Sedona and the duke of Parma ever meet face to face. As you might suspect, there were some problems. For example, when the duke of Medina Sedona's armada of 150 ships arrived in Holland to pick up the duke of Parma's army, there was no harbor in which they could anchor. Perhaps if they had met and talked…

Also, there was no specialization in skills and tools. The land generals were Spain's only military leaders—there was no such thing as a "navy" at that time. The Spanish generals knew from their land battle experience that if you are going to attack fortifications, like coastal forts, then you want to be able to shoot down on those forts with heavy guns. So, they built ships with tall structures and fitted them with heavy guns.

Unfortunately, ships with tall structures can't go to windward very well, and a small but important point in history is that the winds tend to blow down in the English Channel. This means that the Spanish Armada spent most of its voyage to England sailing to windward in ships that couldn't go to windward very well. King Philip II had also given a date on which they were supposed to set sail; unfortunately, there was a northerly storm blowing that day. Sailors, who tend to be humble, would have said, "We'll wait." But the king was the Holy Roman Emperor, so he was close to God; he said, "Go!" so they went. They spent five days going just fifteen miles; they were beat to hell and hadn't gotten anywhere. This is what you get in an autocracy.

Meanwhile, up in England, things are a little different. There's a woman in charge, and Queen Elizabeth wasn't so autocratic; plus she was a much better listener. She had a friend, Francis Drake, whom she called, "My Dear Pirate," and Drake had the Queen's ear (although it is rumored that he had much more than that—because people are people, history is not all boring). Drake convinced the queen that he and his guys were experienced fighting on the sea, and knew something about what works and doesn't work out there. The queen listened, and the specialized command structure, which would later become the Royal Navy, emerged from this relationship between Drake and Queen Elizabeth. Sir Francis Drake was the first commander of the Royal Navy.

They also commissioned Sir John Hawkins, a fellow pirate and friend of Drake's, to design and build the ships. Hawkins' ships were low to the water, narrow and fast, and could go almost directly to windward. Unlike the Spanish ships, Hawkins' ships were not designed to carry an army, and they were fitted with smaller, but longer-range guns.

The British Navy fell down on the Spanish Armada. Beyond the range of the Spanish Armada's heavier, shorter-range cannons, the British fired their long-range cannons, destroyed the Spanish ships and beat it out of there (the phrase "beating it out of there" comes from beating it to windward).

Specialization of skills and differentiation in structure led to the defeat of the Spanish Armada, and it also leads to competitive advantage in a maturing market and maturing business. This is what Alfred Sloan did at General Motors to wrestle competitive advantage from Ford.

However, as you build up vertical and horizontal structure you, by necessity, also build up administrative processes. Thus, we enter the Age of the Administrator.

# 24

# THE AGE OF THE ADMINISTRATOR

*The plan is useless, but planning is essential.*
**Dwight D. Eisenhower**
Supreme commander of allied forces in Europe during WW II, first supreme
commander of NATO, and thirty-fourth president of the United States
1890 – 1969

# NOW WE NEED TO KNOW HOW

many people are working in the hub department, the spoke department, and
the rim department. We need to know their inventory balances and their
production plans. We have entered the Age of the Administrator, and this is
good—to a point—because there needs to be coordination among functions.
Now, we begin to build up the processes of administration, and we have increasing numbers of administrators.

*Figure 21 – The Age of the Administrator*

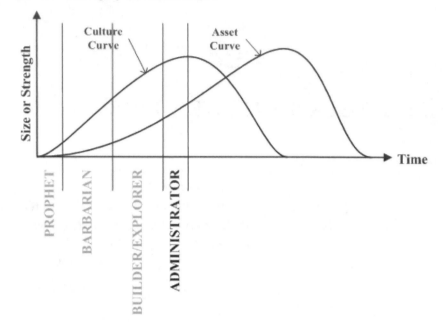

Henry Ford was a prophet in the U.S. auto industry. Later, builder/ explorer Alfred Sloan created differentiation at General Motors, and he integrated that differentiation. Meanwhile, Ford was stuck in the barbarian stage and was getting its butt kicked.

During WWII, there was a function called the "office of statistical control," or OSC, which created a miracle of administration by getting the right boots to the guys in the Pacific versus those in Northern Europe. A couple of guys at the OSC whose work was particularly worthy of note were R. J. Miller and Robert McNamara (McNamara had earned his masters degree from the Harvard Graduate School of Business Administration in 1939). In fact, their work at the OSC had earned them the nickname, "The Whiz Kids."

After WWII, McNamara and Miller decided that some company must need them, and they sold themselves as a team. Ford was a mess, and Henry Ford II bought. Miller and McNamara created order, and there was a renaissance at Ford in the 1950s.

The Whiz Kids were rightfully rewarded and promoted for their success, and with that there was a value shift. Now "real" management became counting and recording, and budgeting, and strategic planning. The budgeting guys and administrators became more powerful in the organization, and there was a power shift—administrators became the dominant decision makers. In fact, in 1960, McNamara became Ford's president—the first president of Ford who was not from the family of Henry Ford.

Unfortunately, with these shifts in values and power, also comes the point where the systems and structure become dominant to the spirit and substance of the mission that propelled the culture up the curve in the first place. Thus, we enter the next stage, the Age of the Bureaucrat, and we can see it in what occupies people's attention and conversation—the new budgeting process, the new positions, the new organization chart, the new forms, the new report, the new system, and so on.

# 25

# THE AGE OF THE BUREAUCRAT

*Whilst marching to Portugal to a position that commands the approach to Madrid and the French forces, my officers have been diligently complying with your requests that have been sent by H.M. ship from London to Lisbon and then by dispatch rider to our headquarters.*

*We have enumerated our saddles, bridles, tents and tent poles, and all manner of sundry items for which His Majesty's Government holds me accountable. I have dispatched reports on the character, wit and spleen of every officer. Each item and every farthing has been accounted for, with two regrettable exceptions for which I beg you your indulgence.*

*Unfortunately, the sum of one shilling and nine pence remains unaccounted for in one infantry battalion's petty cash and there has been a hideous confusion as to the number of jars of raspberry jam issued to one cavalry regiment during a sandstorm in western Spain. This reprehensive carelessness may be related to the pressure of circumstance since we are at war with France, a fact which may come as a bit of a surprise to you gentlemen in Whitehall.*

*This brings me to my present purpose, which is to request elucidation of my instructions from His Majesty's Government, so that I may better understand why I am dragging an army over these barren plains. I construe that perforce it must be one of two alternative duties, as given below. I shall pursue either one with the best of my ability but I cannot do both. Is it to train an army of uniformed British clerks in Spain for the benefit of the accountant and copyboys in London, or perchance, to see to it that the forces of Napoleon are driven out of Spain?*

**General Arthur Wellesley, 1st duke of Wellington in a letter to Whitehall**
British general during the Peninsular Campaign of the Napoleonic Wars, and prime minister of the United Kingdom, 1769 – 1852

The letter above was supposedly written by Wellington to Whitehall[1]

---

[1] Whitehall is a road in London that is lined with government departments and ministries; recognized as the center of HM Government, it has become a metaphor for governmental administration.

275

during the early Napoleonic Wars. I've not been able to verify this letter's authenticity, but I include it nonetheless because it wonderfully illustrates the bureaucratic lifecycle stage in which cultures find themselves when their leadership becomes lazy or complacent—when leadership is no longer aroused to challenge.

Now we have entered that stage of Toynbee's warning that civilizations in decline are consistently characterized by a tendency towards standardization and uniformity.

*Figure 22 – The Age of the Bureaucrat*

When an organization's systems and structure become dominant to the spirit and substance of the organization's mission, then that organization is in the Bureaucratic stage. If the people in your organization spend more time talking about the new budgeting process, the new organization chart, or the new performance review forms, than they do about customers, or new products or services, or current product or service problems, then you are in the bureaucratic stage.

In 53 BCE, Crassus, a moneylender and war profiteer, who had earned his command based not on his battlefield qualifications, led the Roman legions against the Scythians, a tribal people who were skilled horsemen.

The Scythians lured the Legions into an area of hot sand, and through two days of battle, the Romans, who believed they, more than any other people, had perfected the art of warfare, attempted to charge the circling cavalry. The Scythians on horseback easily evaded the Roman foot soldiers, all the while raining arrows into the Roman ranks. Twenty thousand Romans died; another 10,000 were marched into slavery. Like H.G. Wells said, "Money happened to Rome."

This is what happens in other kinds of organizations, too. Back to Ford. While values may have shifted among the company's leadership favoring budgeting and strategic planning, there were those whose loyalty remained to the mission, and they would fly "below the radar" to find ways around the bureaucratic systems and structure in an effort to remain faithful to that mission. Internally, Ford got passive resistance and corruption. What did Ford's customers get? We got the Fairmont—not Ford's best product.

Then, less than five weeks after becoming president of Ford, President-elect John F. Kennedy offered Robert McNamara the role as Secretary of Defense. During this time, the U.S. began filling the void left by France's departure in Vietnam. The Vietnam War was my generation's war, and if we could have killed those bastards with filing cabinets, we would have won that war. There was only one problem. Anytime a barbarian meets a bureaucrat on the battlefield, the battle is over before it even begins, because one is killing while the other one's counting.

Also, in the age of bureaucracy, when systems and structure are dominant, what happens to prophets and barbarians? Who crucifies prophets and barbarians? It's not other prophets or barbarians. It is the bureaucrats--the keepers of the systems and structure, the people who are threatened by the prophets and barbarians' lack of conformance to order. Well-entrenched bureaucrats will drive out the prophets and barbarians—they'll drive out the very mechanisms of creativity that propelled the culture up the curve in the first place.

Finally, we are left with the aristocrats, who look great, but who sit in command of a creativeless hulk.

# 26

# THE AGE OF THE ARISTOCRAT

*It is not because things are difficult that we do not dare;*
*it is because we do not dare that they are difficult.*

**Segoyewatha, (Red Jacket)**

Native American Seneca orator and chief of the Wolf Clan

1750 – 1830

## WE ARE NOW AT THAT POINT IN THE

life cycle where we are caught in a trap. Material wealth may be high, but the culture is low—the spirit and substance that create wealth are gone. We have reached that stage of Jared Diamond's warning:

> *One blueprint for trouble, making collapse likely, is a conflict of interest between the short-term interests of the decision-making elites and the long-term interests of society as a whole—especially if the elites are able to insulate themselves from the consequences of their action. That is, when what is good in the short run for the elites is bad in the long run for the society as a whole, there's a real risk of the elites making decisions that will bring the society down in the long term.[1]*

---

[1] TED Ideas Worth Sharing, "Jared Diamond: Why Societies Collapse," TED2003: http://www.ted.com/index.php/talks/jared_diamond_on_why_societies_collapse.html

*Figure 23 – The Age of the Aristocrat*

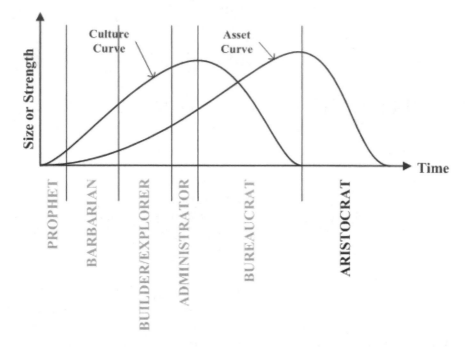

Have you ever seen one of those pictures of guys on a foxhunt? They have gorgeous horses. They have expensive muskets. They're wearing fine, red velvet jackets, polished black leather boots, and helmets. There's another guy who blows a bugle signaling that the foxhunt has begun. What's going on here? It is all a charade; it has nothing to do with reality. These guys are playing at what their great, great, great, great grandfathers did. These are tenth generation dukes and earls, and they are playing at what their ancestors did. The original duke was a big tough guy. He rode into battle on the king's flank and helped him win. After the battle, the king took him aside and said, "You look like a duke to me!" Along with the title, the king also gave the new duke a parcel of land and a buxom wench as thanks and an investment to keep him on his side. It was functionally related.

Does a barbarian go on a foxhunt? I don't think so. If a barbarian wants a fox, he'll have a fox, and he won't be yelling, "Tally Ho!" Anybody yelling, "Tally Ho!" looking for a fox, is definitely in the aristocratic stage. But now, we've got the tenth generation wimps riding around, going, "Tally Ho!" and chasing a fox around a field. In fact, they're really not even chasing a fox. They're chasing hounds who are picking up the scent from a dead fox's tail that's being dragged around by a servant. If those guys actually had to ride their horses into battle, they would be the first to be knocked off. If they actually had to hunt a fox to eat, they would starve.

And at the top of too many of our organizations, we have guys yelling, "Tally Ho!" But, if they had to personally design a product, if they had to personally manufacture a product, if they had to personally look a real customer in the eye and sell a product, they would starve. They are all wrapped up in the symbols of the past, and all they are doing is manipulating the wealth of the past, as opposed to creating new wealth.

Aristocrats lose their grounding with reality—they can lose touch with their customers' realities, they can lose touch with their employees' realities, and they can lose touch with their stockholders' realities. It is interesting to note that every revolution in human history is the result, not of revolutionaries, but of aristocrats who have lost touch. The Renaissance popes produced the Protestant Reformation because they lost touch living in their ivory tower. The American Revolutionaries wanted to be good Englishmen, but the significance of the Townsend and Tax Acts demonstrated that King George III had lost touch with what was going on in their lives. As Barbara Tuchman observes with the opening line in her book, *The March of Folly: From Troy to Viet Nam*, "A phenomenon noticeable throughout history regardless of place or period is the pursuit by governments of policies contrary to their own interests."[2]

It is the leaders who become alienated and aloof—out of touch. That is what leads to revolution; and workers can rebel, customers can rebel, and shareholders can rebel, when leaders lose touch with their realities.

---

[2]   Barbara W. Tuchman, *The March of Folly: From Troy to Viet Nam*, (New York: Alfred A. Knopf, Inc., 1984). p1

# 27

## LIFECYCLE LESSONS

*You can't build a reputation on what you are going to do.*
**Henry Ford**
American founder of the Ford Motor Company and
father of modern assembly lines used in mass production
1863 – 1947

# YOU MAY LOOK AT THIS NORMATIVE
pattern of rise and fall, and find it kind of depressing.

*Figure 24 – Culture Lifecycle Stages*

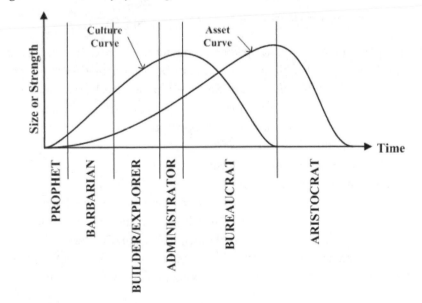

Twenty-one civilizations have gone through this waveform; what can you possibly do? One answer is just to acquiesce and stay the course; this is what I call the "fiddle while Rome burns" option. But, there's a lot to learn from history if we're open to it, and there may be another way. Perhaps, it is possible that day not be followed by night. Maybe there is a way to keep your culture from falling irrecoverably into disintegration and decay. Maybe, it is possible to break out of that wave pattern. Maybe the micro can even be a model for the macro—maybe your department can be an example for your company.

We all know companies that are 150 years old and still conquering and growing. Their leaders are sales people, or manufacturing people, or engineers. Every week they call on customers; not because they think they're better at sales than their salespeople, but to stay in touch with their customers' reality—they know better than to rely solely on reports from the field. Every week they're out on the shop floor; not because they think they're better at manufacturing than their process engineers or production operators, but to stay in touch with their employees' reality—they know better than to rely solely on reports from the floor. They have lunch regularly with hourly employees—they go to the tents of wounded soldiers. Why? To keep in touch with their stakeholders' realities.

There are two key lessons we can learn from this lifecycle analysis that will go a long way to keep us propelled up the curve.

# LIFECYCLE LESSON #1: THE SYNERGIST

It is possible to maintain that upward momentum when we understand the process that leads to health and growth and the process that leads to decay and decline. I don't care if you can find the prophet and barbarian in your organization—this is a metaphor for certain qualities.

There are the qualities of the prophet: the quality of creativity; the quality of vision; the quality of sacrifice.

There are the qualities of the barbarian: dedication, action orientation, get it done now, burn the ships.

There are the qualities of the builder/explorer: love of specialized competency, technical competence. Honda loves engineers. At Disney, the Imagineers are at the top of the cast member food chain. Companies have lost this love for technical competence. They're the Robert McNamara's and they love money. "We're in the business of making money." Wrong! You're in the business of making cars—the money will follow.

There are the qualities of the administrators. We need the ability to integrate the differentiation, the ability to coordinate functions.

We don't need bureaucrats or aristocrats—off with their heads!

My hero is the synergist. The synergist is the leader who is able to keep in balance those qualities that are on the upside of the curve. Any one person is unlikely to have all of these qualities. You may be an administrator; that's okay. What's important is that you don't have nine other administrators on your team. You'll have great plans, everything will be neat and orderly, but you'll never have a great idea or go anywhere. Imagine the sign at your neighborhood McDonald's, "Over one billion planned."

Conversely, would you really want nine H. Ross Perot barbarians on your team? I don't think you do; although it might be fun to watch.

You want to create a team that consists of a balance of those qualities of the prophet, the barbarian, the builder/explorer, and the administrator. This is the secret of the effective team, and this, I would argue, is the only metric of diversity that really matters.

# LIFECYCLE LESSON #2: SHIFT TO WINDWARD

Have you seen one of those pictures of a competitive sailboat sailing into the wind? The boat is turned at an angle to the wind. That side of the boat that is facing away from the wind, the leeward side, is low and cutting into the water, and that side of the boat that is facing the wind, the windward side, is high out of the water. To help cut a stronger angle into the wind, the boat's crew will sit on the windward side, the high side, of the boat, and lean out over the water to affect the boat's center of gravity so it can go more directly to windward.

This is the same thing you want to do with your leadership team. Different qualities are needed at different times depending on where your culture is in the lifecycle. If your organization is weighted more toward the bureaucrat and administrator, the more you need the creativity of the prophet and the action orientation of the barbarian. If you're weighted more toward the prophet and barbarian, then maybe you need to play out the Drake and Hawkins story, or get yourself some Whiz Kid administrators. You never need bureaucrats or aristocrats; they should be purged. The further your culture is to one side, the more you need the qualities on the other side—shift your team composition to windward.

Look at Chrysler; they've tasted bankruptcy twice during my lifetime.

The first was in 1978. Their stock was in the neighborhood of two dollars per share. Lee Iacocca left Ford to take command of Chrysler in 1978 when they were on the mat taking an eight count. Who was Lee Iacocca? I'd say he was a prophet/barbarian. Iacocca brought his vision of the minivan to Chrysler, a concept on which Ford had passed. And, he said his early ad campaign was as much to restore faith inside the company as out—if a team doesn't think it can win, guess what, it can't win. This is what prophets do. Yet in his first year, he fired thirty-three out of thirty-six vice presidents—sounds barbarian to me. And, in the 1980s, there was resurgence at Chrysler.

The second was in 2009. In 2007, the private equity group, Cerberus Capital Management, bought Chrysler from Daimler Benz for about $7.4 billion, about one-fifth of the $37 billion that Daimler paid in 1998. They ended up in bankruptcy, closing facilities, including 800 dealers, and negotiating a deal with Italian automaker Fiat to acquire them in order to qualify for any further assistance from the U.S. government. Having let their sails luft in the wind while they were passed by their competition, these ships' officers ended up throwing crew and assets overboard to reduce their weight in hopes of picking up speed and being more maneuverable. Denominator managers usually have only one play in their playbook—reduce costs—and that's the only play they know how to run.

The lack of market wind is a problem for every ship. Every culture continually experiences challenge that requires a creative response. And each creative response does not lead to a condition of ease, but to a higher order challenge requiring a new and creative response. And, up the staircase of growth and development they go, until their leaders become seduced by a condition of ease, become complacent, lose their creativity, and begin responding to the day's new challenge with yesterday's response. Then, down the staircase of decline and decay they go. Moneylenders, like Carassus and Cerberus, prepare for challenging times differently than barbarians, like Nelson or Iacocca. Moneylenders prepare their people for surrender and sale. Barbarians prepare their people for new ways of battle and competition, because every barbarian knows that while the tools of war may change, victory depends more on the strength of their soul than the strength of their balance sheet.

# PART VI:

# INTEGRATING METAPHORS

# 28

# E = Q X A

*The best moral decision is generally also the best business decision.*
**Earl Bakken**
American businessman and philanthropist, creator of the first wearable pace-
maker, and co-founder of Medtronic
b. 1924

## TOO MANY LEADERS TODAY ARE

smart enough to win every argument; not enough are smart enough to know that
they shouldn't. I give you the equation, E = Q x A, where:

- "E" represents effectiveness.
- "Q" represents quality. For example, did I get it at the least cost? Did I
  produce it with the least scrap, or the fastest cycle time? Did I achieve
  the best ROI? If you grew up with a math, science, or engineering background, or, God help you, you have an MBA, then you may think I've
  defined "E" twice. You may see no difference between E and Q, but there
  is; it's "A," and that's the power of this formula.
- "A" represents acceptance.
- The multiplication sign is there to remind us that anything times zero is
  zero.

Here's an example. What is the value of a brilliant idea that comes out
of headquarters that everyone else is going to hate, oppose, and subvert? The
formula would say high Q, but low A, so forget it—it won't yield much effectiveness. Here's another example. On a scale of one to ten, one solution to a problem

has a Q of eight, but an A of two, thus producing an effectiveness value of sixteen. Meanwhile, another solution to the same problem has a less rigorous, yet still respectable Q of six, but a higher, yet still modest, A of five, thus producing an effectiveness value of thirty. To which solution approach should you give your energy first? This is a little deeper than it looks.

Quality, Q, depends on facts. If you have enough facts, you can always come up with a high quality solution. If you were to analyze the professional schools (e.g., law school, medical school, engineering school, business school, etc.), just about every course in their curriculum is about getting, interpreting, validating, and manipulating facts. That's okay because there are problems in this world that are high Q problems. Problems in your organization's technical systems are typically high Q problems—they're quantitative, linear thinking problems. Take sourcing. It's not trivial. Items have to meet your specs, you've got to get a good delivery schedule, a good price, good terms, but it's not a high A problem. You can use high Q methodologies to solve these problems. You get purchasing algorithms, lists of approved vendors, bid specs, reverse auctions, and so on—no problem.

But a lot of problems in this world are high acceptance, high A, problems. Problems in your organization's social system are high A problems—they're qualitative, non-linear thinking problems. The trouble is that it is very hard to gain acceptance by throwing facts at people. Quality depends mostly on facts, whereas acceptance depends mostly on feelings. Here's a real important lesson: never argue with a person's feelings. I once endured a four-hour lecture on gestalt psychotherapy; the only useful thing I remember from that ordeal is this, "To confront irrationality with rationality will only serve to exacerbate the irrationality." In other words, never throw facts at feelings. However, we like to try; and by "we" I mean two kinds of "we."

One "we" is "we corporate people." Corporations love quality fact stuff. You've got a good boss who says, "I'm wide open. You show me the data where I'm wrong, and I'll change my decision." But if you say, "Boss, I've got a hunch; I've got a feeling that this is the wrong way to go." Your boss will start to wonder what you're talking about, maybe even suspect you of being an astrology nut. So facts are okay for fair fighting in the corporation, but that is not yet the case for feelings.

The other "we" is "we men." I don't think it is any secret that just about every form of empirical and anecdotal data tells us that women are more comfortable using feelings to make decisions than are men. Since men aren't comfortable with it, we deride it and give it cute little names like, "woman's intuition," so we don't have to deal with it. This is true both at work and home.

A husband says to his wife, "Let's go to a movie."

She says, "I'm not in the mood."

"Michael Clayton is showing."

"I know, but I'm not in the mood."

"It was nominated for seven Academy Awards."

"I know."

"Rebecca and Brian saw it. Jess and Josh saw it. They all loved it." (He's going through his facts.)

"I know."

"There's a four dollar special at the mall until 5:00."

"I know."

"Why don't you want to go?"

"I'm not in the mood."

"But give me a reason!"

She gave you a reason; she's not in the mood. But the man thinks that if you don't have a reason to be in that mood, then you shouldn't be in that mood.

Kids of both genders are also very good at using feelings in decision-making until adults help them outgrow it.

A father is putting his child to bed, "Good night; sleep tight."

The child asks, "Please leave the light on."

"Why?"

"I'm afraid of the boogeyman."

The father proceeds to cite twelve true facts, all debunking the myth of the boogeyman. The child listens politely, and at the end says, "Please leave the light on!"

It's very hard to change people's feelings by throwing facts at them, and you just shouldn't do it. If you do, it most often only serves to more solidly entrench them in their feelings. If you've ever trained a dog, you learn that you do not teach a dog to sit by pushing its rump down. When you do that, the dog actually stiffens its legs in resistance. In effect, you are teaching the dog to stand when you give the command to sit. When it comes to feelings, people are much the same.

Leading organizational change is a high-A challenge, and participation is the best way I know to build A. The same idea that people will hate and oppose, if it is stuffed down their throats from above, they will fight to the death defending if they consider it "theirs." However, there is nothing about participation that protects Q. Think of the U.S. president in your voting lifetime who is least impressive to you. That idiot got in under our high-A form of government. On the other hand, nothing about participation prevents Q, either. Think of the most impressive

U.S. president during your voting lifetime. That genius also got in. So, if you run a highly participative initiative, just understand that the Q may vary. And while you may take a more participative approach in order to optimize A, take care not to over-romanticize teams. Teams can do some real stupid stuff, and the trouble with stupid stuff produced by teams is that they like it. That said, I don't worry about high-Q decisions in most corporations because high-Q is most corporations' sweet spot—they never let the Q slip too far. Total quality, continuous improvement, fast cycle time—these are all high-Q initiatives. It's easy to sell high-Q stuff in corporations. The stuff that's hard to sell in corporations is the high-A stuff.

Here's the point: in a multiplicative relationship it always pays to work the side of the street that's low. Imagine a solution where the Q is high, but the A is low. As Q goes up by one, E goes up by one—you're making only additive improvements. There's nothing wrong with that, but if you could spend the same time, money, and cultural energy on A and were able to raise it by one, look what happens to E. When you work the low side of a multiplicative relationship, you get geometric payoffs. This is why I contend that in organizations where you have strong protection for Q you should risk the Q and focus on the A.

Unfortunately, because Q can vary under A, and because A neither protects nor prevents Q, leaders will become frustrated with highly participative methods. Weak leaders who become frustrated will abandon the participative approach and rush to the comfort of autocracy to ensure they get the high-Q they're seeking—at the expense of A and thus E. The strong leader, however, understands that he or she needs both the Q and the A. Unfortunately, getting both requires more strength of leadership than many people in leadership positions possess.

In medicine, can you think of a low-Q/high-A methodology? Some doctors hate it because it works when it shouldn't: placebos—sugar pills. And it's not just the psychosomatic stuff. You can give people sugar pills, and if they believe strongly enough in their curative powers, you will see warts fall off of their faces; peptic ulcers will begin to heal, and you can track the progress with x-rays. In fact, I understand that there are some illnesses where the efficacy of the placebo is essentially the same as that for the treatment that is considered standard of care. How important is a physician's bedside manner in the treatment process? We know that there is a strong correlation between the patient's spirit and the success of the treatment. Some medical schools now teach high-A stuff like bedside manner and forms of holistic medicine.

I'm not saying that A is better than Q. I'm just saying that in a multiplicative relationship there's always more leverage in working the low side of that relationship; and in most organizations that is often the A side.

Another way to think of it is to look at Q like it is the production function and A like it is the marketing function. Organizations will spend months and sometimes years building high-Q solutions, but won't invest even three percent of that on marketing it internally. I offer most SAP[1] implementations as evidence of my point. We say we want to treat anyone who depends on our work to do theirs as our customer, but if they're an internal customer they are more often the victim of customer neglect and even abuse than they are the beneficiaries of good customer service. We know how to market to external customers. Why don't we have an analogous commitment and employ similar methodologies for marketing to internal customers? The only reason I can think of is that you don't care about A. But if you are buying any of what I've been sharing, and you still don't care about A, then you're probably a manipulator.

Here's one last observation. If you look at a good mission statement, you'll find that it gives equal attention to both Q and A. Now go look at your measures, and I'll bet you'll find that your Q stuff is carefully measured, while your A stuff is given token attention. And if you look at your rewards, I'll bet your A stuff gets no attention at all.

---

[1] Founded in 1972 by five former IBM employees, and headquartered in Waldorf, Germany, SAP AG is the world's largest business software company and the third largest software supplier overall. Their SAP R/3 software has been adopted by many companies as their enterprise resource planning(ERP) system, and the track record of implementation borders on legendary—stunning successes and stunning failures. In my opinion, those organizations that understand that purpose comes before process, and that process comes before tools and technology, those organizations that take a benefits based approach to ERP, have more often realized success. Whereas those companies where the implementation of SAP has been treated as an IT project, have more often been less successful than they hoped. There is an age-old adage in IT about projects the caliber of most SAP implementations; it says that if a project is estimated to cost $X, be completed in Y months, and produce Z results, it will actually cost $3X, take 2Y months, and produce ½Z results. Based on my personal experience, and what I remember reading in the trade literature, just about all SAP implementations—including those which are touted as successful—have cost more, taken longer and fallen short of the benefit expectations than those upon which the project was justified.

# 29

# CULTURAL FORCE FIELD MODEL

*Do what you can, with what you have, where you are.*
**Theodore Roosevelt**
Twenty-sixth president of the United States
1858 – 1919

# I WAS INTRODUCED TO THE CUL-

tural Force Field Model at Stephen Covey's Advanced Leadership Seminar[1]; he attributed it to Kurt Lewin[2]. Figure 25 depicts your organization in its current state, along with some desired future state to which you seek to lead it. The reason your organization's current state is where it is, is because there is equilibrium between those forces that are driving change, and those forces that are restraining change.

---

[1] Stephen R. Covey, "Advanced Leadership," (Seminar, Stephen R Covey & Associates, Sundance, UT, Sep. 1988).
[2] Kurt Lewin was a German-born psychologist, and is one of the modern pioneers of social, organizational, and applied psychology. Lewin is often recognized as the "founder of social psychology" and was one of the first researchers to study group dynamics and organizational development.

*Figure 25 – Organizational Force Field: Starting State*

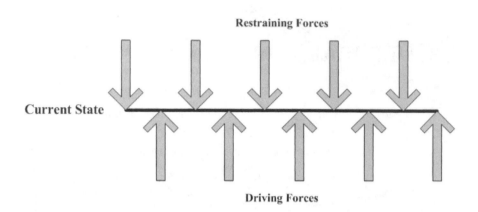

**Desired State**

Restraining Forces

**Current State**

Driving Forces

If you are leading organizational change, to which should you give your energy first: driving forces or restraining forces? Here's a hint: if you are driving your car with one foot on the accelerator and the other foot on the brake, and you want to go faster, which foot should you move first? The obvious answer is that you should first take your foot off of the brake. The same but not as obvious answer when leading organizational change is that you should give your energy first to the restraining forces. Unfortunately, the natural tendency is to simply pile on the driving forces. Rarely are efforts made to deal with the restraining forces at anything more than a superficial level—that would be a lot of work, while adding driving forces is relatively easy.

This model becomes even more interesting when you put it in the context of the equation presented in the previous section, $E = Q \times A$. Driving forces are generally high Q, quantitative in nature; whereas restraining forces are generally high A, qualitative in nature. Put another way, just as intellect drives an organization's technical system so does intellect fuel the driving forces. Similarly, just as emotion drives an organization's social system, so does emotion fuel the restraining forces.

What happens if you neglect the restraining forces and give your energy to the driving forces—can you still affect change? Certainly, but it won't be enduring change; it will be quite temporary. This is because the restraining forces don't go away. As depicted in Figure 26, you can add driving forces, and you will move your current state toward your desired state; but the restraining forces will only compress like springs.

*Figure 26 – Organizational Force Field: Adding Driving Forces*

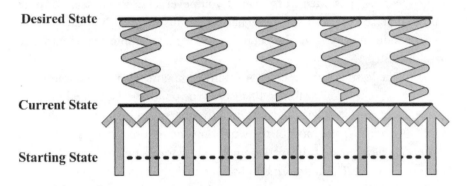

The problem is that unexpressed feelings never die; they only rise up again in uglier, unpredictable ways. In other words, as shown in Figure 27, those restraining forces that have coiled up like springs eventually let loose their compressed energy and propel your current state backwards. In fact, depending on the cultural damage done by ramming the change down people's throats, the compressed energy stored in those restraining forces can often be strong enough to blow your driving forces out of the water and hurl your current state past its original starting point.

*Figure 27 – Organizational Force Field: Restraining Forces Recoil*

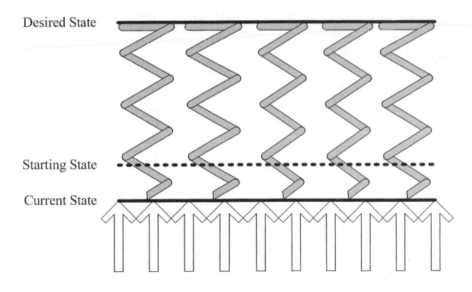

For example, consider your own relationship with someone whom you trust when you learn that they have broken that trust. The devastation to the relationship is often worse than if you never felt a strong sense of trust with that person in the first place. That act of mistrust will hurl the state of your relationship right past the neutral state of no trust into the unworkable state of mistrust.

The lesson of this metaphor is fairly straightforward: give your energies first to the restraining forces. I'll also warn you, however, that you'll need to be patient with it. It will take time, and to others it will look like you're not doing anything. While most of the work on driving forces occurs above soil and in full view, most of the work on restraining forces takes place below soil and out of view. The uninformed observer will see nothing growing above ground and will conclude that you are not driving the change. Persist. You are preparing the soil so your seeds of change can develop a strong root structure; this way the plant that does emerge will be strong and durable.

# PART VII:

# ORGANIZATIONAL TACKING

# 30

# CHARTING YOUR COURSE

*The reasonable man adapts himself to the world;*
*the unreasonable one persists in trying to adapt the world to himself. There-*
*fore, all progress depends on the unreasonable man.*
**George Bernard Shaw**
Irish playwright
1856 – 1950

# YOU CAN'T SAIL DIRECTLY INTO THE

wind. You sail into the wind using a zigzag pattern that involves a nautical process known as "tacking;" tacking is how you sail into the wind. "Tack" is the alignment of a ship with respect to the wind when moving upwind: that is, when the ship's bow is pointed within 90° of the wind. If the wind is to starboard, the ship is on "starboard tack," and if to port, on "port tack." Tacking, or coming about, is the maneuver by which a ship turns its bow through the wind so that the wind changes from one side to the other. For example, if a ship is sailing on a starboard tack (with the wind to starboard) and tacks, it will end up on a port tack, with the wind to port. The better performing your ship and crew, the more directly you can sail into the wind.

When leading an organization, you can't sail directly into the wind, either. Organizational change requires organizational tacking and, the higher performing the organization and the people, the more directly you can sail into the wind. In this and the next two chapters, I share key lessons I've learned, and opinions I've formed about organizational tacking.

## PURPOSE BEFORE PROCESS

At Stephen Covey's Advanced Leadership seminar[1], Blaine Lee, author of *The Power Principle: Influence with Honor*, told a story about a group of teenage boys who skipped school one day to go for a joy ride in a buddy's new muscle car. They took the car out to the country roads so they could "open 'er up." After putting her through her paces, they pulled over by a field to have a few beers. While drinking and joking, they noticed a farmer on a tractor plowing the nearby field. As teenage boys with a couple of beers under their belt will do, they started mocking the farmer, trash-talking his tractor and challenging him to a race with their muscle car. The farmer's plowing pattern brought him close to where the boys were parked, and he couldn't miss the fact that they were clearly enjoying themselves at his expense. However, the farmer, having been young once and being a good sport, pulled his tractor over by the boys and got out of the cab to chat with them.

At first, the boys continued to mock the farmer and his tractor. The farmer admitted that his tractor was built for purposeful work, not speed. But, having a natural interest in all things with an internal combustion engine, he also admired the boy's vehicle and began asking poignant questions about it––questions which not only showed his mechanical prowess but also exhausted theirs. He earned their respect. The boys offered him a beer and they continued their guy-talk.

After a few minutes, the farmer challenged the boys, "I noticed you boys were able to really wind it up on the road. But, do you think you could handle my tractor and plow a row?" Being teenage boys, there was no question in their mind. Reminding the boys that the object was to plow straight rows, not to go fast, the farmer asked them who wanted to try it first. One boy quickly volunteered because he had been watching the farmer as he plowed and noticed that he always kept one of his rear tires in a previously plowed furrow, so he had it figured out. The farmer brought the boys over to the tractor and had the young volunteer climb into the cab. He reminded the boy that it was a manual transmission and tugged at the boy's masculinity by asking him if he knew how to drive a stick. The boy assured him with the air of teenage cockiness one would expect, and the farmer said, "Alright, then your job is to plow this next row. Remember, the furrows need to be straight—parallel with the ones I just plowed."

The boy started off with only a minor jerk as he got used to the trac-

---

[1]  Stephen R. Covey, "Advanced Leadership," (Seminar, Stephen R Covey & Associates, Sundance, UT, Sep. 1988).

tor's clutch and transmission. Off to a proud start, the boy turned around and began watching the one rear wheel to make sure that it stayed in the previously plowed furrow next to him, thus ensuring that the furrow he was plowing would be parallel to it. However, in trying to maintain a steady forward speed while watching the rear wheel, and steering so as to keep that rear wheel in the adjacent plowed furrow, the boy quickly began to over-steer the tractor, making excessive corrections as he tried to keep that rear wheel in the adjacent plowed furrow. With the boy's over-corrections, the tractor's much smaller front tire soon got rutted and stuck. The more the boy over-corrected, the worse the front tire dug in. The boy even stopped and went into reverse to straighten himself out, only to repeat his process and get his front tire dug in once again. Watching the boy's frustration, the farmer was already walking toward the tractor when the boy finally gave up, shut off the engine and climbed out of the cab.

"How'd it go?" the farmer asked with a deserved hint of sarcasm. The boy answered with just a glare: half anger, half embarrassment. So, the farmer asked him how he went about plowing, and the boy answered by telling the farmer that he had been watching him plow and noticed that he always kept one rear wheel in the adjacent furrow. He just tried to do the same and argued that the farmer just had more practice than he—that is the reason he failed, lack of sufficient practice.

"That's a mistake that a lot of beginners make," shared the farmer. "But you never steer by looking behind you. The fact that my rear wheel would track in the furrow I just plowed was an effect, not the cause, of me going straight."

"So, what's the secret, what's the trick?"

"The 'trick,'" the farmer said, "is to pick out a point far in the distance in front of you and focus on it. It will draw you straight towards it. You steer by that, not by watching what's going on behind you."

The same is true in most other things—including leading organizational change. Pick out a point, far in the distance in front of you, focus on it, and it will draw you straight towards it. Your vision, your purpose, your goal, your desired state—steer by that. Keeping your rear wheel in the adjacent furrow is an affect of that process, and steering by a process' affect only leads to over-steering, confusion, frustration, and failure.

Put purpose before process in everything you do. What and how you do something is of little importance until you know why you're doing it. Whether it is organizational change effort on a grand scale, or a small project, the first thing you should do is get clear about why you would do it at all (i.e., the benefits). Before you even ask about <u>how</u> you would do it (e.g., cost and schedule), get clear about <u>why</u> you would want to do it. Too many efforts begin by skipping or short-circuiting that first step in a rush to get to the second. Know how the work you are contemplating contributes to your mission or advances a strategy, because if you can't get clear about that, there's no sense planning and conducting the work. If you can be clear about its purpose, you'll have a shot at being successful, even if it turns out that the work will be tough and ugly. However, if you can't be clear about your purpose, your fate is certain failure.

My experience is that if people want something to work, they'll figure out ways to make it work; and if people don't want something to work, they'll figure out ways to make it not work. People can put up with just about any "what" as long as they understand the "why."

Just like purpose comes before process, just like you shouldn't start re-engineering a process until you're crystal clear as to the larger purpose to be accomplished, so should process come before tools. Too often I have seen people and teams select a software package or other solution before they have addressed the process(es) they seek to automate. Your worry meter ought to sound an emergency alarm any time you see a solution looking for a problem. Here is the three-step approach that I use to get from process to tools: first, simplify; then standardize; then systematize.

A way you can tell if people have this sequence straight is by listening to their language. I know many companies who have implemented SAP. For most, they talked about their SAP implementation project (i.e., it was about the technology, or tool). A few talked about their process re-engineering project (i.e., it is the biggest process re-engineering effort ever attempted). I am aware of no SAP implementation project where the people talked about their "improving-inventory-turns-by-two project," or their "cut-days-sales-outstanding-in-half project" (i.e., the project's purpose).

A key to successful organizational change at any level is to put purpose before process, and process before tools or technology. Of course, in all things, put leadership before management.

# 14 POINTS

Although many people have long since dismissed W. Edwards Deming's book, *Out of the Crises*, as a faded fad, I believe that his fourteen points provide valuable insight and coaching for leading a change effort and transforming an organization. No, it's not a trendy new bestseller; the book was popular in the 1980s, and in truth, Deming's fourteen points date back to WWII. However, they still ring true.

> ***Origin of the 14 points.*** *The fourteen points are the basis for transformation of American industry. It will not suffice merely to solve problems, big or little. Adoption and action on the fourteen points are a signal that the management intends to stay in business and aim to protect investors and jobs. Such a system formed the basis for lessons for top management in Japan in 1950 and in subsequent years.*
>
> *The fourteen points apply anywhere, to small organizations as well as to large ones, to the service industry as well as to manufacturing. They apply to a division within a company.*

1. *Create constancy of purpose toward improvement of product and service, with the aim to become competitive and to stay in business, and to provide jobs.*
2. *Adopt the new philosophy. We are in a new economic age. Western management must awaken to the challenge, must learn their responsibilities and take on leadership for change.*
3. *Cease dependence on inspection to achieve quality. Eliminate the need for inspection on a mass basis by building quality into the product in the first place.*
4. *End the practice of awarding business on the basis of price tag. Instead, minimize total cost. Move toward a single supplier for any one item, on a long-term relationship of loyalty and trust.*
5. *Improve constantly and forever the system of production and service, to improve quality and productivity and thus constantly decrease costs.*
6. *Institute training on the job.*
7. *Institute leadership. The aim of supervision should be to help people and machines and gadgets to do a better job. Supervision of management is in need of an overhaul, as well as supervision of production workers.*
8. *Drive out fear, so that everyone may work effectively for the company.*
9. *Break down barriers between departments. People in research,*

> *design, sales, and production must work as a team, to foresee problems of production and in use that may be encountered with the product or service.*
>
> 10. *Eliminate slogans, exhortations, and targets for the workforce, asking for zero defects and new levels of productivity. Such exhortations only create adversarial relationships, as the bulk of the causes of low-quality and low-productivity belong to the system and thus lie beyond the power of the workforce.*
>
> 11. *A) Eliminate work standards (quotas) on the factory floor. Substitute leadership. B) Eliminate management by objective. Eliminate management by numbers, numerical goals. Substitute leadership.*
>
> 12. *Remove barriers that rob the worker of his right to pride of workmanship. The responsibility of supervisors must be changed from sheer numbers to quality. B) Remove barriers that rob people in management and in engineering of their right to pride of workmanship. This means, inter alia, abolishment of the annual or merit rating and of management by objective.*
>
> 13. *Institute a vigorous program of education and self-improvement.*
>
> 14. *Put everybody in the company to work to accomplish the transformation. The transformation is everyone's job.[2]*

## BEGIN IN THE CURRENT STATE

Every organizational change effort begins by employing the cultural norms of the current state, not those of the desired state. This is arguably counterintuitive; after all, we are taught to lead by example. However, leadership by example is effective only if those being taught will understand and properly interpret the new behavior. My experience with organizational change—especially in those organizations where the people working there have not worked anywhere else—is that they will not understand your new behavior. It will be foreign to them. It will raise suspicion and breed speculation and cynicism. It would be like trying to plant pineapple trees in the arctic—the soil and climate are just not conducive to the crop you seek.

Let's say that command-and-control is currently the dominant man-

---

2   W. Edwards Deming, *Out of Crisis*, (Cambridge: Massachusetts Institute of Technology, Center for Advanced Engineering Study, 1990) pgs 23-24.

agement style of your organization, and you have concluded that your competitive posture would be improved if you adopted a consensus-and-commitment style. Should you immediately try leading by example and begin employing a consensus-and-commitment management style? You should not. It will be foreign and unfamiliar to your people. They won't know who you are. They will wonder what is wrong with you. They will be confused by it. They will be suspicious of it and wonder what you are up to, perhaps even ascribe some dubious motive. You are better advised to continue to use a command and control style and ease your subordinates into consensus-and-commitment.

Put another way, if I speak English and you speak French, and I want to convince you that English is the better language, in which language should I make my argument?

## ORGANIZATIONS ARE NOT HOMOGENOUS

Just as a sea is not a homogenous body of water, but behaves differently depending on the coastline, the weather above and the currents and conveyors below, organizations arc also not a homogenous culture. Organizations are more like a mosaic than a melting pot. The number of subcultures in your organization—the number of tiles in your mosaic—is a function of the organization's dimensions: its breadth, depth, history, function, power structure, and so on. It is possible to have a company that, on the whole, could be fairly characterized as being in the aristocratic life-cycle stage. Yet, within that company you'll be able to find an organization of prophets and barbarians, and another organization of builders and explorers. However, because the prophets, barbarians, builders and explorers do not have critical mass in either numbers or political sway, the bureaucrats and aristocrats will still dominate the company, and those bureaucrats and aristocrats will view the prophets, barbarians, and builders and explorers as a threat, perhaps a cancer. As a result, if they don't leave, self-preservation will drive the prophets, barbarians, and builders and explorers underground—they may go into passive resistance mode, or even practice active resistance below the radar.

Bureaucrats and aristocrats are motivated by the manipulation of wealth rather than the creation of wealth—their motivations are mercenary-like. Meanwhile prophets, barbarians, builders and explorers are motivated by the organization's mission (which they rightly or wrongly may feel that the bureaucrats and aristocrats have hijacked or abandoned), and/or the principles of their profession—their motivations will appear to bureaucrats and aristocrats as revolutionary-like.

Because organizations are not homogenous, because they are a mosaic of cultures, a one-size-fits-all approach to cultural change will not work. The restraining forces will differ among subcultures, thus the prescription for relieving them must necessarily differ as well. Your 10S analysis of each subculture's current state will reveal different results, thus the adjusting action you take must necessarily differ as well.

The fact that organizations are not homogenous and are more like mosaics is one of the chief reasons why the difficulty in leading organizational change increases exponentially as the dimensions of the organization increases. As such, the strength of leadership such organizational change efforts require can often out-strip the leadership capability of the leader and/or leadership team—at which point frustration will set in, and they may even give up and return to the cultural habits of the past, taking comfort in their familiarity.

## CHANGE VS. CONFUSION

In every organizational change effort in which I have been involved, it was inevitable to hear someone remark, "People hate change." Yup, people hate change; humans are built to avoid anxiety and change puts people in a position where they cannot. Yet, it is my experience that people can put up with a lot more change than we give them credit for. What people can't tolerate, however, is confusion.

People can put up with just about any "what," as long as they understand the "why." There is a monumental difference between a journey being hard, and being lost.

## TRIAGE FOR ORGANIZATIONAL PERFORMANCE

Triage is a medical process of prioritizing patients based on the severity of their condition; the term comes from the French verb *trier*, meaning to separate, sort, sift, or select. Triage originated and was first formalized in WWI by French doctors treating the battlefield wounded at the aid stations behind the front. Those responsible for the removal of the wounded from a battlefield, or for their care afterwards, have always divided patients into three basic categories: 1) Those who are likely to live, regardless of what care they receive; 2) Those who are likely to die, regardless of what care they receive; and 3) Those for whom immediate care might make a positive difference in their outcome. The order in which patients receive treatment is: three, one, two.

In doing triage on organizational performance problems, I begin by diagnosing the problem. Is it a premise problem, a process problem, a technology problem, or a people problem? A premise problem is one where the underlying assumptions are wrong. A process problem is one where the process is flawed. A technology problem is one where some technological component, such as an information system, is not operating correctly. If my analysis leads me to believe that the problem is a people problem, then I refer to Covey's habit model (as presented in an earlier chapter and shown again in Figure 28) to determine if it is a knowledge problem, a skills problem, or an attitude problem.

*Figure 28 – Covey Habit Model*

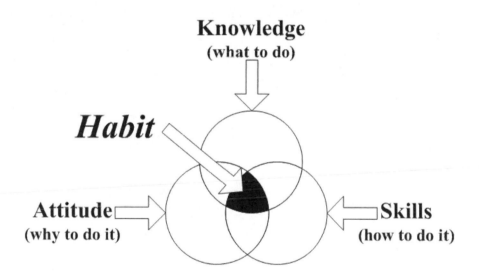

Source: Stephen R. Covey. *The 7 Habits of Highly Effective People* (New York: Simon and Schuster, 1989), p48

Education or training can resolve a knowledge or skill problem; education or training do nothing for an attitude problem. Attitude is about feelings, and generally it is about restraining forces—understanding and addressing an attitude problem usually involves understanding and addressing a restraining force, or more likely a collection of restraining forces. However, there are people who are simply intent on being angry or miserable. Because such attitude problems are infectious, the best therapy for treating them is a shape-up-or-ship-out message, structured and delivered in a way that optimizes the probability that the person will choose to shape up, but with clear understanding as to what will trigger a ship out.

# 31

## OFFICERS AND CREW

*Perhaps our greatest need is for people who are uncomfortable without change.*
**Lewis W. Lehr**
Former chairman of the board and CEO of 3M
b. 1920

## MANAGERS AND LEADERS

Just because a person is a strong manager doesn't mean he or she is a worthy leader. Imagine an organization whose mission is to clear a jungle. There would be teams of machete wielders. There would be teams of debris clearers. There would be teams of machete sharpeners. There would be a team responsible for debris-clearing equipment maintenance. There would be strength and conditioning specialists and classes for machete wielders and debris clearers. There would be a machete, machete wielding, and debris-clearing research and development team. There would be managers who make the clearing plan and schedule. There would be managers who would schedule the machete wielding and debris clearing teams. And the entire operation would run like a Swiss watch. But, that is all management. The person who is a leader is the one who has the clarity of mission and the presence of mind to climb to the top of a nearby tree, scan the terrain and inform the rest of the organization, "Wrong jungle!"

Managers work in the system. Leaders work on the system.

# FROM PIONEERS TO PASSIVE RESISTORS

You must know your crew—their strengths, weaknesses, motivators, and most importantly, their inclination toward change. In regard to the latter, I have found that there are four types.

First, there are the "pioneers." Pioneers are natural change agents, their batteries are charged by change; they seek it out, and will gladly take the lead. They are your scouts, your deep-space sensors, they are the ones who are first to encounter dangerous obstacles and traps, and they are the ones with whom you consult to figure out how to mitigate those dangers. You can tell the pioneers by their scar tissue, and they are the ones you want to enroll first in your change effort. Of course, you need to take care to weed out the crazies—you're looking for Lewis and Clark, not Custer.

Second are the "show me" people. These are the people who are open and willing to change but need to see the way before they will go. Some people are naturally cautious. However, those employees who have not worked at any other company fall into this category, too. It doesn't matter what rank they are, how old they are, what gender they are, or what race they are; if the only baseline they have is their experience at a single company, then they will only know that company's way. Conversely, people who've held jobs at multiple companies at least know and have experienced different ways of doing similar things.

Third are the "evangelists of negativism," and the water cooler is their chapel. Assuming you've tended to the restraining forces, about the only thing you can do with these folks is give them a shape-up-or-ship-out message, and deliver it in a way that hopefully optimizes the odds that they'll choose to shape up. If they don't, they have to be cut.

Finally, there is the most dangerous group—the "passive resistors." Passive resistors usually hide among the show me people. Typically, passive resistors are the keepers of the current systems and structure, the current bureaucracy—by this, I mean they're typically in management. Unfortunately, my experience with these folks is that they are so entrenched that they are impervious to coaching. Their sweat equity and emotional investment in the current systems and structure is often too great for them to let go of it, so be prepared to just let go of them, too.

# PEOPLE MAKE MISTAKES

People make mistakes. As long as people accept that premise, as long as people are willing to doubt a little of their own and each other's infallibility, change isn't hard. Change is really hard, however, in organizations that think they're infallible. If I could adjust one thing in an organization that would make change go easier, it would be how they treat errors and mistakes.

There are people who think they never make mistakes, and they are impossible to work with—nothing works with them. In some organizations, if you make a mistake, they put it on your record, they rub your nose in it, and they never let you forget it. It is very hard to drive any kind of change if that is the attitude the organization has. Further, it is incredibly hypocritical. They tell you they want you to set difficult, risky challenges, but if you don't succeed in one they get all excited. I don't know what your definition of risky or challenging is, but if you are expected to make ten out of ten, then they must not be risky or challenging.

I make about five mistakes each week. If I knew which five they were going to be, I wouldn't do those things. But at the beginning of the week, I don't know which five things will turn out to be the mistakes. This is where my co-workers come in—superiors, peers, and subordinates, alike (and at home this is where family and friends come in—parents, spouse, siblings, and children, alike). It is their job to let me know when I make a mistake. I know I'm making them; I just don't know which ones they are.

This is another reason why it has to be safe for people to risk, and why people need to have the courage to tell truth to power. If it's safe and people have courage, Shannon will come in and say, "Hey, Jim, I've found your fourth mistake this week and it's only Tuesday." That's healthy. If you can get people to tell you about your mistakes, then you can fix them. More importantly, when people feel it is safe to tell someone about a mistake that person made, you'll find that they also feel safe telling others about their own mistakes. This is when real learning occurs.

Here's an exercise for you; try it the next time you do appraisals: tell your employees that when you meet to review their performance you also want them to bring one, two, or three things that, if you changed, would help them do their job better. You don't want them to bring five or ten; but you don't want them to bring zero, either. Make it safe. For too many people, the right amount of criticism to give their boss is zero. Does a subordinate know stuff that would help their boss do their job better? Of course, they do!

A macho culture that doesn't allow reversible mistakes will kill you.

If you don't have a culture where you can gracefully admit that you've made a mistake, then you're only going to take on the 90/10s, as Truman would describe them. Or, if you take on the 51/49s and you know that you're going to get nailed if you fail, then your culture will purge you if you don't purge yourself first. Either way, this is not playing to win; it is playing to not lose.

I use a series of four questions when trying to judge if a person's mistake should be viewed as a problem or as on-the-job training (OJT):

- First, I ask if the action was consistent with the mission. If not, then that's a problem. For example, did they treat a customer in a way that was consistent with our values?
- If their action was consistent with the mission, then the second question I ask is if the person acted within the bounds of their authority. If not, then that's a problem. For example, did they just commit the company to a multi-million dollar, multi-year agreement with a vendor when the limit of their approval authority is $10,000?
- If their action was within the reasonable bounds of their authority, then the third question I ask is if this person makes a habit of such questionable actions. If so, that's a problem.
- Finally, if the behavior is not habitual, then the fourth question I ask is whether learning occurred or not.

If a person makes a mistake, but it was consistent with the mission, within the bounds of their authority, not habitual, and learning occurred, then that mistake was just OJT.

# TEAMS

I'm a big believer in teams because participation is the most effective way to build ownership, and generally a team's IQ is greater than an individual's IQ. However, as I've mentioned before, one must also take care not to over romanticize teams.

If there is a problem to be solved, it makes no sense to gather a group of people with no competency in the area and expect them to solve the problem simply because there is a team of them. I've seen too many cases where, when nobody knew what else to do, they formed a team to figure it out, but in doing so they failed to provide any training, any means for the team members to educate themselves about the problem they were charged to solve. I don't know what their management was thinking; pooling ignorance will not produce a smart solution. (It's tough to be too hard on those managers, though, when they don't have good examples to follow. Pooling the ignorance of individuals onto a team and expecting a smart solution is no more stupid than the boards of directors of dinosaur firms agreeing to merge, thinking their union might somehow produce a gazelle. No matter how mighty your leadership might be, no culture is immune to or can suspend the laws of nature.) If you have a problem to solve, and you can't organize a team of people competent in the area to solve it, then you must be sure to provide the team with commensurate time and resources so they can educate themselves about the problem.

Also, there are some types of work that simply do not lend themselves to a team approach. I don't believe that vision work is best done by teams—I don't care if it is a vision for an organization, a new product or service. These are activities that are best done by a talented and motivated individual, or an individual and their partner, not by teams, and especially not by management teams. Prophets rarely work in teams. A team may support their work, a group of disciples may organize around the prophet's work, the prophet may champion their cause among others, who in turn become champions of the cause, but the prophet's genius is usually singular.

Finally, the kind of team you organize to tackle a problem depends on where your organization is in terms of its interpersonal development (Level II in the 10S Model). If there is high trust among people and high confidence in each other's competency, then you can form a small- and fast-moving team of select members—members who have particular expertise in the subject area and who are held in high regard by their peers. However, if there is low trust and/or low confidence in each other's competency, your team will necessarily gravitate towards one that consists of a representative of each affected constituency. There is another name for such teams where the members are there not because of any distinctive expertise, but because they are representing a particular constituency—such teams are called legislatures and they move at legislative speeds. Given the interpersonal maturity of your organization, this may be the best you can do; that's okay, just calibrate your expectations accordingly.

# YOUR PEOPLE VS. CONSULTANTS

There are two kinds of organizational intervention. When retooling your organization's technical system, the intervention you choose is a function of how much you trust your own people. When replanting your organization's social system, the intervention you choose is a function of the congruence between your culture's heritage and the future culture you seek to create.

When retooling your technical system, if you don't trust your own people, you go outside and bring in McKinsey, Boston Consulting Group, Booz Allen, etc. They push aside and subjugate your people, redo your strategic plan and map your processes. They do some training, and reluctantly and slowly let your people back in. Every organization uses these people at some time—I am not knocking it, and I am certainly not knocking the consultants. But in this case, the impetus for change is outside your organization.

Then, there is the model you use if you do trust your people—you make the assumption that the people who know a job best are the ones doing it; the people who are the experts are the people with their hands on the spot. If that's true, you don't bring in outside experts. You may bring in a consultant who can facilitate the change process, but it is your people who fix the business.

When replanting your social system, if you need to break with the culture of the past, you probably need to replace the keepers of the current systems and structure—by that I mean mostly management. You may have visions of a rose garden, but if your current culture is like a weed patch with bureaucracy choking off any new initiative, or an underground resistance sabotaging your new initiatives, then your first order of business is site clearance—ridding your organization of the keepers of that bureaucracy and that underground resistance. In this case, consultants can provide you with solid interim management team while you repopulate the permanent ranks.

If you find that your culture suffers from mission drift and you need to get it back on course, I'm afraid you'll probably still need to replace the keepers of the current systems and structure—again, I mean mostly management--although perhaps not to the same extent. The good news is that you can usually find new leaders among the existing ranks, although you'll probably have to remove layers of dust and rust that have accumulated on them from their time spent in political exile.

## PARTNERS

As mentioned previously, every person, every organization has a customer—your customer is anyone who depends on your work to do theirs. Consequently, every customer also has a supplier. It is the goal of every supplier to be more than a vendor to their customer; every supplier strives to become a "partner." This is true for companies selling stuff to other companies, and this is true for internal organizations providing products or services to a fellow organization.

Internal providers are a bit of a special case. Often, they mistakenly believe their customer's partnership is their entitlement simply because both work for the same company. The customer/supplier relationship may begin as a partnership because both work for the same company, but it can be lost. An internal service provider gets to keep their partnership status with their customers only if they continue to earn it—it is not an entitlement; once lost, the internal service provider will have to re-earn it just like any other supplier.

So, when does a customer/supplier relationship transform into a partnership, and how can you tell? I contend that a customer/vendor relationship transforms into a partnership when the customer says so. It's that simple. I don't care what the supplier does, and I don't care what criteria the customer uses—it doesn't matter. A customer/supplier relationship becomes a partnership when the customer says so.

The way you can tell if a relationship is a real partnership (vs. one in name only) is by how the two parties negotiate—the give and take. In a customer/supplier relationship, the two parties will continue to negotiate until their individual interests cease to advance, as depicted in Figure 29.

*Figure 29 – Typical Customer / Supplier Relationship*

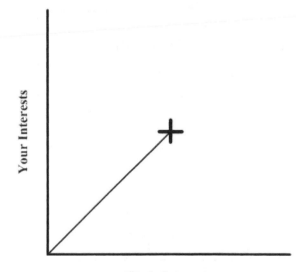

**Their Interests**

In a partnership, the parties will continue to formally negotiate as long as their individual interests are not adversely affected, as the two graphs in Figure 30 illustrate. The other party's interests may continue to advance while yours are standing still, but as long as your interests aren't adversely affected, then that's okay.

*Figure 30 – Partnership Relationship*

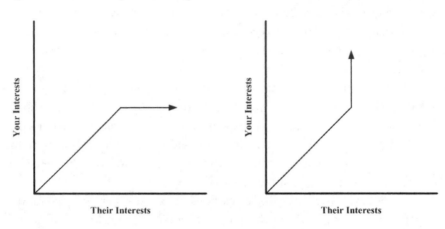

When both parties are willing to continue to negotiate and create benefit for the other party, as long as it doesn't adversely affect their own interests, it opens up a gigantic space where new possibilities can emerge as depicted in Figure 31. This is the beauty of a partnership.

*Figure 31 – Partnership Opens New Opportunities*

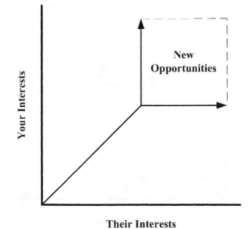

# FAIR VS. EQUAL

During a change effort, people pay extra attention to how they are treated in comparison to others. Consequently, it is helpful to distinguish between "fair" and "equal."

I was about ten years old. My brother, John, was about eight. We were with my mom, Jeanne, and dad, Bill, at the Ben Franklin store in downtown White Bear Lake, MN. My mom and older sisters, Jen and Diane, were shopping. My dad, John and I were waiting for them—well, Dad was waiting; John and I were checking out the toys. John spotted a balsam airplane and asked Dad for twenty-five cents so he could buy it. Dad apparently agreed, because I saw him give my brother a quarter. Seeing this, even though I didn't have a toy I was interested in buying, I asked Dad if I could have a quarter, too.

"Hey, Dad, can I have a quarter, too?"

"Why should I give you a quarter?"

"Because you gave John one!" I held out my hand.

Dad thought for a second, reached in his pocket, and put a dime (ten cents) in my hand.

"What's this?!"

"What's it look like?"

"It looks like it's only a dime! That's not fair!"

"How is that not fair?"

"You gave John a quarter, but you only gave me a dime—that's not fair!"

"How much money did you have before you came to me?"

"None."

"How much do you have now?"

"A dime."

"How have you been treated unfairly?"

With that object lesson, my dad taught me the important difference between fairness and equality. This is not to suggest that one is more important than the other, nor is this a statement about when a person should strive for one versus the other. My dad was simply making the important and pragmatic point that fairness and equality are two different concepts. You can have both fairness and equality, you can have fairness without having equality, and you can have equality without having fairness—just understand that they are different concepts. Because fairness is subjective and equality is not, equality is an easier standard by which to manage.

## INTERPERSONAL PROBLEMS

Organizations do not become angry; people become angry. Organizations do not become happy; people become happy.

The way I was raised, when two people have a problem with each other, their first course of action is not to escalate it to their parents, their bosses, or some other third party. While it is certainly appropriate to discuss the matter with a trusted third party to help you reflect on the problem, it is never appropriate to gossip about an interpersonal problem with, or confess the other party's sins to, anyone other than the person with whom you have the problem. When two people have an interpersonal problem, their course of action should be to seek each other out and make reconciliation. If, after a good faith effort doing that, the problem persists, then it is appropriate to escalate it. If you must escalate the problem, remember that you never go over someone else's head without taking that person with you.

## THERE'S NO SUCH THING AS BYSTANDER LEADERSHIP

In New York City, on the early morning of a March day in 1964, while she was walking the hundred feet from where she parked her car to her apartment, a twenty-nine year-old lady named, Catherine Susan Genovese, or Kitty Genovese to her friends, was repeatedly stabbed, sexually assaulted, and robbed by Winston Moseley. Genovese screamed out, "Oh my God, he stabbed me! Help me!" the *New York Times* reported that thirty-eight individuals nearby had heard or observed portions of the attack, but none came to her aid. Her knife wounds proved fatal.

To be fair, the *Times'* portrayal of the incident was later criticized as inaccurate. However, at the time, people were outraged to think that a lady was being attacked in the presence of others and no one rushed to her rescue because they chose "not to get involved." The circumstances of her murder and the portrayal of neighbors as being fully aware, but completely nonresponsive, prompted investigation into the social-psychological phenomenon that has come to be known as the "bystander effect," or the "Genovese syndrome," or "diffusion of responsibility."

The way I was raised, if we encounter a situation of wrongdoing, and we are in a position to do something about it, then we are ethically compelled to act in whatever way we can to assist, even at the risk of personal injury, stopping short of doing anything stupid.

Do situations analogous to that of Kitty Genovese occur in organizations? Are there times when sins of leadership occur in the presence of fully aware, but completely unresponsive coworkers who make the choice not to get involved? Of course they do. The question, then, is, "How do you respond?" Do you engage, or do you just go about your business? If you are in a position to do something about it, then you are ethically compelled to engage, even at the risk of personal career injury, stopping short of doing anything stupid.

As the Kitty Genovese lesson teaches us, if you become aware of something that is wrong in your organization, or you find something that is broken, and you're in a position to do something about it, then fight to fix it. It may or may not be worth risking your career, but even if you're not in a position to do anything about it, at least make note of it so when the day comes that you are in a position to do something about it, you can. We, especially leaders, are ethically bound to try to right wrongs when it is in our power to do so. If you don't, then who are you?

# 32

# MAKING THE JOURNEY

*It must be remembered that there is nothing more difficult to plan,*
*more doubtful of success, nor more dangerous to manage than the*
*creation of a new system. For the initiator has the enmity of all*
*who would profit by the preservation of the old institution,*
*and merely lukewarm defenders in those who would gain by the new one.*
**Niccolò Machiavelli [*The Prince*]**
Italian diplomat, political philosopher, author, musician, poet, and playwright
1469 – 1527

## LAUNCHING A CHANGE EFFORT

The traditional way to launch a change effort is with a lot of pomp and circumstance. Unfortunately, by doing so, you only deepen the cynicism and skepticism of those who've seen this before, and you scare the hell out of first-timers. This is because too many leaders are great at starting stuff and lousy at completing it; and either they do it so often that people become bored with it, or the leaders really do scare people.

This notion of announcing a change effort is dangerous because everyone takes their cue from their leader. If you announce it with a lot of pomp and circumstance, slogans and exhortations, if you turn it into a big production, your people will treat it with a lot of anxiety—it is tougher to win when your team is anxious. Conversely, if you emulate the calm, cool, collectedness of the aircraft pilot who's informing passengers that the aircraft's engines have been taken out by geese, here's what I'm going to do about it, and here's what I need you to do, then you'll get a much different and much more supportive response. If you're cool, calm, and collected, your people will remain calm, cool, and collected. Over time, you may want to formalize and codify your change effort, but in the beginning, just get on with it like it's no big deal.

I'm not saying to keep your change effort a secret—of course you

323

need to let people know what they need to know. But, the idea that you have to make a big production out of it is a bad one. In fact, one of the single biggest causes of cynicism, skepticism, and jaundice in a work force is that management often drives things with a false sense of urgency and/or an overstated sense of gravity—everything is critical and urgent and it has the same affect as the boy who cried, "Wolf!"

Along with over-hyping change efforts, there is also a tendency toward over-designing them—trying to get everything right the first time. Unfortunately, if you live in an organization where any mistake is fatal, then over-designing is what you get. It's ready, aim, aim, aim... and nobody ever fires. Unless you are somehow privy to divine wisdom, you will not be able to anticipate everything, and you will get stuff wrong. Fortunately, while you won't be able to anticipate everything, you are able to anticipate that there will be stuff you won't anticipate and for which you can put sense and respond mechanisms in place. You'll be amazed at how much of this stuff self-calibrates. Put the ball in play. Trust the people. Don't over-design it, and don't expect it to be perfect. You'll make a lot of mistakes, but it will still be better than if you waited and waited and waited.

By the way, I've found that most people tend not to judge you by the mistakes you make, but by how you respond to the mistakes you make. It is much better to move quickly from concept to practice and adjust course based on information rather than continue to fine-tune a concept based on speculation. Just as Shewhart's PDCA Cycle holds for technical systems, so does it also apply to social systems—just make sure you get past the "plan" part to the "do" part, and don't forget about the "check" and "act" parts.

Finally, when you do make a mistake, own up to it and provide mechanisms for rapid response. Not admitting a mistake—ignoring it or denying it—is the worst mistake you can make.

# MOBILIZING CULTURAL ENERGY

People must enlist in a change effort; they cannot be conscripted or press-ganged into service. One ironic problem is that strong, charismatic-but-autocratic leaders can breed passivity. Mobilizing cultural energy requires a participative approach, some decisions may need to be made autocratically—some times people want their leaders to just make a decision—but the prevalent management style necessarily needs to be one of participation rather than autocracy.

Also, you'll be better off if you avoid putting people into categories. You can talk about your revolution—your quality revolution, your customer-service revolution, your product-development revolution—but you're not going to have a revolution if you put people in lots of little categories: hourly vs. salaried, union vs. non-union, contract vs. permanent, bonus eligible vs. not, etc. When you put people in different categories, you give them a different way to think, a different perspective, a different point of view. The more you do that, the less likely they are to do much in common. For example, some will say that you can't do anything about the hourly vs. salaried, or union vs. non-union, distinctions because those distinctions are regulated by law. Perhaps you can't do anything about those labels, but you can do something about how you treat the people. In a study conducted at GE by GE, as reported by Steven Kerr[1], twenty-five percent of the differences in the way GE treated union folks were caused by the contract and the nature of the work those union folks did. However, seventy-five percent of the differences were caused by management's mindset that union people need to be managed differently—it was GE doing it to GE.

Challenge the categories, and be tough about it. Categorize people if you have to, but make sure you have to, because most of this way of thinking is not your friend.

It is vital to engage the people on the front lines who are actually doing the work—the people with their hands on the spot—because these people know stuff and they just need a chance to share it. Why haven't they shared it in the past? Generally there are two reasons: lack of time and/or lack of safety. By lack of time, I mean more than just giving them the time from the other demands of their job to express their opinions and ideas. I also mean reducing the burden of advancing an idea. Many companies are very good at giving the rank and file opportunities to bring ideas forward to management. However, management has a tough time saying "yes" or "no." Their typical response is something like, "Well, you've certainly given us food for thought." Or there's the more dreaded: "This is very interesting; I'd like you to present it at my next staff meeting." At which point the employee does a quick calculation of the effort-to-results ratio and easily concludes that it isn't worth it.

Management needs to be taught—and be given safety—to make quicker decisions. This means that employees need to bring forward their ideas in small enough chunks that are conducive to a quick decision. For example, the suggestion that process engineering should be relocated from the

---

[1]   Steve Kerr, "Reality-Based Re-engineering and GE's 'Workout'," Speech, The Masters Forum, Minnetonka, MN, 2 Mar. 1993).

office in Singapore to the factory in Penang might be too big to reasonably expect management to give a quick yes or no. However, recommending that a study be conducted to assess the cost/benefit of relocating process engineering is something to which management could be reasonably expected to say yes or no.

Of course, no one wants to make a quick but bad decision just to be dramatic. So, even when given a question or decision to which they should reasonably be able to say yes or no, it is still often too tough for management to do so. I once had a vice president say to me, "I'm uncomfortable with this." That's okay; it wasn't going to kill him. Besides, the object is not to make them—even vice presidents—comfortable. The object isn't joy; the object is to help the business. And, because the shelf life of a bad idea is about the same as the shelf life of a good idea, a quick "no" is every bit as valuable as a quick "yes." However, Mr. Vice President, if you do say no to a recommendation, you must also explain why.

My suggestion is to structure recommendations in this profoundly new way: state the problem or opportunity; state your recommendation; state the action plan for implementing the recommendation (who is going to do what when); and state it all so management can reasonably say yes or no on the spot. If it's too big for a quick yes or no, then break it down into smaller, more management-digestible chunks.

What happens if you do say yes to a bad idea? What happens if, after you start implementing a recommendation, you find out it is a bad idea? One wrong answer is to stay the course and continue to implement the defective recommendation. Another wrong answer is to stop its implementation but not say anything about it in hopes it will fade away. The right answer is to treat people like adults. Get back to those who were involved in making and approving the recommendation, explain that you are stopping its implementation and tell them the reasons why.

There are two rules you can adopt that will go a long way toward making change safe, and they're pretty simple: no blaming and no complaining.

No blaming means forget the past and focus on the future. A particular policy might have been a great idea in 1995; it might have been a stupid idea in 1995—no one knows and no one cares. All we care about is whether it makes sense going forward. Also, while organizations may claim to be big believers in root cause analysis, for too many, root-cause analysis is nothing more than an exercise in assigning blame. When something goes wrong in some organizations, what are the first words to come out of the boss's mouth?

"Who's responsible for this? Who's to blame? Bring me their head! Bring me anyone!"

No complaining means just that. I'm talking about your basic bitch session that doesn't accomplish a thing—it doesn't even make people feel better, it just takes the life out of everyone. Use Eisenhower's doctrine of completed staff work: if you present a problem, you must also recommend corrective and preventative courses of action, and you must do it all in two to three pages. Otherwise, problems without recommendations are just whining, and whining is not allowed.

With the "no blaming" and "no complaining" rules, people are more likely to contribute and will be more open to change—even those people who originally instituted the things you now seek to change.

# MIDDLES ARE THE HARDEST

Most leaders are good at starting changes, but seeing them through is their Achilles heel—they don't have the stamina, they suffer from the management form of attention deficit disorder or Alzheimer's disease, or they just plain lack the strength of leadership. This is the difference between temporary results and enduring results.

The middle of any change effort—of any project—is the hardest. In the beginning everyone is enthusiastic, and at the end, when the goal is in sight, the enthusiasm picks up again. But in the middle is when the effort will tend to wane. It's like Sisyphus pushing the rock up the hill[2]. When you're pushing the rock in the beginning, and you can still see the top of the hill, you're excited by the call to action and you are mentally, physically, emotionally, and spiritually "fresh." But when you get halfway up, you're tired, you can no longer see the top of the hill, you have no idea how much further you have to go or what the terrain ahead looks like—all you can see is the rock.

Any number of bad things can happen in the middle. You'll get tired. You'll lose your resolve and reason that you'll never get there. You could even prematurely decide that you're already there, since you don't know that you're not. Efforts where there is no definition of "done," or no definition of what constitutes success, are particularly prone to people just declaring victory and calling it good. But, when you stop in the middle of the hill and let go of the boulder, it rolls back over the top of you and stops rolling at a point further from the top of the hill than it was when you started. This is particularly true

[2] In Greek mythology Sisyphus was a king who, as punishment from the gods, was cursed to roll a huge boulder up a hill, only to watch it roll down again, and to repeat this throughout eternity.

327

at organizations that always have a new initiative coming down the pike.

It takes special leadership attention to keep people energized and aroused to the challenge—especially in the middle of these initiatives.

# ASSAULT OF COMPETING INITIATIVES

If misaligned measurement systems are the first biggest drag on a change effort, then the second biggest drag is the assault of other initiatives that people are almost always under. Change does not occur in a vacuum; your initiative is competing with an assault of other initiatives (e.g., quality, continuous process improvement, Six Sigma/Lean Sigma, customer satisfaction, empowerment, teaming, diversity, etc.). It's not that these initiatives are necessarily at odds with each other; there can be strong congruence among some of them. It's pretty easy, for example, to draw a line between quality and customer satisfaction, or between teaming and diversity. On the other hand, not everything connects that well. This leaves you with one of two situations: either your initiative may appear to conflict with another; or, even if it doesn't, the shear weight of the collective mass is enough to discourage people.

People can do a lot of things as long as those things seem consistent. But, if one thing seems disjointed from the other things they're asked to do, it gets confusing and frustrating. I can turn eighty bolts per hour, 480 bolts per day, but it doesn't overload me—it may bore me, but it doesn't overload me because they're all the same thing. But, if you have competing initiatives that seem to get in the way of each other, then people get very confused and frustrated.

The answer is to integrate what you can. Then, just as you would manage resources in any other situation, you prioritize (determine the relative importance of the initiatives), schedule (determine the relative urgency of the initiatives), and load level (optimize the utilization of resources, adjusting schedules and bringing additional interim or permanent resources on board as necessary). You must also constantly communicate priorities, schedules, and resource plans so people aren't confused about what and why. If you don't explicitly do this, people will do this for themselves, and you'll lose any semblance of coherence—none of it will fit, or it will fit poorly. Is this hard to do? Certainly it is; but working it will get you further along than if you don't work it.

## DYNAMIC MOTION AND MESS

Do not expect a lot of orderliness when you're going through a change effort. Cultures that are growing, conquering, expanding, and changing are in a state of dynamic motion, and whenever a body is in dynamic motion there is mess. I'm not saying every organization that is a mess is in a state of dynamic motion—they may simply be in a state of confusion. I'm saying that when an organization is in a state of dynamic motion there is going to be mess.

Those with children know this first hand. Children are bodies in a state of dynamic motion. When my daughters were young, if someone were to unexpectedly come to our home and wander into their bedrooms, they would not find things neat and orderly. They would find things in something of a mess—clothing and toys on the floor, unmade bed, books and magazines tossed around, etc. What are the odds that your child would come home, see the mess in their room and say to his or her self, "It makes me so anxious when things aren't in their place." If you have a child like this, you really should have them checked. Children are in a state of dynamic motion; and with dynamic motion comes mess.

The same is true with organizations that are growing, conquering, expanding, and changing—they are in a state of dynamic motion, and this causes a level of mess. Look at most successful start-up companies. There's inventory in the hallways, organization charts may or may not exist, and if they do, they are usually quickly out of date because the structure morphs on the fly. There is a correlation between rapid growth and mess.

Who cares if there is a place for everything and everything is in its place? Old people; well, some old people and almost all accountants. If you are an individual who has a low tolerance for mess, you better not work for a rapidly growing, conquering, expanding, changing organization. You'd better find yourself a nice little bureaucracy that isn't going anywhere—they'll probably even have job descriptions that say what people really do.

## WORK IN HARMONY WITH NATURAL FORCES

Every organization has its own heartbeat, its own natural rhythm, a natural cadence. It is important to work in harmony with this natural rhythm. Any attempt to artificially accelerate or hinder that natural pace will only screw things up.

When earning my private pilot's license, I learned things that went beyond good piloting. For example, I learned that good piloting is all about working in harmony with Mother Nature, and I learned about weather, how to read it, and what it means. I think the same is true about good leadership; it is all about working in harmony with the natural forces of human behavior in general and with the natural forces of that particular culture in specific.

When learning to fly, I also learned to navigate in three dimensions. This was more than a flying lesson; this was an epiphany for me. Prior to this I had always thought about navigation in the context of where other things were in relation to me (i.e., very egocentric). After learning aerial navigation, my perspective flipped, and I found myself thinking about where I was in relation to other things (i.e., very ecocentric). This was a change in perspective that I also found to be very applicable to organizational leadership.

Another important lesson about leading organizational change came when learning aerial combat maneuvers, ACM, from my flying buddies who are ex-military pilots (some with more take-offs than landings). Several of these guys decided to start a business where they would offer ordinary folks, like me, the opportunity to learn about and experience ACM. They purchased two Marchetti SF-260 aircraft (the Marchetti is a high-performance, propeller-driven plane that is capable of pulling between -3Gs and +6Gs; it is also sometimes used as a pre-jet trainer). They equipped these Marchetti's with laser guns to shoot at each other, sensors to detect when you've been shot, and three on-board cameras to record the action for post-flight debriefing.

One weekend, eight of us got together for organized competition. We met on Friday evening to learn ACM basics, to establish rules of engagement, to choose safety pilots (every competing pilot was accompanied by one of the experienced ex-military pilots) and to draw lots for the competition.

The competition was held on Saturday and consisted of a 1½-hour hop against the opponent you drew on Friday night. During the flight from the airport to the practice area, pilots would familiarize themselves with the aircraft, range the guns, and practice maneuvers. The competition consisted of five dogfights: two with you starting on defense (i.e., your opponent on your tail), two with you starting on offense (i.e., you on your opponent's tail), and one starting in the neutral position (i.e., the fight starting after you flew about a mile apart, turned around and flew back past each other). The ex-military pilots kept score, and at the end of your hop you would be taken to a debriefing room where the videos from each of the two planes would be played side by side. The two safety pilots would critique your flying and score the competition; the scores were kept secret until dinner that evening.

Saturday evening we were joined by our spouses and significant others for an award banquet. Dinner was a manly barbeque, each pilot was privately told their own score, and after dinner the pilot with the highest score was revealed and awarded a prize. It was a high testosterone event.

The dog-fighting experience, as latent with testosterone as it was, brought even more lessons that went well beyond flying, and there is one that I think is particularly applicable to the concept of high-performing organizations. A sign that you were getting the most out of your aircraft was when you could feel a slight "tickle" in the stick—it would feel like sand falling on the wings, or like mice running on the wings. If you weren't feeling this "tickle," then you weren't getting the most out of my aircraft. Conversely, if it started to feel like boulders were falling on the wings, or like elephants were running on the wings, that was a signal that you were pushing your aircraft too hard and actually incurring a loss in performance. The secret to achieving peak performance was to find "the tickle."

The tickle was not a function of the plane's mechanics; rather, it was a function of the plane's interaction with the forces of nature (e.g., gravity, the wind, the humidity, the weather, thermals, etc.). Also, it's not the kind of thing where all you have to do is fly the plane so you achieve specific readings on your instruments and you will feel the tickle. The interaction between the plane and the elements was constantly changing; it would change with the ever-changing environmental conditions, with the ever-changing weight of your aircraft as it burned fuel, and with the particular maneuver you were performing. Also, we learned that you don't want to fly your aircraft in a constant state of tickle; this is reserved for times of hyper-competition (e.g., a dog fight).

Finding the tickle is also important to leading a high-performing team. If you can feel the tickle, you are probably driving your organization at peak performance. If you can't feel mice on the wings, then you are probably not getting everything out of it. Conversely, if you feel elephants on the wings, then you are probably pushing it too hard and actually incurring a loss in performance.

In these dogfights, my opponent and I were flying identical equipment, and our training was essentially identical. Finding the tickle could give me an advantage over my opponent; not finding the tickle could give my opponent an advantage over me. For your organization, do you and your competitor have access to similar assets? With global capital markets, global sourcing markets, and global labor markets, you do. Therefore, a key to your team achieving peak performance will be in finding the organizational equivalent of "the tickle."

Also, just as with an aircraft, finding the tickle in your organization is not a matter of achieving some specific set of results in the metrics you use to monitor your organization's technical systems. Rather, just as with an aircraft, finding the organizational equivalent of the tickle is also ever-changing, based on your ever-changing conditions—the tickle is more likely a product of the performance of your organization's social systems.

Finally, don't drive your organization so you constantly feel the tickle; this is reserved for times of hyper-competition (e.g., a product launch). I know there are some who would argue that their particular business is a constant dogfight. That's just testosterone fueled nonsense but, for the sake of argument, let's assume it is true. If you lead your organization as if it is in a continuous, never-ending dogfight, then just understand the toll this will exact. You should expect the useful life of the plane and the life expectancy of the pilot to be dramatically shorter.

# Pay Attention to the Whole Board

I'm a lousy chess player, but it did teach me one lesson that has helped me more in other aspects of life than it has in my chess game. Pay attention to the whole board—a winning strategy cannot be built by focusing on a single piece and a single move. You must pay attention to the whole board, think ahead many moves and think in terms of multiple moves and contingent moves.

This same lesson applies throughout many other aspects of life. For example, I have been riding a motorcycle since I was twelve and learning to drive defensively is all about continually surveying the entire field as you ride (i.e., watching the whole board), thinking ahead many moves (i.e., what lane do I want to be in and when), and thinking in terms of multiple moves and contingent moves (what am I going to do if this car doesn't see me). The same is true about flying: watching the whole board, thinking ahead many moves, and thinking in terms of multiple moves and contingent moves. The same is true playing any sport—you have to pay attention to the whole field of play (there's a runner on second), you have to think ahead many moves (what am I going to do if the ball is hit to me), and thinking in terms of multiple moves and contingent moves (what am I going to do if the runner tries to steal third).

This chess lesson also applies to leading organizational change. When contemplating a change, one needs to look at the whole board—the organization's technical system, its social system, and the streams. Process engineering, Six Sigma, and other such tools are useful in dealing with your organization's technical system. The 10S Model is useful in dealing with your organization's social system and thinking about the streams. However, these things are interdependent, and the chess lesson teaches us that we must deal with these things in an integrated and strategic way—watch the whole board, think ahead many moves, and think in terms of multiple moves and contingent moves.

# P-FACTOR

When learning to fly, you are taught about something called, "P-factor." When taking off in a propeller-driven airplane, asymmetrical thrust is created because the descending propeller blade on the right side of the engine has a greater angle of attack than the ascending blade on the left. This produces greater thrust from the right side of the propeller resulting in a left yaw known as P-factor. To compensate, the pilot has to apply a little right rudder. Too little right rudder and the plane will track to the left; too much right rudder will cause the plane to track to the right. To track straight down the runway, you have to use just the right amount of right rudder.

Organizations experience P-factor, too. For example, if the executive commitment to shareholders and quarterly EPS is stronger than their commitment to the company's mission and all of those with a stake in its success, then that will result in mission drift, a form of organizational P-factor. However, P-factor doesn't emanate only from the top of the organization; it can emanate from any leadership position anywhere within the organizational hierarchy. If your boss either lusts for, or already enjoys, powerful personal motivators like "me first" career advancement or "me first" financial incentives, then he or she will have a tendency to pull his or her whole organization in the direction of their promotion and/or bonus. This is a form of organizational P-factor. Or, you may have the misfortune to be cursed with a clueless boss who pulls your organization in clueless directions. This is another form of organizational P-factor.

When you experience organizational P-factor, no matter how small the team that you lead may be, no matter where you and your team may be in the overall hierarchy, apply a little right rudder. When plans and/or decisions are being formulated that take the organization off course (i.e., mission drift), apply a little right rudder. Apply a little right rudder in the form of proactively advancing your concern in the spirit of "loyal opposition." Apply a little right rudder in your team's own planning and decision-making to the extent you have the latitude to do so. Don't apply too little right rudder; don't be silent. But don't apply too much right rudder; don't be insubordinate, either.

## PYRAMID OF INFLUENCE

In Stephen Covey's seminar, "The Seven Basic Habits of Highly Effective People: Renewal Program,"[3] I learned about the pyramid of influence. Depicted in Figure 32, it illustrates something I suspect we all instinctively realized, and probably experienced.

*Figure 32 – Pyramid of Influence*

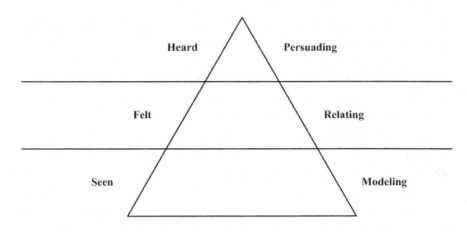

Source: Stephen R. Covey, "Seven Habits of Highly Effective People: Renewal," (Seminar, Covey Leadership Center, Inc., Sundance, UT, Sep. 1991)

The pyramid consists of three levels:

- The base of the pyramid is persuading. This is leadership by example. Your effectiveness at influencing others is a direct function of people seeing you practice what you preach.
- The middle level of the pyramid is relating. This speaks to the quality of your relationship with the person or people you seek to influence. The more strongly people feel that you genuinely relate to them, the stronger your influence with them will be.

---

[3]  Stephen R. Covey, "Seven Habits of Highly Effective People: Renewal," (Seminar, Covey Leadership Center, Inc., Sundance, UT, Sep. 1991).

- The tip of the pyramid is persuasion. This represents overt acts to influence others. The more effective you are at getting people to hear your arguments, the more effective your influence will be.

A pyramid is used because there is a diminishing hierarchical relationship between these three levels. Overt acts of persuasion, the third level, work only when the first two levels are present. If you aren't modeling the behavior you seek in others, and if your relationship with the people you seek to influence isn't strong, any argument, or other overt act of persuasion you might make, will be ineffective. Similarly, if you aren't modeling the behavior you seek in others, your relationship with those people will not be grounded in trust and confidence in each other's competency; therefore, your ability to influence those people will be null.

## FUN IS GOOD

My last but perhaps most important lesson is to remember that fun is good. Have fun playing the game of business, and because people take their cues from their leaders, do it for yourself and do it for them. If you approach your work with a lot of pain, consternation, stress, bloated sense of gravity, and/or false sense of urgency, then so will your people. However, if you approach it as a fun adventure, calm, cool, and collected, then your people are more likely to do so as well.

Every fall, our family takes a long weekend to make our annual sojourn to Minnesota's North Shore on Lake Superior—the water, the rocks, the trees in fall colors, and the hiking trails make for a therapeutic weekend. We've come to stay at a very nice, family-owned hotel in Tofte, MN, The Cliff Dweller on Lake Superior. In their lobby, they have a sign I think is well worth taking to heart, "Life is not a journey to the grave with the intention of arriving safely in a pretty and well-preserved body, but rather to skid in broadside, thoroughly used up, totally worn out, and proclaiming, 'Wow, what a ride!'" This is the attitude with which you want to approach your change effort.

Mike Veeck is an owner of the St. Paul Saints and several other minor league baseball teams, and he's recognized as a maverick marketing whiz. In his book, *Fun Is Good: How to Create Joy and Passion in Your Workplace and Career*, he reminds us, "'Fun is good' isn't just a concept. It's an experience, a feeling, a way of life and an attitude... 'Fun is good' is a philosophy... 'Fun is good' is simply sound business."[4] As my good friend, Bowen White, M.D. author, speaker, consultant, and clown continues to remind everyone, "Normal isn't healthy!"[5]

To give truth-telling, path-finding, and authentic communication air to breathe, the leader must cultivate a culture where it is safe to risk. Playfulness brings cultural safety. Playfulness makes it safe to challenge orthodoxy. Playfulness makes it safe to risk. To steal an observation made in *Star Trek's* 1966 TV episode, "Shore Leave," "The more sophisticated the society, the greater the need for the simplicity of play."

How do you simultaneously promote the value of play and the values of high performance? You already know the answer: leadership by example. In my first job after graduating from college, my father must have noticed me morphing into the stereotypical career warrior and shared this advice with me, "Take what you do very seriously, but don't take yourself too seriously." As the American author, James A. Michener, observed, it is about the art of living:

> *A master in the art of living draws no sharp distinction between his work and his play, his labor and his leisure, his mind and his body, his education and his recreation. He hardly knows which is which. He simply pursues his vision of excellence through whatever he is doing and leaves others to determine if he is working or playing. To himself he always seems to be doing both.*

---

[4]  Mike Veeck and Pete Williams. *Fun is Good: How to Create Joy & Passion in Your Workplace & Career*, (New York: Rodale, Inc., 2005), p1.
[5]  Dr. Bowen F. White, M.D., *Why Normal Isn't Healthy: How to Find Heart, Meaning, Passion & Humor on the Road Most Traveled*, (Center City, MN, Hazelden, 2000).

# Part VIII:

# Life at 30°

# 33

# COMMENCEMENT

*I believe that every right implies a responsibility; every opportunity,*
*an obligation; every possession, a duty.*
**John D. Rockefeller, Jr.**
American businessman and philanthropist
1874 – 1960

## ONE OF MY PURPOSES FOR WRITING THIS

book is to share the lessons I've learned and the opinions I've formed over the course of a career spent leading organizational change—sailing into the prevailing cultural winds, often in choppy internal political waters, to start new organizations, renovate under-performing ones and invigorate neglected ones. We've covered a lot of territory:

- Business has a social purpose: to improve the collective wealth of society, and it does this through the creation of products, services and jobs.
- If an organization's leaders adopt a pattern of decision-making where they create benefit for one of its stakeholders, but at the expense of the others, they devalue the whole organization.
- While an organization's worth may be measured by its production of wealth, its power to produce that wealth lies in its culture.
- The key to an organization's competitive advantage is its culture.
- The key to any organization's culture is leadership.
- The key to leading cultural change is not in implementing a program, but in actualizing a new vision and values.

- History teaches us that cultures die not from murder, but from suicide. An organization is on a suicidal path when there is a conflict of interest between the short-term interests of the decision-making elites and the long-term interests of the organization as a whole—especially if the elites are able to insulate themselves from the consequences of their actions.

- Too many of today's organizations suffer from leadership sins that have created a blueprint for trouble: an abundance of denominator managers and a scarcity of numerator leaders; bosses who are tough on their employees, but not on the competition; the excesses of executive aristocracy, and an absence of shared sacrifice.

- Real leadership—"we" leadership vs. "me" leadership—is strength of vision and strength of values, commitment and loyalty, truth-telling, path-finding, creating safety to risk, and self-interest rightly understood.

- Every organization—be it a government, a political party, a religion, a union, company, a business unit within a company, a function within a business unit, a department within a function, a team within a department, profit or non-profit, public or private, it doesn't matter--is an ecosystem.

- Every organization takes inputs and, through their chain of value-adding processes, creates outputs. If their customers value those outputs, then the organization prospers; if not, then it decays.

- Every organization's chain of value-adding processes is a composite of that organization's technical system (i.e., how it technically does its work: its manufacturing processes, service processes, sales processes, business processes, etc.), and its social system (i.e., how it socially governs the conduct of its work; its culture).

- Because your organization is an ecosystem, and because your chain of value-adding processes is a composite of your organization's technical system and its social system, then to affect enduring change, you must address both the technical system and the social system. If you make changes to one system without making complementary changes in the other, then your organization will reject that change like the human body rejects a transplanted heart.

- Your organization's technical system—your processes—is comprised of discrete, linear systems, which can be worked on directly, and are best served with quantitative methods.

- Your organization's social system—your culture—is a holistic non-linear system, which must be worked on indirectly, and is best served with qualitative methods.

- There is an essential difference between what is technically possible and what is culturally doable; this is why culture is the key to an organization's competitive advantage.
- The organization's culture is defined by the sum of its habits.
- Habit occurs where skill, knowledge, and attitude intersect.
- The goal, then, is to create the organizational habits that will lead to both the organization's success (e.g., speed, agility, quality, continuous improvement, etc.), and the individual's success (e.g., doing valuable work, being valued for doing that work well, trust, friendliness, the ability to practice one's craft in a way that gives one pride, etc.).
- Just as one does not strengthen their heart by exercising it directly, but by exercising the large muscles which in turn exercise the heart, neither does one change an organization's habits directly, but must work on those things that influence those habits.
- Those things that influence an organization's habits, thus its culture, are represented in the 10S Model: shared vision and values, symbols, streams, strategies, structure, systems, style, skills, staff, and self.
- All organizations have shared vision and values, whether they articulate them or not. Too many organizations have two: the vision and values they espouse and the ones they practice. The plaques and banners will tell you what the espoused vision and values are; symbols will tell you the vision and values that are in practice.
- You don't begin organizational change by working on structure, strategies or systems if you don't have the managerial style and skills in place to orchestrate it. Nor do you begin by working on managerial development if your staff doesn't have the trust or the skills necessary to execute. And you do not begin by working on interpersonal development if you don't have the personal wherewithal to lead. Durable organizational change begins with personal leadership—self.
- Organizational cultures have lifecycles just like civilizations. Each one begins with a prophet. It grows and prospers through the ages of the barbarian, builder and explorer, and administrator because they keep it aroused to challenge. It declines and decays through the ages of the bureaucrat and aristocrat when it loses its creativity and responds to new challenges with old solutions, and systems and structure become dominant to the spirit and substance of the mission.
- The more your organization is weighted with administrators, the

more you need prophets and barbarians. The more your organization leans towards the prophet, the more you need builders and explorers and administrators. You never need bureaucrats or aristocrats.

- To keep their organization growing and aroused to challenge, the leader must be a synergist who builds a team comprising the best leadership qualities of the prophet, barbarian, builder and explorer, and administrator, and banishes the leadership qualities of the bureaucrat.

- The equation, E = Q x A, along with Kurt Lewin's Force Field Model provide useful metaphors for pulling it all together, for integrating your thinking regarding the technical system and social system that comprise your organization's ecosystem.

- Finally, I shared the collection of practical lessons for orchestrating cultural change, which I've accumulated through my personal and professional experience.

So, now that you have endured all of this, what is it I recommend you do? That's simple. Put it to work.

I don't care where you are in the organizational hierarchy. I don't care how large your following may be. Take what you've learned and use it to make that corner of this planet that you have the good fortune to lead a better place. Make your organization a model.

Take those things with which you agree and put them to work. Take those things with which you disagree, and put your opposing ideas to the test. Take those things with which you are unsure, and experiment with them. Stop the mental masturbation of debating an idea's merits based on conceptual speculation, and start acting based on the real-world information you gain from pragmatic experimentation—plan, do, check, act, repeat.

# 34

## BEAT TO QUARTERS

*Don't wait for extraordinary opportunities. Seize common occasions and make them great. Weak men wait for opportunities; strong men make them.*
**Orison Swett Marden**
American author, publisher, physician, and hotel owner
1850 – 1924

# "BEAT TO QUARTERS" IS A DRUM PAT-

tern that was used to signal the crew of a ship. Beating to quarters was called whenever the ship or crew might face danger beyond that which was normally expected of them in a life at sea. Quarters were called during storms, battles, or random sightings in the fog. The general philosophy is that of preparedness. If a ship is to face the danger of the elements, or should happen upon an enemy, it is much better to be prepared.

In addition to sharing, my other purpose for writing this book is one of preparedness—to sound the beat to quarters. I've been fairly direct about my concern that the leadership in too many of our organizations today is pretty messed up—the blueprint for trouble cited by authorities like Arnold Toynbee and more recently by Jared Diamond, is playing out at many levels. Of course there are exceptions, but too many of today's leaders—especially in business, and especially in publicly traded businesses—are leading with all of the instincts of overfed lemmings, except they have parachutes and their followers do not. I want to reach out to those parachute-less followers in hopes that when it is their turn to lead they will choose a direction other than towards a cliff. It was "me first" leadership that put organizations on a bad course, and it will take "we" leadership to get them back on course. I have little faith that this course correction will come from the insulated top-down, so I am encouraging it from the middle out. I think the micro can be a model for the macro. I think the micro *must* be a model for the macro.

You know that you lead by your example whether you choose to or not. So, don't be a mollusk—have a backbone, stand for something. And don't be a lemming—blind obedience may be a way to get ahead, but it is no way to live or to lead. Choose to be a noble and worthy example. Remember the lessons of Alexander and Nelson. The ability of leaders to influence their people is the key. Alexander and his men, Nelson and his, were unified and trusted one another. Alexander and Nelson innovated; they took risks by attempting new tactics and new methods. Alexander and Nelson delegated; they relied on the abilities of their fellow officers. Alexander and Nelson created advantage through training, human competence, and commitment. In short, Alexander and Nelson created the stronger cultures. This is what leaders do.

Strength of vision and strength of values, commitment and loyalty, truth-telling, path-finding, and creating safety to risk is the stuff leaders are made of. But, those things are not enough to get us where we need to go; the leadership ingredient that has impoverished us by its absence is self-interest rightly understood. It begins with your personal leadership, and you should not expect others to follow you without you demonstrating some measure of mastery over self. Your capacity and capability for authentic organizational leadership will never be any stronger than your capacity and capability for authentic personal leadership.

My guess is that your people have had to endure superficial, psych-up change efforts inflicted upon them by your predecessors, and maybe one of those predecessors is the old you. So, be prepared for any change effort you try now to be met with cynicism and skepticism from people suffering with organizational jaundice. If you're new to your team, if you have no "street cred" with the people you now lead, they probably view you as just one more boss who is just passing through. As far as they're concerned, you're just a blip on the curve and all they have to do is bunker-in and wait for you to go away––experience has taught them that you, too, shall pass. Most organizational change today is going to be born with the original sin begat by the disingenuous, half-hearted, management-fad-of-the-month programs perpetrated upon them by your predecessors, and this kind of original sin can't be baptized away. Neither a person nor an organization can talk itself out of a problem it behaved itself into.

So, don't announce your change effort with a lot of pomp and circumstance. You'll only exacerbate the cynicism and skepticism; you'll come across as clueless, and insult the intelligence of the people you seek to lead. Just quietly get to work and understand that there's no quick fix. While the effect of your efforts may be imperceptible at first, persist. As English writer and Anglican clergyman, Sydney Smith, argued, "It is the greatest of all mistakes to do nothing because you can only do a little."

Your experience will be like strength conditioning. You may have to begin by lifting weights that seem embarrassingly light, but as your change effort builds muscle, you can add weight. At first, you'll add a little weight, and then a little more, and over time you will be lifting a respectable, then an admirable amount of weight. You won't notice, nor should you expect to see, any immediate results. But, after six to twelve months, you just may find yourself and others observing that your organization is now somehow different—they won't be able to cite to any one event, decision or point in time as the cause, they'll just notice that things are different. Perfect!

This is a great time to be leading because it is a time of great challenge and rapid change. Yesterday's "me first" leaders have been leading their organizations like lemmings toward the cliff, while they parachute to safety. Today's "we" leaders are creating an amazing transition—a transition in which doing well and doing good are convergent, where they had previously been divergent. As Woodrow Wilson, twenty-eighth president of the United States so eloquently put it, "You are not here merely to make a living. You are here in order to enable the world to live more amply, with greater vision, with a finer spirit of hope and achievement. You are here to enrich the world, and you impoverish yourself if you forget the errand." It is this transition that will keep us going up the curve, rather than off the cliff.

On Wednesday, April 8, 2009, at approximately 7:15 a.m. local time, more than 300 miles off the coast of Somalia, pirates attacked the 508-foot, 17,000-ton, American-flagged, cargo ship, Maersk Alabama, which was on a humanitarian mission carrying food aid to Mombasa in Kenya. The unarmed, twenty-man crew had been drilled by their captain, Richard Phillips, on what to do in the event of such an attack. While Captain Phillips and three other sailors met the pirates on the bridge, most of the crew hid for ten hours in sweltering safe rooms below. The power was cut and all the lights went out. The crew escaped harm after Captain Phillips offered himself as a hostage, and was taken at gunpoint into the lifeboat in which the pirates fled. Happily, U.S. Navy Seals rescued Captain Phillips unharmed in a daring operation in the Indian Ocean on Sunday, April 12, thus ending the five-day standoff between U.S. Naval forces and the small band of brigands in the eighteen-foot, covered, orange lifeboat off the Horn of Africa.

345

There are people like Crassus the Money Lender, Michael Eisner, and John Thain, performing daily acts of self-aggrandizement at all levels in most organizations. There are also people like Alexander, Nelson, and Captain Richard Phillips, performing daily acts of quiet heroism at all levels in most organizations. I don't know which of these two leadership models your organization rewards, but I know the one that will allow you to sleep better. The question is, "To which one do you aspire?"

I don't know the organizational winds and political seas in which you sail. It doesn't really matter. Whatever your situation may be, whatever kind of organization yours may be, no matter where you and your organization are in the hierarchy, no matter how big the group may be that you have the good fortune to lead, the question to you is, "To which of these two leadership models do you aspire?" Your answer establishes the North Star by which you will navigate your career.

Competitive sailors will talk about "life at 30°." The reference is to the angle of the mast when tacking into the wind. In a dead calm, the mast is perpendicular to the plane of the water. Think of those pictures of a sailboat tacking into the wind with the crewmembers leaning out over that high side of the boat. When you tack into the wind, your mast does not stay perpendicular to the water; as you tack more aggressively into the wind the angle of the mast, relative to its original perpendicular position, increases. The reason the crew positions itself on the high side of the boat, and leans out to throw their weight over that high side, is to offset the changing center of gravity thus enabling the boat to tack more aggressively into the wind. Often the crew will get wet from the spray, and they prepare for that. Of course, you can tack so aggressively that you capsize your boat—hence the phrase, "life at 30°."

So you think you're a leader, and you want to change your organization? My closing suggestion to you is to learn to lead your life at 30°. It's a journey that promises both adventure and adversity. It is a necessary journey. In the words of one of my favorite philosophers, Dr. Seuss, "Unless someone like you cares a whole awful lot, nothing is going to get better. It's not."

A ship may be safe in the harbor, but that is not what ships are for. So, if you and your team have been anchored in the safety of some organizational harbor, prepare for sea. If you've just been lazily sailing with the political winds, and you're headed in a direction your leadership compass tells you not to go, prepare to change course.

Your change effort will take several years. If you begin now you'll start seeing results in one or two years, but if you wait three years to begin, you won't start seeing results for four to five years; and if you wait five years to begin, you won't start seeing results for six to seven years. I'm not necessarily suggesting a revolution; an evolution is okay—just make sure your evolution starts tomorrow at 8:00 a.m.

Prepare to go to windward and embrace life at 30°. Godspeed, fair winds, and following seas...

# Part IX:

# Extra Provisions

# APPENDIX A

## EXAMPLE OF A BUSINESS UNIT INFORMATION TECHNOLOGY ORGANIZATION'S OPERATING PRINCIPLES

# Business Unit Information Technology Operating Principles

## In addition to the company's

mission and our business unit's charter, there are certain operating principles that guide not only how our IT organization conducts its work, but also how we govern the conduct of our work. These are the IT Operating Principles.

## Our License to Exist

Our business unit fights cardiac disease. Our IT organization exists only to the extent we are able to help our business unit fight cardiac disease. There is no entitlement that guarantees our IT organization's right to exist. The day we begin to believe that we are entitled to our business unit's IT work, is the day we begin to decline and decay as an organization.

Through our trustworthiness and distinctive competencies we will earn our business unit's IT business. We do not strive to be our business unit's IT provider of force. We strive to be our business unit's IT provider of preference. In fact, our goal is not to simply meet our business unit's expectations; it is to create expectations to which any would-be competitor must respond.

# OUR PURPOSE

The purpose of IT is to bring understanding of the business, along with expertise in business process engineering, information technology, and organizational/cultural change, to bear on business problems and opportunities in ways that:

- Improve product or service quality for business unit customers.
- Improve the quality of life at work for business unit employees.
- Avoid or reduce costs, protect or increase revenue, and mitigate risk for company shareholders.
- Improve the quality with which our business unit can transact with our suppliers.
- Strengthen our business unit's citizenship in the many communities to which we belong.

# OUR MARKET(S)

Our primary market is our business unit. Our secondary market is the company's other businesses. While helping our business unit fight cardiac disease is our primary purpose, we also have an obligation to the company's other business units—this obligation is especially strong because our business unit is the company's largest.

For this reason, we will develop new solutions and support existing solutions in ways that certainly meet our business unit's business needs, but also accommodate the interests of the company's other businesses to the extent they do not diminish our business unit's interests.

# OUR VALUE PROPOSITION & ALIGNMENT IN THE COMPANY'S IT COMMUNITY

We do not believe that our business unit's interests are best served by a monolithic IT organization. We believe that the pace and highly dynamic nature of our business requires an environment where multiple parties can do IT work concurrently, and unbeknownst to each other.

In fact, IT capability has naturally evolved in the company's ecosystem in three ways:

- In Corporate IT.
- In our IT and the other business unit IT organizations.
- In non-IT departments where technical personnel perform IT-like work.

In our company's IT world, we believe:

- The primary value proposition of Corporate IT is low cost, which requires operational excellence.
- The primary value proposition of business unit IT organizations, including our own, is high service, which requires customer intimacy.
- The primary value proposition of the technical personnel and teams in non-IT departments and cost centers is product leadership, which requires innovation.

Because our IT organization must operate in both the business ecosystem, and the company's global IT ecosystem, we will conduct ourselves in ways that are responsibly independent and effectively inter-dependent. Toward this end:

- IT work will be directed to and led by that IT organization whose value proposition is best suited to the work.
- Our IT organization will avoid participation in areas where we cannot make a distinctive and worthy contribution.

To leverage the creativity, flexibility, speed, and strength of the various geographic teams within our global IT organizations, Corporate IT, and the other business unit IT organizations, the working relationship we will cultivate is a peer-to-peer one. We do not subscribe to a working relationship that would put one organization at the top of a hierarchy, or at the center of a hub-and-spoke.

## Our Clients and Good Client Service

We use the term "customer" to refer to our company's customers. We use the word "client" to refer to the customers of our IT organization.

Our client is anyone who depends on our work to do theirs. A client may be another department or a person in the next office. Our IT management's clients are our IT staff.

    Good client service is not:

- Giving the client whatever they ask for, whenever they ask for it, however they ask it to be.
- Indentured servitude.

    Good client service is:

- Listening: Understanding the client and ensuring that they feel understood.
- Kindness and courtesy: Treating the client the way you'd like to be treated, even when they are not treating you that way.
- Keeping the promises you make: Honoring your explicit commitments.
- Managing expectations: A met expectation has the same effect as a kept promise. An unmet expectation has the same effect as a broken promise.
- Communicating: Keeping clients apprised on the status of commitments.
- Not being duplicitous: Not talking behind another person's back or confessing another person's sins.
- Humility: Apologizing if you blow any of the above.

## Our Distinctive Competencies

Because our value proposition is based on high service, which requires customer intimacy, we put client service before our own administrative efficiency. To provide the kind of service that our clients value, we must have distinctive competency in:

- The character traits and inter-personal skills required in cultivating and maintaining working relationships with our clients that are based on mutual trust and mutual confidence in each others' competency.
- Our knowledge of our clients' business (e.g., their purpose, their processes, their measures of success, their organization, their key opinion leaders, etc.)—and we must know them in practical ways, not just conceptual ways.
- Our knowledge of the company's industry and the regulations to

which our clients must adhere—and how our Quality System supports that compliance.

- Moving at the speed of our clients' business—we cannot be a constraint in the speed of their business.
- The language of our clients, as we will communicate with them in the terms and conditions of their profession, not ours.
- Discerning client requirements:
  - Sometimes our clients prefer to express their requirements in the form of a solution design. However, because we are responsible for the integrity of the solutions we develop, we must reserve our right to design. Therefore, when a client prefers to express their requirements in the form of a solution design, we will listen actively and politely, and then reverse engineer the client's requirements from their expressed solution design.
  - Whatever form they may take, client requirements come in four kinds:
    - Expected: the kind the client assumes to go without saying.
    - Expressed: the kind that the client articulates.
    - Emergent: the kind the client discovers, or that emerges during the development process.
    - Energizing: the kind that shows that we are in tune with the client, and brings the client back to work with us again.

Because solutions we develop or support must inter-operate with solutions developed elsewhere by others unbeknownst to us, we must also have distinctive competency in:

- Business process engineering. We do not implement technology for the sake of technology; we put purpose before process, and process before technology. For example, we do not conduct a project to implement an ERP system; we conduct a project to improve supply chain management—that project may happen to involve implementing an ERP system. In other words, we will first understand the business purpose and value of the solution we seek to devise. Second, we will engineer the business processes and rules by which our solution will operate. Third, we will apply information technology, as necessary,

to enable those business processes and enforce those business rules. Further, as we drive our solutions from process engineering to enabling technology, we will follow these three steps in order:
- • Simplify.
- • Standardize.
- • Systematize.
- • Existing and emerging information technologies.
- • Information systems concepts, methods, and tools including:
  - • Common architectural rules (e.g., data architecture, technical architecture, process architecture, etc.).
  - • Development and support methods and tools.
- • Project management methods and tools.
- • Organizational/Cultural Change. We understand that the durability of our solutions is more a function of what is culturally doable than what is technically possible. We must have distinctive competency in organizational/cultural change principles, methodologies, and tools.

# OUR WORK AND WORK PRODUCTS

In a dynamic, fast moving environment, the preeminent criterion in our work and work products is "resilience." When something is resilient, it possesses two qualities:

- • It is highly reliable. By "highly reliable" we mean:
  - • It never or rarely breaks (breakage is defined as anytime intervention is required to return a product or process to normal operation).
  - • Should it break, it is quick and easy to diagnose and repair.
- • It is highly adaptive to change. By "highly adaptive to change," we mean it is quick and easy to change in terms of capacity and capability—without jeopardizing reliability.

We need resilience in the:

- • Products we manufacture and the services we deliver.
- • Processes we use to manufacture those products and deliver those services.
- • Processes we use to manage those manufacturing and service deliv-

ery processes.
- Most importantly, we need resilience in our people.

# OUR CULTURE

We will make our IT organization a great place to work by:

- Producing products and delivering services that add value for our clients (Clients believe a product or service adds value when they are willing to pay for it or are willing to convince others to pay for it.):
  - Bold thinking. We will open our hearts and minds to new ideas and insights. We will not be constrained by conventional thinking; we are willing to explore and experiment––we are willing to be entrepreneurial.
  - Speed of process. We will drive the actual cycle time of our business processes to as near the theoretical minimum as possible. We believe speed is important because:
    - Speed is valued by our clients. Speed is required when serving a fast paced and dynamic business––we must be able to move at our clients' speed; our speed cannot be a constraint on our clients.
    - Speed improves our skills. The only way to get better at anything is to practice, and if we can perform a process in half the time of a competitor, then we will get twice the practice at that process as our competitor in the same amount of time.
    - Speed keeps us cost effective. Faster processes are less expensive processes.
  - Continuous improvement. We will be a learning organization, always improving our own processes. We understand that research and development are essential to advancing the state of our profession
  - Cost effectiveness. We will eliminate waste in how we manage our resources, perform our processes, and imposition our co-workers' time. We will not squander whatever opportunities with which we are entrusted.
- Respecting each other's competency and work by cultivating:
  - An honorable work ethic in each other and ourselves:

- Showing respect for each individual.
- Conducting ourselves with unconditional integrity.
- Practicing on going personal and team development to constantly make ourselves more useful.
- An environment where we each may practice our craft with pride and with balance.
- Egalitarianism and meritocracy (versus aristocracy and autocracy):
    - Preferring a culture of consensus and practicing a command management style only in times of crises.
    - Distinguishing between importance and urgency, and recognizing fabricated crises.
    - Encouraging each other to speak their mind, respectfully, but without regard to rank.
    - Making decisions based not on a person's rank, but on the merit of their argument.
- A professional work ethic while also valuing a balanced life style. We are not bound by a traditional 8:00 – 5:00, Monday through Friday work schedule. Rather, our work is bound by the clients we serve and the commitments we make.
- Trusting each other and making it safe to take risks by:
    - Telling people what they need to know to do their jobs, not what we think they want to hear.
    - Making commitments and setting expectations with thoughtful care, mutual agreement as to outcomes, and pre-defined measures of success.
    - Doing what we say we are going to do.
    - Fearing not failure, only missed opportunity; and recognizing an error as a failure only if:
        - It is incongruent with our mission, or
        - Learning does not occur, or
        - It dramatically exceeds the bounds of the party's authority, or
        - It becomes habitual.
    - Being friendly and authentic with each other:
        - Respecting the legitimate differences among us and the many cultures in which we serve.
        - Preferring simplicity and being authentic in our communications, rather than being fancy or complex.

- Taking what we do very seriously, but not taking ourselves too seriously—having fun at "the game of business."
- Being good citizens in the many communities to which we belong.
- Leading by example.

# OUR JOBS

Each person's job responsibility is simply: "Use your best judgment at all times to serve our clients in ways that are congruent with the company mission, the business unit charter and our IT operating principles."

Every person has five roles in which they are expected to contribute:

- Producer: Delivering products and services to clients in ways that:
    - Are on or under budget.
    - Are on or ahead of schedule.
    - Meet or exceed client expectations
    - Meet or exceed standards for quality.
    - You can be proud of.
- Resource Manager: Whether responsible for a team or for only one's self, each of us is responsible for planning, acquisition, allocation, and management of the financial, physical, and human assets necessary for us to sustain operations and achieve future goals.
- Entrepreneur/Innovator: Continuous improvement of our products, services, and processes—increasing the value of IT to our clients.
- Personal & Team Developer: Continuous improvement of the capability and capacity of yourself and your co-workers on both individual and team levels.
- Good Citizen: Showing "good citizenship" in the many communities to which we belong (e.g., organizational, professional, etc.).

# APPENDIX B

## GOOD FAMILY CITIZENSHIP

## ALLOWANCE AGREEMENT

## DRIVING CONTRACT

# Good Family Citizenship

# January 1996

## By "good citizenship" in our

family, we mean that behavior which is necessary to:

> *Have a family and home of honesty and integrity, caring and nurturing, order and safety, and friendliness and fun. Where each member acts in ways that are responsibly independent and effectively interdependent. So we may each and together do well and do good.*

We believe that our personal freedom and rights end only when they begin to interfere with the freedom and rights of another. However, to make this possible, we put duty before rights; team before self. That is, our duty to ourselves and each other is more important than our personal rights.

We also recognize that there is a difference between what is "right" (i.e., morally or ethically correct) and what is "legal" (i.e., what is technically or legally correct). Our mutual expectation is that we will do more than what is just "legal," but we will do that which is "right." For example, a person may be within their "legal rights" to not share a personal possession—and there are times when it is reasonable and appropriate not to share; however, there are other times where kindness and courtesy argue that sharing is the "right" thing to do.

On this basis, the following points are intended to outline the spirit and substance of what we mean by "good family citizenship." That is, these points do not represent an exhaustive list of the attributes of good family citizenship; rather they are examples—hopefully sufficient—to get the idea across:

- Take personal responsibility—you are the creative force in your life and you are responsible for your actions and your decisions.
- Take care of yourself:
  - Physically (e.g. your body—your personal hygiene and appearance, your physical condition and exercise, etc.).
  - Intellectually (e.g., your brain—your school grades, your "intellectual exercise," etc.).
  - Emotionally (e.g., your heart—your relationships with family, friends, and others, your "emotional exercise," etc.).
  - Spiritually (e.g., your conscience and soul—your values, your "spiritual exercise," etc.).
- Take care of your possessions and respect the possessions of others:
  - Keep your possessions neat and orderly, and in a well cared for condition.
  - Receive permission before you borrow something from another person, and return borrowed things in the same or better condition than you received them.
- Take care of each other:
  - Treat people with kindness and courtesy, even if they may not be treating you that way.
  - Certainly defend yourself, but do not use force (physical or psychological) to make your point or get your way.
  - If you have an inter-personal problem with another, then seek that person out and make reconciliation.
- Do more than "your fair share" in the care and upkeep of our family and home, and in the many communities in which we each belong (e.g., Woodbury, Mounds Park Academy, Guardian Angels Church, etc.):
  - Understand that there is a difference between fairness and equality. We strive for fairness over time.
  - Judge what is fair based, not on what or how much you do in comparison to what or how much others do, but on what and how much you give of yourself in comparison to what and how much you receive.

- Let your word be your bond and honor your commitments. Understand that there are explicit commitments (called promises), and implicit commitments (called expectations):
    - Keep the promises you make.
    - Manage your expectations of others, and others' expectations of you knowing that a missed expectation is little different than a broken promise.
- Take pride in yourself and your family. Build and protect yours and our family's good name and reputation.
- Apologize and do whatever you can to make things right if you "blow" any of the above.

# ALLOWANCE AGREEMENT

# JANUARY 1996

- **{CHILD'S NAME} WILL RECEIVE** an allowance of $25 per week.
- The only condition governing her receipt of this allowance is that she shows "good family citizenship."
- What is meant by "good family citizenship" is explained in the attached.
- Mom and/or Dad will be the sole judge(s) of her citizenship.
- Failure to comply may result in the loss of some or all of her allowance.
- {Child's name} will be responsible for her own "day-to-day expenses."
- Mom and Dad will continue to cover the following expenses:
- School tuition, books, lunches, supplies, and other education related expenses.
- Purchase of winter/school clothing, once annually
- Purchase of summer/non-school clothes, once annually.
- The purchase of additional parent purchased items (e.g., clothing, school supplies, etc.) due to changed style/fashion preferences, or due to mistreatment or neglect shall be at [child's name]'s expense.

- The cost for other, "non-day-to-day expenses," not specifically listed above (e.g., People To People fees, ski equipment, etc.) are, by default, [child's name]'s responsibility. However, Mom and Dad are open and willing to share in these expenses (ranging from 0 to 100%) depending on [child's name]'s "good family citizenship."

# AGREED:

_____

{Child's Name}                                   Date


_____

{Mother's Name}                                  Date


_____

{Father's Name}                                  Date

# DRIVING CONTRACT

# MARCH 1996

# WHAT YOU CAN EXPECT OF MOM & DAD:

- Payment for professional driver's training, and practicing with [child's name] so she gains the driving experience necessary to be a safe and courteous driver and to qualify to take her driver's license tests.

- Use of a family vehicle when circumstances and conditions permit. Mom and Dad will make a family vehicle available for [child's name]'s use. However, there may be circumstances (e.g., Mom's or Dad's vehicle is in for extended maintenance or repair) when Mom's or Dad's use of family vehicles will take priority over [child's name]'s use. In addition, there may be conditions (e.g., severe weather) when Mom or Dad may deem it unsafe for [child's name] to use any family vehicle.

- Use of a family cellular phone when driving and when circumstances and conditions permit. Mom and Dad will make a cellular phone available for [child's name]'s use when she is using a family vehicle. However, there may be circumstances (e.g., Mom's or Dad's cell phone is in for extended maintenance or repair) when Mom's or Dad's use of family cell phones will take priority over [child's name]'s

371

use. *[Ed's note: this contract dates back to the time when cell phones cost an arm, and cell minutes cost a leg.]*

- Payment of expenses for the vehicle's routine maintenance.
- Payment of reasonable cellular phone expenses. That which constitutes "reasonable cellular phone expenses" will be determined by Mom and Dad based on their review and judgment of [child's name]'s cellular phone usage as reported in the monthly cellular phone invoices (which itemize both incoming and outgoing calls, the phone number called, the time and the duration of the call).
- Payment of the base auto insurance premium (the base premium is that which covers [child's name] as a licensed driver of the family vehicles and is discounted by those amounts earned for meeting the insurance company's definition of a good student, a non-smoker, and a safe driver).
- A $25 per week increase in [child's name]'s allowance to cover regular fuel expenses. *[Ed's note: this contract dates back to the time when $25 would fill the tank more than once.]*

# WHAT MOM & DAD EXPECT OF YOU:

- Research and arrange for her own driver's training, obtaining Mom and Dad's approval of the program and schedule selected.
- Show "good family citizenship" as explained in the attached.
- Maintain good grades (i.e., whatever grade point average is required to qualify for a "good student discount" in auto insurance premiums, or a B- average, whichever is greater).
- Execute an S.A.D.D. (Students Against Drunk Driving) contract.
- Do not use tobacco products, or drugs.
- Obey the laws of the land, and the rules of the school.
- No one other than a member of the family, covered by the vehicle's insurance policy, is to operate the vehicle.
- All vehicle occupants are to use their seat belt, and the vehicle is to carry no more passengers than there are seat belts.
- Use the vehicle and cellular phone for responsible purposes, at responsible times, and in responsible ways. Do not use either the vehicle or cell phone for frivolous purposes (e.g., joy riding, etc.), at inappropriate times (e.g., after a reasonable hour, during dangerous weather conditions, etc.), or in dangerous ways (e.g., speeding, reck-

less driving, etc.).

- Be ready, willing, and able to do "driving errands" for the family (e.g., drive your sister to school or an appointment; go to the store; etc.).
- Pay for your own fuel.
- Ensure that the vehicle is maintained in good operating condition, including routine maintenance performed on a properly scheduled basis in accordance with the vehicle's owner's manual. (Mom and Dad will pay for such maintenance, but [child's name] is expected to see that it gets done.)
- Pay for any traffic violations that you might incur.
- Pay for the repairs required as a result of any accident occurring while the vehicle and/or cellular phone are in your charge.
- Pay for any increase in auto insurance premiums due to a loss of discount (e.g., good student discount, non-smoker discount, etc.), or due to any driving violation or accident.
- Pay for any and all cellular phone expenses deemed by either Mom or Dad to be unreasonable.
- Understand that failure to meet these expectations, based on Mom or Dad's judgment, may result in the loss or restriction of some or all of your driving privileges.

# AGREED:

_____

{Child's Name}                                    Date


_____

{Mother's Name}                                   Date


_____

{Father's Name}                                   Date

# REFERENCE MATERIALS

*Never confuse book learnin' with education.*
**Bill Ruprecht**
Engineer, jazz musician, and author's father
1922 – 1997

# IT IS SAID THAT EXPERIENCE IS A

tough teacher because it gives you the test first and the lessons after, so I thought you might find it useful to see a partial list of the resources from which I've drawn the various lessons reflected in this book. I'm an avid reader in general, and have been a serious student of leadership and organizational change for most of my thirty-plus-year career, so although it is a partial list it is a long one. However, even if you merely skim the list, you will also notice that it is an eclectic collection. This has been by design, and I know it is also a bit ironic. Frankly, while I have set the context of this book in business organizations, I have learned more useful lessons from non-business books. In fact, over the course of my career I found myself navigating away, weaning myself, from traditional business authorities and their publications. With notable exceptions, I found traditional business literature to be typically linear, often myopic and, in aggregate, quite repetitious—the same old topics just presented with different coats of paint. I have found it far more interesting, pertinent, and thus beneficial to draw upon a broader and more eclectic base of resources and experience—some mainstream, but most not. I have found it far more helpful to take lessons and insights from history, philosophy, science, sports, world religions, and fiction, and apply those lessons to organizational life.

With those caveats, below is a list of resources you might also enjoy.

# Resources

Ackoff, Russell L. *Ackoff's Fables: Irreverent Reflections on Business and Bureau-cracy.* New York: John Wiley & Sons, Inc, 1991.

Adams, Scott. "The Dilbert Principal." Speech. The Masters Forum, Min-netonka, MN. 5 Aug. 1997.

Adams, Scott. *The Dilbert Principle: A Cubicle's Eye View of Bosses, Meetings, Management Fads, & Other Workplace Afflictions.* New York: HarperCol-lins Publishers, 1996.

Adams, Scott. *Dogbert's Top Secret Management Handbook.* 1 ed. New York: HarperCollins Publishers, Inc, 2006.

Albrecht, Karl, and Ron Zemke. *Service America! Doing Business in the New Economy.* Homewood, IL: Dow Jones--Irwin, 1985.

Allen, Michael W. *Creating Successful E-Learning: A Rapid System For Getting It Right First Time, Every Time.* San Francisco: Pfeiffer, 2006.

Ambrose, Stephen E. *Band of Brothers: E Company, 506th Regiment, 101st Air-borne from Normandy to Hitler's Eagle's Nest.* 3rd ed. New York: Simon & Schuster, 2001.

Anderson, Elmer L., and Sturdevant, Lori, *A Man's Reach.* Minneapolis, Min-nesota: University of Minnesota Press, 2000

Applegate, Lynda M., F. Warren McFarlan, and James L. McKenney. *Cor-porate Information Systems Management: The Challenges of Managing in an Information Age.* 5 ed. Michael W. Junior. New York: Irwin McGraw-Hill, 1999.

Arthur, John. *Morality In Our Age: Human Rights & Civil Rights.* Knowledge Products. Robert Guillaume. Audio Cassettes.

Auerback, Ernest. *Joining the Inner Circle: How to Make It as a Senior Executive.* New York: John Wiley & Sons, 1990.

Autry, James. "Finding the Balance in Life and Work." Speech. The Mas-ters Forum, State Theatre, Minneapolis, MN. 14 Nov. 1995.

Bakken, Earl E. *One Man's Full Life.* Minneapolis: Medtronic, Inc, 1999.

Balabkins, Dr. Nicholas. *Great Economic Thinkers: The German Historical School of Economics.* Knowledge Products. Louis Rukeyser. Audio Cassettes.

Bardwick, Judith M. "Between Entitlement and Fear: The Psychology of Earning." Speech. The Masters Forum. Minnetonka, MN. 4 Aug. 1992.

Bardwich, Judith M. *Danger in the Comfort Zone: From Boardroom to Mailroom--How to Break the Entitlement Habit That's Killing American Business.* New York: Amacom, 1991.

Bardwick, Judith M. "Finding Comfort in Endless Danger." Speech. The Masters Forum, Minnetonka, MN. 21 Oct. 1997.

Bardwick ,Judith M. *The Plateauing Trap: How to Avoid It In Your Career...and Your Life.* New York: Amacom, 1986.

Bartlett, Christopher. "Changing the Role of Top Management: Beyond Strategy to Purpose." Speech. The Masters Forum, Minnetonka, MN. 9 Apr. 1996.

Bazerman, Max. "Negotiating Rationally." Speech. The Masters Forum. Ted Mann Concert Hall, University of Minnesota. 2 Nov. 1994.

Begley, Sharon. *Train Your Mind Change Your Brain.* New York: Ballantine Books, 2007.

Belasco, Ph.D., James A. *Teaching the Elephant to Dance: Empowering Change in Your Organization.* New York: Crown Publishers, Inc, 1990.

Belasco, Ph.D, James A, and Ralph C. Stayer. *Flight of the Buffalo: Soaring to Excellence, Learning to Let Employees Lead.* New York: Warner Books, 1993.

Benko, Cathleen, and F. Warren McFarlan. *Connecting The Dots: Aligning Projects with Objectives in Unpredictable Times.* Boston: Harvard Business School Press, 2003.

Bennett Amanda. *The Death of the Organization Man.* New York: William Morrow and Company, Inc, 1990.

Bennis, Warren. "From Manager to Leader: The Four Keys of Effective Leadership." Speech. The Masters of Executive Excellence. Minnetonka, MN. 29 Sep.1989.

Bennis, Warren. *On Becoming a Leader.* Reading, MA: Addison-Wesley Publishing Company, Inc, 1989.

Bernstein, Ross. *America's Coach: Life Lessons & Wisdom for Gold Medal Success: A Biographical Journey of the Late Hockey Icon Herb Brooks.* Eagan. MN: Bernstein Books, LLC, 2006.

Blanchard, Ph.D., Kenneth, Donald Carew, Ed.D., Eunice Parisi-Carew, Ed.D. *The One Minutes Manager: Builds High Performing Teams.* New York: William Morrow and Company, Inc, 1990.

Blanchard, Ph.D., Kenneth and Norman V. Peale. *The Power of Ethical Management: Integrity Pays! You Don't Have to Cheat to Win.* New York: William Morrow and Company, Inc, 1988.

Bowen, Catherine D. *Miracle at Philadelphia: The Story of the Constitutional*

*Convention May to September 1787.* Boston: Little, Brown and Company, 1986.

Brands, H. W. *The First American: The Life and Times of Benjamin Franklin.* Collector's ed. Norwalk, CT: The Easton Press, 2002.

Brash, Sarah, and Britten, Loretta, eds. *Our American Century: Events That Shaped the Century.* Alexandria, VA: Time-Life Books, 1998.

Brassard, Michael. *The Memory Jogger Plus+.* 1 ed. Methuen, MA: GOAL/QPC, 1989.

Brokaw, Tom. *The Greatest Generation.* New York: Dell Publishing, 1998.

Buckingham, Marcus, and Donald O. Clifton, Ph.D. *Now, Discover Your Strengths.* New York: The Free Press, 2001.

Buckingham, Marcus, and Curt Coffman. *First, Break All the Rules: What the World's Greatest Managers Do Differently.* New York: Simon & Schuster, 1999.

Burke, James. "Connections: An Alternative View of Change." Television Documentary Series. Produced by the BBC. 1978.

Byham, Ph.D., William C. *Zapp! The Lightning of Empowerment: How to Improve Quality, Productivity, and Employee Satisfaction.* New York: Harmony Books, 1988

Cannadine, David ed. *The Speeches of Winston Churchill.* London: Penguin Books, 1990.

Campbell, Joseph, and Bill Moyers. *The Power of Myth.* New York: Doubleday, 1988.

Carey, John. *Eyewitness to History.* Cambridge, MA: Harvard University Press, 1987.

Carlin, George. "Language Complaints." Speech. National Press Club. Washington, DC. 13 May 1999.

Carroll, Andrew, ed. *Letters of a Nation: A Collection of Extraordinary American Letters.* New York: Broadway Books, 1997.

Cash, James I and F. Warren McFarlan. "Competing Through Information Technology." Video Course. Harvard Business School Video Series. Nathan/Tyler Productions. Boston, MA. 1989.

*A Century of Innovation: The 3M Story.* St. Paul: 3M Company, 2002.

Cerf, Christopher, and Victor Navasky. *The Experts Speak: The Definitive Compendium of Authoritative Misinformation.* New York: Pantheon Books, 1984.

Champy, James. "Reengineering Management." Speech. The Masters Forum, State Theatre, Minneapolis, MN. 6, Jun. 1995.

Chandler Jr., Alfred D, and James W. Cortada, eds. *A Nation Transformed by*

*Information: How Information Has Shaped the United States from Colonial Times to the Present.* York: Oxford University Press, 2000.

Christensen, Clayton M. *The Innovator's Solution: Creating and Sustaining Successful Growth.* Boston: Harvard Business School Press, 2003.

Christensen, Clayton. "The Opportunity and Threat of Disruptive Technologies." Speech. The Masters Forum, Minnetonka, MN. 18 May 1999.

Coffee, Captain Gerald. "Beyond Survival." Speech. The Masters of Executive Excellence. Minnetonka, MN. 24 Jan. 1990.

Coffee, Captain Gerald. *Beyond Survival: Building on the Hard Times-A POW's Inspiring Story.* New York: G. P. Putnam's Sons, 1990.

Collins, James. "Building a Visionary Company." Speech. The Masters Forum, Minnetonka, MN. 21 Feb. 1996.

Collins, Jim. "Getting From Good To Great." Speech. The Masters Forum, Minnetonka, MN. 24 Oct. 2000.

Collins, Jim. *Good to Great: Why Some Companies Make the Leap...and Other's Don't.* New York: HarperCollins Publishers, 2001.

Cooper Ph.D, Robert K. "Executive EQ." Speech. The Masters Forum, Minnetonka, MN. 5 Aug. 1997.

Cooper Ph.D., Robert K. "The Performance EDGE." Speech. The Masters of Executive Excellence. Minnetonka, MN. 7 May 1991.

Cooper Ph.D., Robert K. "Personal Best: Some Uncommon Thinking on the Art and Science of Personal Effectiveness Under Pressure." Speech. The Masters Forum. Minnetonka, MN. 8 Dec. 1992.

Covey, Dr. Stephen R. "Advanced Leadership." Seminar. Stephen R Covey & Associates. Sundance, UT. Sep. 1988.

Covey, Dr. Stephen R. "Advanced Leadership Renewal." Seminar. Stephen R Covey & Associates. Sundance, UT. Oct. 1989.

Covey, Stephen R. *The 7 Habits of Highly Effective People.* New York: Simon and Schuster, 1989.

Covey, Stephen R. "Living The Seven Habits." Speech. The Masters Forum. Minnetonka, MN. 7 Dec. 1993.

Covey, Stephen R. *Principle-Centered Leadership: Teaching People How to Fish.* Provo, UT: Executive Excellence, 1989.

Covey, Stephen R. "Principle Centered Living: Timeless Principles of Effectiveness," Seminar. Covey Leadership Center, Provo, UT. 1991.

Covey, Stephen R. "Restoring the Character Ethic." Speech. The Masters of Executive Excellence. Minnetonka, MN. 5 Mar. 1991.

Covey, Dr. Stephen R. "Seven Basic Habits of Highly Effective People."

379

Seminar. Stephen R Covey & Associates. Sundance, UT. Sep. 1988.

Covey, Dr. Stephen R. "Seven Habits of Highly Effective People Facilitator Training & Certification." Seminar. Stephen R Covey & Associates. Sundance, UT. Feb. 1989.

Covey, Dr. Stephen R. "Seven Habits of Highly Effective People: Renewal." Seminar. Covey Leadership Center, Inc. Sundance, UT. Sep. 1991.

Covey, Stephen R. "The Seven Habits Of Highly Effective People." Speech. The Masters of Executive Excellence. Minnetonka, MN. 28 Feb. 1990.

Covey, Stephen R. "Transformational Leadership." Speech. The Masters of Executive Excellence. Minnetonka, MN. 5 Dec. 1989.

Crupi, Dr. James. "Making a Diference: The Key to More Effective Leadership." Speech. The Masters Forum. Minnetonka, MN. 14 Sep. 1993.

Csikszentmihalyi, Mihaly. *Flow: The Psychology of Optimal Experience.* New York: Harper & Row, Publishers, 1990.

Csikszentmihalyi, Mihaly. "Steps Toward Enhancing the Quality of Life." Speech. The Masters of Executive Excellence. Minnetonka, MN. 7 May 1991.

Cusumano, Michael A. *Japan's Software Factories: A Challenge to U.S. Management.* New York: Oxford University Press, 1991.

Dalton, Gene W., and Paul H. Thompson. *Novations: Strategies for Career Management.* Glenview, IL: Scott, Foresman and Company, 1986.

Davidson, Dr. Paul. *Great Economic Thinkers: Struggle Over the Keynesian Heritage.* Knowledge Products. Louis Rukeyser. Audio Cassettes.

Davidson, William H. "Transforming Your Business Today to Succeed in Tomorrow's Economy." Speech. The Masters Forum. Minnetonka, MN. 8 Dec. 1992.

Davis, Stan. "The Monster Under the Bed." Speech. The Masters Forum, State Theatre, Minneapolis, MN. 9 May 1995.

Davis, Stan, and Bill Davidson. *2020 Vision: Transform Your Business Today to Succeed in Tomorrow's Economy.* New York: Simon & Schuster, 1991.

Davis, Stan, and Christopher Meyer. *Blur: The Speed of Change in the Connected Economy.* Warner Books ed. New York: Warner Books, 1999.

DeGeorge, Dr. Richard. *Morality In Our Age: thinking About Moral Issues.* Knowledge Products. Cliff Robertson. Audio Cassettes.

Deming, W. Edwards. *The New Economics for Industry, Government, Education.* 2 ed. Cambridge: Massachusetts Institute of Technology, Center for Advanced Educational Services, 1994.

Deming, W. Edwards. *Out of the Crisis.* Cambridge: Massachusetts Institute of Technology, Center for Advanced Engineering Study, 1990.

DePree, Max. *Leadership Is An Art.* New York: Dell Publishing, 1989.

DePree, Max. *Leadership Jazz.* New York: Doubleday, 1992.

Diamond, Dr. Arthur. *Great Economic Thinkers: Frank Knight and the Chicago School.* Knowledge Products. Louis Rukeyser. Audio Cassettes.

Diamond, Jared. *Guns, Germs, and Steel: The Fates of Human Societies.* New York: W. W. Norton & Company, 1999.

Dickinson, Brian. *Developing Quality Systems: A Methodology Using Structured Techniques.* 2 ed. New York: McGraw-Hill, Inc, 1989.

Dickinson, Brian. *The Principles of Business Engineering.* Seminar ed. *Strategic Business Engineering: A Synergy of Software Engineering and Information Engineering.* Brisbane, CA: LCI Press, 1992.

Doidge, MD, Norman. *The Brain that Changes Itself: Stories of Personal Triumph from the Frontiers of Brain Science.* New York: Penguin Group, 2007.

Donovan, John J. *Business Re-engineering with Information Technology: Sustaining Your Business Advantage--An Implementation Guide.* Mary P. Rottino. Englewood Cliffs: Prentice-Hall, Inc, 1994.

Downes, Larry, and Chunka Mui. *Unleashing the Killer Ap: Digital Strategies for Market Dominance.* Boston: Harvard Business School Press, 1998.

Driver, Stephanie S. *The Declaration of Independence. Manifesto: Words That Changed the World.* Edited by Neil Turnbull. Hauppauge, NY: Barron"s, 2004.

Drucker, Peter F.. *Managing for the Future: The 1990s and Beyond.* New York: Penguin Books, 1992.

Eason, Ken. *Information Technology and Organizational Change.* New York: Taylor & Francis, 1988.

Ellis, Joseph J. *American Founding Brothers: The Revolutionary Generation.* New York: Alfred A Knopf, 2001.

Ellis, Joseph J. *American Sphinx: The Character of Thomas Jefferson.* Collectors ed. Norwalk, CT: The Easton Press, 2000.

Etzioni, Amitai. *The Moral Dimension: Toward a New Economics.* New York: The Free Press, 1988.

Faulkner, Charles, Dr. Gerry Schmidt, Robert McDonald, Tim Hallbom, Suzi Smith, and Dr. Kelly Gerling . "Neuro-Linguistic Programming: The New Technology of Achievement." Audio Course. Nightingale-Conant Corporation. Chicago, IL. 1991.

Ferrell, O. C., and John Fraedrich. *Business Ethics: Ethical Decision Making and Cases.* 2 ed. Diane McOscar. Boston: Houghton Mifflin Company,

1994.

Fisher, Roger. "The Getting Together: Building a Relationship That Gets to Yes." Speech. The Masters of Executive Excellence. Minnetonka, MN. 27 Apr. 1989.

Fisher, Roger, and Scott Brown. *Getting Together: Building a Relationship That Gets to Yes*. Boston: Houghton Mifflin Company, 1988.

Fisher, Roger, William Ury, and Bruce Patton. *Getting to Yes: Negotiating Agreement Without Giving In*. 2 ed. New York: Penguin Books, 1991.

Flexner, James Thomas. *Washington The Indispensible Man*. Collectors ed. Norwalk, CT: The Easton Press, 2002.

Forester, Cecil Scott, *Hornblower Series*, New York: Little, Brown and Company, 1937-1967.

Frankl, Viktor E. *Man's Search for Meaning: An Introduction to Logotherapy*. New York: Simon & Schuster, 1984.

Friedman, Benjamin M. *Day of Reckoning*. New York: Random House, Inc, 1988.

Friedman, Milton, and Rose Friedman. *Free To Choose: A Personal Statement*. New York: Avon Books, 1979.

Friedman, Thomas L. *The World is Flat: A Brief History of the Twenty-first Century*. New York: Farrar, Straus and Giroux, 2005.

Fritz, Robert. *Creating*. New York: Ballantine Books, 1991.

Fritz, Robert. "Learning to Become the Creative Force in Your Own Life." Speech. The Masters Forum. Minnetonka, MN. 3 Mar. 1992.

Fritz, Robert. *The Path of Least Resistance: Learning to Become the Creative Force in Your Own Life*. New York: Ballantine Books, 1989.

Fulghum, Robert. "A Finite Gesture Toward Infinite Concerns." Speech. The Masters Forum, Minnetonka, MN. 2 Dec. 1997.

Fulton, Jane. "Ethics and the 21st Century Manager." Speech. The Masters Forum, Minnetonka, MN. 10 Sep. 1996.

Gabor, Andrea. *The Man Who Discovered Quality: How W. Edwards Deming Brought the Quality Revolution to America--The Stores of Ford, Xerox, and GM*. New York: Times Books, 1990.

Galbraith, Jay. "From Recovery to Development: Structuring Today's Organization to Meet Tomorrow's Challenges." Speech. The Masters of Executive Excellence. Minnetonka, MN. 1 Nov. 1990.

Garfield, Charles. *Peak Performers: The New Heroes of American Business*. New York: Avon Books, 1986.

Garvin, David A. "Competing Through Quality." Video Course. Harvard Business School Video Series. Nathan/Tyler Productions. Boston, MA.

1989.

George, Bill. *Authentic Leadership: Rediscovering the Secrets to Creating Lasting Value.* San Francisco: Jossey-Bass, 2003.

George, Bill. *True North: Discover Your Authentic Leadership.* New York: John Wiley & Sons, 2007.

Ghiselin, Dr. MIchael. *Science & Discovery: Darwin & Evolution.* Knowledge Products. Edwin Newman. Audio Cassettes.

Gladwell, Malcolm. *Blink: The Power of Thinking Without Thinking.* New York: Little, Brown and Company, 2005.

Gladwell, Malcolm. *The Tipping Point: How Little Things Can Make a Big Difference.* New York: Little, Brown and Company, 2002.

Glahe, Dr. Fred. *Great Economic Thinkers: The Keynesian Revolution.* Knowledge Products. Louis Rukeyser. Audio Cassettes.

Gleick, James. *Chaos: Making a New Science.* New York: Penguin Books, 1988.

Goldratt, Eilyahu M.. *Critical Chain.* Great Barrington, MA: The North River Press, 1997.

Goldratt, Eliyahu M, and Jeff Cox. *The Goal: A Process of Ongoing Improvement.* Revised ed. Croton-on-Hudson, NY: North River Press, 1986.

Goodwin, Doris K. *Team of Rivals: The Political Genius of Abraham Lincoln.* New York: Simon & Schuster, 2005.

Gordon, David and George H. Smith. *The U.S. Constitution: On Liberty and Vindication of the Rights of Woman.* Knowledge Products. Graig Deitschmann. Audio Cassettes.

Greene, Brian. *The Elegant Universe: Superstrings, Hidden Dimensions, and the Quest for the Ultimate Theory.* 1st ed. New York: W. W. Norton & Company, 2003.

Halberstam, David. *The Reckoning.* New York: William Morrow and Company, Inc, 1986.

Haley, Alex. "Find the Good and Praise It." Speech. The Masters of Executive Excellence. Minnetonka, MN. 30 Jan. 1991.

Hallahan, William H. *The Day the American Revolution Began: 19 April 1775.* New York: William Morrow and Company, 2000.

Hamel, Gary. "Competing For the Future." Speech. The Masters Forum. Ted Mann Concert Hall, University of Minnesota. 12 Apr. 1994.

Hamel, Gary. "Corporate Imagination and Expeditionary Marketing." Speech. The Masters Forum. Minnetonka, MN. 8 Sep. 1993.

Hamel, Gary. "Leading the Revolution." Speech. The Masters Forum, Minnetonka, MN. 26 Oct. 1999.

Hamel, Gary. *Leading the Revolution: How to Thrive in Turbulent Times by Making Innovation a Way of Life*. New York: Penguin Group, 2002.

Hamilton, Alexander, James Madison, and John Jay. *The Federalist Papers*. 9th ed. New York: New American Library, 1961.

Hammer, Michael. "Beyond Reengineering." Speech. The Masters Forum, Minnetonka, MN. 30 Jan. 1996.

Hammer, Michael. *Beyond Reengineering: How the Process-Centered Organization is Changing Our Work and Our Lives*. New York: HarperCollins Publishers, Inc, 1997.

Hammer, Dr. Michael. "Designing and Implementing High-Performance Processes: Creating World Class Capability." Seminar. Hammer and Company. Boston, MA. Jan 1998.

Hammer, Dr. Michael. "Implementing the Process of Change: Tools for Organizational Transformation." Seminar. Hammer and Company. Boston, MA. Jan 1998.

Hammer, Dr. Michael. "Reengineering Certification Program." Seminar. Hammer and Company. Boston, MA. Jan 1998.

Hammer, Michael. "Reengineering the Corporation." Speech. The Masters Forum. Ted Mann Concert Hall, University of Minnesota. 2 Mar. 1994.

Hammer, Michael, and James Champy. *Reengineering the Corporation: A Manifesto for Business Revolution*. New York: Harper Business, 1993.

Hammer, Michael, and Steven A. Stanton. *The Reengineering Revolution: A Handbook*. New York: Harper Business, 1995.

Hammond, Josh. "The Stuff Americans Are Made Of: The Seven Cultural Forces That Define Americans." Speech. The Masters Forum, Minnetonka, MN. 28 Jan. 1997.

Harrigan, Kathryn Rudie. "Business Strategies for the Year 2000." Speech. The Masters of Executive Excellence. Minnetonka, MN. 5 Nov. 1991.

Hart, David Kirk. "Excellence and Ethics: Management by Good Character." Speech. The Masters of Executive Excellence. Minnetonka, MN. 18 Jul. 1989.

Hart, David Kirk. "Quality With Tears: An Ethical Anchor for Leadership." Speech. The Masters Forum. Minnetonka, MN. 10 Nov. 1993.

Haseltine, Dr. William. "The Biotech Revolution." Speech. The Masters Forum, Minnetonka, MN. 2 Apr. 2001.

Hawkins, Daniel. "Problem Solving & Decision Making." Seminar. Kepner Tregoe. Bloomington, MN. Jul 1996.

Hawking, Stephen W. *A Brief History of Time: From the Big Bang to Black Holes.* New York: Bantam Books, 1988.

Hazlitt, Henry. *Economics In One Lesson.* Knowledge Products. Louis Rukeyser. Audio Cassettes.

Hebert, Dr. Robert. *Great Economic Thinkers: Alfred Marshall & Neoclassicism.* Knowledge Products. Lous Rukeyser. Audio Cassettes.

Heidger, Dr. Paul M. *Science & Discovery: Medical Science.* Knowledge Products. Edwin Newman. Audio Cassettes.

Heifetz, Ron. "Leadership Without Easy Answers." Speech. The Masters Forum, Minnetonka, MN. 4 Mar. 1996.

Highsmith III, James A. *Adaptive Software Development: A Collaborative Approach to Managing Complex Systems.* New York: Dorset House Publishing, 2000.

Hill, Sam. "Radical Marketing." Speech. The Masters Forum, Minnetonka, MN. 21 Mar. 2000.

Hoover, R.A. "Bob," and Mark Shaw. *Forever Flying" Fifty Years of High-Flying Adventures, from Barnstorming in Prop Planes to Dogfighting Germans to Testing Supersonic Jets.* New York: Pocket Books, 1996.

Houlgate, Lawrence D. *Morality In Our Age: The Family.* Knowledge Products. Cliff Robertson. Audio Cassettes.

Hultkrantz, Ake. *Religion, Scriptures & Spirituality: Native Religions of the Americas.* Knowledge Products. Ben Kingsley. Audio Cassettes.

Hummel, Jeffrey Rogers. *The U.S. Constitution: The Bill of Rights & Additional Amendments.* Knowledge Products. Walter Cronkite. Audio Cassettes.

Hummel, Jeffrey Rogers. *The United States At War: The War of 1812.* Knowledge Product. George C. Scott. Audio Cassettes.

Hummel, Jeffrey Rogers. *The United States At War: The Mexican-American War.* Knowledge Product. George C. Scott. Audio Cassettes.

Hummel, Jeffrey Rogers. *The United States At War: The Civil War, Part 1.* Knowledge Products. George C. Scott. Audio Cassettes.

Hummel, Jeffrey Rogers. *The United States At War: The Civil War, Part 2.* Knowledge Products. George C. Scott. Audio Cassettes.

Hunter, James C. *The World's Most Powerful Leadership Principle: How to Become a Servant Leader.* New York: Crown Business, 2004.

Hurst, Sue Miller. "Dialogue." Speech. The Masters Forum, State Theatre, Minneapolis, MN. 10 Oct. 1995.

Hurst, Sue Miller. "The Learning Edge Is The Leading Edge." Speech. The Masters Forum. Minnetonka, MN. 15 Sep. 1993.

Iacocca, Lee. *Iacocca.* New York: Bantam Books, 1984.

Iacocca, Lee, and Sonny Kleinfield. *Talking Straight*. New York, NY: Bantam Books, 1988.

Imagineers, The. *Walt Disney Imagineering: A Behind the Dreams Look at Making the Magic Real*. New York: Hyperion, 1996.

Imai, Masaaki. *Kaizen: The Key to Japan's Competitive Success*. 1 ed. New York: McGraw-Hill, 1986.

Iten, Shannon F. "Attention Deficit Disorder and Leadership." Master of Arts in Organizational Leadership diss., Bethel University, June 2006.

Jackson, Dr. Ian. *Science & Discovery: Chemistry & The Enlightenment*. Knowledge Products. Edwin Newman. Audio Cassettes.

Jackson, Dr. Ian. *Science & Discovery: Exploring and Mapmaking*. Knowledge Products. Edwin Newman. Audio Cassettes.

James, Jennifer. "Diversity: The New Intelligence." Speech. The Masters Forum. Minnetonka, MN. 1 Sep. 1992.

James, Jennifer. "Peak Performance: The Personal Side of Management." Speech. The Masters of Executive Excellence. Minnetonka, MN. 12 Jun. 1990.

Jaynes, Julian. *The Origin of Consciousness in the Break-Down of the BiCameral Mind*. Boston: Houghton Mifflin Company, 1990.

Jenks, James M, and John M. Kelly. *Don't Do. Delegate!: The Secret Power of Successful Managers*. New York: Ballantine Books, 1985.

Johnson MD, Spencer. *Who Moved My Cheese?: An A-Mazing Way to Deal with Change in Your Work and in Your Life*. New York: G. P. Putnam's Sons, 2002.

Joiner, Brian L.. *Fourth Generation Management: The New Business Consciousness*. New York: McGraw-Hill, Inc, 1994.

Juran, J. M. *Juran On Leadership For Quality: An Executive Handbook*. New York: The Free Press, 1989.

Kanter, Rosabeth Moss. *The Change Masters: Innovation & Entrepreneurship in the American Corporation*. New York: Simon & Shuster, Inc, 1984.

Kanter, Rosabeth Moss. *Confidence: How Winning Streaks & Losing Streaks Begin & End*. New York: Crown Business, 2004.

Kearns, David T., and David A. Nadler. *Prophets in the Dark: How Xerox Reinvented Itself and Beat Back the Japanese*. New York: HarperBusiness, 1992.

Keegan, John. *The Mask of Command*. New York: Penguin Books, 1988.

Kelly, Mark. *The Adventures of a Self-Managing Team*. 3 ed. Raleigh: Mark Kelly Books, 1990.

Kennedy, Paul. *The Rise and Fall of the Great Powers*. New York: Random

House, 1987.

Kepner, Charles H, and Benjamin B. Tregoe. *The New Rational Manager*. Princeton, NJ: Princeton Research Press, 1981.

Kerr, Steven. "Reality-Based Re-engineering and G.E.'s 'Workout'." Speech. The Masters Forum. Minnetonka, MN. 2 Mar. 1993.

Kets de Vries, Manfred. "Life and Death in the Executive Fast Lane." Speech. The Masters Forum, Minnetonka, MN. 17 Jun. 1997.

Kim, W. Chan & Renèe Mauborgne. *Blue Ocean Strategy: How to Create Uncontested Market Space and Make the Competition Irrelevant*. Boston: Harvard Business School Press, 2005.

King, Bob, and Dr. Helmut Schlicksupp. *The Idea Edge: Transforming Creative Thought Into Organizational Excellence*. 1 ed. Methuen, MA: GOAL/QPC, 1998.

Kirzner, Dr. Israel. *Great Economic Thinkers: Early Austrian Economics*. Knowledge Products. Louis Rukeyser. Audio Cassettes.

Klamer, Dr. Arjo. *Great Economic Thinkers: Monetarism & Supply Side Economics*. Knowledge Products. Louis Rukeyser. Audio Cassettes.

Koestenbaum, Peter. *Leadership: The Inner Side of Greatness*. San Francisco: Jossey-Bass Publishers, 1991.

Koestenbaum, Peter. "Leadership: The Inner Side of Greatness." Speech. The Masters Forum. Minnetonka, MN. 12 Oct. 1993.

Kolbe, Kathy. *The Cognitive Connection: Uncovering the Link Between Who You Are and How You Perform*. New York: Addison-Wesley Publishing Company, Inc, 1990.

Kotter, John. "The Leadership Factor." Speech. The Masters Forum. Ted Mann Concert Hall, University of Minnesota. 7 Jun. 1994.

Kouzes, James. "Credibility—How to Get It, How to Lose It, and Why It Matters." Speech. The Masters Forum. Ted Mann Concert Hall, University of Minnesota. 16 Aug. 1994.

Krisco, Kim H. *Leadership & the Art of Conversation: Conversation as a Management Tool*. Rocklin, CA: Prima Publishing, 1997.

Kuhn, Thomas S. *The Structure of Scientific Revolutions*. 2nd ed. Chicago: The University of Chicago Press, 1970.

Kuntzleman Ed. D., Charles T. *Maximizing Your Energy & Personal Productivity*. Chaska, MN: Nordic Press, 1992.

Kushner, Rabbi Harold. "When All You've Ever Wanted Isn't Enough." Speech. The Masters Forum, Minnetonka, MN. 10 Dec. 1996.

Lainhart IV, John W. "Data Processing Auditor Certification Program." Seminar. The EDP Auditors Foundation. St. Paul, MN. Sep. 1979.

Lawler III, Edward E. "Building High Invovement Organizations." Speech. The Masters Forum. Minnetonka, MN. 22 Jun. 1993.

Lawler III, Edward E. *High-Involvement Management.* San Francisco: Jossey-Bass Publishers, 1988.

Lawler III, Edward E. *Strategic Pay: Aligning Organizational Strategies and Pay Systems. Jossey-Bass Management Series.* San Francisco: Jossey-Bass Publishers, 1990.

Lawler III, Edward E. *The Ultimate Advantage: Creating the High-Involvement Organization.* San Francisco: Jossey-Bass Publishers, 1992.

Lee, Blaine. *The Power Principle: Influence with Honor.* New York: Simon & Schuster, 1997.

Lee, Dr. Blaine. "The Power Principle: Influence with Honor." Seminar. Covey Leadership Center, Inc. Sundance, UT. Jul. 1997.

Lee, Blaine. "The Seven Basic Habits of Highly Effective People." Speech. The Masters of Executive Excellence. Minnetonka, MN. 23 Feb. 1989.

Leonard, George. *Mastery: The Keys to Success and Long-Term Fulfillment.* New York: Penguin Group, 1991.

Levering, Robert. *A Great Place To Work: What Makes Some Employers So Good (And Most So Bad).* New York: Random House, 1988.

Levinson, Jay Conrad. *The Way of the Guerrilla: Achieving Success and Balance as an Entrepreneur in the 21st Century.* Boston: Houghton Mifflin Company, 1997.

Levitt, Steven D., and Stephen J. Dubner. *Freakonomics: A Rogue Economist Explores the Hidden Side of Everything.* Revised and Expanded ed. New York: William Morrow, 2006.

Levine, Rick, Christopher Locke, Doc Searls, and David Weinberger. *The Cluetrain Manifesto.* Cambridge: Perseus Publishing, 2000.

Lewis, Michael. *Moneyball: The Art of Winning an Unfair Game.* New York: W. W. Norton & Company, 2003.

Loewen, James W. *Lies My Teacher Told Me: Everything Your American History Textbook Got Wrong.* New York: Simon & Schuster, 1996.

Lynch, Richard L and Kelvin F. Cross. *Measure Up! Yardsticks for Continuous Improvement.* Cambridge, MA: Basil Blackwell, Inc, 1991.

Maas, James. "Asleep in the Fast Lane." Speech. The Masters Forum, State Theatre, Minneapolis, MN. 14 Nov. 1995.

Mackay, Harvey. *Swim With the Sharks Without Being Eaten Alive: Outsell Outmanage Outmotivate and Outnegotiate Your Competition.* New York, NY: William Morrow and Company, Inc, 1988.

MacKenzie, Gordon. *Orbiting the Giant Hairball.* New York: Penguin Group, 1996.

MacMillan, Margaret. *Paris 1919: Six Months That Changed the World.* New York: Random House, 2003.

Madaras, Larry and James M. SoRelle. *Clashing Views on Controversial Issues in American History.* 9th ed. *Taking Sides.* Vol. II, Reconstruction to the Present. Guilford, CT: McGraw-Hill/Dushkin, 2001.

Mahowald, Mary. *Morality In Our Age: Lying, Secrecy & Privacy.* Knowledge Products. Cliff Robertson. Audio Cassettes.

Malamud, Bernard, *The Natural.* New York: Farrar, Strauss and Cudahy, 1952.

Manchester, William. *Visions of Glory 1874-1932. Winston Spencer Churchill: The Last Lion.* I, New York: Dell Publishing, 1989.

Manchester, William. *Alone 1932--1940. Winston Spencer Churchill: The Last Lion.* II, New York: Dell Publishing, 1989.

Mandaville, Dr, Jon. *Science & Discovery: Science In Antiquity.* Knowledge Products. Edwin Newman. Audio Cassettes.

Matthews, Richard K. *The Radical Politics of Thomas Jefferson: A Revisionist View.* Lawrence, KS: University Press of Kansas, 1984.

Maxfield, Otis. "A Garden in Which to Bloom: How Managers Can Create an Environment for Peak Employee Performance and Well Being." Speech. The Masters of Executive Excellence. Minnetonka, MN. 6 Jun. 1989.

Mayo, Anthony J, and Nitin Nohria. *In Their Time: The Greatest Business Leaders of the Twentieth Century.* Boston: Harvard Business School, 2005.

McCall, Jr, Morgan W, Michael M. Lombardo, and Ann M. Morrison. *The Lessons of Experience: How Successful Executives Develop On The Job.* Lexington: Lexington Books, 1988.

McCullough, David. *1776.* New York: Simon & Schuster, 2005.

McCullough, David. *John Adams.* Collectors ed. Norwalk, CT: The Easton Press, 2002.

McDonald, Forrest. *Alexander Hamilton: A Biography.* Collectors ed. Norwalk, CT: The Easton Press, 1995.

McElroy, Wendy. *The U.S. Constitution: The Ratification Debates.* Knowledge Products. Walter Cronkite. Audio Cassettes.

McElroy, Wendy. *The United States At War: The Vietnam War, Part 2.* Knowledge Products. George C. Scott. Audio Cassettes.

McGraf, Michael E . *Setting the Pace in Product Development: A Guide to Product and Cycle-time Excellence.* Boston, MA: Butterworth- Heinemann, 1996.

McLean, Bethany, and Peter Elkind. *The Smartest Guys in the Room: The Amazing Rise and Scandalous Fall of Enron*. New York, NY: Penguin Group, 2003.

McNally, David. *Even Eagles Need a Push: Learning to Soar in a Changing World*. Eden Prairie, MN: TransForm Press, 1990.

Merlyn, Vaughan, and John Parkinson. *Development Effectiveness: Strategies for IS Organizational Transition. Ernst & Young Information Management Series*. New York: John Wiley & Sons, Inc, 1994.

Merrill, A. Roger, and Rebecca R Merrill. *Connections: Quadrant II Time Management*. Salt Lake City: Publishers Press, 1987.

Merrill, Roger. "Translating Values Into Action: Quadrant II Time Management." Speech. The Masters of Executive Excellence. Minnetonka, MN. 14 Mar. 1989.

Merrill, A. Roger. "Translating Values to Action." Speech. The Masters of Executive Excellence. Minnetonka, MN. 29 Mar. 1990.

Meyer, Christopher. *Fast Cycle Time: How to Align Purpose, Strategy, and Structure for Speed*. New York: The Free Press, 1993.

Meyer, Christopher. "Speeding Products to Market." Speech. The Masters Forum. Minnetonka, MN. 13 Apr. 1993.

Miller, Irwin. *A Primer on Statistics for Business and Economics. The Primer*. Peter L. Bernstein. New York: Random House, 1968.

Miller, Lawrence M. *American Spirit: Visions of a New Corporate Culture*. New York: William Morrow and Company, Inc, 1984.

Miller, Lawrence M. *Barbarians to Bureaucrats: Corporate Life Cycle Strategies: Lessons from the Rise and Fall of Civilizations*. New York: Clarkson N. Potter, Inc., 1989.

Miller, Lawrence M. *Competing in the New Capitalism: How Individuals, Teams and Companies are Creating the New Currency of Wealth*. Bloomington, IN: AuthorHouse, 2006.

Miller, Lawrence M. "Design For Total Quality." Seminar. The Miller Consulting Group. Atlanta, GA. Oct. 1990.

Miller, Lawrence. "Managing for Tomorrow: Visions of a New Corporate Culture." Speech. The Masters of Executive Excellence. Minnetonka, MN. 22 Aug. 1989.

Miller, Lawrence M. "Managing Quality Through Teams." Seminar. The Miller Consulting Group. Atlanta, GA. Oct. 1990.

Miller, Lawrence, M. "The New American Spirit: Winning Through Teamwork." Audio Course. Nightingale-Conant Corporation. Chicago, IL. 1984.

Mills, D. Quinn. "Facing the New Competition." Speech. The Masters of Executive Excellence. Minnetonka, MN. 21 Aug. 1990.

Moore, Geoffrey A. *Inside the Tornado: Marketing Strategies from Silicon Valley's Cutting Edge.* New York: Harper Business, 1995.

Morris, Tom. "True Success." Speech. The Masters Forum, State Theatre, Minneapolis, MN. 11 Sep. 1995.

Moss, Dr. Lawrence S. *Great Economic Thinkers: Joseph Schumpeter and Dynamic Economic Change.* Knowledge Products. Louis Rukeyser. Audio Cassettes.

Murphy, Emmett C. *The Genius of Sitting Bull: 13 Heroic Strategies for Today's Business Leaders.* Englewood Cliffs, New Jersey: Prentice-Hall, Inc., 1993.

Musashi, Miyamoto. *A Book of Five Rings: The Classic Guide to Strategy.* Woodstock, NY: The Overlook Press, 1974.

Naisbitt, John. *Megatrends: Ten New Directions Transforming Out Lives.* New York: Warner Books, Inc, 1982.

Naisbitt, John, and Patricia Aburdene. *Megatrends 2000: Ten New Directions For the 1990's.* New York: William Morrow and Company, Inc, 1990.

Naisbitt, John, and Patricia Aburdene. *Re-inventing the Corporation: Transforming Your Job and Your Company for the New Information Society.* New York: Warner Books, 1985.

Nalebuff, Barry. "Game Theory and Strategy: Competition." Speech. The Masters Forum, Orpheum Theatre, St. Paul, MN. 15 Aug. 1995.

Negroponte, Nicholas. *Being Digital.* New York: Alfred A. Knopf, Inc, 1995.

Newman, Maurice S. *Financial Accounting Estimates Through Statistical Sampling by Computer. Systems and Controls for Financial Management.* Robert L. Shultis & Frank M. Mastromano. New York: Wiley & Sons, Inc, 1976.

Nichols, Edwin J. "Cultural Diversity in the Workforce 2000." Speech. The Masters of Executive Excellence. Minnetonka, MN. 23 Jul. 1991.

Nohria, Nitin. "Beyond Hype to Real Effectiveness." Speech. The Masters Forum, Minnetonka, MN. 12 Nov. 1996.

Norton, David L. *Personal Destinies: A Philosophy of Ethical Individualism.* Princeton, NJ: Princeton University Press, 1976.

Oech, Roger von. *A Kick In The Seat Of The Pants: Using Your Explorer, Artist, Judge, & Warrior To Be More Creative.* New York: Harper & row, Publishers, 1986.

Oncken, Jr, William. *Managing Management Time.* Englewood Cliffs, NJ: Prentice-Hall, Inc, 1984.

O'Toole, James. "The Executive's Compass." Speech. The Masters Forum.

Ted Mann Concert Hall, University of Minnesota. 13 Sep. 1994.

Panati, Charles. *Extraordinary Origins of Everyday Things.* New York: Harper & Row, Publishers, 1987.

Pascale, Richard Tanner. *Managing On The Edge: How the Smartest Companies Use Conflict To Stay Ahead.* New York: Simon and Schuster, 1990.

Pascale, Richard Tanner. "The Role of Conflict in Continuous Learning." Speech. The Masters of Executive Excellence. Minnetonka, MN. 8 Oct. 1991.

Pascale, Richard Tanner, and Anthony G. Athos. *The Art of Japanese Management: Applications for American Executives.* Warner Books ed. New York: Warner Books, 1981.

Pascale, Richard and Tony Athos. "The Art of Reinvention." Speech. The Masters Forum, State Theatre, Minneapolis, MN. 7 Mar. 1995.

Pasmore, William A.. *Designing Effective Organizations: The Sociotechnical Systems Perspective. Organization Assessment and Change.* Edward E. Lawler III and Stanley E. Seashore. New York: John Wiley & Sons, 1988.

Peck, M. Scott. "Community by Choice, Not Chance." Speech. The Masters Forum. Minnetonka, MN. 8 Apr. 1992.

Peck, M.D., M. Scott. *The Road Less Traveled: A New Psychology of Love, Traditional Values and Spiritual Growth.* New York: Simon & Schuster, 1978.

Peters, Tom. "Business Survival Strategies for the 21st Century." Speech. The Masters Forum. Minnetonka, MN. 26 Apr. 1993.

Peters, Tom. "Embracing Chaos: How to Shake Things Up and Make Things Happen." Audio Course. Nightingale-Conant Corporation. Chicago, IL. 1993

Peters, Tom. *Liberation Management: Necessary Disorganization for the Nanosecond Nineties.* New York: Alfred A. Knopf, 1992.

Peters, Tom. "Thriving on Chaos." Video Lecture. Produced by Public Broadcasting System. 15 Dec 1989.

Peters, Tom. *Thriving on Chaos: Handbook for a Management Revolution.* New York: Alfred A. Knopf, 1988.

Peters, Tom and Bob Waterman. "In Search of Excellence: Passion for Excellence." Video Lecture. Nathan/Tyler Productions. Boston, MA. 1985.

Peterson, Dr. William H. *Great Economic Thinkers: Thorstein Veblen and Institutionalism.* Knowledge Products. Louis Rukeyser. Audio Cassettes.

Peterson, Dr. William H. *Great Economic Thinkers: The Austrian Case for the Free Market Process.* Knowledge Products. Louis Rukeyser. Audio Cassettes.

Poirier, Charles C, Michael J. Bauer, and William F. Houser. *The Wall Street*

*Diet: Making Your Business Lean and Healthy*. San Francisco: Berrett-Koehler Publishers, Inc, 2006.

Porter, Michael E. *Competitive Strategy: Techniques for Analyzing Industries and Competitors*. New York: The Free Press, 1980.

Porter, Michael. "Michael Porter on Competitive Strategy." Video Course. Harvard Business School Video Series. Nathan/Tyler Productions. Boston, MA. 1988.

Prager, Dennis. "Happiness is a Serious Problem." Speech. The Masters Forum, Minnetonka, MN. 5 Aug. 1997.

Prahalad, C. K, and Venkat Ramaswamy. *The Future of Competition: Co-Creating Unique Value With Customers*. Boston: Harvard Business School Press, 2004.

Pritchett, Price. *The Employee Handbook of New Work Habits For a Radically Changing World: 13 Ground Rules for Job Success In the Information Age*. Dallas: Pritchett & Associates, Inc, 1994.

Pritchett, Price. *Fast Growth: A Career Acceleration Strategy*. Dallas: Pritchett & Associates, Inc, 1997.

Pritchett, Price. *Mind Shift*. Dallas: Pritchett & Associates, Inc, 1996.

Pritchett, Price. *Teamwork: The Team Member Handbook: 16 Steps to Building a High-Performance Team*. 5 ed. Dallas: Pritchett & Associates, Inc, 1997.

Quinn, James Brian. "Intelligent Enterprise." The Masters Forum. Speech. Ted Mann Concert Hall, University of Minnesota. 18 May. 1994.

Raico, Ralph. *The U.S. Constitution: Communist Manifesto and Social Contract*. Knowledge Product. Craig Deitschmann. Audio Cassettes.

Raico, Ralph. *The U.S. Constitution: Democracy in America*. Knowledge Products. Craig Deitschmann. Audio Cassettes.

Raico, Ralph. *The United States At War: World War 1, Part 1*. Knowledge Products. George C. Scott. Audio Cassettes.

Ramsay, David. *Great Economic Thinkers: Karl Marx: Das Kapital*. Knowledge Products. Louis Rukeyser. Audio Cassettes.

Reich, Robert R. "The Vanishing Nation." Speech. The Masters of Executive Excellence. Minnetonka, MN. 4 Dec. 1991.

Renault, Mary. *The Nature of Alexander*. New York: Pantheon Books, 1975.

Restak, MD, Richard. *The Brain*. New York: Bantam Books, 1984.

Rich, Ben R, and Leo Janos. *Skunk Works*. Boston, MA: Little, Brown and Company, 1994.

Rosenblatt, Roger. "A Perspective on Leadership." Speech. The Masters Forum. Minnetonka, MN. 28 Jan. 1992.

Rosenblatt, Roger. *Children of War*. New York: Doubleday, 1992.

Rosenblatt, Roger. "The Power of the Story." Speech. The Masters Forum, State Theatre, Minneapolis, MN. 24 Jan. 1995.

Ross, Richard. "Leading and Managing in Learning Organizations." Speech. The Masters Forum. Minnetonka, MN. 2 Jun. 1992.

Ross, Rick. "A Systems Thinking Toolbox." Speech. The Masters Forum, Minnetonka, MN. 8 Apr. 1997.

Rubin, Harriet and Avram Miller. "Personal Power and Leadership Miracles." Speech. The Masters Forum, Minnetonka, MN. 4, Aug. 1998.

Russo, J. Edward, and Paul J.H. Schoemaker. *Decision Traps: The Ten Barriers to Brilliant Decision Making & How to Overcome Them*. New York: Doubleday, 1989.

Saffo, Paul. "Coming Next: Things That Think." Speech. The Masters Forum, Minnetonka, MN. 9 Feb. 1999.

Salinger, J.D. *The Catcher in the Rye*. New York: Little, Brown and Company, 1951.

Sanders, Dr. Jack. *Science & Discovery: Medieval Science*. Knowledge Products. Edwin Newman. Audio Cassettes.

Sanders, John T. *Science & Discovery: Dimensions of Scientific Thought*. Knowledge Products. Edwin Newman. Audio Cassettes.

Sanders, John T. *Science & Discovery: Einstein's Revolution*. Knowledge Products. Edwin Newman. Audio Cassettes.

Savill, Agnes. *Alexander the Great and His Time*. New York: Barnes & Noble Books, 1993.

Schaef, Anne Wilson, and Diane Fassel. *The Addictive Organization: Why We Overwork, Cover Up, Pick Up the Pieces, Please the Boss & Perpetuate Sick Organizations*. San Francisco: Harper & Row, Publishers, 1988.

Schlesinger, Leonard A. "Achieving Breakthrough Service." Speech. The Masters Forum. Minnetonka, MN. 18 May 1993.

Schmidt, Dr. Allen H. "Strategic Planning for Information Systems." Seminar. Harvard University. Cambridge, MA. Jun. 1981.

Schrag, Dr. Brian. *Morality In Our Age: Civility & Community*. Knowledge Products. Robert Guillaume. Audio Cassettes.

Schroth, Richard. "The 21st Century Leader." Speech. The Masters Forum, Minnetonka, MN. 6 Aug. 1996.

Schwartz, Peter. "The Long Boom." Speech. The Masters Forum, Minnetonka, MN. 27 Feb. 2001.

Sears, Stephen W. *Gettysburg*. Boston: Houghton Mifflin Company, 2003.

Seldes, George. *The Great Thoughts: From Abelard to Zola, from Ancient Greece to contemporary America, the ideas that have shaped the history of the world.*

New York: Ballantine Books, 1985.

Seligman, Martin. "Learned Optimism." Speech. The Masters Forum State Theatre, Minneapolis, MN. 14 Nov. 1995.

Senge, Peter M. "The Art and Practice of the Learning Organization." Speech. The Masters Forum. Minnetonka, MN. 6 Oct. 1992.

Senge, Peter M. *The Fifth Discipline: The Art & Practice of the Learning Organization*. New York: Doubleday, 1990.

Senge, Dr. Peter. "Leadership & Mastery." Seminar. Innovation Associates, Inc. Boston, MA. Jan. 1993.

Shechtman, Morris. "Working Without a Net." Speech. The Masters Forum, Minnetonka, MN. 2 May 1996.

Sidey, Hugh. *Portraits of the Presidents: Power and Personality in the Oval Office.* Kelly Knauer. New York: Time Books, 2000.

Simons, Robert. "Rooting Out Risk." Speech. The Masters Forum, Minnetonka, MN. 26 Mar. 2002.

Skousen, W. Cleon. *The Five Thousand Year Leap: The 28 Great Ideas That Are Changing the World.* 5th ed. Washington, DC: National Center for Constitutional Studies, 1981.

Sloan, Jr, Alfred P. *My Years With General Motors.* John McDonald with Catharine Stevens. New York: Doubleday, 1972.

Slywotzky, Adrian. "Value Migration." Speech. The Masters Forum, Minnetonka, MN. 6 May 1997.

Smart, Ninian. *Religion, Scriptures & Spirituality: The Religion of Small Societies.* Knowledge Products. Ben Kingsley. Audio Cassettes.

Smith, George H. *The U.S. Constitution: The Constitutional Convention.* Knowledge Products. Walter Cronkite. Audio Cassettes.

Smith, George H and Wendy McElroy. *The U.S. Constitution: The Federalist Papers.* Knowledge Products. Craig Deitschmann. Audio Cassettes.

Smith, George H and Wendy McElroy. *The U.S. Constitution: Two Treatises of Government.* Knowledge Products. Craig Deitschmann. Audio Cassettes.

Smith, George H. *The U.S. Constitution: The Text of the United States Constitution.* Knowledge Products. Walter Cronkite. Audio Cassettes.

Smith, George H. *The U.S. Constitution: Common Sense and The Declaration of Independence.* Knowledge Products. Bill Middleton. Audio Cassettes.

Smith, George H. *The U.S. Constitution: Civil Disobedience and The Liberator.* Knowledge Products. Bill Middleton. Audio Cassettes.

Smith, George H. *The U.S. Constitution: The Wealth of Nations, Part 1.* Knowledge Products. Dan Church, Travis Hardison, Joe Keenan, and Paul

Meier. Audio Cassettes.

Smith, George H. *The U.S. Constitution: The Wealth of Nations, Part 2*. Knowledge Products. Dan Church, Travis Hardison, Joe Keenan, and Paul Meier. Audio Cassettes.

Smith, George H. *The U.S. Constitution: The Prince and Discourse on Voluntary Servitude*. Knowledge Products. Craig Deitsschmann. Audio Cassettes.

Smith, George H. *The U.S. Constitution: Communist Manifesto and Social Contract*. Knowledge Product. Craig Deitschmann. Audio Cassettes.

Smith, George H. *The U.S. Constitution: Reflections on the Revolution in France and Rights of Man*. Knowledge Product. Craig Deitschmann. Audio Cassettes.

Smith, George H. *The U.S. Constitution: Leviathan*. Knowledge Products. Craig Deitschmann. Audio Cassettes.

Smith, George H. *The United States At War: The American Revolution, Part 1*. Knowledge Products. George C. Scott. Audio Cassettes.

Smith, George H. *The United States At War: The American Revolution, Part 2*. Knowledge Products. George C. Scott. Audio Cassettes.

Solomon, Dr. Jon David. *Religion, Scriptures & Spirituality: Classical Religions & Myths of the Mediterranean Basin*. Knowledge Products. Ben Kingsley. Audio Cassettes.

Sommer, Dr. Jack. *Science & Discovery: Natural Science & The Planet Earth*. Knowledge Products. Edwin Newman. Audio Cassettes.

Spradley, James and David W. McCurdy. *Conformity and Conflict: Readings in Cultural Anthropology*. 9th ed. New York: Longman, 1997.

Startwell, Crispin. *Morality In Our Age: Punishment*. Knowledge Products. Cliff Robertson. Audio Cassettes.

Stern, Lou. "The Future of Marketing." Speech. The Masters Forum, Minnetonka, MN. 30 Mar. 1999.

Stewart, James B. *Disney War*. New York: Simon & Schuster, 2005.

Stewart, Jon. *America (the Book): A Citizen's Guide to Democracy Inaction*. New York: Warner Books, 2004.

Stoessinger, John G. "An Immigrant Looks at America." Speech. The Masters Forum. Ted Mann Concert Hall, University of Minnesota. 25 Jan. 1994.

Stoller, Martin. "The Going Gets Rough: Issue Management and Crisis Communication." Speech. The Masters Forum. Ted Mann Concert Hall, University of Minnesota. 11 Oct. 1994.

Stromberg, Joseph. *The United States At War: The Spanish-American War, World War 1, Part 1*. Knowledge Products. George C. Scott. Audio Cassettes.

Stromberg, Joseph. *The United States At War: World War 2, Part 1.* Knowledge Products. George C. Scott. Audio Cassettes.

Stromberg, Joseph. *The United States At War: World War 2, Part 2.* Knowledge Products. George C. Scott. Audio Cassettes.

Stromberg, Joseph. *The United States At War: The Korean War, The Vietnam War, Part 1.* Knowledge Product. George C. Scott. Audio Cassettes.

Sutton, Ph.D., Robert I. *The No Asshole Rule: Building a Civilized Workplace and Surviving One that Isn't.* New York: Warner Business Books, 2007.

Takeuchi, Hirotaka. "The Knowledge-Creating Company: How Japanese Companies Create the Dynamics of Innovation." Speech. The Masters Forum, Minnetonka, MN. 25 Jun. 1996.

Tapscott, Don. "Creating Wealth in the Digital Economy." Speech. The Masters Forum, Minnetonka, MN. 15 Oct. 1996.

Tapscott, Don. *The Digital Economy: Promise and Peril in the Age of Networked Intelligence.* New York: McGraw-Hill, 1996.

Teichgraeber III, Richard F. *'Free Trade' and Moral Philosophy: Rethinking the Sources of Adam Smith's Wealth of Nations.* Durham: Duke University Press, 1986.

Thurow, Lester. *Head to Head: The Coming Economic Battle Among Japan, Europe, and America.* New York: Warner Books, 1993.

Thurow, Lester. "Keeping America Competitive." Speech. The Masters of Executive Excellence. Minnetonka, MN. 6 Dec. 1990.

Thurow, Lester. "The Emerging World Economic Order." Speech. The Masters Forum. Minnetonka, MN. 26 Jan. 1993.

Tichenor, Harold. *The Blanket: An Illustrated History of the Hudson's Bay Point Blanket.* Toronto, Ont: Madison Press Books, 2002.

Tichy, Noel. "A Teachable Point of View." Speech. The Masters Forum, Minnetonka, MN. 15 Sep. 1998.

Tichy, Noel M. "Transformational Leadership for the 1990's." Speech. The Masters of Executive Excellence. Minnetonka, MN. 4 Jun. 1991.

Tichy, Noel M, and Eli Cohen. *The Leadership Engine: Building Leaders at Every Level. The Thought Leader.* Dallas: Pritchett & Associates, Inc, 1998.

Tichy, Noel M and Mary A. Devanna. *The Transformational Leader.* New York: John Wiley & Sons, 1986.

Tiger, Lionel. "Ethics, Evolution and the Industrial System." Speech. The Masters Forum. Minnetonka, MN. 4 May 1992.

Tiger, Lionel. *The Manufacture of Evil: Ethics, Evolution and the Industrial System.* New York: Marion Boyers, 1991.

Tocqueville, Alexis de. *Democracy in America (Abridged).* Ware, Hertfordshire:

Wordsworth Editions Limited, 1998.

Toffler, Alvin. *Future Shock.* Bantam ed. New York: Bantam Books, 1971.

Toffler, Barbara L. *Tough Choices: Managers Talk Ethics.* New York: John Wiley & Sons, 1986.

Tong, Dr. Rosemarie. *Morality In Our Age: Unity In Diversity.* Knowledge Products. Robert Guillaume. Audio Cassettes.

Toynbee, Arnold J. *A Study of History: Abridgement of Volumes I - VI by D.C. Somervell.* Oxford: Oxford University Press, 1946.

Toynbee, Arnold J. *A Study of History: Abridgement of Volumes VII - X by D.C. Somervell.* Oxford: Oxford University Press, 1946.

Treacy, Michael. "Sustaining Value Leadership." Speech. The Masters Forum, Orpheum Theatre, St. Paul, MN. 11 Apr. 1995.

Treacy, Michael. "Value Leadership, Strategic Agility and Organizational Greatness." Speech. The Masters Forum, Minnetonka, MN. 27 Oct. 1998.

Treacy, Michael, and Fred Wiersema. *The Discipline of Market Leaders: Choose Your Customers, Narrow Your Focus, Dominate Your Market.* Reading, MA: Addison-Wesley Publishing Company, 1995.

Tuchman, Barbara W. *The March of Folly: From Troy to Viet Nam.* New York: Alfred A. Knopf, Inc., 1984.

Twain, Mark. *Adventures of Huckleberry Finn.* New York: Penguin Classics, Penguin Putnam, Inc., 1994.

Ury, William L. "Principled Negotiation." Speech. The Masters of Executive Excellence. Minnetonka, MN. 9 Apr. 1991.

Veeck, Mike, and Pete Williams. *Fun is Good: How to Create Joy & Passion in Your Workplace & Career.* New York: Rodale, Inc., 2005.

von Oech, PhD, Roger. *A Whack on the Side of the Head: How to Unlock Your Mind for Innovation.* New York: Warner Books, Inc., 1983.

Walker, Dr. Donald. *Great Economic Thinkers: The Vision of Leon Walras.* Knowledge Products. Louis Rukeyser. Audio Cassettes.

Wallace, Doug. "Ethical Leadership and the Manager: Leading in the Midst of Ambiguity." Speech. The Masters of Executive Excellence. Minnetonka, MN. 16 Aug. 1990.

Walton, Mary. *The Deming Management Method.* New York: The Putnam Publishing Group, 1986.

Ward, Geoffrey C., and Ken Burns. *Baseball: An Illustrated History.* 1 ed. New York: Alfred A Knopf, Inc, 1994.

Ward, Geoffrey C., and Ken Burns. *The War: An Intimate History 1941 - 1945.* 1 ed. New York: Alfred A Knopf, 2007.

Ward, Geoffrey C., Rick Burns, and Ken Burns. *The Civil War: An Illustrated History*. New York: Alfred A. Knopf, Inc, 1991.

Warner, Terry C. "Bonds of Anguish, Bonds of Love: Applying the Principle of Agency in Relationships." Speech. The Masters Forum, Minnetonka, MN. 17 Nov. 1993.

Waterman Jr, Robert H. *Adhocracy: The Power to Change: How to Make Innovation a Way of Life*. Masters of Executive Excellence.

Waterman, Robert H. "How to Make Innovation a Way of Life." Speech. The Masters of Executive Excellence. Minnetonka, MN. 10 Sep. 1991.

Waterman, Robert. "The Renewal Factor." Speech. The Masters of Executive Excellence. Minnetonka, MN. 31 Oct. 1989.

Waterman, Jr, Robert H. *The Renewal Factor: How the Best Get and Keep the Competitive Edge*. New York: Bantam Books, 1988.

Weill, Peter, and Jeanne W. Ross. *IT Governance: How Top Performers Manage IT Decision Rights for Superior Results*. Boston: Harvard Business School Press, 2004.

Weinberg, Gerald M. *Quality Software Management. 1, Systems Thinking*. New York: Dorset House Publishing, 1992.

Welles, Orson, and Mankiewicz, Herman J.. *Citizen Kane*. Screenplay. USA: 1 May 1941.

West, Dr. E.G.. *Great Economic Thinkers: The Classical Economists*. Knowledge Products. Louis Rukeyser. Audio Cassettes.

Wheatley, Margaret J. *Leadership and the New Science: Learning about Organization from an Orderly Universe*. San Francisco: Berrett-Koehler Publishers, 1992.

Wheatley, Margaret J. "Quantum Thinking: Leadership and the New Science." Speech. The Masters Forum. Ted Mann Concert Hall, University of Minnesota. 19 Jul. 1994.

Wheeler, Donald J. *Understanding Statistical Process Control*. Knoxville: SPC Press, Inc, 1990.

Wheeler, Donald J. *Understanding Variation: The Key to Managing Chaos*. Knoxville: SPC Press, Inc, 1993.

Wheeler, William B and Susan D. Becker. *Discovering the American Past: A Look at the Evidence*. 9th ed. Vol. II, Since 1865. Boston: Houghton Mifflin Company, 2002.

White, M.D., Bowen F. *Why Normal Isn't Healthy: How to Find Heart, Meaning, Passion & Humor on the Road Most Traveled*. Center City, MN: Hazelden, 2000

White, Dr. Roger. *Science & Discovery: Complexity & Chaos*. Knowledge Products. Edwin Newman. Audio Cassettes.

Wiersema, Fred. "Customer Intimacy." Speech. The Masters Forum, Minnetonka, MN. 9 Sep. 1997.

Wilder, Thornton. *The Skin of Our Teeth: A Play in Three Acts*. French's Standard Library Edition. New York: Samuel French, Inc., 1999.

Wilkins, Alan L. "Developing Corporate Character." Speech. The Masters of Executive Excellence. Minnetonka, MN. 25 Sep. 1990.

Wills, Garry. "Certain Trumpets: The Call of Leaders." Speech. The Masters Forum, Orpheum Theatre, St. Paul, MN. 11 Jul. 1995.

Wirth, Annalisa M. "Women and Leadership: Overcoming Old Obstacles, Exploring New Opportunities." Doctor of Philosophy diss., Graduate School of the University of Minnesota, July 2005.

Woodward, Bob, and Carl Bernstein. *The Final Days*. New York: Simon & Schuster, 1976.

Yergin, Daniel, and Joseph Stanislaw. *The Commanding Heights: The Battle for the World Economy*. New York: Simon and Schuster, 1998.

Young, Nedtrick and Smith, Harold Jacob. *Inherit the Wind*. Screenplay. USA: 1 Nov 1960.

Zachman, John. "A Framework for Information Systems Architecture." Speech. IBM. Los Angeles, CA. Jun. 1984

Zander, Rosamund Stone, and Benjamin Zander. *The Art of Possibility: Transforming Professional and Personal Life*. New York: Penguin Group, 2002.

Zeithhaml, Valarie A., A. Parasuraman, and Leonard L. Berry. *Delivering Quality Service: Balancing Customer Perceptions and Expectations*. New York: The Free Press, 1990.

Zemke, Ron, and Dick Schaaf. *The Service Edge: 101 Companies that Profit from Customer Care*. New York, NY: Penguin Group, 1990.

Zohar, Danah. "Is Business Using Its Brain?" Speech. The Masters Forum, Minnetonka, MN. 14 Sep. 1999.

Zyman, Sergio. *The End of Marketing As We Know It*. New York: Harper Business, 2000

# ABOUT THE AUTHOR:
# JIM RUPRECHT

*No one ever saw a motorcycle parked at a psychiatrist's office.*
**T-shirt at Sturgis 2005**

ALTHOUGH JIM'S DEGREE IS IN QUAN-
titative Methods/Operations Research, his career has been one of leading increasingly challenging transformations--building new organizations, renovating under-performing ones, and revitalizing neglected ones. Most of Jim's career has been spent leading technology organizations at an eclectic variety of large and small, centralized and decentralized, and public and private firms, during economic conditions ranging from times of dramatic growth to times of dramatic cost and competitive pressure.

From his beginning creating the IS Audit function in 3M's Internal Auditing Department, to creating the IT function in Medtronic's Neurological business during their start-up, to renovating the Information Systems organization at the Star Tribune newspaper, to creating the Factory Systems organization in Seagate Technology's Recording Heads Operations business, to building two management consulting firms, to revitalizing the IT function in Medtronic's Cardiac Rhythm Disease Management (CRDM) business, to leading the development of the next generation programming strategy, product line and project plan in Medtronic CRDM's Product Development organization, Jim has come to be regarded as a pragmatic leader, not constrained by conventional thinking, with a track record of building high-performing organizations that use technology to add value.

Jim has led through his ability to formulate and align strategy, process, technology, and organizational design, to move quickly from concept and theory to pragmatic issues, to explain complex topics in everyday language, and to build relationships with, build consensus among, and communicate naturally with people regardless of their level or background.

Jim has been seasoned by leading through the spectrum of business conditions—ranging from the dramatic growth of new startups, to the downsizing that accompanies cost and competitive pressures and economic downturns. Further, he's gained experience managing in a variety of corporate cultures—large and small, centralized and decentralized, hierarchical and matrix, public and private.

Jim's career also includes a unique blend of corporate and consulting experience, leading teams throughout the U.S., Northern Ireland, The Netherlands, Switzerland, Malaysia, Singapore, and Thailand.

Jim was fortunate to be honored with Medtronic's highest award for leadership, the Win Wallin Leadership Award. He shares his experience by serving on the boards of several small organizations, through articles and speaking engagements, consulting engagements, as a mentor in the various organizations at which he worked, and in the Mentiuum Minnesota 100 mentoring program.

Jim is the father of two daughters, and his therapist is Dr. Harley Davidson.